ATLAS OF MAN AND HIS WORLD

Aldus Books London

ATLAS OF MAN AND HIS WORLD

Shirley Carpenter

Editorial Coordinator: John Mason
Art Editor: Grahame Dudley
Designer: Janey Sugden
Editor: Damian Grint
Research: Sara Butler

ISBN 0490 004555
© 1979 Aldus Books Limited London
First published in the United Kingdom
in 1979 by Aldus Books Limited
17 Conway Street, London W1P 6BS
Printed and bound in Hong Kong by
Leefung-Asco.

Introduction

It is more important now than ever before to be informed about parts of the world other than our own. In an age of jet travel and fast communications, events move with a rapidity more startling than at any period in the world's long history. An incident of political or economic importance in some remote part of the world can rapidly develop to the point where it profoundly affects international and commercial relationships and our own everyday lives. *Atlas of Man and his World* gives the reader the background information against which the possible consequences of the changing scene can be set. There is a wealth of relief and political maps, aerial and satellite photographs, color photographs of cities, landscapes, and people, and detailed information on all the world's countries. All these are combined in a way that enables the reader to explore the colorful variety of our modern world.

Contents

Chapter 7
Africa and Arabia

Africa is the world's second largest continent.
Its desert belt stretches across the north
and into the Arabian peninsula. The many
new nations created from former colonies
are now entering upon a new phase of
political and cultural development.

Page 161

Chapter 8
North America

North America is a region of amazing
variety of landscape and life style, with vast
wealth, both tapped and potential. It
presents every kind of natural challenge,
from icy waste and mountain barrier to
burning desert and steaming swamp.

Page 199

Chapter 9
Central America and the Caribbean

The long, mountain ranges of Central
America that stretch from the Rockies to
the Isthmus of Panama, plunge eastward
into the sea to emerge again as the vast arc
of Caribbean islands. Out of this region has
grown a richly varied civilization.

Page 229

Chapter 10
South America

Lying mostly in the tropics, South America
contains jungle, rich grasslands, rainless
deserts, active and dormant volcanoes,
snowfields and high plateaus. Its natural
resources, too, are as varied as its landscape
and its climate.

Page 247

Chapter 11
Australia and Oceania

The Pacific Ocean is studded with islands,
many still under Western influence. In the
southwest corner lies Australia and New
Zealand — both of which are major
producers of wool, beef, and dairy cattle,
and in Australia, copper, uranium, and
bauxite.

Page 267

Chapter 12
The Polar Lands

The Arctic, which takes in the north coasts
of Eurasia and North America, is an area
of high strategic and economic importance.
By contrast the vast, equally inhospitable
continent of Antarctica is the setting for
much international research and cooperation.

Page 287

Chapter 1
The Creation of the World

How did our world and the universe come into being? Where did mankind come from? Man has long sought the answers to these questions. For centuries archaeologists have dug deeply into the past and philologists and religious historians have examined the myths and beliefs of ancient peoples. The evidence they have uncovered contains fascinating insights into the views of primitive man about the origins of himself and his world. Remarkably, many of these early observations are very close to conclusions reached by the latest scientific discoveries. There is, of course, much that still puzzles us about the creation of the universe, the world, and man. Perhaps, after all, the solution to some of the puzzles lies buried in those ancient accounts of the beginnings of all things.

Left: God, seen as supreme architect of the universe, an illustration taken from a 13th-century edition of the Old Testament. The Bible – the revealed word of God to Jews and Christians – declares that God created the universe, the world, and man. But long before the Bible was written, far back in prehistory, stories were told to account for the existence of the world and man – of some original divine creator who brought order out of chaos.

The Earliest Creation Myths

Man has a questioning nature, so it would hardly be surprising if his earliest questions were about the origin and nature of himself and his world. Every culture so far investigated, however primitive, provides some framework to account for the creation of the universe, the earth, and mankind. Some of these accounts are in the form of myths that try to explain how the physical world came into existence, how something came from nothing, how diversity came from unity, order from chaos. Others put forward the idea of an "Unmoved First Mover" standing outside his creation, a god who created the world and man by an act of will and for a specific purpose.

It was the modern American historian of mythology, Joseph Campbell, who distinguished four types of primitive creation story: in the first and oldest the world is born of a goddess without the aid of a consort; in the second the world is born of a goddess after sexual union with a consort; in the third it is a male warrior god who fashions the world from the body of a goddess; and in the fourth type the world is created by the unaided power of a male god alone.

On the evidence of prehistoric carvings and pictures – and also taking into account what is known of present-day primitive peoples in a similar stage of evolution – historians have suggested that the worship of an earth goddess as the embodiment of fruitfulness was probably man's first religion. The tribal woman who renewed the tribe was parallelled with the great earth mother who renewed all creation.

Below: a Neolithic statuette from about 6000 BC of a mother goddess, worshiped as a symbol of fertility and creation by the ancient Anatolians of Asia Minor. Many ancient peoples believed that the world itself was created from the body of a great primeval goddess.

There is no doubt that between 10,000 and 40,000 years ago the unmistakably pregnant female, as depicted in such carvings as the Venus of Laussel, was held in awe by primitive peoples. And it seems very likely that there was also a time when males were unaware that they played any part in procreation. Whether there ever was a time when society was entirely matriarchal is a much debated question but scholars are agreed that the absolute ascendancy of the male was a late development.

Above: the Venus of Laussel, a 30,000-year-old rock carving found in France and probably the oldest representation of a deity yet discovered. The head and feet are barely sketched in, whereas the hips and bust are more fully molded – emphasizing the figure's creative role.

It is not difficult to imagine how the male's status would have changed when the connection between sex and the production of young eventually dawned on him. He would have realized that he too was a creator, that he was a partner in the miracle of birth. In his mythological thinking mother earth could now be complemented by father sky, the earth goddess by the sky god. And it would be hardly surprising if the male tended to compensate for his former inferior position by belittling that of the female.

The overturning of the role of the great primeval goddess is found in the myths that contain elements of both the second and third of Joseph Campbell's categories, such as the creation myths of Sumer and Babylon that date from as far back as 2000–3000 years BC. The Sumerian myth begins by relating how the air-god Enlil tore apart the cosmic mountain, the base of which was the female principle, *Ki*, and the summit the male principle, *An*, and which hovered above the primordial watery abyss. This tearing apart was the

Below: the Japanese sky god Izanagi and the earth goddess Izanami depicted in this late 19th-century Japanese illustration standing on the "floating bridge of heaven." With a jeweled spear Izanagi stirs the waters of chaos until they thicken and congeal into an island. On the island – which becomes the "central pillar of earth," the two deities perform the marriage ritual. From their union all the gods were created.

creation of heaven and earth, and it was followed by the appearance of the gods who, as men do on earth, enjoyed physical pleasures and cultivated their heavenly fields. They found that farming was a burden, so the god Enki created servants to carry out the gods' tasks for them. Enki was the lord of the watery abyss and his goddess-spouse was the earth-mother, and it was from her that he fashioned man.

In the *Enuma Elish*, the Babylonian Creation epic, the primeval gods, Apsu and Tiamat, are seen as personifications of the river waters and the great sea, and the original state of things is envisaged as a watery chaos. From the waters, and the commingling of Apsu and Tiamat, the great gods were born, but they became such a great annoyance to Apsu that he re-

solved to kill them. The gods became aware of his plan, and the leader among them, Ea, devised and successfully carried out a plan to kill Apsu. He then settled down to a peaceful life with his wife Damkina, and eventually they had a son, Marduk, "the wisest of the wise, most knowing of the gods."

Angry that Ea had usurped Apsu's place, Tiamat planned revenge. She, the personification of the sea and the primal chaos, spawned a brood of terrible monsters, and proceeded to rally them all for a great battle against the gods.

The gods agreed that Marduk should be supreme among them if he defeated Tiamat. A titanic struggle, which is described vividly in the epic, ended with Marduk's victory and Tiamat's death. Then Marduk split her into two halves. He suspended one half above the other, and thus created heaven and earth. There are close correspondences between these myths and the ancient Greek creation myths.

In the beginning there was only open and empty space. Then appeared the first divinity, Gaea, the

earth-goddess. She then created the mountains and the sea and through the mating of the sky-god Uranus with his mother, Gaea, were born 12 Titans, the three one-eyed Cyclopes, and finally three monsters. Uranus shut his horrible offspring away in the depths of the earth, which made Gaea so angry that she conspired with her son Cronus, the last-born of the Titans, to mutilate Uranus while he slept. Using a sickle, the son emasculated his father and cast the bleeding genitals into the sea.

Cronus now liberated the other Titans and the work of creation proceeded apace. But an oracle had predicted that Cronus would be supplanted by one of his children, and it was Zeus, who upon attaining manhood, drove Cronus from the sky and imprisoned him in a region beneath the earth and the sea. But now the Titans became jealous of Zeus and the new generation of gods, and a mighty war was waged which resulted in the defeat of the Titans. The Titans were then cast deep below the earth and the three monsters set to guard them. But Gaea, the earth-mother, would not accept the defeat of her children, and in a final attempt to overcome Zeus she produced a terrifying monster, Typhoesus, at the sight of which all the gods except Zeus trembled with fear and fled to Egypt. Zeus lost the first round of the struggle with Typhoesus, but he finally overcame the monster with his thunderbolts and crushed him.

Here, then, is primitive man's account of how order originally emerged, by degrees and after many struggles, out of chaos. The mythologies were told or written in a naïve, symbolical way suited to the understanding of primitive people. They look back to a time far back in the racial memory when the elements were wild and unpredictable, when the earth shook, the mountains quaked, and the seas heaved in tumult. They transformed aspects of the rebellious elements into the giants and various monsters, while the elements themselves are represented by the sea and earth-goddesses. Scholars have long since learned not to dismiss these ancient myths, for inside many lie historical facts expressed in symbolical or figurative terms.

Above: Cronus devouring one of his children. Worried that he would be overthrown by one of his children – as he overthrew his own father, Uranus – Cronus swallowed each of his children as his wife Rhea gave birth. When Zeus was born, Rhea substituted a stone for him, and reared the future supreme god in secret.

The Genesis Account

Jews and Christians believe that the world was created by God. The basis for their belief is the creation story from the Bible as related in the Book of Genesis. Genesis in fact has two accounts of creation. In Chapter 1 there is the story of the six days of Creation and in Chapter 2 the story of Adam and Eve and their expulsion from the Garden of Eden. The second is the older account dating from about 950 to 850 BC. The story of the six days of Creation dates from some 400 years later and comes from what is known as "the priestly source."

"In the beginning," Chapter 1 of Genesis tells us, ". . . the earth was without form, and void; and darkness was upon the face of the deep. And the Spirit of God moved upon the face of the waters. And God said, let there be light: and there was light." This idea of "creation from nothing" is fundamental to the Jewish-Christian tradition, and it is vividly symbolized in an engraving by Robert Fludd, the 17th-century English mystic and artist, in which the Spirit of God, represented by a dove, is released by creative command and establishes an area of light in the enveloping darkness. Before the divine command was issued, however, there existed the primeval waters, "the deep," and this is an idea found in the beliefs of other civilizations. In the Babylonian Creation epic, the *Enuma Elish*, for instance, the primeval waters are identified with the goddess Tiamat, from whose name scholars have maintained the Hebrew word for "the deep," *tehom*, was derived. Another idea common to many creation stories is that of the separation of heaven from earth. On the second day, according to Chapter 1 of Genesis, "God made the firmament, and divided the waters which were under the firmament from the waters which were above the firmament."

The account goes on to tell how on the third day God separated the land from the sea and created vegetation. On the fourth day he created the sun and the moon, and therefore day and night. On the fifth day he created fish and birds, and on the sixth all the animals and finally man and woman, who he created "in his own image" and commanded to "Be fruitful, and multiply, and replenish the earth, and subdue it." Then he surveyed his creation, felt satisfied with it ("behold, it was very good"), and withdrew to rest.

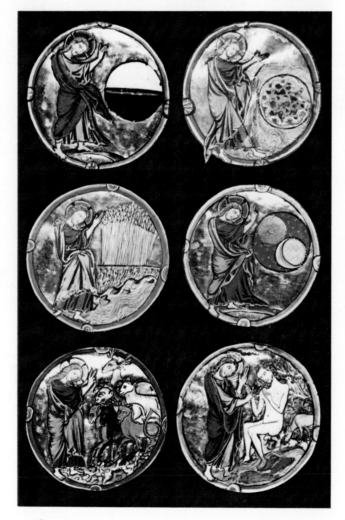

Above: God creates the first woman, Eve, seen here rising from the side of the sleeping Adam, the first man.
Left: the creation story from a French Bible of around 1250. The top two scenes depict the division of light from dark, (left), and the creation of dry land among the waters (right). Center, the creation of seed and herbs (left) and Sun, moon, and stars (right). Bottom, the creation of the animals (left) and finally, man (right).

The much older Chapter 2 of Genesis appears to take up the story where the priestly first chapter left it, only shifting the focus of interest to man. God, we learn, "formed man of the dust of the ground, and breathed into his nostrils the breath of life"; then he put him in the Garden of Eden, "to dress it and to keep it," and to give him company he created first of all the animals and then the female, Eve, whom he fashioned out of Adam's rib.

In this account the animals are created after man, and woman is fashioned from his rib, whereas in Chapter 1 the animals appear first and man and woman are created simultaneously. But it is not only in such details that the two Genesis accounts differ. They set out to explain different things: the origins respectively of the physical world and its life forms, and of man and human nature.

These then are the stories that have become a fundamental part of Western culture and consciousness, and in consequence, European literature and art in particular are full of reconstructions of the biblical creation story. *Paradise Lost*, by the English poet John Milton, the *Creation* oratorio by the Austrian composer Joseph Haydn, and the paintings in the Sistine Chapel in Rome by the Italian artist Michelangelo are just a few of these reconstructions.

By applying the categories of creation accounts invented by the American historian of mythology Joseph Campbell, we can place the Genesis accounts in the context of worldwide primitive creation stories. We then see that both Genesis stories come under the heading "the world created by the unaided power of a male god alone." This indicates their late composition, and that they are already the product of a male-dominated culture that had obliterated the much earlier concept of the earth goddess. Indeed, all analogy to human sexuality has been removed from their attitude

Above: Adam and Eve, tempted by the evil serpent, eat the forbidden fruit (left). For the sin of disobedience they are expelled from the Garden of Eden (right).

to Creation, and a concept of creation through the word – the command – has been substituted.

The fact that the Genesis stories have similarities with myths from surrounding cultures in no way invalidates the views of those who hold the traditional Jewish-Christian beliefs in the biblical Creation. Our primitive ancestors were seeking answers to the same questions that man asks today about his origin, his destiny, his culture. And the answers are always proportioned to the level of man's knowledge. In the language of the era when Genesis was compiled it would naturally be simple and figurative, a language adapted to the understanding of less-developed people, that could be rapidly decoded and understood by its hearers. It is not the language of today, however, which is why scholars and scientists are needed to discover the truths that they contain.

Although critics of the biblical view of the Creation point out that the compilers of the first of the Genesis stories were certainly not scientists, it is important to establish that nothing in the "priestly source" contradicts the findings of science. It is quite possible for the religious man to believe in the synthesis of life occurring in the biblical "waters under the heavens." That with the creation of land the two forms of life took place: plant and animal. That animal life branched into every "living creature that moves, which the waters brought forth abundantly . . . every winged bird" and "cattle and creeping thing and beast of the earth." There is the same chronological sweep of creation from galaxy to man. In the words of the British scientist Dr A. R. Peacocke, "from the primeval mass of hydrogen and helium atoms in the 'hot big bang' up to man himself we see a seamless web."

The Big Bang Theory

Above: an engraving from a book by the English physician and mystic Robert Fludd, published in 1617. It depicts hot, cold, dry, and moist "elements" seething in an original chaos, out of which God created the universe and everything in it including man himself.

According to the Bible, in the beginning God created the heavens and the earth. But according to many 20th-century scientists, in the beginning there was a Big Bang. It is an interesting point that both believers and scientists concede that there had to be a beginning – a moment of creation. Nor are the two views on what happened at the beginning incompatible either. Indeed, in 1951 Pope Pius XII adopted the big bang theory as the official theory of the Roman Catholic Church.

It was in fact a Belgian astronomer-priest, the Abbé Georges Lemaître, who suggested the big bang theory of the universe in 1927. According to him all matter in the universe was once condensed into one huge mass that became unstable and exploded. Other scientists, basing their work on recent astrophysical observations, have worked out that at the moment of the explosion a huge, intensely hot fireball of radiation was produced and began to expand rapidly. After hundreds of thousands of years, the fireball cooled sufficiently for atoms to form. Eventually, gravity gathered the matter together into galaxies in which individual stars formed. These galaxies, made up of millions, sometimes billions, of stars are not only moving away from each other, but do so at increasing velocities.

There are, of course, many theories other than the big bang that fit the events of an expanding universe. A serious opponent for many years was the steady state theory – a continuous creation universe where matter is being formed all the time from nothing to take the place of those galaxies that hurtle away at ever-increasing speeds and disappear from the universe.

Another theory, developed by the Swedish physicist Hannes Alfven, is that of an oscillating universe in which an immense cloud of gas contracts under its own gravitational attraction. As the cloud contracts, a succession of galaxies condense and then move out in hyperbolic orbits. Eventually they fall back into the center, diffuse, and the cycle starts again. We on earth are witnessing the expanding phase.

Despite the attraction of these theories, however, much of the latest evidence from outer space tends to favor the big bang theory. It is a somewhat sobering thought that while some astrophysicists are confident they know the origin and structure of the universe there are still many aspects of our own solar system that puzzle us. Astronomers are still not sure how it was formed. The strongest theory is that the solar system was created from recycled material from some exploded star. Massive stars formed in the galaxies burn rapidly then explode, scattering elements such

Above: the Crab Nebula, the result of a supernova explosion that occurred in 1054 AD. Such phenomena occur, it is believed, when an abundance of hydrogen suddenly reaches the center of an aging star causing a cataclysmic explosion. The Crab Nebula can be seen only as an expanding patch of gas.

as carbon, oxygen, and uranium into space. Gravity takes hold of this enriched debris and shapes it into new stars and planets. Did the atoms from one of these stars that blew itself apart form our sun, the entire solar system, and eventually, man himself?

Although we know very little about those early steps in the formation of the sun and planets, we do know with reasonable accuracy when the process took place. Studies of radioactive elements in the rocks on earth and also of meteorites, have enabled scientists to calculate that the earth was formed between 4500 and 5000 million years ago.

When the earth finally condensed as a solid sphere, the atmosphere surrounding it probably contained hydrogen, water, ammonia, methane, and hydrogen sulfide. Under the sun's heat the water would have been continually dissolved into hydrogen and oxygen. Because the earth's atmosphere is not strong enough to retain free hydrogen atoms they

escaped – as they still do – from our atmosphere. The oxygen that remained combined with other gases and elements to produce new substances. Gradually the atmosphere and surface of the earth became more oxydized as the planet cooled. Large amounts of water were released into the crust and onto the surface from the *mantle*, the layer of rock between the molten inner core of the earth and the outer crust. In the course of thousands of years water slowly collected in hollows and depressions of the earth's surface to form the oceans. Then, as the land developed, rainwater and rivers dissolved salts and other substances from the rocks and carried them down into the oceans, which is what gives them their salty character.

During this time, when the earth's surface was being shaped, many different organic compounds were being formed through the action of sunlight, atmospheric electricity, and radioactivity. Then, a few hundred million years ago, quite complicated organic compounds with big molecules were formed – among them amino acids and simple proteins, the basic building blocks of living substances. Some of these compounds began to build onto themselves and form more and more complicated structures and it was at this stage that life began. Later, a green substance known as *chlorophyl* was formed. It was the formation of chlorophyl that enabled plants to carry on their life processes by *photosynthesis*, – that is, they could use non-living material as food. Because plants liberate oxygen into the air, they in turn made it possible for animals to evolve. Photosynthesis, in fact, made life as we know it possible on earth.

When conditions were ripe for the spread of green plants they transformed the surface of the globe. The formation of organic substances was no longer haphazard, but a chain reaction that has covered every fertile land with a huge variety of green plants and filled land and ocean with a multitude of living forms.

Above: rock formations of the Giant's Causeway, Northern Ireland – the result of molten rock cooling rapidly near the earth's surface. Stresses in the crust split the rock into six-sided columns.

Right: a cloud of intergalactic gas and dust known as the Dumbbell Nebula. From such gas and spacedust new stars are formed.

Overleaf: the Trans-Americana Highway in Brazil. Trees and all green plants have functioned as oxygen factories since the dawn of life, constantly renewing this vital gas.

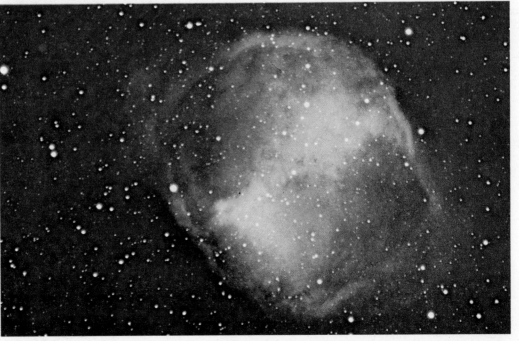

Chapter 2

The World Before Man

As soon as mankind became reconciled to the fact
that the world was really a vast globe moving
around the sun through almost empty space
scientists began investigating the shape and structure
of our planet, and although there is still much to
be discovered, they have pieced together a
surprisingly large amount of information.
We know that the earth is a globe because the
particles that make it up attract each other and cling
together, and the tightest, compactest form they
can assume is a sphere. Forces deep within this sphere
constantly act to make the earth an ever-changing
globe. Mountains are thrust up, surface forces
such as rain, wind, and ice all affect its structure. Our
earth is changing all the time. It is never still.

Opposite: an eruption on Heckla,
the active volcano in southern
Iceland. Iceland lies across the
Mid-Atlantic Ridge, formed where
a crack in the earth's crust
separates the great American and
Eurasian continental plates.

The Shifting Plates

It is the crust, the thin 12-mile-thick outer skin of our planet that has been the feature most familiar to mankind. But just how much do we know about it? The earth's crust is made up of a great variety of rocks that fall into two major groups: the light rocks, rich in silicon that make up the continents, and the heavier basaltic rocks, containing much iron and magnesium that form the foundations of the ocean floors and extend under the continents – and possibly right around the earth.

Important forces affect the crust, one of which originates in the mantle. This layer, between the earth's crust and the core, is hot and acts like a very thick liquid. Gradually, part of the mantle under the

crust cools, then expands, welling up through the crust to pour out over the surface and form great mountain chains, vast plateaus, and deep ocean trenches. These are the *tectonic* – or building and shaping – forces that originate deep inside our planet. The finer details, the molding of the features, are the results of the forces of erosion by weather or due to deposition by rivers and floodwaters.

The lighter continental rocks of the earth's crust appear to float on the denser basaltic layer and as material is gradually added to them from the mantle, so they become heavier and sink lower into the dense layer. On the other hand, as material is eroded from the continental rocks and they become lighter they rise again. When the continents become heavier and sink, the sea level rises. The seas then erode the coastlines of the continents, which get lighter, and rise up again, and the sea level drops. At the same time, material washed down from the continents is added to the ocean floors, which in turn makes the water level rise. There is, then, a continual movement up and down of the land masses, and a continual movement up and down of the sea level.

In 1915 a German meteorologist, Alfred Wegener, published a book that suggested that the continents

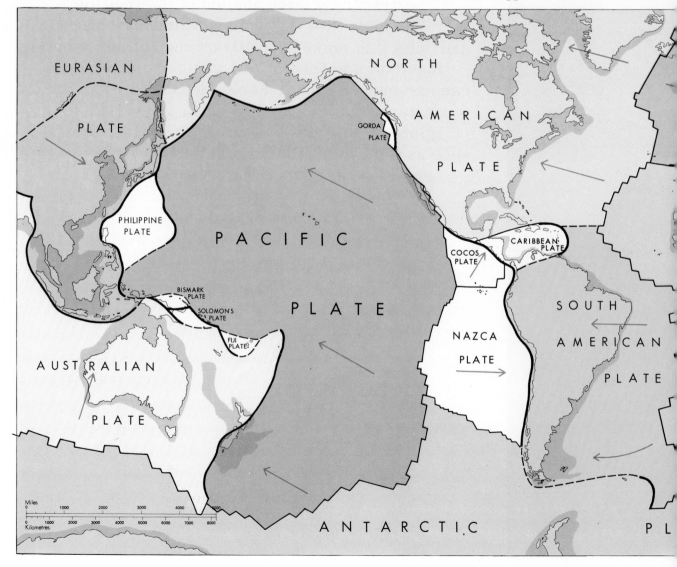

had gradually drifted apart, and that the process was still continuing. Wegener's theory is considered by earth scientists to be basically right. According to the latest evidence the crust is made up of several rigid plates with the continents embedded in them. At the plate boundaries, which coincide with the mid-oceanic ridges, new material is constantly welling up out of the earth and pushing the plates slowly away from the central ridge. Where two plates of crust meet, one overrides the other and material is "lost." As the lower plate descends to mix again with the molten interior of the earth, great hollows or trenches are formed and the areas are subject to intense volcanic activity.

Where one plate meets another that has a continent on its leading edge – as seems to be happening on the west coast of South America – a trench forms close to the coast. The continental crust is too buoyant to be sucked down and so buckles, throwing up mountain ranges like the great chain of the Andes which were probably formed in this way. If both plates have continents on their leading edges, then vast mountain ranges are thrown up as the lighter continental rocks are buckled – which is probably what happened when the plate carrying the Indian subcontinent collided with the Eurasian plate, forming the Himalayas. Some inland mountain ranges, such as the Ural'skiy Khrebet (Urals), probably mark the margins of ancient plate activity and may indicate the boundaries of ancient oceans that no longer exist.

Evidence of the drift of continents has come from recent oceanographical research. The research drilling and coring vessel *Glomar Challenger* has brought up sediments from the sea bed laid down over 200 million years ago to be examined and dated. But the most important evidence to support the concept of ocean-spreading has come from the study of the magnetism of the rocks.

The study of the rocks on either side of the Mid-Atlantic Ridge showed that they were arranged in bands of alternating intensity of magnetization, which fits in with the knowledge that the polarity of the earth's magnetic field reverses from time to time. This indicates that as basaltic liquid poured out of the crack down the center of the ridge, it solidified on either side, to be magnetized in the then prevailing direction of the earth's magnetic field. New material forced up through the crack pushed the original solidified bands on either side farther apart, and the new material in turn solidified.

Left: world map showing the crustal plates that make up the solid surface of the earth. Molten material from deep within the mantle keeps the plates in constant motion.

Below: the European Alps, stretching from southeastern France, through to Yugoslavia, were forced up when the Eurasian and African plates collided.

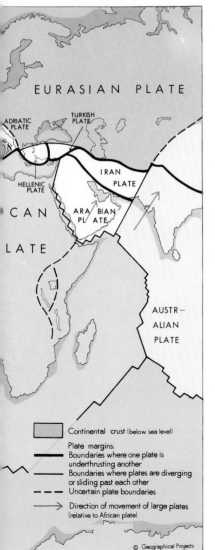

EURASIAN PLATE

ADRIATIC PLATE

TURKISH PLATE

HELLENIC PLATE

IRAN PLATE

ARABIAN PLATE

CAN

LATE

AUSTR–ALIAN PLATE

Continental crust (below sea level)

Plate margins:
Boundaries where one plate is underthrusting another
Boundaries where plates are diverging or sliding past each other
Uncertain plate boundaries
Direction of movement of large plates (relative to African plate)

© Geographical Projects

23

World Structure

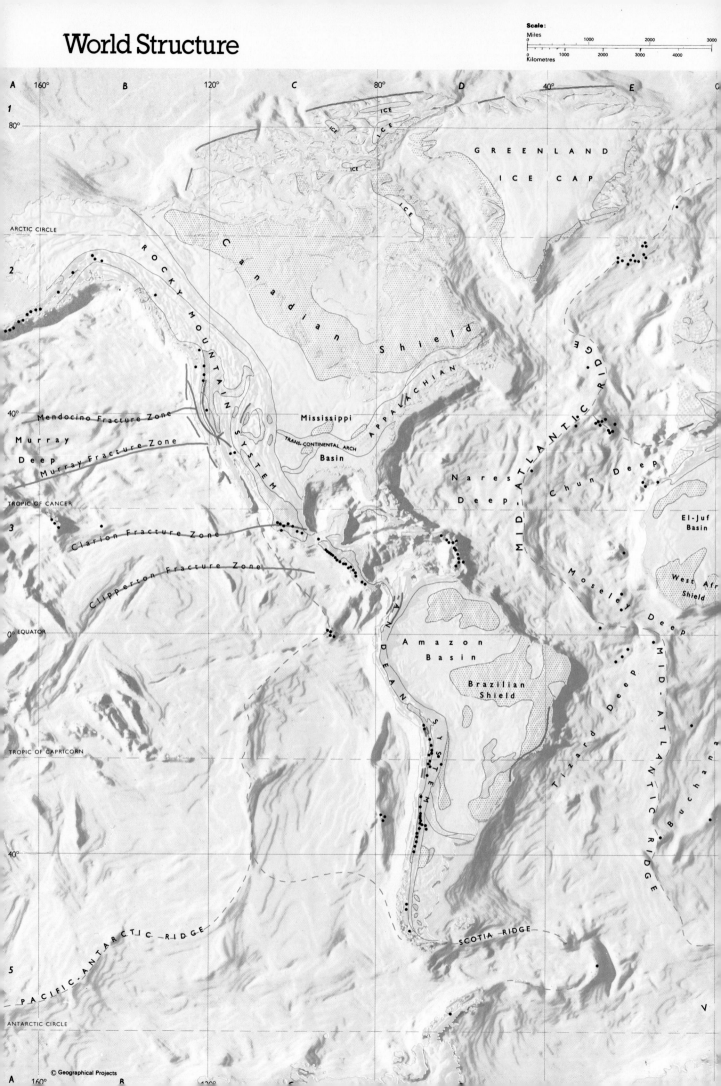

Scale:
Miles
Kilometres

A 160° B 120° C 80° D 40° E

1
80°
ARCTIC CIRCLE

G R E E N L A N D
ICE   CAP

ICE

2

R O C K Y   M O U N T A I N   S Y S T E M

C a n a d i a n   S h i e l d

MID-ATLANTIC RIDGE

40°
Mendocino Fracture Zone
M u r r a y
APPALACHIAN
Mississippi
Deep
TRANS-CONTINENTAL ARCH
Basin
Murray Fracture Zone
Narest
TROPIC OF CANCER

Deep · Chun · Deep

3
Clarion Fracture Zone
MID-ATLANTIC RIDGE
El-Juf
Basin

Clipperton Fracture Zone
Moseley   Deep
West Afr
Shield

0° EQUATOR
A
N
D
E
A
N
Amazon
Basin
Tizard Deep
MID-ATLANTIC RIDGE
Buchana

S
Y
Brazilian
Shield

TROPIC OF CAPRICORN
S
T
E
M

40°

PACIFIC·ANTARCTIC·RIDGE
SCOTIA RIDGE

5
ANTARCTIC CIRCLE

A 160° B 120°

Below: the map shows the structural features of the earth's crust, both in the islands and continents and the ocean floors. The dots indicate areas of crustal instability – earthquakes and volcanoes – which generally follow the belts of comparatively recently formed mountains such as the Alps, Himalayas, Rockies, and Andes.

Fossils and Forests

Although we know little about the first 4000 million years of the earth's history we have begun to build up the story of the last 500 million years or so from the record left by fossils.

Geologists divide the life of earth into four intervals of time they call *eras*. The first era, from the origins of the planet to about 500 million years ago, is termed Pre-Cambrian and is an era for which there is virtually no fossil evidence of life. The next is the Palaeozoic, lasting from 500 to 225 million years ago, and is the first era of which we have any detailed knowledge. Thirdly comes the Mesozoic era, from 225 to 65 million years ago, and finally the Cenozoic, or Cainozoic era, from 65 million years ago to the present day. Such enormous time spans have been subdivided into *periods* for greater accuracy when dating deposits or fossils.

A time of intense activity or earth movements within a geological period is known as an *epoch*. During the Pre-Cambrian there were six epochs of mountain-building, known as *orogenies*, and there have been three epochs since. The various orogenies are usually named for the location where the movements took place.

Slight traces have been found of the three earliest orogenies yet identified in the Pre-Cambrian: the earliest is in Manitoba, the next is found both in South Dakota and near the White Sea in northern Europe, and the third is again in South Dakota, around the Great Bear Lake in Canada and also in Western Australia. The first period of which there is clearer evidence of intensive mountain-building is known as the Laurentian orogeny, from the range in eastern Canada. The activity took place about 1000 million years ago, but apart from eastern Canada, few of these mountains remain, most have long since been worn away and hidden under deposits. Little evidence of life has so far been found from the Pre-Cambrian era, though a fossil impression of a primitive organism, more than 600 million years old, has been found in South Australia.

The early Palaeozoic era, which followed, was one of almost continuous erosion and deposition, the sea covered great areas of the earth's surface and although there were no major mountain-building phases there were series of minor movements. During the early periods, the Cambrian and Ordovician, many groups of marine plants and animals developed and life advanced in complexity. Some of the organisms developed rigid bodies, or shells, and their protective coverings were preserved in the sediments to leave us a fossil record that gives a clear picture of their evolution.

The end of the Silurian period, almost halfway through the Palaeozoic era, was marked by a massive mountain-building episode, known as the Caledonian orogeny after the ancient name for Scotland, where geologists first found the evidence. Traces have since been discovered in Norway and in North America, in the Appalachians, where it is termed Older Appalachian. In the latter half of the Palaeozoic era – the Devonian, Carboniferous, and Permian periods – a number of small earth movements culminated in the gigantic Hercynian orogeny, known in North America as the Younger Appalachian. As with earlier periods of mountain-building, the mountains have long since been obliterated by wind, rain, and ice, and there is little evidence now of these great mountain chains, except in some areas of the Appalachians, in central Europe, and Ireland.

By the end of the Palaeozoic some animals had developed an internal rod – a spinal cord – instead of a shell, and from these animals the first vertebrates evolved rapidly. Some animal forms landed on the shores and survived. With the cooler and drier times during periods of earth movements, some creatures migrated to dry land and became the first amphibians. In the warm, dry Devonian period plants evolved and clothed the land in forests of tree ferns, giant horsetails, and many other strange trees. Toward the end of the Carboniferous period, the sea again inundated the land, eventually drowning great tracts of forest and decaying swamp vegetation, burying them under

Above: a fossilized ammonite shell from the Palaeozoic era. Rocks from this era contain a large number and variety of fossils of sea creatures. Upheavals in the crust during the era created important mountain systems such as the Appalachian and Caledonian mountains.

Above: part of a peat-bog in Galway, Ireland. Peat is the partly decayed plant matter that collected in swamps and marshes over very long periods of time. It provides a valuable heating resource especially in a country like Ireland that has neither extensive forests or coal deposits.

layers of sediments. As the land alternately rose and sank, the process was repeated, the deposits became compressed and hardened, and the vegetable matter formed coal. The great coal deposits of the Northern Hemisphere were all formed during the Carboniferous period. The last period, the Permian, named for the Russian province of Perm, where rocks from this age were well developed, was a period of violent contrast and change. Deserts cut off salt seas in the north, while glaciers moved over the land in the south.

The next era, the Mesozoic, was again one of almost continuous erosion and deposition. The first period, the Triassic, saw the development of reptiles, mammals, and birds. The reptilian advance marked one of the most important biological innovations, the appearance of plant-eating vertebrates, for until then vertebrates had been carnivores. Also, earth scientists believe that during the Triassic the lands of the world, which until then comprised one single supercontinent of Pangaea, began to split apart.

By the end of the Triassic, the split between the northern land mass, Laurasia, and the southern, Gondwana, was complete, though the two remained close together, or even in contact, near a position now represented by the Strait of Gibraltar. About the same time, a large mass detached itself from Gondwana and began its long journey northward to its present position as the Indian subcontinent. Africa detached itself and moved north, North America and South America moved westward separately, causing great upheavals along their western margins and opening up the great rift that now forms the Atlantic Ocean. Throughout the Triassic and the following Jurassic and Cretaceous periods, there was a rapid evolution of reptiles, but by the end of the Mesozoic era there occurred the extinction of all the giant reptiles – one of the most dramatic biological events ever to have hap-

Above: this Brazilian rain forest recalls the lush vegetation that covered vast areas of the earth during the Carboniferous period. Plants grew in profusion, with giant cone-bearing scale trees reaching a height of 100-or-more-feet. From the decaying of these and other vegetation the great coal-bearing seams around the earth were laid down.

Overleaf: the wavelike dips and crests in a massive upfold of the earth's crust are the result of an upwelling of molten rock in the earth's mantle that buckled a large mass of crustal rock – which gives some idea of the tremendous forces at work within the crust of the earth.

Above: During the Pleistocene Ice Age, nearly 2,000,000 years ago, four great icecaps formed over the northern part of the world and four glacier systems developed over the world's high mountains.

pened and an event we still cannot explain satisfactorily.

The movements of the continents continued slowly throughout the Cenozoic era, the Atlantic widened; India completed its journey and piled itself up against the massive continent of Eurasia; Australia became detached from Antarctica and moved gradually northward; the Pacific shrank. It was in the Cenozoic that the last great orogeny occurred. This was the Alpine, (in America referred to as the Circum-Pacific), which began about 50 million years ago and ended about 20

million years ago – although from the recent evidence of earth tremors, many doubt that the Alpine orogeny has yet finished. It was during this mountain-building period that all the great mountain chains, the Rockies, the Andes, the Alps, Bolshoy Kavkaz (Caucasus) and Himalaya, came into being.

By the Cenozoic era two major variations had developed in the animal kingdom; placental and marsupial mammals were able to feed their offspring with milk secreted by the mother and the mammals also developed a covering of fur. Their fur, warm blood, and consequent ability to maintain body temperature at a constant level, were to give mammals a distinct advantage in a world that was to grow cold. In the first two periods of the Cenozoic, the Eocene and

ly, then contracted, shaping and carving the land by the sheer weight of the ice as it retreated. The Ice Age began just over one million years ago and ended about 10,000 years ago. The ice advanced and retreated in four main cycles, causing worldwide changes in climate and alterations of sea level. These cycles of abnormally cold climate, alternating with periods in which the climate was warmer, are known respectively as glacial and interglacial periods. With the onset of a glacial period, the snowline gradually advanced down the mountain sides, the glaciers became established on mountains where normally they were absent and existing glaciers enlarged and advanced into the lowlands. With the approach of an interglacial period this process went into reverse, the glaciers and ice-sheets dwindled and retreated, the sea level rose as the ice melted, and meltwaters flowed rapidly down to the coasts.

In the glaciations of the Pleistocene Ice Age, the ice covered approximately 25 percent of the earth's land area. Just over 10,000 years have elapsed since the last retreat of the ice and today the remains of the last Ice Age cover only some 10 percent of the land surface, mostly comprising the vast ice sheets of Greenland and Antarctica. We may at present be in the early centuries of an interglacial, which could be followed by yet another glacial period that could obliterate much that man has built and achieved.

Above: curved slopes of this valley in Waterton Lakes National Park, Alberta show where a glacier has broadened and deepened the original V-shape into a typical U-shape of a glacial valley. The action of glaciers greatly changes the appearance of the land.

Oligocene, two developments occurred in the plants that were to play an important role in the subsequent history of the biosphere and the crustal rocks. The first of these was the appearance of a tiny plant form, the diatom, a single cell in a shell of silica. These minute plants became the grass of the seas, the energy base of marine food chains, and it is deposits formed from their shells that produce the light porous rock known as diatomite. The second plant development was the arrival of grass on the land, which favored the development of grazing animals.

In the most recent period, the Pleistocene, the Northern Hemisphere witnessed a great epoch of glaciation, the ice sheets and glaciers expanded great-

Right: Loess, a kind of silt, covers immense areas of central and northwestern parts of the United States, eastern Europe, and eastern China. It forms fertile farm-lands, like this seen here in Kansas. The main source of loess is the mud left behind after the last ice age. Winds carried the dried mud to cover vast areas of flat grassland.

The Physiography of Our World

The Shaping of the Land

The surface of our earth is continually changing. The greatest instrument of change is the movement of the crustal plates, while the longer-term shaping is carried out by the earth's atmosphere and oceans.

The movements of the crustal plates cause pressures and tensions to build up, and the crust bends, warps, folds, and fractures. The forces that cause these major landforms are twofold; there are vertical forces that cause parts of the crust to be lifted up or dropped down, and horizontal forces that cause complex folding. There are of course also the deformations caused by earthquakes and volcanic action.

Warping and faulting are usually the result of vertical forces in the crust. As the crust cracks along the lines of weakness, displacements occur in the rock layers and sometimes fault scarps – cliffs – form along these lines. In a normal fault the two sides move in opposite directions and if cliffs form, the cliff face inclines backward. One of the most spectacular examples of a normal fault is the San Andreas fault in California, where the land on the western coastal side has moved northward and the land to the east has moved southward. With a reverse fault, the forces move toward each other and the cliff face inclines forward and may even overhang.

If vertical faulting continues over a long period, fault blocks are raised up to form mountains or plateaus such as the Sierra Nevada in the western USA. If a fault block drops down, a rift valley, or graben, is formed. The most extensive rift system in the world is in East Africa where it starts in the region of the confluence of the Shire and Zambezi rivers and stretches north, dividing into two gigantic arms through East Africa, then continuing through Ethiopia, the Red Sea to the Jordan valley, and finally north into Syria – a distance of some 3000 miles.

When the tectonic activity results in folding, the horizontal layers of the crust are deformed into a simple series of waves. The top of a wave's arch is known as the anticline, the bottom the syncline. If the pressures are great the folds become more complex. The anticlines can lean over or even lie on top of the neighboring fold so that the layers are once more horizontal and form what are known as recumbent folds.

Earthquakes, too, cause deformations of the crust, although on a smaller scale than tectonic activity. They can shake the ground, and in severe shocks, topple buildings, rupture river banks, and actually split the ground open. A whole series of deep gashes marking the edges of crustal plates encircles the Pacific. It is a ring of instability that often results in earthquakes and volcanic eruptions. The Chilean earthquake of 1960 caused one of the longest tears in the earth's surface, shaking an area of over 1000 square miles. When an earthquake occurs on the deep ocean floor, however, the only disturbance on the surface thousands of feet above is usually no more than a series of small waves, perhaps a foot high, but often stretching in arcs over 200 miles long. These waves travel at incredible speeds across the Pacific and when they approach the shores are transformed into tidal waves or tsunamis – killer walls of water, often over 100 feet high, which crash down on the land and cause widespread destruction.

Volcanic action is not always accompanied by violent eruptions. Often fluid, basaltic lava pours out through ruptures in the earth's surface creeping and spreading slowly over the surrounding land. In this way an area of about 200,000 square miles in the Columbia basin of northwest USA was inundated by molten lava in the Cenozoic era, and at the same time, the Deccan of India was also subject to vast outpourings.

The final modeling of the features of our earth is due to the processes of weathering and erosion. There are two main types of weathering: physical, which causes rock disintegration without changing the chemical constituents, and chemical, where some, or all, of

Above: the meandering Uruguay river in South America. The slow-moving currents eat into the outer bank of each bend developing them into huge loops.
Left: this man's garden collapsed when the sea undermined a nearby cliff on England's east coast. His house, too, will fall victim to the encroaching sea.

the minerals in the rock are altered. It is rare, if ever, that either process acts alone. Physical weathering is caused by temperature changes and crystallization. The temperature changes lead to minute internal fractures – always greater in the surface layers because rock is a bad conductor of heat. Crystallization is a result of water or salts that penetrate the rocks then freeze and thaw, at the same time changing in volume and causing stresses inside the rocks. Chemical weathering is the result of chemical change of the minerals in the rocks due to the varying rates in which they take up water, or reactions such as those caused by the acids in rainwater. If the minerals change, then the rocks are subject once again to stresses that cause them to break down. When this

happens the material is in a form that can be transported by water, ice, or wind.

Water is both the main force of erosion and the agent primarily responsible for the removal of the waste material produced by weathering. As the water falls on the land, it drains down the slopes and this run-off is effected by the angle of the slope, the amount of vegetation covering the land, and the underlying rocks.

Where water collects in hollows, it flows downhill as a stream, gathering more and more side streams until it becomes the early stages of a river. As a river moves downhill to the sea, it picks up and drops sediment again and again, until near the coast its course flattens, its speed drops, and so does the size of the particles it carries. At the end of its course, the now slow river deposits first the coarse material, then the

Overleaf: the Grand Canyon, in Arizona was gouged out of the living rock of the Colorado Plateau over tens of thousands of years by the Colorado river.

35

fine particles of sand and finally the clays. The old river meanders across its plain in a series of loops and, reaching the sea, may build up new land at its mouth as some of the material is deposited to form a delta, such as the vast area created by the river Nile where it enters the Mediterranean.

The shorelines of land masses are constantly being altered by water. Its effect on the shape of the shore, depends upon the hardness of the rock involved, on the nature of the sands, and the ability of both to withstand the combined pressure of wind and water. The most important and most obvious of the coast-shaping forces are the waves. Their erosive effect is due partly to the impact of water against the rock and partly to the action of the material removed by the waves as they scour or deposit. Tides and currents also play some part in erosion. The final result of all these erosive forces depends on the type of coast, whether it is a rocky one with cliffs, or a low-lying, sandy shore. The wave action can be destructive, weakening the cliffs and removing material; or constructive, piling up sediment to form new features such as sand spits. While the sea devours part of a coast it may help to build land outward elsewhere.

The efficiency of water in its liquid form as a shaping and transport agent is only matched by water in its solid form, as ice. During the Pleistocene Glaciation vast ice sheets covered large areas in the Northern Hemisphere and shaped much of its landscape. The main scouring action usually happens beneath the middle of the ice sheet. As the ice moves outward, it crushes the surface rocks underneath it and gradually carries the debris to its margins. Here the material that piles up is known as moraine. If the ice advances again the moraine is pushed forward; if it retreats, the moraine is left behind indicating the ice's former position. When the ice sheet finally disappears the landscape it leaves behind is completely changed into a confused relief where the ice has stripped off the weathered rock, eroded hollows, and deposited material in a haphazard manner. The drainage pattern is nearly always destroyed and the final terrain is likely to be ill-drained, boggy, and dotted with innumerable lakes – such as can be seen today in Finland.

The effects of ice on a mountainous landscape are much more dramatic and spectacular. High up in the mountains, above the snowline, the snow accumulates in hollows and valley heads, settling under its own weight until it becomes compressed into ice. The hollows are enlarged as the rock around the sides shatters and the ice begins to move downhill under gravity. The basis of the hollows are deepened to form a cirque or corrie. The rivers of ice move on down the valleys, cutting and grinding their way, removing loose bedrock and pushing it ahead of them or to one

Top: this bedrock has been smoothed and deeply scored by the abrasive action of rock embedded in a glacier.
Left: the main glacier has retreated from this Greenland valley, leaving tributary glaciers flowing into it. Dark areas at the edge of the ice are rocks carried in the ice.

side, or carrying it along in the lower levels of the ice. The glacier moves by sliding at the base. When the glacier moves over a steep change in slope, its speed increases and cracks or crevasses develop, some of which may be very deep.

When the glaciers retreat up their valleys, the rubble or moraines they leave behind may be wholly or partially swept away by the rivers of meltwater and eventually distributed along the length of the valleys, over the lowlands, or as outwash fans at the ends of the valleys.

Winds are the third great force of erosion. When loaded with sand and dust, as they are in arid regions, winds can be powerful abrasive agents. Wind erosion has carved bizarre shapes in rocks and many beautiful formations are found in Nevada and Arizona in the southwest United States, and in the mountainous regions of Ahaggar and Tibesti in North Africa. In another kind of erosion, deflation, the wind lifts and removes particles of sand leaving behind a surface strewn with gravel as is found over vast areas in the Sahara.

Like water and ice, wind deposits as well as erodes. Its deposits form features that can vary in size between the small ripples like those left in the wet sand when the tide goes out, and the vast sand dunes that can reach to a height of over 100 feet. These dunes can move forward, burying everything in their path, then move on again leaving behind them a bare landscape. In areas where the wind has been shedding its load over a long period, immensely thick layers of loess, as the wind-blown dust is called, accumulate, often reaching a depth of several hundred feet. In northern China, where large amounts of loess are found, it varies in depth between 400 feet and 1000 feet.

Below: a desert landscape shaped by the action of the wind. Heating and cooling loosen rock particles which are then picked up by the wind so that they sandblast other rocks, smoothing their surfaces and also turning the particles into rounded sand grains.

The Climate of Our World

ARCTIC CIRCLE

TROPIC OF CANCER

EQUATOR

TROPIC OF CAPRICORN

ANTARCTIC CIRCLE

1 Tropical climates	1b Savanna	1d Semi-desert	2 Sub-tropical	3 Mid-latitude	3a(ii) Humid cool	3c Semi-desert	4 Polar climates	5 Mountain climates
	Humid climate	*Dry climate*	climates	climates	summers	3d Desert	4a Polar	5 Mountain climates
1a Rainy	1c Highland	1e Desert	2a Mediterranean	3a(i) Humid warm	3a(iii) East coast	3e Sub-polar	4b Ice caps	
Humid climate	*Humid climate*	*Dry climate*	2b Humid	summers	3b Marine west coast			

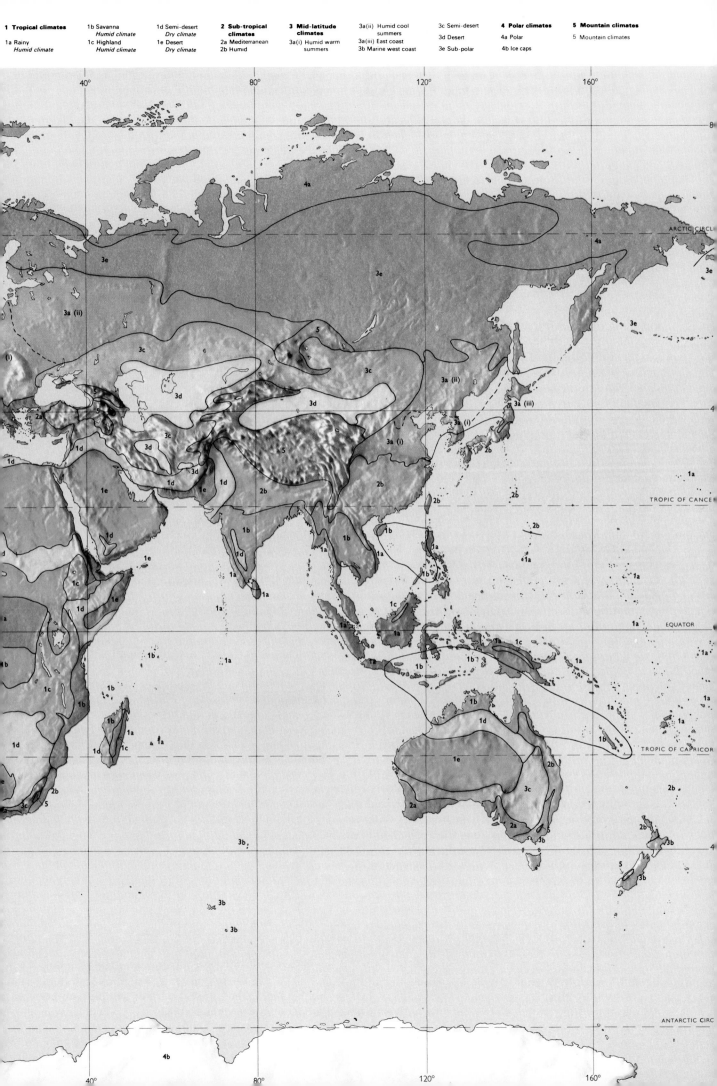

Our World and Its Weather

Because the earth is a sphere, the sun's rays hit the surface at different angles. The effect is to make the climate hotter near the Equator, where the sun's rays are more direct, and colder near the poles, where the rays are slanting to the earth's surface. The amount of sunlight received is therefore largely determined by latitude, although the length of day, which is itself partly controlled by latitude and partly by the season of the year, is also of some importance. But before solar radiation reaches the earth it has first to pass through our atmosphere.

Less than half the amount of radiation from the sun received by the ionosphere, the outer margins of our atmosphere, actually reaches the earth's surface. Some of the energy is scattered and lost by dust particles as it passes through the atmosphere, some is absorbed by water vapor and gases, and finally, some is reflected back by the actual surface of the earth. It is in fact the radiation reflected back by the earth that is trapped and heats our atmosphere, so that it acts as a giant greenhouse. Our atmosphere can also be said to be a gigantic factory in which the winds, storms, and rain are manufactured.

Moisture exists in the atmosphere though it is not until millions of droplets of water collect and form clouds that it is obvious to observers. This moisture exists as gas, liquid, and solid and changes from one form – water vapor, water droplets, ice crystals – to another very frequently. The air is continually receiving, and returning, moisture to the earth's surface. It receives it by evaporation from all water surfaces – from oceans to tiny dewdrops – and by transpiration as land plants lose their water vapor. It returns water in the form of rain, snow, or hail, and as with so many happenings on earth, this is a never-ending cycle.

If the humidity or moisture content of the air is low, strong evaporation occurs, if the humidity is high there is little evaporation because the air is unable to take up much more moisture. Once the air is saturated it will release its moisture. Warm air can hold more moisture than cold air, so that when air is cooled it releases its moisture. Temperature changes, then, are the main factors in precipitation.

The very hot air of equatorial latitudes holds lots of moisture, and rises quickly to a great height, where it cools rapidly and releases its moisture in the form of the torrential rains that are typical of such regions. Mountainous areas are also often well supplied with rain because when clouds are blocked by high ground,

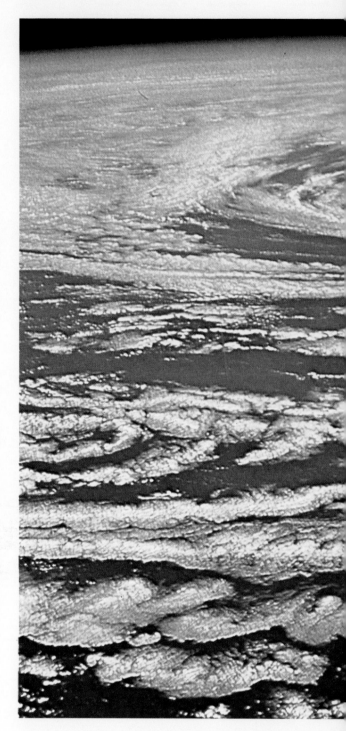

Above: a visible reminder of the invisible atmosphere that encapsulates our earth – a giant "pin wheel" weather system above the Pacific Ocean as photographed from the Apollo 9 spacecraft. It is the 6–10-mile thick layer of air nearest the earth that contains most of the atmospheric water and the turbulent currents that create the weather.

they are forced to rise – an action that cools the air releasing its moisture onto the higher slopes. When the now dry air passes over the mountain range and moves down the other side it is once more warmed and again begins to draw up moisture from the land. When air is warmed as it moves from a cool region to a hot one it absorbs all the moisture from the land instead of releasing it, and in areas where this happens continually the land becomes a desert.

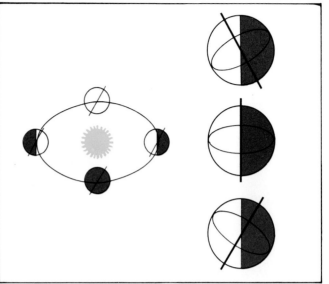

Pressure is an important property of the earth's atmosphere. The pressure of the air at sea level is high, whereas in the higher reaches of the air the pressure is lower. In addition, warm air is lighter than cold air and so exerts less pressure. It is these differences in air pressure that cause air movement, or winds. Three important factors affect the pattern of winds produced: the rotation of the earth, which deflects wind to the right in the Northern Hemisphere and to the left in the Southern Hemisphere; the tilt of the earth's axis, which means that the sun is not always overhead at the same latitude; and the unequal distribution of land and sea, which causes contrasts in the air temperature because land takes up, and loses, heat more rapidly than does water.

Areas where the atmospheric pressure is high are called anticyclones, or highs, and where it is low, cyclones, or depressions. In an anticyclone the air is sinking and gives rise to periods of relatively stable conditions, clear skies, and often extremes of heat or cold. In a cyclone, the warm air rises and the cold air moves in to take its place causing unstable conditions, cloud, and rain.

The boundary zone between a belt of cold air advancing into a warm air area is known as a cold front. The zone between warm air and the next area of cold air over which it is being pushed is known as a warm front.

Weather, then, is determined by all the changing conditions of temperature, humidity, pressure, rainfall, cloudiness, and wind. Climate, on the other hand, is governed by latitude, by relative positions of land and sea, and by local geographical conditions. Different types of climate are brought about by these various elements and by the pattern of seasons in different combinations. The seasons are chiefly due to the pattern of changes in temperature caused by the inclination of the earth's axis and revolution of the earth around the sun. The pattern is not the same everywhere. In the tropical zone the temperature is always high and the season depends upon rainfall. In some tropical areas there is only one season, hot and wet; in others there are three seasons, cool, hot, and wet; these are the monsoon regions. In polar regions temperature is the prime factor; there are two seasons, hot and cold, and the change from one to the other is very abrupt. But in the intermediate latitudes, where the change from hot to cold is more gradual, there are four seasons of almost equal duration, the hot, the cold, and the two seasons that mark the change between them – in other words, summer and winter, fall and spring.

Chapter 3

Northwest Europe

Northwest Europe, with its cool summers and generally mild winters, varied soils and valuable mineral deposits, is made up for the most part of densely populated states. The climate encourages crop growth and animal rearing, while the mining of coal and iron ore and the extraction of oil and natural gas encourages a wide range of industries. With the decline of the Mediterranean lands as the center of world civilization, this highly developed corner of the great Eurasian land mass came to lead the world in ideas, power, and material progress. Many of its people have been seafarers and explorers. As a result, Northwest Europe has been for almost 400 years a prosperous cultural center for much of the world.

Opposite: this industrial center in a major coal-mining region, Saarbrücken in Germany, is typical of many areas in the heavily industrialized northwest corner of Europe.

Europe: Political

Scale:
Miles
0   100   200   300   400   500   600   700
0   100   200   300   400   500   600   700   800   900   1000   1100
Kilometres

Lands of the North

A broken chain of very old mountains, formed about 400 million years ago, stretches along the north-western seaboard of Scandinavia, across Scotland and over the northern part of Ireland. These mountains, formed during the Caledonian orogeny, have since been fractured by successive waves of earth movements and worn down by the forces of erosion. Only the hardest rocks remain, so that streams are forced to cut their valleys along fracture and fault lines in the rocks. North of the Caledonian belt in the British Isles are the remains of an ancient shield, considered by some geologists to be the eastern edge of the great Laurentian Shield of Canada. To the south along the southern edges of what is really the western extremity of the great North European Plain, the warped and much folded uplands that were created in the Hercynian mountain-building epoch of the late Paleozoic, appear in the British Isles in the Pennines, South Wales, and southern Ireland.

The British lowlands are made up of rocks that are much younger than the mountains and these lowland rocks lie in alternating hard and soft layers. The result is a special kind of landscape: where hard beds reach the surface the hills are low with one steep slope – the scarp – and one gentle slope – the dip; where the soft rocks occur, the rivers have worn wide valleys. In Scandinavia, the lowland rocks are ancient crystalline rocks from Pre-Cambrian times, and millions of years older than the Caledonian highlands – so old, in fact, that they have been worn away until they are almost flat. They slope south and southeast, dipping under the newer sediments deposited during the Pleistocene and more recent periods. This buried extension of the shield forms the vast area of the North European Plain and the lowlands of Russia, from the Gulf of Finland to the Black Sea.

The spectacular scenery in the mountains of Northwest Europe is a result of the erosive powers of the ice that carved the rocks and carried away vast quantities of debris during the Pleistocene Glaciation. Scandinavia, Iceland, and nearly all the British Isles were covered by ice during this time. The glaciers that moved down from the mountains and along the river courses gouged out the characteristic, deep U-shaped valleys. The last retreat of the ice began 20,000 years ago, after four successive periods of advance and retreat.

On the mainland of Europe the ice completely overwhelmed Scandinavia, covering almost three million square miles, reaching as far south as latitude 40°N.

At its maximum extent in the British Isles the ice covered the whole of Ireland, Wales, and reached as far south as the Midlands and East Anglia. When eventually the ice melted, the combination of water from the melting ice and the rise of the land after it had shed its heavy burden resulted in a rise of sea level of some 300 feet, drowning the coastlines and flooding the valleys to form long, narrow inlets – the fjords of Norway and the sea lochs of Scotland.

In some parts of Sweden and Finland the ice swept the surface clean and exposed the bare rock. Lakes formed where glaciers had scoured out hollows in the rocks or where moraines had dammed streams and changed the drainage patterns. In the British Isles, in the southeast where the glaciers merged and ice sheets covered the land, a thick deposit of glacial drift, known locally as boulder clay, was left covering much of Ireland, the Midlands, and East Anglia. Iceland is only 60 million years old, a youngster by the geological calendar. It is situated at the northern end of the Mid-Atlantic Ridge, on the junction of the North American and Eurasian plates. The island is made up almost entirely of volcanic rocks, the oldest being of Tertiary (early Cenozoic) age, and has many volcanoes that are still active. Along with the volcanoes there are geysers and hot springs from which the capital, Reykjavik, gets its hot water supply. Much of the island is desolate or under snow, so that the population lives in only a quarter of the country's total area.

Above: this fiord, like many around the coasts of Scandinavia, was probably formed by earth movements that caused cracks in the mountains. Glacial movement during the Ice Age accounted for their final shaping.

47

Europe

Above: a fishing port in Norway in winter. Norway's ports are ice free – warmed by the Gulf Stream.

Iceland and Northwest Europe are warmed in winter by the North Atlantic Current, the eastern end of the Gulf Stream, which comes across the Atlantic from the neighborhood of the Florida coast. Norway's ports are ice-free all winter and even at latitude 71°N the sea never freezes; in contrast, the St Lawrence river estuary in North America, which is much farther south between 47° and 50°N, freezes over for four months in winter. Prevailing onshore westerly winds pass over the warm water of the Gulf Stream and pick up a lot of water vapor, when they reach the land and are forced to rise, they lose this. The annual rainfall at Bergen on the west coast of Norway is 80 inches, but on the eastern side of the mountain ranges, at Stockholm in Sweden, it is only 22 inches.

The climate of the British Isles, on the other hand, shows a most delicate adjustment between warmth and coolness, between the hotter climate of south Europe and the colder lands of Scandinavia. A small shift northward of the westward passage of the cyclones can bring in the warm, hot sunny days of a Mediterranean summer. A southerly shift of these depressions can allow cold Arctic air to flow south over the land. The combination of such a finely balanced climate and the varying relief of the land encourages a variety of vegetation, from the bare, treeless slopes of the mountains of the Scottish Highlands to the sheltered, lush lowlands facing the English Channel where vines can be raised. The British people are made up of a fusion of the main streams of invaders from the mainland of Europe: Saxons and Angles from what is now Germany and Denmark; Vikings from Scandinavia; and, later, Normans from France.

Variety is the main feature of the British Isles – in land use, mining, industry, trade, and transportation, and human development.

Since earliest times London has held its own as the hub of the country, the center of government and commerce, within easy reach of the continent of Europe. Although linked with northern Europe through the European Economic Community (EEC), its position as the unifying force within the United Kingdom is challenged by the surge of nationalism and desire for devolution in Scotland and Wales.

In Norway, Sweden, and Finland, the terrain is not so hospitable: the rugged mountainous area of much of the region allows little room for agriculture; the scoured surface of the Baltic Shield in lowland Sweden and Finland is not naturally a rich farming area. These countries cannot support a large population and the peoples are concentrated along the coasts and in the southern lowlands of Sweden and Finland.

In Norway, many of the people have been forced to turn to the sea for their livelihood and the lucrative fishing and shipping industries support a great percentage of the population. Discovery of oil under the floor of the North Sea is an added source of wealth for Norway. Scandinavians lack the traditional fuel, coal, but utilize water power to the full. Once the installations are paid for, hydroelectric power is very cheap and has been put to good use in a flourishing timber industry, the production of aluminum from imported bauxite, chemical factories, and in refining ores such as iron, zinc, nickel, silver, and copper.

Below: logging in Bjornoff Fiord, Sweden. It is the most heavily wooded of the Scandinavian countries. The forests of Sweden, which cover the northern, central, and western parts of the country, are its richest resource.

Plains and Polders

The hills and plains of northern Europe embrace one of the most technologically and industrially advanced areas in the world, and also one of the most densely populated. The region spreads out from the southern shores of the North and Baltic seas in three west-east bands. First, the North European Plain; secondly, the central highlands of the Ardennes, the Harz, the Erzgebirge, and the Sudety; and thirdly, the southern uplands and scarplands that stretch from the Vosges eastward, in front of the northern limit of the Alps. The second and third bands are the remnants of the Hercynian mountain-building epoch of about 225 million years ago. Across the bands flow four great rivers, the Rhine, the Elbe, the Oder, and the Wisla (Vistula), which empty into the North and Baltic seas. The greatest of the water highways is the Rhine which is navigable by barges from the Swiss frontier to its mouth on the North Sea coast.

Climatically, the hills and plains of northern Europe can be divided into halves, one half benefits from the effects of the Gulf Stream, the other half shows all the extremes of a continental climate regime. The Gulf Stream affects the north and west and the prevailing westerly winds and barometric disturbances bring the Atlantic air far into the continent in summer. Summer rainfall is much the same from Paris to Moskva (Moscow) but in winter, cloud, rainfall, and snowfall increase on the higher ground to the south of the region and especially on western coasts. The annual rainfall amounts to between 25 and 30 inches. Farther to the east the climate is less maritime, it becomes drier and colder. The rain falls mainly in the summer months and in Warszawa (Warsaw) over 14 inches of the annual rainfall of some 22 inches falls in the summer. Precipitation in winter is mainly in the form of snow, which often lies on the ground for many weeks at a time, while rivers freeze over and the temperature rarely rises above freezing point.

The roughly wedge-shaped North European Plain stretches from its narrow end in Belgium in the west, where the Ardennes come down to within 100 miles of the sea, to more than 2000 miles eastward and then northeast to the Ural'skiy Khrebet (Ural Mountains), the mountain chain that forms the demarcation line between the continents of Europe and Asia. The plain is generally flat, masked by glacial drift, with slight hills and ridges of morainic material a few hundred feet high. Soils are sandy and produce wide stretches of heathland with pine and birch trees such as are found on the Luneburger Heide, south of Hamburg. Farmers can only cultivate this land by using huge quantities of chemical fertilizers. But there are some patches of fertile soil, for example, along the alluvial plains of the valleys of the great north-flowing rivers.

In parts of Germany and Poland the rivers zig-zag across the plain where glaciers diverted them from their south-north course into east-west channels, and lakes have formed in the ill-drained hollows. Linking canals have been cut across the broad, swampy areas between the rivers, in order to provide a communication system between east and west. Along the North Sea coast there are many sandy islands formed when the incessant action of the sea and the wind broke up the sand dunes. On the other hand, the Baltic coast is smooth and the sand has been moved to form long spits enclosing the mouths of many of the rivers.

The landscape of Belgium and the Netherlands is a mature one and the rivers, the Schelde, Meuse, Rhine, and their tributaries, are slow meandering streams that have built up huge deltas of silt and alluvium. Much of the land between these rivers is only just above sea level and floods easily if the water in the rivers rises due to melting snows or exceptionally high run-off far to the south, near their sources in the great Alpine chain. Floods also occur if, as in 1953, there are exceptionally high spring tides combined with storm-force winds blowing south across the North Sea. Then the water is "piled up" along the southern coastlines and soon penetrates the sea defenses and surges through to drown the low-lying ground.

Because the Dutch live so precariously near to sea level they have for centuries had a continual struggle against the sea. They have developed a unique water control and drainage system to get rid of the water and keep the reclaimed land dry and habitable. First, to keep out the water from both sea and flooding rivers, they build dikes – there are over 2000 miles of dikes in a country that is less than 200 miles from north to south – then they pump the land dry. Afterward the soil is fertilized to eliminate salt and acidity. A large number of modern pumping stations and hundreds of windmills work day and night, especially in winter to pump out the excess water, and the dikes and protective dunes need constant attention to ensure they keep the water out.

More than 50 years ago the Dutch began their famous Zuiderzee project and by 1932 the dike was completed, cutting off the North Sea and enclosing the water that formed a freshwater lake, the Ijsselmeer. Since then five tracts of land, or polders, have been completed. Ring-shaped dikes are first thrown up in the water, which is then pumped out of the center. Then the long and lengthy process begins of draining the polder, treating the soil, cultivating the ground, and bringing in the installations necessary for habitation. The most recent project, the Delta Plan, was derived to provide an answer to the terrible calamity caused by the 1953 floods when some 1800 people were

Above: an aerial view of some of the 550,000 acres of reclaimed land that once lay beneath the shallow Zuiderzee, or IJsselmeer. Now corn, sugar beet, flax, and fodder crops are grown there. Grouping houses along the road gives farmers equal access to land.

drowned and most of the islands in the southwest were inundated. This project provides for the closure, by means of massive dams, of four broad, deep-sea inlets near the mouths of the Schelde, Meuse, and Rhine; for the building of secondary dams; and for the heightening and strengthening of existing dikes and defenses. At the same time, adjustable flood barriers are planned for the Meuse and Rhine and two of its branches to allow the ice, which comes downriver after severe winters, to reach the sea. The Delta Plan is now nearing completion and in addition to ensuring the safety of southwest Holland it will also result in an improvement of the region's freshwater supply, as indeed the Zuiderzee project did in the more northerly part of the country.

Northwest Europe is one of the main areas in the world for the intensive, commercial mixed farming of cereals, rootcrops, hay, and animal produce. This type of farming arose because available farming land is scarce and the area's large population demands varied types of food. Good transport systems enable perishable commodities to reach markets easily, and a reliable climate means that there is rarely a poor harvest.

Farther south, the Rhine flows through the rift valley between the Vosges and Schwarzwald highlands and in its valley are some of the most fertile soils in Germany. The scarplands, which are also good farmlands, lie east of the Schwarzwald. Both these areas are dry and warm enough for grapes to ripen and they produce some of the most famous wines. Heaped against the mountains is the loess, an accumulation of wind-blown dust and silt, mainly composed of glacial material that was deposited when the ice sheet retreated. This loess makes an extremely fertile soil and stretches in a belt from the hills of France, across Germany, and eastward through Russia, to China.

The main industrial belt also stretches in a band from the United Kingdom in the west, through northern France and Belgium, southern Holland, the Federal Republic of Germany, and the German Democratic Republic to southern Poland. It forms the second of the world's great industrial areas (the first being in the northeast of the United States) and is concentrated on the coalfields and largely based on the iron and steel industry. The three other main classes of industry that exist in the important industrial areas, such as the Ruhr, are textile manufacturing, chemicals, and engineering.

Overleaf: steel being poured into ingot molds in a steelworks in northern Britain. Steel, coal, iron ore, and scrap, the foundations of industrialized societies, were the first important commodities to be embraced in the European Coal and Steel Community in 1952.

Mont Blanc "the white mountain," is the highest mounta[in]
in the European Alps. It rises on the border between Franc[e,]
Switzerland, and Italy. It is about 30 miles long, 10 mil[es]
wide, and 15,780 feet high.

Europe's Mountains

The Alps, one of Europe's major mountain ranges, curve east from the Mediterranean Sea to the river Danube, with hundreds of peaks of over 10,000 feet high and the largest glaciers on mainland Europe. The Alps were formed during the great Alpine mountain-building epoch of the Cenozoic era when the present major mountain chains on our planet were formed. The system extends from Gibraltar in the west to the Himalaya and East Indies in the east. It originated in a long, wide depression that developed between the northern foreland of Eurasia and the southern foreland of Africa, Arabia, and India, and which developed into the sea known to geologists as the Tethys Sea. Pressure, mainly from the south, pushed the sediments into complex recumbent folds and nappes that were driven northward far from their original position.

In some places two main sets of ranges originated, separated by a sea or plain. In places the Alps encroached on the eroded, hard Hercynian uplands, driving them upward in gigantic, crystalline splinters to form peaks, such as the 15,780-foot-high Mont Blanc and the Aiguilles Rouges. Alpine rivers cut deeply into the underlying rocks, and where parts of the young, recumbent folds have been eroded, the exposed rocks enable geologists to work out some of the complicated formations that have resulted from · this massive orogeny.

Austria, about two thirds the size of New York State, is at the northeastern end of the Alpine arc. It is a mountainous country with snow, glaciers, and pretty mountain villages. The Austrian Alps are less than 10,000 feet high, much lower than the mountains of Switzerland. Valleys are longer, wider, and easier to travel along than those in the Swiss Alps. The only lowland areas are in the northeast along the Danube valley and in the fertile basin around the capital, Wien (Vienna), between the Alps, the Böhmerwald, and the Carpathians. Wien, a center of trade, banking, and commerce, is a linking point at the crossroads between east and west, and between north and south Europe.

Although Switzerland gives the appearance of being entirely mountainous, only just over two thirds of the country is Alpine and only some 12 percent of the population live there. The Swiss Alps reach heights of between 13,000 and 15,000 feet and in the Ice Age formed the center of an icefield that moved outward in every direction, encroaching onto the lower-lying lands. The Alpine valleys are deep and U-shaped; the tributary streams often enter the main valleys as waterfalls tumbling down from the hanging valleys. Forests, usually fir and pine, cover the valley sides to a height of about 6500 feet on the northern slopes and as high as 7500 feet or more on the warmer southern faces. In summertime the herdsmen take their flocks to graze on the highland pastures above the forests.

Most Swiss live on the relatively flat central plateau north of the main Alpine ranges. The plateau is about 1300 feet above sea level, just south of the Jura mountains, but rises to over 3000 feet as it reaches the foothills of the Alps. Part is forested, but there is considerable pasture and crop land and the whole area is patterned with rivers and lakes. The Jura mountains to the north are formed of limestone and are a good example of fold mountains. Switzerland is a highly industrialized country and in some areas over three quarters of the mountain farmers commute every day to the factories in the valley floors, leaving their women and children to do the bulk of the farm work. The maintenance of mountain agriculture has become a problem for the government, which is trying to emphasize other kinds of employment such as the tourist industry, which will not completely destroy agriculture.

The Alps curve down into southeast France to form one of the five highland regions of the country. These regions lie like spots on a five-spot domino and between them are the lowland basins that all border the sea. In the south the Rhône flows down to the Mediterranean through a broadening funnel of lowland, the shape of an inverted Y. North of this, between the Massif Central in the west and the Alps in the east, the Rhône-Saône corridor forms one of the lowland routeways linking the two areas of different climates and products – the North European Plain and the southern Mediterranean lands.

In the north lies the Paris basin, like a shallow stack of saucers that get broader the deeper they are. The deepest layer is limestone, then the beds rise one on top of the other, clay, limestone, clay, and a surface layer of chalk with patchy deposits of alluvium, silt, and loess. Erosion has worn away the softer beds so that the harder ones stand out like ribs around the basin, making a series of gently curving scarps, especially well formed south of Paris. Clay valleys lie between the scarps. The French call the porous chalk region "Dry Champagne" and the clay valley to the southeast "Wet Champagne." Champagne, the famous French wine, comes from this area. In the west, the Aquitaine basin borders the Bay of Biscay and here it is warm enough for grapes to ripen in the summer temperatures of around 70°F – winter temperatures range between 40° and 50°F.

The Massif Central is the middle of the "domino." It is about 3000 feet high and dotted with broken-down cones of extinct volcanoes, called puys, which reach as high as 5000 feet. The volcanoes were formed from lava that was unable to flow far from the vent, result-

Northwest Europe

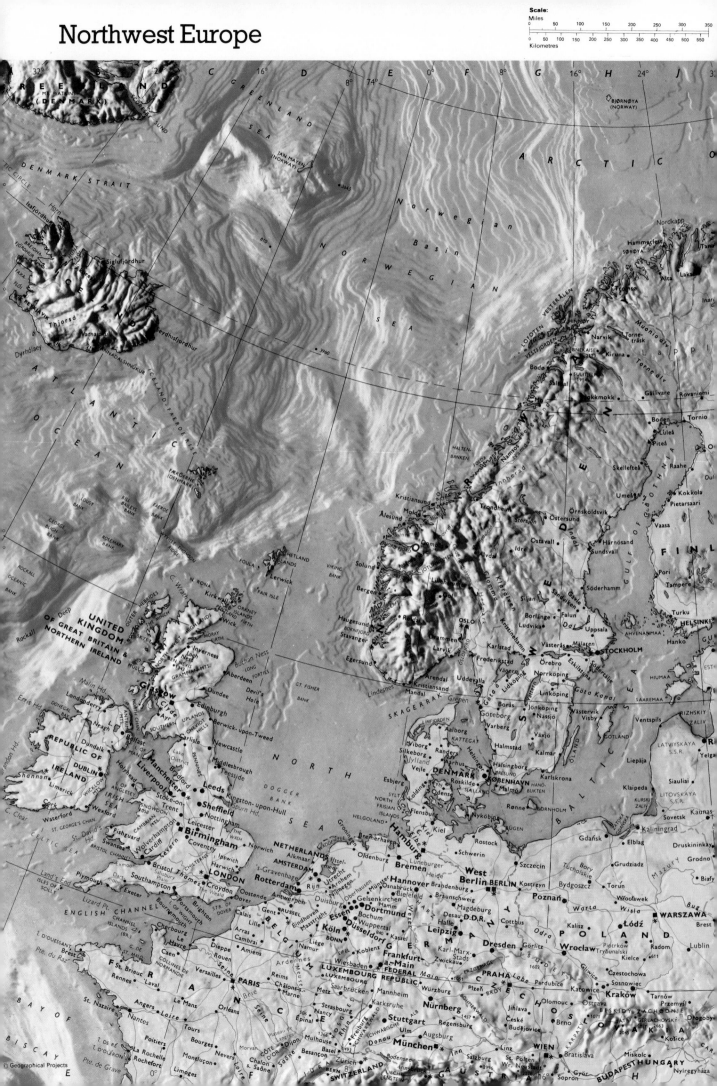

Scale:
Miles
0 50 100 150 200 250 300 350
0 50 100 150 200 250 300 350 400 450 500 550
Kilometres

© Geographical Projects

Above: the 12th-century cathedral of St. Michel
d'Aiguilhe at Le Puy, the chief town in the Velay region of
France, is built on a spectacular puy, or volcanic cone.
Similar cones, known as the Monts du Velay, dot this area
of south-central France.

S, through the Carpathians and the Stara Planina to
the shores of the Black Sea. Straddling this eastern
extension of Alpine ranges in a northwest-southeast
direction are Czechoslovakia and Hungary, occupying an area that can be divided into three parts. To the
northwest is the high basin of the upper Elbe, enclosed by the heavily eroded Hercynian mountains
of the Böhmerwald, Erzgebirge, and Sudety. To the
southeast is the central European plain of the middle
Danube and its tributary, the Tisza. Finally, ringing
this plain is the great arch of the folded mountains of
the Tatry and Carpathians, which have been thrust
into the northeast over the Hercynian front and the
deposits of the Russian lowlands.

The mountains and plateaus of western Czechoslovakia are particularly rich in wildlife largely because
much of the area has retained a forest cover – mainly
coniferous – in spite of cutting and reforestation over
the centuries. A large area of Czechoslovakia falls in
the great industrial belt of western Europe and the
northwestern part of the country is densely populated.
The flatter areas of the plateau and valley floors have
been intensively cultivated. The ancient crystalline
rocks have been disturbed by later formations and
volcanic activity, resulting in bizarre pillar-shaped
formations in the encircling mountains of the Böhmerwald and Sudety and many isolated peaks scattered
over the flatter ground. The Carpathians, with the
exception of the Tatry, are not so high as the Alps and
only the highest peaks are above the treeline. These
mountains were not covered by an ice sheet in the last
glaciation though probably they had many large
glaciers. Today they are completely ice free and only a
few snow patches remain throughout the summer in
sheltered places on north-facing slopes. The Tatra,
lying mainly in Czechoslovakia, have their northern
slopes in southern Poland and are the highest range
in the eastern Alpine system, rising to over 6000 feet.
They support a rich mountain flora and fauna.

The Hungarian plain is an isolated outpost of the
great Russian steppe. It has a typical continental
climate of cold winters and hot summers because of its
position in the center of the land mass of Europe, cut
off from the warming effects of the Gulf Stream. The
rich sediment on the floor of the plain, deposited when
the area was covered by sea and later enriched by the
alluvium brought down by the rivers as the area rose
above sea level, form the basis for the famous black
earth soil known as tschernozem. This rich loose soil
has been cultivated intensively, so that little of the
original typical steppe grassland vegetation now
remains. Over the area the great river Danube and its
tributaries meander slowly, providing an invaluable
water supply for farmers as well as for the surrounding
areas.

Right: the freezing and thawing of snow on the slopes of
the Matterhorn, viewed from Zermatt, in Switzerland
shattered rocks, carving ice-filled hollows that dug deeply
into its flanks. This resulted in steep rock walls separated
by frost-sharpened ridges.

ing in steep-sided, sometimes even bulbous, domes
being built up immediately over the outlets and choking them. These domes, or plugs, remain as resistant
rock long after the outer layers have been cracked and
worn away.

The Pyrenees in the southwest and peninsular
Brittany in the northwest are the two remaining spots
of the "domino." The Pyrenees, formed at the same
time as the Alps, are part of the great Alpine system.
Brittany, on the other hand, is a low plateau with an
irregular coastline caused by the rise in sea level after
the river valleys had been drowned during the Ice Age.
Inlets formed in this way are known as rias and differ
from fjords in that they are not steep-sided and that
they gradually deepen toward the sea.

The eastern continuation of the massive Alpine
system is cut through twice by the Danube river as it
curves around in two great loops, forming an inverted

Fisheries and Farms

Farming in Northwest Europe owes much to the favorable climate that exists throughout the region. Most of the region lies between the latitudes of 40° and 60°N, which means that Northwest Europe is free from both tropical and polar extremes of climate. The absence of any great mountain ranges along its western seaboard also means that there is no deficiency of rainfall over the continent. But it is the ocean, warmed by the Gulf Stream, that gives Northwest Europe such a favorable climate of warm, but not too hot, summers, mild winters, and a well-distributed rainfall.

Because the peoples that live in the area are technologically advanced, techniques have been introduced that have created methods of farming not totally controlled by the environment. In general, a system of mixed farming is practiced, an intensive commercial type of farming that specializes in cereals, rootcrops, and animal produce. The mixed farms, with both arable and pasture land, have many advantages. An obvious one is that the farmer can feed his animals on the fodder crops he grows and then use the animals' manure to fertilize the land.

Cows are grouped in pens according to their grade of milk in this intensive-rearing dairy farm.

Northwest Europe is also fortunate in its wide variety of fertile soils. Some of the richest are in the Aquitaine and Paris basins, East Anglia, the Hungarian plain, and on the loess belt that stretches eastward across the southern boundary of the North European Plain. Arable farming predominates, with wheat, potatoes, sugar beet, barley, and clover as the main crops. But large areas of the flat English Fenlands also grow vegetables for the national market and are known for their flowers, bulbs, and soft and hard fruits. Bulb growing is also a traditionally famous and important industry in the Netherlands. In the Aquitaine basin the summer is warm and dry enough for corn and tobacco crops to thrive as well as for grapes to ripen. The vine also grows on the hillsides in the valleys of the upper Seine, Meuse, Moselle, Rhine, and Neckar.

Denmark and the Netherlands specialize in dairy farming. In these countries cattle can graze out of doors nearly all year on the good pastures. Grain and root crops are grown for supplementary fodder, especially in Denmark. Hog raising often goes along with the dairy farming, because hogs can be reared on dairy by-products such as skim milk and whey. Danish butter and bacon and Dutch cheeses are famous all over the world.

In the north of the region, along the highland fringes of western Ireland, northwest Britain, northern Sweden, and Finland are small patches of lowland. In these areas an average of 30 inches of rain falls annually and the summers are short. The land is mostly pasture, but hay, barley, and root crops are also grown for local supply. Lowland Ireland has a lot of pasture and farmers there concentrate on dairy cattle and produce. The air is always moist, and after rain the ground dries out slowly so that the grass is lush and green throughout the year – which is why Ireland is often called the "Emerald Isle."

The soils of the uplands of Northwest Europe are too thin and poor and the slopes too steep for crop growing. The weather is harsh in winter and stock raising is the only kind of farming possible. Sheep, which provide both meat and wool, are raised in the highlands wherever there is enough pasture and the winters are not so severe that snow lies on the ground for long periods. Large flocks graze on the uplands of Wales, Scotland, and northern England, as well as farther south in the Pyrenees, the Massif Central, and the Alps.

In Lapland, in the extreme north of Scandinavia large herds of reindeer graze on the tundra – the bleak and almost treeless land where the subsoil is always frozen and the only vegetation is mosses, lichens, and other dwarf plants. In recent years the nomadic herdsmen have tended to settle in the river valleys and breed the reindeer. They have found that high prices are offered for meat, skins, and antlers. In the uplands of southern Norway, as well as in the Swiss and Austrian Alps, the farmers keep herds of goats.

Forests cover huge areas of Sweden, Finland, and

Czechoslovakia, so forest products form a large part of the manufacturing and exports in these countries. Nearly all Finland's wealth comes from her forests, which cover almost three quarters of the country's land surface. Thousands of trees, mainly conifers, go every year to make pulp for paper and to feed the sawmills, and the plywood and hardboard factories.

The continental slope is the true boundary between the continental land mass and the ocean. The continental shelf, which extends to an average depth of 600 feet (100 fathoms), is the area where fishing and other marine activities are most intensive, especially on the north Atlantic continental shelves. In Northwest Europe, the continental shelf is wide and extends west of the British Isles and the coast of Norway and also includes the North Sea and Baltic Sea. Once the home of many kinds of fish – cod, haddock, redfish, flounder, plaice, sole, halibut, turbot, herring, mackerel, and others, the rich fishing grounds are now seriously depleted. The leading fishing country in Northwest Europe, apart from Iceland, is Norway, whose fleets fish both inshore waters and, like Britain and Germany, much farther afield. Norway's whaling fleets – it controls half the world's whaling industry – sail regularly far south to the Antarctic.

Below: using the latest sonar fish-detecting devices, these three Norwegian trawlers meet in the North Sea to handle a huge catch of fish. Fishing in the European countries bordering the North Sea is now a highly organized and sophisticated industry.

Industrial Europe

Northwest Europe was the world's first industrialized area. Even before the Industrial Revolution itself there was a fairly highly developed industrial structure. The high density of population in the area provided a labor force that had a tradition of skills that went back to the development of the craft industries in the Middle Ages. Power, vital to industry, is in ample supply in the region.

Britain led the way in mining development, and after a period of decline rich coal seams were discovered along the eastern edge of Yorkshire. There are also coalfields all along the northern margins of the ancient block mountains in central Europe; in northeast and central France, Belgium, the Netherlands, the Ruhr in the Federal Republic of Germany, Saxony in the southern part of the DDR, and Silesia in southern Poland. The Ruhr is Europe's largest coalfield and still has resources great enough to last for centuries.

Below: an industrial scene in South Wales, one of the coal-rich regions in the British Isles, where the Industrial Revolution began.

Scandinavia, in the north of the region, and southern France, Switzerland, and Austria to the south have no coal but plenty of water, the chief source of hydroelectric power. Scandinavia has developed more than one third of its potential and Sweden even exports electricity to Denmark by a cable under the narrow strait of Øresund between the two countries. Nuclear power is the most recent development, and stations have been built all over Northwest Europe to provide electricity. The minerals required to produce this power, uranium and thorium, are not found in the region, of course, and have to be imported.

The natural gas found in southwest France has been exploited for some years and is piped to areas as far away as Paris. The full effect on Europe of the discovery of the oil and natural gas in the North Sea has yet to be felt, but it is believed to be so significant that in some quarters it is being called a second Industrial Revolution. Today over 90 percent of Britain's gas comes from the southern North Sea and the Netherlands also receives the bulk of its gas from nearby fields or from the large field discovered on the North Sea coast, near Groningen. In spite of immense technical problems, oil is being brought ashore from fields in the North Sea to the surrounding countries.

Deposits of nonferrous ores are inadequate in Europe but the continent has good iron ore supplies for iron and steel. Only ores rich in iron are commercially important, and Swedish magnetite ores contain over 70 percent iron. In Lorraine, in northwest France, the ores contain up to 30 percent iron, but they remain of high commercial value because they occur in large quantities in beds near the surface. Bauxite, used in

making aluminum, is found throughout Europe, although deposits at Les Baux, from which the mineral gets its name, have been worked out and France now only meets a small part of Europe's needs. Common salt and lignite deposits form the basis of chemical industries in the Leipzig area of the DDR.

Industrial Northwest Europe falls into two zones, "black" and "white." The "black" zone, mainly centered on coalfields or where there are raw materials, takes in Britain, northeast France, and a band stretching eastward to southern Poland. These areas are full of coal mines and tips, foundries and factories making all kinds of iron and steel goods. In the Ruhr coalfield area seven industrial towns, all with populations of more than 250,000 as well as about a dozen others with more than 100,000 inhabitants, have grown up close together within a radius of about 40 miles. Good rail and river communications have helped to accelerate their growth.

Some areas concentrate on textiles. Lancashire, in England, is famous for cotton goods, Yorkshire for its wool industry. Northeast France makes both wool and cotton goods. Factories in Belgium and Northern Ireland, originally dependent on local flax supplies, manufacture millions of square yards of linen every year. Since the introduction of synthetic fibers all the textile areas have been forced to adapt to these new materials and as well as traditional fabrics they now also produce entirely synthetic weaves in addition to mixtures.

The "white" industrial zone is to north and south, in the mountainous areas of Scandinavia, Finland, Switzerland, and Austria. The major power source is electricity, not coal, so industrial towns are clean and free from smoking factory chimneys. The electrochemical and electrosmelting industries need large amounts of electricity and it is these that are prominent in the "white" zone. There are aluminum factories everywhere as well as smelters making certain metals for steel alloys. Nitrogen, extracted from the atmosphere, forms the basis of a wide variety of these electrochemical products.

Transportation of raw materials and finished goods in the "white" zone is important, as indeed it is in any industrial center. Water transport is easiest and cheapest and is highly developed in Northwest Europe. The canal system in France is considered one of the best in the world. All the major rivers are navigable for long distances upriver from their mouths. The rail system also provides a dense network but since the 1930s the development of the motorway has meant the transfer of a large proportion of the manufactured goods from rail to road transport.

The continued growth of other industrial areas throughout the world is bound to affect European industry. But products like Swedish glass, Scottish tweeds, Italian leather, and Swiss watches continue to show an extremely high standard of European craftsmanship and skill. These products remain competitive in a world market dominated by mass production.

Above: a giant turbogenerator being constructed in a nuclear power plant. Turbogenerators are now the basic power-producing machines of the electrical age.

65

People and Politics

Although the continent of Europe is less than half the size of North America, its average population density is five times greater. Its total population, excluding the USSR, is about 473 million and of these about half live in Northwest Europe – a large population for a comparatively small region. The density of population is especially high in Britain, Belgium, the Netherlands, and parts of France and Germany where the growth has been so great that towns and cities have often expanded to join one another. These huge urban areas occur mainly in a broad, industrial arc running from Liverpool, Manchester, and Leeds in England through northern France and eastward to southern Poland. By contrast, some other countries, such as Norway and Finland, are thinly populated.

Throughout history Northwest Europe has been a region to which migrants have come from the east, many pouring across the North European Plain, the great east-west routeway. Some were drawn by the milder climate and richer farmlands of the region, others came to escape fresh waves of invaders that bore down on them from still farther east. Some braved the North Sea and others ventured even farther, so anticipating the great Age of Discovery and the time when Northwest Europe would become a springboard for fresh migrations to Africa, the Orient, the Americas, and Australasia.

The recurrent themes in the story of mankind are movement and change. As men wandered, they changed their lifestyles, adapting to their new environments, and mingled with others who were themselves moving and changing. The age-old process is now so advanced, especially in western Europe, that we cannot really identify any country by a single physical type, although we can often point to distinctive characteristics. Scandinavians are usually tall and have fair hair and complexions. Southern Europe has its "Mediterranean" peoples, distinguished by their medium height, fine bone structure, and darker complexions. The fringe peoples of Northwest Europe – the Bretons, Irish, Welsh, and Scots – are often short, dark, and stocky and usually speak a Celtic language. They are thought to be the descendants of the earliest inhabitants who moved north from Mediterranean lands and were later driven farther and farther west by successive waves of migrants.

The diversity of languages also reflects the movement of peoples. French, Spanish, and Italian have their roots in Latin, the language of the Roman Empire and its dialects. English, Dutch Flemish, and German are basically related, but English contains many words derived from Latin through French and at least two, cocoa and tomato, from the Aztec language. Such diversity has not helped the spread of thought and knowledge in Europe or the growth of understanding between nations. Some countries have language differences to overcome inside their own frontiers. For example, the people of north Belgium are mostly Flemings speaking Flemish, while those of the south are Walloons who speak French. In Switzerland four languages are spoken – German, French, Italian, and Romansh.

Sometimes differences between peoples or within countries have been accentuated, or even created, by political events. A good example in Europe is the partition of Germany at the end of World War II. This, and the building of the Berlin Wall later, made West Berlin an island of West German territory in Communist East Germany. Another is the division of Ireland. Northern Ireland is part of the United Kingdom; the south is the independent Republic of Ireland.

Northwest Europe has been developing politically for hundreds of years. Its forms of government include constitutional monarchies like Belgium, Denmark, the Netherlands, Norway, Sweden, and the United Kingdom, where the head of state is a king or queen; and republics like Austria, Finland, France, Ireland, Iceland, and the Federal Republic of Germany, where the head of state is an elected president. In the center and the east are Communist countries such as the East-German DDR, Czechoslovakia, Hungary, and Poland, who are ruled through the permanent committees of the Communist Party.

Above: a natural gas drilling rig in the North Sea. The discovery of natural gas under the North Sea has been one of the most important industrial developments for Europe since the invention of the steam engine. Such natural gas deposits unleash new sources of fuel and raw materials.

Above: the 26-mile long Berlin Wall, built by the Communist East Germans to seal off their sector of the city – where, as in the East German Democratic Republic generally, the standard of living is lower and the cost of living higher than in the West German Federal Republic.

Material living standards in Northwest Europe – excepting the Communist countries – are high. Only in the United States, Canada, Australia, and New Zealand are they higher in terms of wealth per person. Most people live in well-built houses or apartments, and the symbols of an affluent society – cars, refrigerators, washing machines, televisions, and other luxury goods – are found everywhere.

There are several reasons why Northwest Europe has become one of the four most densely inhabited and affluent regions of the world – its favorable geographical position and climate, its abundance of natural resources, and the enterprising ability of its people to make the most of these. The same reasons go far to explain Northwest Europe's importance as a center of world influence and ideas.

Until the discovery of America in 1492, European influence in world affairs centered on the Mediterranean, where Western civilization itself had been born. But with the rapid growth of nations across the Atlantic, the balance increasingly shifted to Northwest Europe, to vigorous trading and empire-building nations such as Britain, France, and the Netherlands. This movement was decisively confirmed by the use Northwest Europeans made of their considerable mineral resources, especially coal and iron ore. Coupled with the energy of hardworking and inventive

craftsmen and technicians, these resources made Northwest Europe the world's first great industrial area.

The rapid growth of industry and population soon outstripped agricultural production. Today Northwest Europe imports more than three quarters of its food. Another vital import is petroleum. Although more and more oil and gas are being obtained from under the North Sea, the bulk of the requirements still have to come from abroad. But while Northwest Europe imports it also exports. Few regions can match its output of manufactured goods.

With industrial expansion came the development of transportation and communications. There were immediate natural advantages. Most rivers in western Europe flow west or north, to the Atlantic or to the North or Baltic seas, providing easy inland communication and cheap freight transport. A lot of the region is plains country and, except for the Caledonian mountain system along the northwest edge and the Alpine system in the south, there are no impassable mountain barriers. Today an excellent road, rail, waterway, and air network covers all of Europe.

The importance of overseas trade is reflected in the number of large towns in Northwest Europe that are also ports. Rotterdam and London are the leaders; then come Hamburg and Antwerpen (Antwerp). The many busy river or sea ports include Glasgow, Liverpool, Bristol, Bordeaux, Le Havre, Bremen, København, Oslo, Göteborg, and Gdynia. Three quarters of the world's shipping moves in and out of these European ports.

After World War II the west European nations moved toward unity. They believed that many postwar economic problems could be solved by abolishing trade barriers. In 1952 the organization of the European Coal and Steel Community (ECSC) was formed to pool the resources of coal, steel, and iron ore of the countries of France, Belgium, Luxembourg, the Netherlands, the Federal Republic of Germany, and Italy. This paved the way for the Treaty of Rome, in March 1957, which was signed by the same six nations, and the European Economic Community (EEC) – or Common Market as it is generally known – was created. In 1951 another free trade zone had been formed when the European Free Trade Association (EFTA) came into being and included Austria, Denmark, Iceland, Norway, Portugal, United Kingdom, Sweden, and Switzerland, with Finland as an associate. Later the United Kingdom and Denmark joined the EEC and the majority of the other members have applied

Left: molten steel pouring from a 1200-ton mixer furnace in a steel works in Monmouthshire, West England. There are many kinds of steel, each designed for the job it has to do. One type may have to be corrosion-resistant, another capable of receiving a fine cutting edge, and yet another capable of withstanding changing stresses. Britain, together with much of Northwest Europe, is heavily industrialized, one of the factors that enables its peoples to enjoy high material living standards.

Left: the signing of the treaty that set up the European Economic Community in Rome, March 1957. The six original countries were Belgium, France, Germany, Italy, Luxembourg, and the Netherlands.

Below: United States, Canadian, and European forces on a NATO exercise in Turkey. NATO was set up in 1949 against possible communist aggression and is the Western counterpart of the Warsaw Pact forces.

to be admitted. If this happens then EFTA will disappear. The nine-member EEC is now one of the largest trading blocs in the world and is exerting a powerful influence on the economic well-being of many of the Third World countries.

Western European countries have joined one another and North America in various other cooperative organizations. In 1949, the USA and Canada joined western Europe in the North Atlantic Treaty Organization (NATO), a mutual defense pact against possible Communist aggression. In 1951, the European Atomic Energy Community (EURATOM) was set up to integrate and promote development of nuclear energy for peaceful purposes.

Meanwhile Western imperialism was retreating. Since World War II the great powers have gradually lost their colonies and in Africa, Asia, and elsewhere independent states have emerged. In some cases a special relationship between the old imperial power and the former colony has been preserved. For example, France maintains associations with many of her former colonies through the sometimes loose links of the French community. The United Kingdom has ties with the 35 other member nations of the Commonwealth that are situated in every part of the inhabited world and take in almost a quarter of the world population. Not all countries formerly under British rule have chosen to join the Commonwealth, but the heads of state of the member nations meet regularly, every two years, and there are frequent ministerial consultations and cooperation.

The tradition of European genius in literature and music, art and science, remains as strong as ever. Europe is still the focus of Western culture; scientists and technicians are making important contributions in research and industrial development. But in world affairs generally European influence has been overshadowed and diminished by the United States and the USSR. Their size and wealth of natural resources alone are sufficient to make them preeminent, although no one can afford to ignore Europe's role in world politics.

North Sea Oil and Gas Fields

Below: map shows division of North Sea into "fields" for exploitation of its vast reserves of oil and natural gas.

Legend:

- – – – Median Lines
- Oilfields & wells
- Gasfields & wells
- —— Oil pipelines
- ·········· Projected oil pipelines
- —— Gas pipelines
- ·········· Projected gas pipelines
- ⊼ Rigs drilling during period 1972-3

Miles
0 50 100 150 200 250

Kilometres
0 50 100 150 200 250 300 350 400

© Geographical Projects

The Countries of Northwest Europe

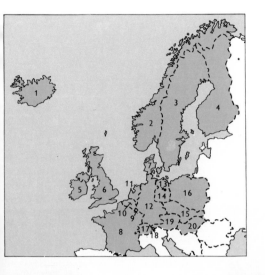

1 Iceland	13 West Berlin
2 Norway	14 German Democratic Republic
3 Sweden	15 Czechoslovakia
4 Finland	16 Poland
5 Ireland	17 Switzerland
6 United Kingdom of Great	18 Liechtenstein
Britain & Northern Ireland	19 Austria
7 Denmark	20 Hungary
8 France	
9 Luxembourg	
10 Belgium	
11 Netherlands	
12 Federal Republic of Germany	

ICELAND (Island)

Area: 39,702 square miles
Population: 220,500
Capital: Reykjavik
Language: Icelandic
Religion: Lutheranism
Monetary Unit: Krona

History and Government: Iceland was settled by Scandinavia and North British peoples from around AD 874. It united with Norway in 1262, then with Denmark in 1380. It revoked the Act of Union with Denmark in 1944, when it became an independent republic. It is governed by a cabinet of a prime minister and six other ministers responsible to the *Althing*, which is a parliamentary assembly of 60 members. The country has a recent history of coalition governments from center-left parties. It is a charter member of both the United Nations and NATO.

Economy: Because almost all the necessities of life have to be imported and paid for by exports of fish, the maintenance of fish stocks around their coasts are of extreme importance to the Icelanders. Reaction to the dangers of overfishing by British and West German fleets led to a long drawn-out dispute over Iceland's extension of the limits of its territorial waters to 200 miles from its coasts. In Iceland, 80 percent of the population live by fishing and by processing fish, especially herrings and cod. Shipyards are also important, and there are a few chemical and textile industries, but fish represents practically all Iceland's exports.

NORWAY (Norge)

Area: 125,052 square miles
Population: 4,000,000
Capital: Oslo
Language: Bokmeal or Riksmaal, Nynorsk or Landsmaal
Religion: Lutheranism
Monetary Unit: Krone

History and Government: Norway became a separate nation at the end of the Viking Age in the mid-11th century and at one time in the 18th century controlled an empire that included Iceland, Greenland, the Faeroes, Shetlands, Orkneys and Hebrides islands. The population is largely Nordic in appearance, with over 60 percent having pure blue eyes. Alpine and Mediterranean characteristics appear from settlements of those peoples in the southwest of the country. Norway is now a constitutional hereditary monarchy founded in 1905 when Norway ended its 91-year-old union with Sweden. For 500 years before 1905 Norway was politically united with Denmark. The king is the administrative head of the government and selects his own cabinet. The passing of all government decrees into law is done through the parliament, or *Storting*, which is elected by the people.

Economy: The chief industries are agriculture and fishing. Cereals, potatoes, vegetables, and fruit are the main products of agriculture and there is a thriving timber and wood pulp industry based on the coniferous forests. Norway has a higher catch of fish in normal years than any other European country – the USSR excepted. Mineral resources are modest, but oil production in the North Sea fields is assuming increasing importance. In addition, Norway is rich in hydroelectric power, leading to the development of the metallurgical industry (especially refined aluminum) and electrical engineering and chemical industries. The cellulose and paper industries and shipbuilding are of worldwide importance. The Norwegian merchant navy is the fourth largest in the world. A nationwide referendum in 1972 rejected a proposal to join the EEC, but Norway is a member of EFTA.

SWEDEN (Sverige)

Area: 173,648 square miles
Population: 8,200,000
Capital: Stockholm
Language: Swedish
Religion: Lutheranism
Monetary Unit: Krona

History and Government: Toward the end of the 12th century the provinces of Sweden were united under a single king and remained an independent sovereign state until the Kalmar Union which united Norway, Denmark and Sweden between 1397 and 1523. The country is now a constitutional monarchy with the role of the king reduced to that of a figurehead. The *Riksdag*, or parliament, is a single-chamber legislative body of 350 members elected for three years. The Social Democratic Labor Party has formed the government since 1923. Sweden is considered the most advanced model of "industrial democracy." Social democracy has given the country some original features: an all-embracing system of social security, progressively severe taxation, and attention to social problems, varying from the workers' environment and work rhythms to pollution. In the economic field, rigorous planning is imposed on private enterprise (95 percent of the industries are privately owned). Sweden's foreign policy is independent of the policies of the other Western nations.

Economy: Compared with the rest of the world Sweden is a country at the height of prosperity. Due to mechanization and the organization of cooperatives, agriculture has a very high level of productivity. The chief crops are cereals, potatoes, sugar beet, oil-seeds. Animal husbandry is also important and supplies the cheese-making industry. The vast extent of forests has made possible the development of a large paper industry and Sweden is among the world's greatest producers of timber. It is also a country rich in minerals

Below: Fair-haired, blue-eyed people are found in large areas of Scandinavia, northern Germany, Denmark, and Holland.

– especially good quality iron ore, copper, zinc, manganese, gold, and tungsten. There is a very extensive development of manufacturing industry, from iron and steel to engineering, electrical engineering, chemicals, textiles, and paper. Fishing is important and supplies the canning industry.

FINLAND (Suomi)
Area: 130,128 square miles
Population: 4,700,000
Capital: Helsinki (Helsingfors)
Language: Finnish or Swedish
Religion: Lutheranism
Monetary Unit: Markka

History and Government: Finland has been settled by peoples from the Baltic and Scandinavian races for some 5000 years. From being part of Sweden from the 12th century until 1809, Finland became a Russian Grand Duchy until the Revolution of 1917 when it declared its independence. The republic has been ruled since then through a single chamber parliament. Its close proximity to the USSR has a strong influence on Finland's foreign policy, so that its neutrality is conditioned by continual compromise with its mighty Communist neighbor – which, for instance, opposed Finland's entry into the EEC. The president of the republic is elected for six years by secondary stage voting.

Economy: Finland's greatest source of wealth is in the forests that cover 70 percent of the land. It is among the biggest producers in the world of timber, wood pulp, and newsprint. Among the industries besides paper and wood, metallurgy and engineering are well developed, and chemicals, textiles, cement, glass, and porcelain are also of importance. In 1973 an agreement was drawn up with COMECON. Finland is also an associate member of EFTA.

IRELAND (Eire)
Area: 27,136 square miles
Population: 2,900,000
Capital: Dublin (Baile Atha Cliath)
Language: Gaelic or English
Religion: Catholicism
Monetary Unit: Irish Pound

History and Government: The island was invaded by Celts around 500 BC and was split between various warring kings and chieftains. It was Christianized in the 5th century AD by St. Patrick and was later invaded by Norman

Lords from England. The English ruler Oliver Cromwell subdued all Ireland and colonized the northern part with Welsh, Scots, and English settlers. Made into Irish Free State in 1922, it gradually loosened its ties with the British Crown until 1937 when it was declared an independent sovereign state within the British Commonwealth. Ireland became a republic with no allegiance to the British Crown or Commonwealth in 1949. The country is ruled through a parliament, *oireachtas*, consisting of a president and two houses, a House of Representatives from which the *Taoiseach*, or Prime Minister, and the government is drawn and an upper house, the Senate.

Economy: The Irish economy is heavily dependent on agriculture, which engages 27 percent of the working population. Cereals, root crops, and hay are produced, but the basic industry is animal rearing – cattle, sheep, pigs, horses, and ponies – and provides a large part of the exports. There is also a substantial fishing industry. Ireland has been a member of the EEC since 1973

UNITED KINGDOM OF GREAT BRITAIN & NORTHERN IRELAND
Area: 93,026 square miles
Population: 56,000,000
Capital: London
Language: English
Religion: Anglicanism
Monetary Unit: Pound Sterling

History and Government: Inhabited by Celtic speaking tribes, who were conquered first by the Romans, later by Nordic tribes. Eastern and northern parts gradually formed into Wales and and the independent kingdom of Scotland, while central and southern parts formed the kingdom of England. Parliamentary system of government introduced into the United kingdom of England and Wales in 1295. In 1707 Scotland joined the Union and the name Great Britain was adopted for both island and kingdom. The country is ruled as a constitutional monarchy. Parliament has two legislative chambers, the House of Commons, whose members are elected for five years by the uninominal system, and the House of Lords, composed of members who are hereditary or appointed for life. The House of Commons inaugurates legislation. After the end of World War II, the United Kingdom divested itself of its colonial empire. Since then, the modern Commonwealth has evolved and there are now 36 member nations. Not all the countries formerly under British rule

Above: a vast network of docks, warehouses, and transport links reaches as far up London's Thames river as Tower Bridge, seen here in the background. London is one of the world's greatest ports.

chose to join, and South Africa and Pakistan have withdrawn since its formation.

Economy: It is a highly developed country, the first to effect an "Industrial Revolution," but has suffered economic repercussions since its change in role from being a major international power. The manufacturing industries, on which the economy is based, are very flexible and the country has an important position in the manufacture of cars, industrial vehicles, aircraft, chemicals, textiles, foodstuffs, and in shipbuilding. Among the most important mineral resources are coal, largely used to supply electric power stations, and iron. Rich oil deposits discovered in the North Sea are expected to boost the economy. Agriculture, although it does not meet all the needs of the home market, has a high level of production. It is a member of the EEC.

Religion: Lutheranism
Monetary Unit: Krone
History and Government: Denmark, the ancient European kingdom which includes the Faeroes and Greenland, is a constitutional monarchy. Its peoples are a racial mixture of European types with the Nordic characteristics of fair hair and blue eyes predominating. Executive authority rests jointly with the monarch and parliament, or *Folketing.* Parliament is a single-chamber legislature of 179 members, including two from Greenland and two from the Faeroe Islands, both of which also have their own parliaments.
Economy: Agriculture is all important. There are very high levels of productivity and as a result a flourishing processing industry. The principal products are cereals, vegetables, and fruits. Fodder is also very widely grown for stock-rearing, which provides a large proportion of the exports such as dairy produce and bacon, especially to the EEC countries. Forestry and fishing are also important. The lack of raw materials has conditioned industrial development, but many of its sectors are competitive on an international level. Denmark became a member of the EEC in January 1973.

Population: 53,000,000
Capital: Paris
Language: French
Religion: Catholicism
Monetary Unit: Franc
History and Government: Most of the area formerly occupied by the Romans and known as Gaul, was united under the kingdom of the Salian Franks, who gave their name to France. During the 15th–16th centuries, royal rule was strengthened and centralized. The monarchy was overthrown in 1789 and there followed a period during which the constitution changed several times between republic, monarchy, and empire before finally becoming a republic in 1870. The Fifth Republic of France is governed through a parliament made up of a Senate and a National Assembly. The prime minister and cabinet are appointed by the president of the republic, who is supreme executive head of government. There is also a constitutional council which is responsible for supervising elections and referenda, and must be consulted on all constitutional matters. Administratively, France is divided into 95 departments and there are also four overseas departments – Guadeloupe, Martinique, French Guiana, and Réunion and other territories – New Caledonia, Wallis and Fortuna Islands, French Polynesia, and St Pierre and Miquelon Islands.
Economy: Agriculture employing around 13 percent of the working population is the richest in western Europe. Chief agriculture products in France are: cereals, beet, potatoes, fruit, and vines. Stock-rearing and the resulting dairy products are also important; fishing, too, plays an important role in the economy. The public participation in industry, either by the nationalization or the ownership of shares, is large. Among the mineral resources are iron, some bauxite, uranium, natural gas, and coal. France is among the leaders in the iron and steel and chemical industries, but engineering, electrical engineering, and electronics are also very advanced. In the other sectors, textiles, clothing, and foodstuffs are dominant, and perfumes and cosmetics are traditional industries. France comes third in Europe, after Spain and Italy, in the tourist industry. It is one of the founder-members of the EEC.

DENMARK (Kongerig et Danmark)
Area: 17,000 square miles
Population: 5,000,000
Capital: Copenhagen (København)
Language: Danish

**FRANCE
(La Republique Française)
Area:** 213,000 square miles

**LUXEMBOURG (Grande-Duché de Luxembourg)
Area:** 1000 square miles

Population: 350,000
Capital: Luxembourg
Language: French and Letzeburgesch
Religion: Catholicism
Monetary Unit: Luxembourg and Belgian Francs
History and Government: Luxembourg has been a separate political unit since the 10th century although it has come under the control of many of the surrounding states in its long history. It was finally established as an independent state in 1815. Because Luxembourg is at the crossroads of Belgium, France, and Germany its peoples are a historic mix of Celts, Ligurians, Romans, Franks, and Belgics. The Grand Duchy is a constitutional monarchy ruled through a single-chamber parliament of 59 deputies. Legislation is submitted to a council of State before becoming law.
Economy: The chief industry is iron and steel and Luxembourg is among the biggest producers in Europe of steel, cast iron, and iron alloys. The most widespread agricultural crops are cereals, potatoes, and vines; the cultivation of roses is traditional. Animal husbandry is also practiced. For commercial purposes Luxembourg works in close collaboration with Belgium. It was one of the six original member nations of the EEC.

BELGIUM (Royaume de Belgique)
Area: 11,781 square miles
Population: 9,800,000
Capital: Brussels (Brussel, Bruxelles)
Language: Flemish and French (Walloon)
Religion: Catholicism
Monetary Unit: Belgian Franc
History and Government: Belgium has been an independent state since 1830, created from the bringing together of four French-speaking states occupying the southern part of the country and four Flemish-speaking states in the north and a German-speaking minority in the southeast. It has been a constitutional monarchy since its creation. The country is governed through a two-chamber parliament consisting of a Chamber of Representatives, elected by the people and a partly elected, partly nominated, Senate. Government programs of "regionalization" have been enacted to ease friction between French and Flemish-speaking Belgians. Belgium divested itself of its overseas African territories when the Belgian Congo became the independent state of Zaire in 1960, and Ruanda-Urundi became the independent states of Rwanda and

Burundi in 1962. It joined The Netherlands and Luxembourg in 1948 in an economic union called Benelux.
Economy: Production is mainly industrial and Belgium has a well-established position in international markets. There are rich coalfields and the country is one of the world's largest manufacturers of steel, cast iron, and ferro-alloys, zinc, lead, and copper for which it uses imported minerals. The engineering, chemical, textile, and electronic industries are also very highly developed. Mixed farming is practiced, specializing in the production of beet, flax, cereals, potatoes, as commercial crops mainly for export. One of the main types of farming is stock-rearing. It is one of the original member nations of the EEC.

NETHERLANDS (Koninkrijk der Nederlanden)
Area: 15,891 square miles
Population: 14,000,000 and the Court
Language: Dutch
Religion: Catholicism and Protestantism
Monetary Unit: Florin or Guilder
History and Government: The Dutch are a mixture of the Frisians, Angles, Saxons, and Franks who occupied the area. Famous for their freedom of thought, their cities have long attracted refugees expelled from their homelands through religious or political pressure. The struggle against the sea has imposed a certain asceticism on the lifestyle of the northerners in contrast to the more relaxed lifestyles of the southerners. Dutch independence began in 1581 when the northern provinces revolted against Spanish rule. The present constitution dates from 1815 and is defined as a constitutional monarchy which, with the former colonies of Surinam and the Netherlands Antilles form the kingdom of the Netherlands. The monarch rules in conjunction with ministers through a two-chamber States-General, or Parliament of 150 members directly elected and 75 members elected by the councils of the 11 provinces. There are a large number of political parties.
Economy: The Netherlands has a well-balanced economy, with both very advanced industry and intensive agriculture. It also has a flourishing export trade. In the agricultural sector the production of cereals, potatoes, beet, and flax is among the highest in the world. Horticulture is traditionally of great importance, both the production of bulbs and the growing of flowers. But

the most lucrative activity is animal husbandry with the consequent dairy products – Holland is among the biggest exporters of butter in the world. Fishing, too, is well developed and linked with a prosperous processing industry. The most important industrial sectors are iron and steel, engineering, electrical engineering, shipbuilding, textiles, chemicals, and foodstuffs. Traditional industries are diamond-cutting and the processing of imported raw commodities, such as tobacco, quinine, vegetable oils and rubber, mainly from Indonesia and other former colonies. It is one of the original members of the EEC.

FEDERAL REPUBLIC OF GERMANY (Bundesrepublik Deutschland)
Area: 95,794 square miles
Population: 61,000,000
Capital: Bonn
Language: German
Religion: Protestantism and Catholicism
Monetary Unit: Deutsche Mark
History and Government: The Federal Republic of Germany was founded in 1949 from the 10 western states of the former German nation – which for hundreds of years before the late 1800s consisted of many separate states ruled by princes. The Federal Republic became a sovereign independent country in 1955 after the Occupation Structure was revoked by the High Commissioners of the UK, the USA, and France. The 10 states that make up the republic are known as Länder, each of which has a large measure of autonomy in finance and labor, education, justice, and civil rights. A president is head of state, but his powers are largely ceremonial. The federal government, presided over by the Chancellor, is answerable to the Federal Diet (*Bundestag*) which with the Federal Council (*Bundesrat*), formed of members of the governments of the Länder, constitutes the parliament. The Federal Diet is elected for a term of four years. The treaty of 1972 tackled the problem of relations with the eastern DDR and in 1973 both the Federal Republic and the DDR were admitted to the United Nations.
Economy: Rapid industrial development has ensured the Federal Republic's position as the main industrial power on the continent, but has proved unfavorable to agriculture, from which labor has been drained away. There are vast forests that supply the cellulose, paper, and construction industries. The country has important deposits of coal,

lignite, iron, potassium salts, and recently oil has been discovered. Industry has developed enormously since World War II and in many sectors is of worldwide importance. It is a founder-member of the EEC.

WEST BERLIN
Area: 186 square miles
Population: 2,000,000
Monetary Unit: Deutsche Mark
History and Government: It comprises the three sectors of the former capital of prewar Germany, occupied after World War II by United States, British, and French troops. Its legal position is controversial; according to Bonn it is a "Länd," separated from the territory of the Federal Republic; according to the DDR it is an autonomous entity. West Berlin is administered by a Chamber of 200 members (the 73 seats reserved for the representatives of East Berlin, however, remain permanently vacant), which elects the burgomaster, and a Senate of 16 members, which holds the executive power.
Economy: The population is largely engaged in industry – engineering, electrical engineering, electronics, and clothing – and in services.

Below: the Rhine, longest and busiest water highway in Western Europe is navigable from Basle in Switzerland to the North Sea.

GERMAN DEMOCRATIC REPUBLIC (Deutsche Demokratische Republik, DDR)
Area: 41,767 square miles
Population: 17,000,000
Capital: East Berlin (Berlin)
Language: German
Religion: Mainly Protestantism
Monetary Unit: Mark
History and Government: The DDR occupies the area of the former eastern states or provinces of Saxony, Brandenburg, Anhalt, Mecklenburg, and Thuringaria in the old German nation. The DDR was set up in 1949 by the USSR. The People's Council of the Soviet occupied zone, appointed in 1948, was converted into a provisional People's Chamber. According to the Social Constitution of 1968, the law-making body is the People's Chamber (*Volkskammer*), which appoints the council of state, the supreme organ of state power. The chairman of the council of state represents the state in international law. The only party recognized is the Marxist-Leninist party known as the Socialist Unity Party (SUP). In December 1972, a treaty was signed outlining the basis of relations between the two German republics, and they were both admitted to the United Nations in 1973.
Economy: The DDR is the second industrial power in the Communist bloc. Strict planning achieved a rapid development, especially in the production

of electrical power, iron and steel, engineering, and chemicals. The great thrust forward of industrialization had an unfavourable effect on agriculture, which employs only 12 percent of the labor force, whereas industry employs more than 50 percent. Stock-rearing is considerable and there are fairly substantial areas of forest, but the DDR depends on imports for food.

CZECHOSLOVAKIA (Československá Socialistická Republika)
Area: 49,373 square miles
Population: 15,000,000
Capital: Prague (Praha)
Language: Czech and Slovak
Religion: Mainly Catholicism
Monetary Unit: Koruna
History and Government: The homeland of two Slavic peoples, the Czechs, who live in two western areas of Bohemia and Moravia, and the Slovaks, who live in the eastern area of Slovakia. The Slovaks were ruled by the Hungarians from the 10th century until 1918, and the Czechs came under Austrian rule in the 16th century until they combined with the Slovaks in 1918 to form the present nation. After World War II, the country was reconstituted and territories taken by the Germans, Poles, and Hungarians were restored to Czechoslovakia. It has been governed since 1948 by the Communist Party. The Constitution of 1950 invests the

legislative power in the National Assembly, elected every six years, which nominates the council of ministers and the president of the republic. After an attempt at democratization in 1968 Warsaw pact countries invaded Czechoslovakia and brought the reforms to an end. The country is now governed as a federation of the Czech Socialist Republic and the Slovak Socialist Republic each with its own government, although Foreign Affairs, constitution, and currency are the responsibility of the Federal Administration.

Economy: Industry, in particular heavy industry, is the most important productive element. Besides iron and steel, which is very highly developed, the main industries are engineering (machinery and automobiles), electrotechnics, and precision instruments. After these come the industries concerned with the processing of agricultural products, textiles, chemicals, cement, and footwear. Traditional industries are glass and ceramics. Mineral resources are modest, apart from uranium. The main agricultural products are cereals, beet, potatoes, and hops. There are large forests that supply a flourishing paper industry.

POLAND (Rzeczpospolita Polska Ludowa)
Area: 121,000 square miles
Population: 4,000,000
Capital: Warsaw (Warszawa)
Language: Polish
Religion: Catholicism
Monetary Unit: Zloty
History and Government: The Polish people are descended from the western Slavs who occupied the plains (pole means "field") between the Oder and Warta rivers in the 10th century. It was an important and powerful kingdom in medieval times but disastrous wars in the 17th century led to a loss of much of its accumulated territory. The first constitution of the Polish republic dates from 1921, laying down conditions for a parliamentary democracy. The republic was dismembered during World War II. It was liberated in 1945 by the Red Army of the USSR, and owes its present position and boundaries to the annexation of the territories of the former German Reich, which were east of the Oder-Neisse rivers, and the restitution to the USSR of the territories that now form parts of Ukrainskaya and Belorusskaya. The former were finally accepted in 1970 by the Federal Republic of Germany. Poland is a "people's democracy," according to the Constitution of 1952, and has a

single legislative chamber parliament, the *Sejm*, elected for four years by all citizens over 18 years of age. The Sejm appoints the council of state and a council of ministers. The titular head of the state is the chairman of the council of state. Dissatisfaction with the regime and conditions of life led to strikes and riots in 1970, after which the "new road" policies of Edward Gierek has led to a greater liberalization and significant changes in economic policy.

Economy: Agricultural production is among the most important in Europe for rye and oats, potatoes, and flax. Poland is also among the foremost countries in Europe for stock-rearing, much of which goes for export, and the very first for the rearing of horses. There are rich forests too, which place Poland among the largest producers of timber and paper. The country has rich mineral resources of coal, lignite, copper, lead, zinc, nickel, rock salt, sulfur, potassium salts, and cadmium. In the manufacturing industries, iron and steel has developed most, followed by engineering, chemicals, and textiles. There are also significant food, tanning, and glass industries. More than 50 percent of the labor force is engaged in industry.

SWITZERLAND (Schweizerische Eidgenossenschaft)
Area: 15,950 square miles
Population: 6,500,000
Capital: Bern (Berne)
Language: French, German, Italian, Romansh
Religion: Protestantism and Catholicism
Monetary Unit: Franc
History and Government: The Swiss republic dates from 1291 when the Forest Cantons of Uri, Schwyz, and Unterwalden, then part of the Holy Roman Empire, formed an anti-Hapsburg league. Other cantons joined the league and expanded their territories. By the 15th century they were virtually independent. It is now a confederation of 25 cantons, or districts, and is characterized by its international neutrality and by the fact that its highest power is vested in the electorate, that is, everyone over 20 years of age. The parliament, or Federal Assembly, has two chambers, a National Council of 200 members and a Council of States of 44 members. The president of the Confederation, elected by parliament, remains in office for 1 year and is not immediately eligible for reelection. He also has the functions of the head of state. Executive power is invested in a Federal Council. Universal suffrage

Above: the Matterhorn's jagged peak towers over this view of Zermatt – a view like thousands more in Switzerland, where the picturesque is carefully preserved as a tourist attraction.

Above right: the Europa Bridge in Austria. It carries a major highway from northern Europe through Austria into Italy. It spans 2752 feet.

was introduced in 1971 when the vote was extended to women.

Economy: The country's great prosperity arises from historical, political, and geographical factors: for example, the high immigration of labor, especially from Italy; the powerful claims on foreign capital; and the immense sums of money available, far beyond the restricted limits of local economy. The chief agricultural activity, employing 10 percent of the working population, is animal husbandry, which in turn supplies the cheese, chocolate, and textile industries. Swiss industry enjoys worldwide preeminence in various sectors: engineering, electrical engineering, chemicals, and pharmaceuticals. The clock-making industry has an almost world monopoly, but other branches of precision engineering are also exceptionally highly developed. Tourism is very important.

LIECHTENSTEIN (Furstentum Liechtenstein)
Area: 65 square miles
Population: 24,000
Capital: Vaduz
Language: German
Religion: Catholicism
Monetary Unit: Swiss currency
History and Government: In 1719, the lordship of Vaduz and the countship of Schellenberg, both in the hands of the Liechtenstein family, were renamed the principality of Liechtenstein in the Holy Roman Empire. The state belonged to the Austrian customs union before the collapse of the Hapsburg monarchy in 1918. It later joined the Swiss customs union and also adopted Swiss currency and postal administration. It is a constitutional monarchy with a legislative assembly of 15 members, elected by universal suffrage. Its diplomatic relations are conducted through Switzerland.
Economy: Stock-rearing and agriculture are practiced, and its main industries are metal goods and the textile industry. Tourism is also important. The influx of foreign capital, attracted by the relaxed financial legislation, is important.

AUSTRIA (Österreich)
Area: 32,373 square miles
Population: 7,500,000
Capital: Vienna (Wien)
Language: German
Religion: Catholicism
Monetary Unit: Schilling
History and Government: It was the Emperor Charlemagne who erected the former Slovenian kingdom of the Avars

into a border state – the East Mark or Osterreich – and it later came into the possession of Rudolf of Hapsburg in 1278. It remained under Hapsburg rule until 1918. After being formally absorbed in the German Reich from 1938 to 1945 under the name Ostmark, and then occupied by the Allies from 1945, Austria finally regained its sovereignty with the Austrian State Treaty of 1955, signed by the UK, USA, USSR, and France. Austria is now a federal republic composed of nine provinces: Vienna, Lower Austria, Salzburg, Tyrol, Vorarlberg, Carinthia, Styria, and Burgenland. The president of the republic is head of state and elected for six years by direct universal suffrage; he nominates the chancellor, who is head of government and answerable to parliament, which is a National Assembly of 183 deputies. Social tensions have been lessened by a practical collaboration between industrialists, trade unions, and the government. In foreign policy, the treaty of 1955 guarantees neutrality.
Economy: The country is highly industrialized with agriculture developed only in a limited area. Apart from stock-rearing which supplies the dairy industry, there are forests that provide a valuable contribution to the nation's economy, and supply the cellulose and paper industries. Mineral resources are good – lignite, iron, magnesite, lead, and copper – and have facilitated the development of an advanced iron and steel industry. Other important industries are engineering, chemicals, textiles, food, and tourism. Austria was an original member state of EFTA and since 1972 has been an associated state with the EEC, which has done much to boost its economy.

HUNGARY (Magyarország)

Area: 36,000 square miles
Population: 10,500,000
Capital: Budapest
Language: Hungarian
Religion: Mainly Catholicism
Monetary Unit: Forint
History and Government: The Hungarian peoples – of Finno-Ugrian and Asiatic Turkish origin – conquered and settled their lands in the 9th century AD. It became an independent kingdom and was converted to Latin Christianity by around AD 1000. Hungary was later divided between the Ottoman empire and Austria, and in the 17th century came directly under the Austrian Hapsburg rule until some autonomy was restored in 1867, when the Dual Monarchy of Austria-Hungary was formed. After the collapse of the Hapsburg empire, the independent republic, then kingdom, of Hungary was proclaimed. The country was ruled by a pro-Axis Regent until the end of World War II. The "People's Democratic Government" was instituted in 1949, three years after the proclamation of a republic. The constitution is typical of eastern European countries; the supreme power is vested in parliament, which elects the presidential council and this council undertakes the functions of parliament in the intervals between sessions. The chairman of the council is also head of state.
Economy: Both industry and agriculture are almost entirely state-controlled. Agriculture is important both for crop growing and stock-rearing. The chief crops, which are also exported, are cereals, potatoes, beet, and vines. Hungary is famous for its horses and is the main producer of pigs in Europe. Raw materials include oil, large amounts of bauxite, brown coal, some natural gas, iron ore, and uranium. The industries are well developed and employ more than 50 percent of the labor force. Besides iron and steel, the textile, chemical and petrochemical, engineering and electrical engineering industries are particularly advanced.

Chapter 4

The Mediterranean Lands

The name "Mediterranean" means quite literally "the middle of the earth" and for the greater part of the history of man it was the center of his known world. The sea is deep and tideless, and has only one natural outlet to the open ocean, the Strait of Gibraltar at its western end between North Africa and the western extremity of mainland Europe – the Iberian peninsula. About 10 miles wide, the strait links the Mediterranean with the Atlantic Ocean. The northeastern outlet, the long narrow passage called Canakkale Bogazi (Dardanelles) leads only to the Sea of Marmara and from there by the Karadeniz Bogazi (Bosporus) to the Black Sea. At the southeastern corner of the Mediterranean is a man-made outlet, the Suez Canal, which cuts across over 100 miles of desert to the Red Sea, providing a route to India and the Far East.

Opposite: the rocky peninsula of Gibraltar separated from the coast of Africa by the narrow Strait of Gibraltar, lies at the western entrance of the Mediterranean Sea. This busy seaway was the center of life in the ancient world and today serves as an important world trade route.

Southern Europe and the Mediterranean

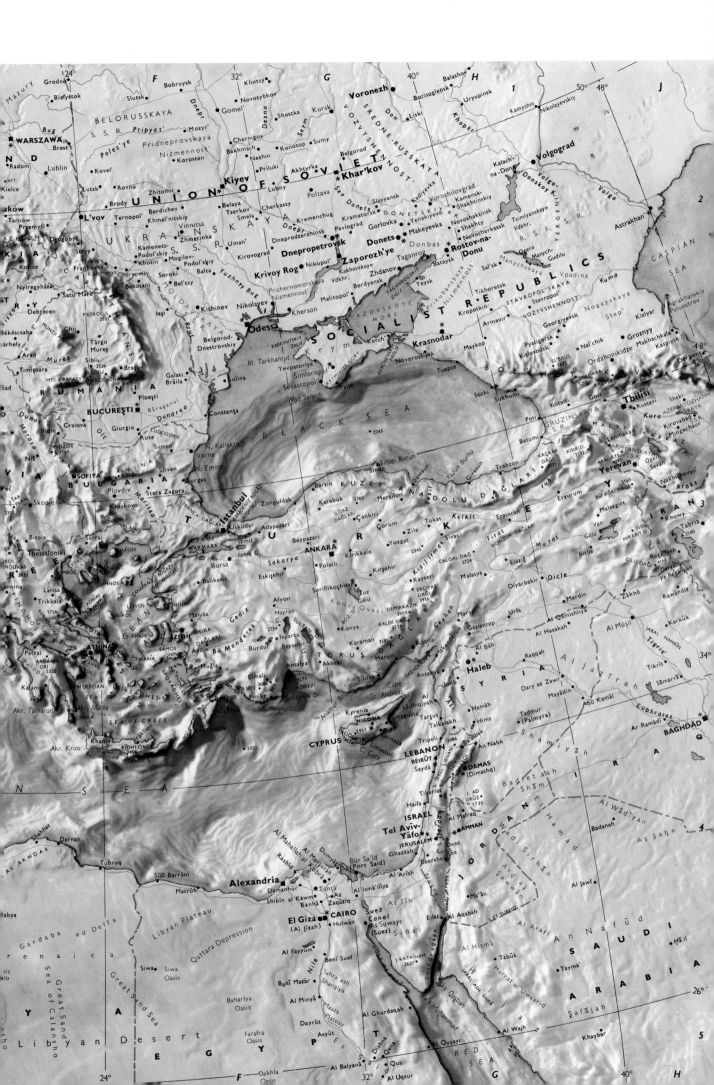

The Mediterranean Sea

Only one state has ever succeeded in dominating the Mediterranean from end to end and in ruling all the hinterland too. That state was the Roman Empire. The Romans had adopted and adapted much of what was best in the earlier Greek civilization and carried it westward to Italy and eventually throughout their empire. By the early 5th century BC the Roman Empire began to collapse in the face of the invading hordes pouring into Europe from the east. The eastern part of the Empire survived in southeastern Europe and southwestern Asia – the area of the eastern Mediterranean and provided the vital link between the civilization of Rome and that of Medieval Europe.

Between AD 632 and 732 the armies of Islam spread their culture along the southern shores of the Mediterranean and then westward across the Strait of Gibraltar into Spain and mainland Europe. The Frankish

sufficient to replenish the amount of water lost from the sea by evaporation. In fact, the level of the Mediterranean Sea would drop by 55 feet each year if it were not for the in-flow from the Atlantic at the Strait of Gibraltar. Once into the Mediterranean this water flows along the north coast of Africa and then fans out. At the western end of the Mediterranean water piles up against the lip of the strait until it overflows into the Atlantic. Without this flow and counter-flow the Mediterranean would become a stagnant and rapidly diminishing lake.

Because the Mediterranean is almost landlocked the currents are comparatively sluggish and, in most places, the tidal range is only a few inches. Ever since 1000 BC – when the inhabitants of Cyprus mined copper to sell to the Phoenicians and tipped the unwanted material into the sea – the Mediterranean has been used as a dumping ground for industrial wastes. But because of its poor circulation and its one narrow link with the world circulatory system, it is not efficient enough to cope with all that has been, and is being poured into it. Many scientists believe that the Mediterranean Sea is dying, choking to death on the by-products of our industrial world.

In the Mesozoic era a great geosyncline was submerged beneath the Tethys, the sea that separated Laurasia and Gondwana. The small oceanic areas of the Mediterranean and Black Sea are, most likely,

Above: Seville cathedral, Spain, is built on the site of a Moorish grand mosque.
Right: Pont du Gard, France, impressive relic of the once mighty Roman Empire.

ruler Charles Martel eventually halted the Islamic armies at Tours in France, but the Moslems continued to control the Mediterranean Sea until the end of the Middle Ages. Their stranglehold was finally loosened by the rise of maritime powers such as Venezia (Venice) and Genova (Genoa). Even so, it was not until the end of the 19th century that European powers again controlled the waterway of the Mediterranean.

The Mediterranean Sea is more than 2300 miles from end to end and the average depth is 5000 feet, but there are extensive areas with depths of over 10,000 feet. It is surrounded by warm, dry countries and the amount of rainfall, combined with the runoff from rivers, is not

remnants of this larger ocean lying between the plates of Eurasia and Africa. During the late Tertiary Alpine orogeny, as the plates moved toward each other, the two sides of this geosyncline were folded, contorted and pushed up. The rugged, high mountains of the Alpine system border both sides of the western Mediterranean, the Haut Atlas and Atlas Saharien to the south, the Pyrenees and Alps to the north. Along the northern boundary of the eastern Mediterranean, the system continues eastward in a series of near-parallel ranges, through Greece, Asia Minor, Iran, to the Himalayas and beyond. Along the southern and eastern shores, from the Sicilian Channel to Syria, is the

Above: Mount Vesuvio with the ruins of the ancient Roman town of Pompeii in the foreground.
Right: casts from the bodies of three of the citizens of Pompeii; choked to death by fumes and buried under volcanic ash when Vesuvio erupted in 79 AD.

ancient African Shield. Thus the contrast between the western and northern shores and the southern and eastern shores is marked, the complexity and variety of the folded mountains and indented coastline on the one hand and the low plateaus and smooth coastline on the other.

The Mediterranean is also an unstable region, an area subject to earthquakes and where there are active volcanoes such as Etna, Vesuvio (Vesuvius), and Stromboli. The majority of these volcanoes are of the explosive type that eject both ash and lava and often have many subsidiary vents. Etna, the largest volcano in Europe, has hundreds of these secondary vents. Many of the islands in the Isole Lipari, north of Sicilia (Sicily), are volcanic and exhibit different types of eruptions according to the pressure and quantities of gas and the type of lava. In some, where the pent-up gases escape spasmodically, the explosions are rhythmic and may even be continuous. Stromboli behaves in this way, erupting for a few minutes, or maybe for an hour, very frequently, often daily. In other types the more viscous lava crusts over between eruptions. This means that the gases accumulate for longer periods, until the pressure causes the top to blow off with greater violence.

In types such as Vesuvio, there is a combination of

violent explosions, when magma is ejected, and alternating dormant periods of quiescence or only mild activity. The famous eruption of Vesuvio in AD 79 that buried the Roman towns of Pompeii and Herculaneum under several feet of volcanic ash, was followed by many centuries of quiescence. It erupted again in 1631 and since then has been active in cycles that have varied from 11 to 40 years, the last being in 1944. It has changed its profile several times, building up subsidiary cones inside the main crater, blowing off parts of the crater wall and emitting lava from various vents, resulting in flows down the mountain sides.

Lands and Peoples

Spain and Portugal together make up the Iberian peninsula, a peninsula isolated geographically from the rest of Europe. Most of this massive, square peninsula is plateau country about 2000 feet high, called *Meseta*. It is an ancient Hercynian massif, worn down by successive cycles of erosion. But it is also criss-crossed by numerous mountain ranges that in places rise to 6000 feet and more. To the southeast are Spain's highest mountains, the Sierra Nevada, which exceed 11,000 feet and may be snow-tipped even in midsummer.

Most of the people in this hot, dry peninsula, live in the predominantly agricultural river valleys and coastal lowlands such as the central Tajo (Tagus) valley, the lower Guadalquivir and the coastal plains round Barcelona, Valencia, and Cartagena. Spain has a long history of mining that attracted Phoenicians, Cretans, Carthaginians, Romans, and others. Among the many minerals mined are copper, tin, lead, silver, zinc, and mercury. There is, however, a shortage of coal, which affects widescale industrialization The

deposits of iron in the northern coastal region, between Santander and Bilbao, represent the largest export item, and is shipped chiefly to Britain and the Ruhr. The main industrial areas are in this northern belt, between Oviedo in the west and Bilbao in the east, near the French frontier, and on the Mediterranean coast in Catalonia where textile and engineering predominate.

Portugal, the other country that shares the peninsula with Spain, has no Mediterranean seaboard. To all purposes it has turned its back on the Meseta, and looked to the ocean for its livelihood in the past. In every way Portugal's maritime outlook has strengthened her connections with Northwest Europe and the Americas, as well as Africa and the East, where she first established her empire.

Portugal is still predominantly an agricultural country, producing cereals and wines. Forest products are especially important, the oil from the olive, cork from the cork oak, and the resin and timber from pines.

Right: a Mediterranean beach. Pollution is so serious that bathing is now forbidden in many areas.
Below: Portuguese workers strip the bark from a cork oak. Portugal produces half the world's cork.

Fishing is a major occupation but industries are chiefly concerned with the processing of agricultural, forest, and fishing products.

Italy is probably the most Mediterranean in character of all the countries bordering this sea. It thrusts southeast like a boot about to kick a ball. The Appennini (Apennines) mountains run down the whole length of the boot and bend around, linking with the great curve of the Alps, like a reversed question mark. The ball is the once-fertile island of Sicilia (Sicily). Geologically it is a young country, the mountains were forced upward during the Alpine orogeny, and the recent sediments that cover the floor of the Po river basin in the north are the result of successive stages of erosion, when great thicknesses of material were removed from the encircling Alps and Appennini (Apennines).

In contrast to the Iberian peninsula, the narrowness of the Italian peninsula ensures that it and the islands enjoy a typical Mediterranean climate of warm, wet

winters and hot, dry summers. There is, however, a fundamental difference between peninsular Italy and continental Italy where climatic conditions are less favorable. The Alps act as a screen to the valley of the Po against the severe winter conditions that prevail in central Europe. The ring of mountains, almost completely circling the valley, receives the heaviest rainfall and snowfall, between 40 and 60 inches a year, but the valley gets progressively drier to the east. It is along the Ligurian coast in the northwest, the north of Corse (Corsica) and the north of Sardegna (Sardinia), that the local violent northerly winds, known as the bora – and in the Rhône valley of France as the mistral – often occur. They are most prevalent in winter, when the pressure is high over the continent and a particularly deep depression develops in the western Mediterranean. These very strong winds, funneled down the river valleys, are accompanied by clear skies, low humidity, and very low temperatures.

Italy can be divided into three main regions, the north, the center, and the south and islands. In the north, between the westward curve of the Appennini and the much higher ranges of the Alps, is the large fertile plain of Lombardy, drained by the Po and its tributaries. Over the years these rivers have brought down in their flood waters the fine silt that makes the plain's soil fertile. It is a densely populated area and economically the most important region of Italy. Below Ferrara the Po has built a huge delta, sticking out into the Adriatic. To the north is a lagoon, on the northern end of which the ancient city-seaport of Venezia (Venice) stands on a cluster of islands. But the region's chief city is Milano (Milan), an important commercial, transport, and industrial center, the second largest city in Italy. Another important industrial center and route focus of the north is Torino (Turin).

The central region is dominated by the rugged Appennini, with their bare, rocky hillsides, and the patches of lowland are confined to coastal areas. It is traditionally the cultural and authoritarian center of Italy. In southern Italy, and on the islands of Sardegna (Sardinia) and Sicilia (Sicily), the land is not fertile enough to support the population. As well as geographical considerations, historically the area has been one of alternating colonization and devastation from the time of the Phoenician settlements and Greek colonies. But since World War II the government has made determined efforts to improve the situation, by land reform and by making available a special development fund to help restore the fertility of the soil and increase agricultural productivity.

Looking toward Italy, across the Adriatic Sea, are Yugoslavia and Albania, generally considered with Greece to form the Balkan peninsula. It is largely a mountainous area bordered in the north by the Danube river that flows across the Plain of Hungary then east to the Black Sea. In Tertiary times the plain was a lake, but after the Alpine orogeny it was gradually drained. The folded mountain ranges of the Alpine system run in a crescent. In Yugoslavia they are the Dinara Planina (Dinaric Alps) then south through Albania to Greece where their extension is the Pindhos mountains, which disappear beneath the Aegean Sea in a scatter of islands. The eastern folded zone includes the Stara Planina (Balkan mountains) and the Rodopi Planina (Rhodope mountains), which reappear again in Asia Minor.

The Dinara Planina takes in the famous *karst* region of Yugoslavia, a name geologists use to describe the particular landscape associated with limestones that develop more distinctive relief features than any other type of rocks. In Yugoslavia they have been worn away to rugged plateaus and are much lower than the main Alpine mountain ranges. Water sinks quickly through the porous rock, and the fissured surface is usually barren and dry. Caverns and streams lie underground. But here and there on the plateaus are long, flat-floored basins called *poljes*, often covered with comparatively fertile soil. These are thought to be mainly tectonic in origin and the floors of the depressions, being nearer to the water table, or level of saturation, are usually more fertile.

In the Balkan peninsula the climate shows the same sort of contrast between the Mediterranean coastlands and the interior as is shown in the Iberian peninsula. This contrast is most marked in Yugoslavia where only a narrow coastal strip, Dalmatia, enjoys pleasant Mediterranean conditions. The mountains have extremely severe, snowy winters, but the inland areas, though having cold winters, do enjoy hot summers and a summer rainfall maximum.

There is also a contrast historically between the Mediterranean coasts and the interior. The former have been subject through the centuries to a series of cultural influences from the Mediterranean powers; the interior, and in particular the eastern part, was for many centuries under Ottoman domination, although in the last 200 years Slovenia and Croatia, in Yugoslavia, were controlled by the Hapsburgs. Since World War I the separate Balkan states that emerged have been overshadowed by more powerful neighbors and today both Yugoslavia and Albania are mainly influenced by the USSR.

In the three Balkan countries of Yugoslavia, Albania, and Greece, agriculture is still the dominant occupation in which more than 50 percent of the people are engaged. By far the larger proportion of these are peasant farmers, growing cereals, vegetables, olives and wines and in Greece tobacco and currants also. A large number of the populations of Greece and Albania engaged in industry are concerned with handicrafts. In Greece the largest section of industry is that which deals with the processing of the agricultural products, although marine engineering is increasing in importance. Yugoslavia has a wide

variety of mineral resources from coal, iron ore, bauxite, lead, antimony, mercury, copper, and zinc. Most of its industry is located in the northwest of the country.

The extreme eastern Mediterranean is hemmed in by the vast land masses that exert a great influence on the climate, much more so than do the land areas in the western Mediterranean. To the north is Asia Minor, an area of great structural complexity that has been subject to tectonic movements since the Cretaceous period and was then again severely folded and faulted during the Alpine mountain-building epoch. Along the shores of the Black Sea are the Kuzey Anadolu Daglari (Pontine mountains) and to the south on the Mediterranean hinterland the Taurus Daglari (Torus mountains). These ranges continue eastward through Iran. It is essentially an unstable area, subject to volcanic activity and earthquakes, and several times within recent years whole villages on the Anatolian plateau have been devastated.

To the south, underlying much of the Near East and northeast Africa, are the ancient crystalline shields of the Pre-Cambrian era, covered for the most part by sedimentary rocks that have been extensively faulted. Between these two major zones is the transitional area of the "Fertile Crescent," from the Nile delta to the Persian Gulf, where the sedimentary rocks have been disturbed by the Alpine orogeny.

Above: harvesting wheat in Greece. Much has been done to increase areas under cultivation since World War II. **Left:** the Pyrenees, the mountain chain that forms a barrier to overland commerce between France and Spain. They cover an area of more than 20,000 square miles and are the source of iron, lead, silver, and cobalt.

Yet again the climate is characterized by wetter, more maritime coastlands and arid, hotter interior. Turkey, lying in both Asia and Europe, occupies the great plateau and folded mountains of Anatolia – Asia Minor – and a relatively small area to the north of the Sea of Marmara controlling both the Canakkale Bogazi (Dardanelles) and the Karadeniz Bogazi

(Bosporus). The northern coastline, bordering the Black Sea, receives up to 60 inches of rainfall a year and the mountains are heavily forested with deciduous trees. The Aegean and Mediterranean coastal areas have the typical Mediterranean climate, but inland extremes of cold, severe winters and hot summers are experienced. It is arid with less than 20 inches of rainfall, much of which is in the form of snow. Over 80 percent of the population is dependent on agriculture or pastoralism. Wheat is grown as well as citrus fruits, olives, and figs, and tobacco, hemp, cotton, and rice are grown in the valleys. Minerals, such as copper, antimony, and mercury, are mined in Turkey, which is also the world's chief producer of chrome.

The eastern shoreline of the Mediterranean is characterized by the smooth coastlines of Syria, Lebanon, and Israel. East of these is the flat-floored, steep-sided rift valley through which the river Jordan slowly meanders. At the lowest part of the valley the Jordan empties into the Dead Sea, 1287 feet below sea-level. This sea is so much saltier than ocean water, due to the high evaporation, that even the poorest swimmers float on it like corks. The rift is the northern section of the great East African rift system, here it marks the boundary zone between the African plate to the west and the smaller Arabian plate to the east.

The humid coastal strip supports the most intensive agricultural systems in the Mediterranean and the arid hinterland, which varies from steppe to semi-desert, is dominated by low-grade cereal production and pastoralism. However, there are oases and irrigated areas in the interior that are cultivated extensively, for example, the areas round Damas (Damascus). Since the middle of the third millennium BC, the timber of the now denuded forests on the slopes of the Jebellibna has been famous and highly prized. A plan to reforest the area is under way. The coast plains have been well irrigated and devoted to the cultivation of wheat, vegetables, and citrus fruits, bananas, and pineapples, and, on the lower mountain slopes, figs, mulberries, and the stone fruits.

The state of Israel, formed in 1948, has added a new dimension to the Near East. It is in essence a European state set in the middle of a unified Moslem region. It is surrounded by Arab states: to the north Syria and Lebanon, to the east Jordan, and to the southeast Egypt. Conflict has been inevitable. Israel, supported by capital from abroad, rich in expertise and technological skills, has developed the agricultural potential of the area to the full and far outstripped its neighbors. It has in kibbutzim the most advanced collective agricultural system in the world. Although natural resources are few, industry has not been neglected. Chemicals, engineering, and the manufacture of light consumer goods are of greatest importance.

Overleaf: a scene outside a peasant farm in eastern Anatolia, Turkey. Anatolia is a dry region and although the soil is good, it is thin, and much of it has been washed away. Nevertheless, wheat, barley, corn, rye, oats, and opium poppies are grown there.

87

The Mediterranean's Southern Coasts

The southern shores of the Mediterranean fall into two sharply defined areas: in the west the mountainous regions of Morocco, Algeria, and Tunisia, and to the east the almost level plateau lands of Libya and Egypt. The mountains of the Atlas system in the west were formed in the great Alpine mountain-building epoch. Along the Mediterranean coastal lands the rainfall is adequate, being over 25 inches a year, mainly in the winter months. The higher ground to the south of the strip is in many ways a zone of transition between the true Mediterranean lands of the coastal strip and the vast Sahara desert south of the mountains.

In the east the monotonous tabular plateaus of ancient crystalline rocks, overlain with sedimentary rocks, come right down to the coast. There is a small winter rainfall along the narrow coastal strip, but in other parts the rainfall is very small and in parts of the Libyan Desert there is none at all. Temperatures are unusually high and apart from the coast, the Nile valley, and the oases, the land is a wilderness, sometimes shifting sands, sometimes barren rocks.

Below: goats climbing an argan tree to graze on the foliage. Overgrazing by goats has been perhaps the most important factor among many that have helped to create the arid landscapes of North Africa as well as contributing to the enormous extension of the Sahara Desert.

Above: the High Dam at Aswan, Egypt, built to control the floodwaters of the Nile river. Since its completion in 1970 the Dam has provided enormous benefits for the Egyptian economy by greatly increasing the area under cultivation – as well as providing Cairo's electricity.

Morocco has a variable landscape ranging from the Mediterranean seaboard in the northeast to the Haut Atlas in the southwest, and from the marshy areas bordering the Atlantic in the west to the true desert in the south. The country becomes more arid to the southeast away from the influence of the moist winds blowing from the Atlantic and Mediterranean and into the rain shadow of the Atlas ranges. The forests of oak, cedar, and juniper are replaced by scrub wherever the precipitation falls below 24 inches and many places have suffered from deforestation and are reduced to maquis, consisting of wild olive and myrtle. The many herds of goats are among the greatest denuders of the land. They graze indiscriminately, devouring all vegetation – even climbing into trees – and creating a surface that is easily eroded when the rains come. Large-scale dams are improving agricultural output and there are drainage and reforestation schemes such as those in the Moyen Atlas (Middle Atlas) and in the river Dra.

Algeria falls clearly into three zones: the well-watered coast, the ranges of the Atlas Saharien (Saharan Atlas) behind the coastal area, and the arid desert plateaus to the south. The population of these southern plateaus is mainly pastoral and semi-nomadic, although the various groups tend to have bases where they supplement their economy by agriculture. It is the discovery of oil that is having the greatest effect on the economy. Oil was first shipped in commercial quantities from the country in 1958 and by 1960 Algeria was in a position to supply half of France's requirements. Since then production has increased, and a pipeline has been built to the Mediterranean coast at Bejaia (Bougie).

Tunisia, another former French protectorate, is at the eastern extremity of the Atlas system. In this country the French colonizers did not play such an important role as in Algeria. Tunisia was principally in the hands of the local people who created large-scale holdings, then let out portions. The road system has been developed from the major town and port of Tunis to the interior in order to bring phosphates, olives and olive products, cork and fruits to the coast for export.

The discovery of oil in the 1960s and the subsequent military revolution of 1969 have wrought many changes in the state of Libya. The income from the oil is a great boost to the economy for less than eight percent of the country is considered productive and this, apart from the desert oases, is a narrow strip a few miles wide along the coast. Even this strip is really marginal in that the rains can fail completely with the consequent disastrous results to the grain harvest. Exploitation of oil and natural gas has brought benefits especially to the isolated oases far to the south in the desert. Concessions are often leased on condition that a percentage of the profits are used to initiate schemes concerned with water and agricultural resources. In the Kufra Oasis, far to the southeast, an oil company has drilled wells to bring up sweet water well suited to an irrigation project. Successful experiments have been carried out, using this water for the cultivation of wheat, barley, and clover and using the latter for sheep grazing.

Egypt resembles Libya in many respects. Almost 96 percent of the land is desert, with some small areas of marsh, and into the remaining four percent are crowded over 33 million people. They occupy the narrow Nile valley, the delta, a thin coastal strip, and various oases dotted throughout the western desert. The overriding problem is the pressure of this vast population on the very limited resources. There is not enough land to go around. But since the revolution of 1952 and the end of the monarchy, agrarian reform, nationalization and expansion of industry and the great projects such as the Aswan Dam and land reclamation, especially in the delta area and along the Mediterranean coast, have all combined to improve the lot of the people. In the industrial field Egypt is the second most industrialized state in Africa, after the Republic of South Africa. There has been massive investment in plant producing cement, fertilizers, and oil refining, as well as in the old-established industries based on agricultural products such as cotton.

Farming Lands

The climate of the Mediterranean lands has three main characteristics. Firstly, the rainfall falls in the winter months and the summer is almost completely dry. The amount of rainfall is on an average 30 inches a year but may be as little as 5-10 inches along the north-eastern African coast and in the extreme east of the region. For example, Gibraltar in the west has 35 inches, Malta in the center has 20 inches, and in the eastern Mediterranean Athinai (Athens) has 15 inches and Alexandria only 8 inches. Secondly, the winters are very mild, the temperature rarely falling below 50°F, and never below 40°F, and the summers are hot with an average July temperature of over 70°F and as high as 85°F in North Africa. Thirdly, there is little cloud, even in winter, and the bright sunny skies are ideal for ripening the many fruits and have far-reaching effects on human development. In fact the classic description of a Mediterranean type climate is "warm, wet winters, hot, dry summers."

The land of the Mediterranean region is mostly difficult to cultivate. There are many steep slopes and only small pockets or strips of lowland. Farmers often have to terrace the slopes to stop the torrential rains – when they come – from washing away the precious topsoil. Crops grown for local use include wheat and corn, where the winters are wet enough. Rice is grown

Above: terrace cultivation, practiced here in Mirador, Majorca, is a way of conserving precious topsoil. A series of low embankments are formed across the slopes so that water soaks into the land instead of teeming down the hill carrying soil with it.

Above: the flood plain of the Po river in Italy. Engineering skill and perseverence have kept the soils drained yet not too dry, and a wide variety of crops are grown there.
Right: These Spanish olive groves and citrus orchards in Andalusia, are typical products of Mediterranean lands.

in the Po valley, the Rhône delta, and in southeast Spain; melons in southern Spain, Italy, and Israel, and tomatoes everywhere.

Farmers concentrate on goat and sheep raising as these animals do not require lush pasture and goats, in particular, will graze the almost bare hillsides and forage successfully for themselves in scrubland. In some Mediterranean lands, in summer, the shepherds often take their flocks to higher pastures where it is cooler and moister. But the danger is always that the animals may overgraze – as they have done in Morocco – loosening the dry soil, which is then washed away by the winter rain. Except in a few limited areas in north-west Spain, parts of the Alps, the Appennini (Apennines), and Dinara Planina (Dinaric Alps), there are few cattle and people usually do not eat butter.

The substitute for animal fats is provided by the olive. It flourishes in almost all soils, but demands many hours of sunshine, a dry summer, and a frost-free winter. The gnarled, twisted trees have very long roots that can draw moisture from deep below the parched, brown surface. The trees can live for hundreds of years, regularly producing thousands of fruits resembling small plums. Few of these are eaten fresh in Mediterranean lands. Most are used to make cooking oil. Eating olives are carefully handpicked, but nut olives are beaten from the trees with long poles and pulped into a paste. This paste is spread on esparto grass mats, which are then put through a hydraulic press to force out the oil. The best oil comes from the first pressing.

Another characteristic tree is the cork oak. This evergreen is remarkable because its outer bark can be stripped off every 10 years without damaging the tree itself, which may go on producing cork for 150 years. Portugal is famous for its cork, but there are

also valuable cork forests in Morocco and Algeria.

Vineyards on terraced hillsides are another common feature of the Mediterranean landscape. Although vines tend to lose a lot of water because their leaves are large, thin, and soft, they compensate by drawing up moisture through deep roots. Vine roots sometimes push down 20 feet or more into the ground. Mediterranean lands have many famous wines, such as the sherry from southeast Spain, and the port from the Douro valley in Portugal. In the eastern Mediterranean, where it is drier and sunnier, grapes are slowly dried in the open to provide raisins, sultanas, and currants.

Citrus and other fruits are widely grown. Citrus trees can withstand drought, but farmers usually practice irrigation to produce better quality crops. Sicilia (Sicily) is noted for its lemons, Spain for the oranges named for Sevilla (Seville), and Israel for its grapefruit and Jaffa oranges. Other fruits grown for export include Italian peaches and pears, the dried figs for which Turkey had always been known, Israeli avocados and pineapples, and dates from the oases of Libya, Tunisia, and Algeria.

In Egypt the twice-yearly crop rotation has been replaced by a three-crops-a-year rotation, made possible by the building of the Aswan Dam, and the consequent control of the Nile. The change from large estates rented out in tiny plots, to vast fields each entirely under one crop such as maize, clover, or cotton has meant higher yields. Peasant farmers work under the control and direction of the village cooperative, which ensures the same crop is grown in each field, the correct application of fertilizer and pesticides, and the correct use of the irrigation water. This cooperative system is responsible for much of Egypt's improved yield and recent agrarian success.

Above: Algerian street sellers surrounded by piles of dates – the only really valuable fruit to grow in the desert.
Left: Lemons being harvested on the Greek island of Corfu. The Mediterranean is one of the principal fruit-growing areas of the world.

Industry and Resources

The industrial economy of an area is based mainly on its production of iron and steel and its possession of adequate fuel and power resources. The Mediterranean lands have few mineral resources and no large deposits of coal. Therefore, most Mediterranean countries are not highly industrialized. Mineral wealth is usually found in old rocks where the deposits have been built up over a long period of time. But the mountains of the Atlas and Alpine systems are geologically young. Fuel and power have always been a problem. It was not until the discovery and development of the important new oilfields in Algeria, Libya, and Egypt in the last two decades that the region was able to boast a source of power.

Hydroelectric power on a large scale can only be developed in mountain districts where melting snow and ice keep rivers flowing, even in the dry summer months. France and northern Italy make good use of such power. One of the most important recent schemes is the Rhône development plan, which includes a

Below: workers in an automobile plant, Turin. Turin is the chief city of Piedmont and fourth city in Italy – coming after Rome, Milan, and Naples. Its industries include engineering, textiles, and chemicals.

navigable channel from Lake Leman (Geneva) to the Mediterranean, on which 20 power stations are planned. Rivers in Portugal, Spain, southern Italy, Yugoslavia, Greece, and Turkey are also now being harnessed.

Italy and Spain are the only Mediterranean countries with any large-scale industry. Italy's greatest industrial area lies in the north. Here the early growth of cities like Venezia (Venice), Milano (Milan), and Torino (Turin) was based on trade routes. Later readily available cheap labor, and coal imported through seaports conveniently close by, encouraged industrial development. Further expansion has occurred with the transmission of hydroelectricity from the Alps and, still more recently, natural gas from local fields mainly near the Po delta has been used to power some factories. In this part of Italy the medieval silk industry has grown into the manufacture of all kinds of textiles, from silk to man-made fibers. The chemical industry figures prominently in another part of Italy, in the island of Sicilia (Sicily). Here, mainly along the coastal strip around Syracuse, south of Catania, the recent industrial development has included an oil refinery and a chemical plant that makes fertilizers from the island's sulfur and potash.

Above: a cement factory in full production near Cairo, Egypt. There are industrial sites both north and south of this city, which is the capital of Egypt and the largest city in Africa.

The barren Spanish plateau, where the rocks are older than in most parts of the region, has a long history of mining. Its deposits include copper, tin, lead, silver, zinc, mercury, and wolfram. Spain's chief coalfield is in the north near Oviedo. This coal, with the iron ore from the Cordillera Cantabrica, is used in the iron and steel plants and engineering works in Oviedo and in Bilbao farther east. In spite of the absence of local coal and raw materials, other than potash, Barcelona has become an important industrial center. It is Spain's second largest city and the chief seaport. It is also Spain's foremost engineering center and specializes in electrical equipment, diesel engines, and railway vehicles, as well as textiles (especially cotton), glass, chemicals, and food processing. Cables carry hydroelectric power from the Pyrenees 50 or 100 miles to the city.

In Yugoslavia, which has a wide variety of mineral

Below: the port of the manufacturing and trading city of Barcelona, Spain. The towers on the left support an aerial lift to carry tourists across the docks.

resources such as iron ore, manganese, lead, and certain precious metals, attempts have been made to divert a surplus rural manpower into industry. Successful efforts have been made to increase power supplies and expand the steel, engineering, and chemical plants. Most of the industry is in the northwest of the country and here too the shipyards of Rijeka have expanded to provide useful exports.

It is perhaps in Egypt that the most spectacular advances have been made in recent years. In 1966

Above: the Portuguese tourist resort of Albafeira. Portugal has around 500 miles of level sandy coastline that attracts vacationers from many parts of Europe – especially the less-sunnier northwestern parts.

industry was responsible for a quarter of the national income and it is now rapidly overtaking agriculture as the main component – an enormous feat considering that industry was almost absent in the 1930s.

Of course, one of the major industries of the Mediterranean lands is tourism. The "raw materials," of which the Mediterranean has ample supply, are sunshine and scenery. In summer tourists crowd the shores of southern Europe and North Africa, coming mainly from the cooler, densely populated countries in Northwest Europe. Tourism is highly organized and attracts heavy investment in new hotels, villas, motels, and types of entertainment. Among the most popular resorts are the Costa Brava and Islas Baleares (Balearic Islands) in Spain, the French and Italian Rivieras, the Adriatic coasts of Italy and Yugoslavia, the Greek islands, and, more recently, the coastal resorts of Tunisia and Morocco.

95

History and Culture

The Mediterranean has a unique place in the story of mankind. It was the cradle of Western civilization. The seeds of that civilization were sown about 5000 years ago in Crete, the island home of the cultured Minoan seafarers, and later took root in mainland Greece. Greek traders and colonists in turn spread knowledge of science, art, and philosophy throughout the Mediterranean.

Other places and peoples added their contributions. Rome's vast empire contributed the Roman system of law, which forms the basis of many of the present-day legal systems; a vast network of roads, which circled the Mediterranean and stretched from Mesopotamia in the east to the Scottish border in the northwest; and, above all, the art of administration. Palestine, in the Levant, was the birthplace of Christianity. From Italy, many centuries later, came the glories of Renaissance philosophy and culture. Portugal and Spain, two great seafaring nations of the region, sent out explorers to find new trade routes to the East and new lands across the oceans. It was their success which led to the decline in the importance of the Mediterranean in the Middle Ages. Its lands and waters were no longer the highways for the spices, silks, and other Eastern luxuries. As the peoples of the Iberian peninsula turned their backs to the Mediterranean, so the initiative moved to Northwest Europe and for a time it seemed that the Mediterranean would become a backwater, no longer a world center of ideas and power.

The situation was radically changed by the opening of the Suez Canal in 1869. This man-made link between the eastern Mediterranean and the Red Sea – the entrance to the Indian Ocean – was vitally important to the colonial powers of Northwest Europe, Britain and Holland, whose empires embraced territories in East Africa, India, and the Far East on the one hand and the vast archipelago of the East Indies on the other. It also gave added significance to British Mediterranean bases like Gibraltar and Malta. Britain's hold on the Suez Canal itself did not end until 1956 when Egypt seized control. In 1967 came the Arab-Israeli war and the Suez Canal was blocked by scuttled freighters. It was only after several years that plans were put into operation to clear the canal and both widen and deepen it. It reopened in 1974. Meanwhile giant oil tankers used the Cape of Good Hope route to Europe thus cutting off a source of income to Egypt by not using the canal.

96

Most people around the Mediterranean belong to one racial, or ethnic, group. They are the various branches of the Mediterranean race that first spread, most probably from the southeast of the region, along the shores of North Africa and into southern and western Europe. They are short, dark-haired, with olive or brown skins. In North Africa they were followed later by the Semitic peoples from Arabia who reached the Strait of Gibraltar where they crossed into Europe. The Arabian influence, marked by greater height and slighter build, became predominant in these southern Mediterranean lands.

Above: a Venetian *albergo*, or hotel, built when Venice was a great city-state and "mistress of the Mediterranean Sea" in the 15th–16th centuries. Although no longer the greatest trading center of the Mediterranean, Venice is still a great port and an even greater tourist attraction.

In southern Europe there are signs of Alpine influence. The people are still short and stocky but have lighter skins and hair. These people moved into eastern Europe from the highland areas and plateaus of Asia and later groups of Alpine peoples drifted westward across the North European Plain and along the natural highway of the Danube valley. In the western Mediterranean, some small groups, such as the isolated Basques in the western extremity of the Pyrenees, have kept their own separate characteristics and languages intact. Their origin is something of a mystery, but it is thought that they are a remnant of one of the earlier groups of Mediterranean peoples who reached the Iberian peninsula before 1500 BC. In the Maghrib, as the western half of the North African Mediterranean lands is termed, live another unique

eople, the Berbers. They are the oldest settled people
f the region, some of the early Mediterranean peoples
who spread across North Africa long before the fam-
us Phoenician colony of Carthage was founded. They
ave since mixed with the invading peoples, especially
he Arabs, from whom they are now barely distin-
uishable. But there are still several enclaves, es-
ecially in the west, where the Berbers have main-
ained their language, customs, and clan organization.
n Morocco these so-called pure Berbers represent
bout 40 percent of the population. In Algeria 30
ercent but in Tunisia only two percent.

Great empires of the past have left their marks on
ll the languages spoken in the Mediterranean region.
Modern Greek is confined within the borders of the
ountry, but Latin influences have spread through all
he languages of southern Europe – Italian, Portu-
uese, and Spanish. Arabic is spoken in the whole of
he vast region that stretches from the Arabian
eninsula, both westward across North Africa and
orthward to the Anatolian plateau. In Israel Hebrew
as become a living language again. For centuries the
ews left their homeland in Palestine and set up com-
unities all over Europe and the Americas, where they
ept their language alive in their religious studies.
But since the formation of the state of Israel in 1948,

many of their descendants have returned, bringing
modern skills and techniques and making their historic language, Hebrew, become once more a spoken
language.

At the eastern end of the Mediterranean, in the
Middle East, there arose three of the world's greatest
religions – Judaism, Christianity, and Islam. Of these,
Judaism is the oldest living religion of the Western

Right: the Ka'aba (cube), containing the Black Stone
acred to Moslems, is in Makkah (Mecca) birthplace of
slam's founder, Mohammed.
Below: Berbers, descendants of an early people who
ettled the Sahara and North Africa centuries ago.

world and historically the parent of Christianity. Islam is considered the most powerful religious force outside Christianity and is regarded by many as chief competitor for spiritual dominance of the world. It is Christianity and Islam that dominate the Mediterranean lands.

Christianity, born in Palestine about AD 29, soon attracted people and spread to Antakya (Antioch) and thence westward across Europe. Although derived from 2000 years of Judaism, within 100 years it became predominantly non-Jewish. Two of Christianity's three major sects are based in the Mediterranean: the Eastern Orthodox Church, whose spiritual head, the Ecumenical Patriarch, lives in Istanbul, has most of its adherents in Greece, Russia, and the neighboring countries of Europe; and the Roman Catholic Church, whose spiritual head, the Pope, rules the 109-acre independent Vatican State in Rome, is the dominant religion in Portugal, Spain, France, Belgium, and Italy. The third sect, the Protestant, is the main religion of Northwest Europe.

Islam, the name of the faith founded by Mohammed in Makkah (Mecca) and Al Madinah (Medina) between AD 620 and 630, spread rapidly throughout the Middle East and west across North Africa, and into

Above: the Vatican City, Italy, is the residence of the pope, head of the world's 600 million Roman Catholics.

Below: Moslems at prayer. The followers of the religion of Islam are based in the Middle East, North Africa, and Southeast Asia.

outhern Spain, as well as east to India. The Arabs uilt mosques with minarets and onion-shaped domes nd even today some Spanish architecture still eflects Arab influence. Turkey is also a Moslem ountry and there are small groups of Moslems in Greece, Bulgaria, and Yugoslavia. Islam, is in fact the ominant religion of two-thirds of the area encircling ne Mediterranean.

Living standards in lands around the Mediteranean Sea are low when compared to North America nd Northwest Europe. Only northern Italy aproaches the living conditions and prosperity of Northwest Europe, but this area is really borderline Mediterranean, with its strong industrial bias and rbanization. Everywhere else, through Portugal, pain, southern Italy, Greece, Turkey, and across the ridth of North Africa, people live without the comrts that are taken for granted as part of everyday life n Northwest Europe.

The system of property ownership goes a long way to xplaining the lack of modern agricultural techniques nd the gap between rich and poor. Often wealthy, bsentee landlords own large estates worked by farm aborers who are paid very low wages. Since 1950 and reforms have been instituted in southern Italy nd Sicilia, aimed at expropriating some of the large states and dividing them into economically-sized oldings that can be cultivated under supervision and vith a set agrarian scheme. Similar reforms have aken place in Morocco and Algeria, where former 'rench estates have been treated in a similar manner, nd also in Egypt, where long established small oldings are now controlled by village cooperatives. Clsewhere, farmers who own or rent their own small creages, of often infertile land, barely grow enough o feed their own families. They grow a little grain, orn, keep a few sheep, goats, and chickens, perhaps ave some olive trees and a small vegetable garden. Many people in rural areas live in rude houses made of nud bricks or boulders from the mountains, with only he simplest necessities for comfortable living.

It is not surprising that many people, especially talians, have emigrated to the United States and the etter job opportunities in Northwest Europe. As yet, t is the peoples of the northern Mediterranean countries who have moved away, the peoples from the eastern Mediterranean and North Africa have been nore reluctant to leave their homelands, although ome from the Maghrib have moved to France. Recently, however, there has begun a surge northward o the industrial areas of Europe from Turkey and the Arab countries.

In Yugoslavia agrarian reform has helped to narrow he gap between rich and poor. Here the government again has broken up big estates and reallocated land o peasants. Spain has also taken the first steps toward lealing with this enormous problem. Israel has, peraps, found the best solution with kibbutzim, land nits that are worked communally. The land is owned oy the community and the members of the kibbutz

Above: young Jews at work on a kibbutz at Eliat, Israel. These collective settlements have been at the forefront in the reconquest of the desert areas since the State of Israel was established in 1948.

offer their labor in return for whatever economic support and social services the commune can afford. The people work, eat, and have their leisure communally and the children are cared for by the kibbutz, which provides nurseries, schools, and other services.

In the Mediterranean, as in many other regions, there have been many political changes since World War II. In the east the state of Israel has been created from part of Palestine (a name that no longer exists politically) and Cyprus has become independent only to be torn in two internally by friction between its Greek and Turkish populations. Malta, marking the division of the Mediterranean into western and eastern basins, is also independent. The former French territories in the Maghrib – Morocco, Algeria, and Tunisia – have won independence too, and the first of these, Morocco, has absorbed the former state of Spanish Morocco and the international territory of Tanger (Tangiers). Recently it has taken over part of the former Spanish Sahara. Economic links between these countries and Europe, however, continues to remain strong.

The Mediterranean is still strategically important to both the United States and the USSR. It is one of the major waterways between the two powers and gives access to the Black Sea where the USSR has its only ice-free winter ports and, consequently, bases a large proportion of its navy in that sea.

99

Atlantic Ocean

© Geographical Projects

The Countries of Southern Europe and the Mediterranean

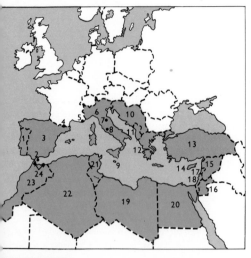

1 Portugal
2 Gibraltar
3 Spain
4 Andorra
5 Monaco
6 Italy
7 San Marino
8 Vatican City State
9 Malta
10 Yugoslavia
11 Albania
12 Greece
13 Turkey
14 Cyprus

15 Syria
16 Jordan
17 Lebanon
18 Israel
19 Libya
20 Arab Republic of Egypt
21 Tunisia
22 Algeria
23 Morocco
24 Ceuta & Melilla

PORTUGAL (Republica Portuguese)

Area: 35,378 square miles
Population: 8,600,000
Capital: Lisbon (Lisboa)
Language: Portuguese
Religion: Catholicism
Monetary Unit: Escudo

History and Government: The original inhabitants of Portugal, the Lusianians, were conquered by Rome in the 2nd century BC. The country was overrun by Visigoths in the 5th century AD, and later, by Moslems. It became an independent kingdom in the 12th century and expelled the Moors from southern parts in the 13th century. Portuguese explorers opened up African coasts and colonized Brazil. The monarchy was overthrown in 1910 and a period of great political instability followed, which was resolved by the rise to power of Oliveira Salazar, who by 1933 had brought the country out of the bankruptcy it had suffered since the early 1900s. Salazar's closed, patriarchal dictatorship was continued by his successor until a military coup d'état in April 1974 attempted to restore parliamentary democracy. A period of political turmoil followed, but Legislative Assembly elections brought the Socialist party to power in 1976, resulting in greater political stability.

Economy: The main agricultural products are cork, wheat, rye, corn, oats, barley, and rice as well as almonds, olives, oranges, lemons, and figs. Portuguese wines are widely exported and Portugal is among the leading producers in the world of olive oil. The production of cork (about half the total world production), resin, and turpentine are important, and so is fishing, especially for sardines, tuna, cod, and whales. Mineral resources are scarce and the country is only moderately industrialized. There are some textile, footwear, and clothing industries, as well as agriculture and fishing, linked with winemaking and sardine canning.

GIBRALTAR

Area: 2.3 square miles
Population: 28,000
Monetary Unit: Pound Sterling
History and Government: First fortified after its capture by Tariq, a Moslem invader of Spain in 711 AD it was recaptured by the Spanish in 1462. Gibraltar was then taken by the British in 1713. A referendum held in 1967 resulted in an overwhelming vote to retain the British connection. In 1969 a new Constitution was introduced providing for a House of Assembly largely elected by the people. Executive authority is exercised by the governor. Gibraltar is a naval base of great strategic importance and is gradually changing in character from a fortress to an important holiday center.

Economy: The inhabitants, mostly Spanish, are mainly engaged by the UK departments of the government. Others are in trade and tourism.

SPAIN (España)

Area: 194,883 square miles
Population: 35,500,000
Capital: Madrid
Language: Spanish
Religion: Catholicism
Monetary Unit: Peseta

History and Government: Greeks and Phoenicians colonized the southern and eastern coasts, which were later ruled by Carthage. Under Roman dominion from 201 BC and invaded by vandals in 409 AD, Spain then settled down to a long period of Moslem rule from North Africa between the 8th and 13th centuries. The Moslem-held regions were gradually reconquered by the Christian states of Castile and Aragon and united in 1469. Spain acquired large possessions in America in the 16th century. Gradually it lost its overseas possessions. Between 1931, when the last monarch left Spain, and 1936 a republican Spain was ruled through a single-chamber assembly. Following the counter revolution of 1936 and subsequent civil war, the government passed into the hands of the victorious military-fascist Nationalists under the leadership of General Francisco Franco Bahamonde. At the death of Franco Spain became a monarchy under King Juan Carlos I of Bourbon. In Spain's

Above: harvesting oranges. Spanish citrus groves are mainly in the east and south of the country.

first elections since 1936 the center-left coalition won a majority and formed the government, with the Spanish Socialist Worker's Party as the main opposition.

Economy: The country has large tracts of fertile ground suitable for many kinds of agriculture especially for growing such fruits as grapes, lemons, bananas, pomegranates, apricots, and Spain is among the foremost wine, olive oil, and orange producers in the world. Industrial crops are also well developed, especially beet. Stock-rearing, fishing and the production of resins and cork are also important. The mineral resources, such as iron, lead, zinc, tin, sulfur, and mercury, are largely exported. One of the most important industrial sectors is the car industry. Other flourishing industries are shipbuilding, chemicals, textiles, foodstuffs, paper, and cement. Spain is the European country that attracts the greatest number of tourists.

ANDORRA (Valls d'Andorra)
Area: 175 square miles
Population: 30,000
Capital: Andorra (Andorra la Vella)
Language: Catalan
Religion: Catholicism
Monetary Unit: French and Spanish currencies
History and Government: Autonomous since the 13th century, the principality of Andorra falls under the joint sovereignty of two "princes" – the President of France and the Spanish Bishop of Urgel. The two co-princes can veto certain decisions of the parliament – the council of 24 members that rules Andorra – but cannot impose their own decisions on the council.
Economy: The principal economic activity is tourism, favored by the absence of customs duties and taxes. Relatively important also are stock-rearing and forestry.

MONACO (Principaute de Monaco)
Area: 0.69 square miles
Population: 24,500
Capital: Monaco-ville
Language: Monegasque and French
Religion: Catholicism
Monetary Unit: French currency
History and Government: This is a tiny principality surrounded by, and having a customs link with France. Probably settled first by Phoenicians, it has been in the hands of the ruling Grimaldi family since the 10th century. It has a hereditary monarchy and is ruled through a national council of 18 members, a council of government, a president, and three state counsellors.
Economy: It has lived for decades on the profits from the roulette tables. In the last few years it has increased and diversified its income, due to foreign investments in industry, attracted by financial concessions, and an intensive building program. The predominant industries are electrical engineering, foodstuffs, and pharmaceuticals. Tourism is important.

ITALY (Repubblica Italiana)
Area: 131,000 square miles
Population: 56,000,000
Capital: Rome (Roma)
Language: Italian
Religion: Catholicism
Monetary Unit: Lira
History and Government: Firs united under the Roman Octavian an the center of a vast empire that onc included all southern Europe, Britai North Africa, Asia Minor, norther coast of the Black Sea, Armeni southern Caucasus, Mesopotami Syria, Palestine, and part of Arabi Italy fell to barbarian invasions in th 4th and 5th centuries AD. It became par of the Holy Roman Empire in 962 bu gradually split into petty states. Partl united under Napoleon, it eventuall achieved fullest union under leader ship of kingdom of Sardinia, to becom kingdom of Italy. In 1946 Italy becam a republic and ended its connectio with the House of Savoy which ha ruled as kings of a united Italy sinc 1860. Parliament consists of the Cham ber of Deputies and the Senate. Th Chamber is elected for five years by un versal and direct suffrage, the Senat is elected for five years on a region: basis. The president of the republic i elected for seven years in a joint sessio of the Chamber and the Senate. Sinc the end of World War II, there has bee an increase in the formation of revolu tionary extraparliamentary organiza tions, leading to an escalation of urba violence. Since 1953 government ha been through a series of mainly shor lived coalitions.
Economy: Monetary resources an energy supplies are very low, agricu ture and stock-rearing are partly ur developed and insufficient to satisf domestic needs. Industry is highly d veloped in the north, helped in no sma measure by the availability of labo from the poor, overpopulated regions (the south. The sectors where there ha

been expansion are those of the production of cars, domestic electrical appliances, clothes, chemicals, and refined oil.

SAN MARINO (Repubblica di San Marino)
Area: 23.5 square miles
Population: 21,000
Capital: San Marino
Language: Italian
Religion: Catholicism
Monetary Unit: Italian currency
History and Government: This little republic, whose first statutes go back to 1200, is the oldest free state in Europe. Since 1862 it has had a treaty of friendship and a customs union with Italy. The constitution provides for a Great and General Council, a legislative body of 60 members, elected for five years by popular vote. Two of the Council are appointed every six months to act as regents, "Capitani reggenti," exercising the functions of heads of state.
Economy: At an economic level integration with Italy is almost total. The population lives mainly on tourism: stock-rearing and agriculture (wheat and vines) are also practiced. Valuable sources of revenue are the issue of postage stamps for collectors as well as remittances from emigrants – about 20,000 emigrants in all.

Above: Florence, Italy, and Valletta, Malta (below), attained their original importance by being situated on important trade routes.

VATICAN CITY STATE (Stato della Citta del Vaticano)
Area: 0.17 square miles
Population: About 1000 inhabitants
Monetary Unit: Papal Coinage and Lira
History and Government: Situated within the capital city of Rome, it enjoys extraterritorial rights based on the 1929 treaty with the state of Italy. Constitutionally it is an absolute monarchy. The Pope, elected by secret conclave of the College of Cardinals, holds legislative, executive, and judicial power, which he delegates to the organs of the Roman Curia. At the head of the administration is the Secretariat of State, which is responsible for international relations. The Vatican City State has legal status distinct from the Holy See, but is integrated with it.
Economy: The reason for the existence of the state is to provide an extraterritorial base for the Holy See, which is the government of the Roman Catho-

lic Church. Apart from the issue of postage stamps and the printing of books by the Vatican library there is no source of revenue other than the Church.

MALTA
Area: 122 square miles
Population: 318,000
Capital: Valletta
Language: Maltese and English
Religion: Catholicism
Monetary Unit: Malta Pound
History and Government: Originally a Phoenician and Carthaginian colony, Malta has passed under the dominion of Rome, Byzantium, the Saracens, the Knights of St. John, Napoleon and, in 1814, the British. It has been an independent state within the Commonwealth since 1964. The Constitution is of the parliamentary type consisting of a House of Representatives and a Cabinet. The importance of the island lies in its strategic position in the center of the Mediterranean Sea.
Economy: Agriculture plays a significant role in the island's economy, with potatoes, onions, tomatoes, cabbages, and cauliflowers, as the main crops. The state-owned dry docks are the leading industry and there are local manufacturers of textiles, furniture, electronic equipment, rubber products, and carpets. Tourism is expanding.

YUGOSLAVIA (Socijalisticka Federativna Republika Jugoslavije)
Area: 98,766 square miles
Population: 21,300,000
Capital: Belgrade (Beograd)
Language: Serbo-Croat, Slovenian and Macedonian
Religion: Mainly Eastern (Greek) Orthodox
Monetary Unit: Dinar
History and Government: A great variety of religious, political, and social traditions lie behind the territories that now make up Yugoslavia – their uniting force being the South Slav languages. Orthodox and Byzantine influences were behind the Serbs, 1000 years of Roman Catholicism and a Latin-Teutonic civilization were behind the Croats and Slovenes, and Moslem traditions behind the south and east Turkish and Albanian groups. The kingdom of the Serbs, Croats, and Slovenes was declared in 1918 on the collapse of the Austro-Hungarian empire. Its name

was changed to Yugoslavia in 1929. The monarchy was repudiated in 1943 and the Socialist Federal Republic of Yugoslavia was proclaimed in 1945. It is composed of six republics – Bosnia and Herzegovina, Crna Gora (Montenegro), Croatia, Macedonia, Serbia, and Slovenia, and two autonomous provinces from former Serbian territory: Vojbodina and Kosovo. The Federal Assembly is the supreme organ of government. There is a ruling body of eight members (from the six republics and two provinces) called the presidency, whose members rule with Josip Broz Tito, who was elected President for Life in 1974. After Tito's death, the eight members will elect one of their number to be president of the republic for a period of 12 months only. In effect the presidency will rotate among the eight members. However, according to the Constitution the people are the sole holders of power.

Economy: Nearly half the population is engaged in agriculture but there has been a rapid expansion of industrial production – which has grown sevenfold since 1939. The principal agricultural products are wheat and corn and there are important fruit crops also. Stock-rearing and forestry also deserve mention. The production of minerals is increasing (it is the first country in Europe for copper) and also the generation of electricity. Remarkable development has taken place in many industries – iron and steel, engineering, textiles, chemicals, canning, furs, and timber. Tourism is important.

ALBANIA (Shqiperise)
Area: 11,100 square miles
Population: 2,500,000
Capital: Tirana (Tiranë)
Language: Albanian
Religion: The first self-proclaimed atheist state
Monetary Unit: Lek
History and Government: Albania was the home of an ancient Mediterranean people, overrun by Goths in the 4th and 5th centuries, and part of the Byzantine empire and later of the Ottoman empire. It became independent in 1917, and was made a kingdom in 1928. The country fell to German forces in World War II, but was liberated from the Nazis by efforts of the Partisans (November 1944). In 1945 it constituted itself a People's Republic. The supreme legislative body is the single-chamber People's Assembly, which meets twice a year and delegates its day-to-day running to a presidium. The titular head of state is the chairman of the presidium; effective rule is by the Albanian Labor

Party, that is, the Communist Party.
Economy: The extreme backwardness of the country made the process of development very difficult. Agricultural methods were medieval and industry primitive. Both have been developed appreciably, however, and excessive imbalance between the various sectors of production has been avoided. The principal crops are beet, cotton, and tobacco. In the mineral field, deposits of oil, lignite, copper, and nickel are important and Albania is one of the main producers of chromite in Europe. The exploitation of hydroelectric power is increasing. The most important industries are the processing of agricultural products and textiles.

GREECE (Hellas)
Area: 50,961 square miles
Population: 8,700,000
Capital: Athens (Athinai)
Language: Greek
Religion: Eastern (Greek) Orthodox
Monetary Unit: Drachma
History and Government: The Balkan peninsula was invaded by Greeks around 1500–1000 BC, and settled as many independent city-states, which never achieved unity. It was conquered by Rome, later by Byzantium, then became part of the Ottoman empire in 1456. The modern Greek kingdom achieved independence from Turkey 1821–29. It was overrun by German troops in 1941, and liberated by Greek and British troops in 1944. A military coup d'état in 1967 suspended parliamentary government and eventually also abolished the monarchy. After a series of crises the army chiefs relinquished power and parliamentary democracy was restored in 1974. A referendum rejected the king in favor of a republic and a new Constitution came into force in 1975.
Economy: Greece is still largely an agricultural country – employing about a fourth of the working population. Tobacco is the most important crop followed by wheat, cotton, sugar, and rice. For the production of vines, olives, and currants, Greece is among the foremost in the world; it leads the world in sponge fishing. Mineral resources are modest, those principally mined are nickel, bauxite, iron ore, chrome, lead, and zinc; oil has recently been found in the Aegean. The main industries are textiles, chemicals, cement, shipbuilding, tobacco, paper, rubber, and leather. The merchant navy, with 15,329,000 gross tonnage, is among the largest in the world, but the majority of its ship fly Panamanian or Liberian flags. Tourism is expanding.

TURKEY (Turkiye)
Area: 300,946 square miles
Population: 40,000,000
Capital: Ankara
Language: Turkish
Religion: Islam
Monetary Unit: Turkish Lira
History and Government: In the 13th century a group of Turks from central Asia entered Anatolia and gradually established an empire on both sides of the Dardanelles. This became the Ottoman empire, which lasted from the 14th to the 19th centuries. The Turkish Republic was proclaimed in 1923 after the disintegration of the Ottoman empire in 1922. In 1960, the army overthrew the government and the Grand National Assembly was dissolved. A new Constitution was approved in 1961 and general elections held. Legislative power is vested in the Grand National Assembly and executive power in the president and Council of Ministers. The president is elected for seven years and not eligible for reelection. The 1961 Constitution has approved many modernizing reforms, especially in the ending of polygamy and the abolition of old-style religious education.
Economy: Agriculture employs the majority of the working population and agricultural commodities account for more than half Turkey's exports. The cultivation of cereals produces low yields, but Turkey leads the world for raisin production, and grapes, figs, and olives are exported. Animal stocks are high, especially sheep and goats. Little of its considerable mineral wealth has been exploited, except for copper and chromium ore. The iron and steel industry is modest but cement, paper, textile, food, and tobacco industries are being developed. Foreign investment has been encouraged to develop exploitation of the petroleum resources.

CYPRUS (Kibris, Kypriaki)
Area: 3572 square miles
Population: 640,000
Capital: Nicosia (Leukosia, Lefkosa)
Language: Greek and Turkish
Religion: Eastern (Greek) Orthodox and Islam
Monetary Unit: Cyprus Pound
History and Government: Cyprus was colonized by Phoenicians and ancient Greeks and ruled by all great Mediterranean empires from Assyria to Byzantium and for a long time by the Turks from 1571 to the 19th century –

when it was administered by Britain. It has been independent since 1960 and a member of the Commonwealth. An attempt at a coup d'état, inspired by the regime of the Greek colonels, in 1974 caused the flight of President Makarios – who was following a policy of international non-alignment – and the armed intervention of Turkey, which occupied the northern part of the island. Legislative power is with the House of Representatives.

Economy: The principal economic activity is agriculture – wheat and barley, potatoes, grapes, citrus fruits, melons, carobs (pods of a Levantine tree), and olives. But for export, minerals are of most account: iron and copper pyrites, asbestos, chromium ore, and chalk. There are a few industries chiefly concerned with the processing of agricultural and mineral products.

SYRIA (Al-Jamhouriva al Arabia as-Souriva)
Area: 71,497 square miles
Population: 7,700,000
Capital: Damascus (Dimashq)
Language: Arabic
Religion: Islam
Monetary Unit: Syrian Pound
History and Government: This, the northern part of the ancient territory known as Syria, was conquered by Egypt around 1471 BC, then became part of the Babylonia, Assyrian, and Persian empires, was conquered by Alexander the Great, and by the Roman Pompey, and by the Ottoman Turks in 1516. It was administered by the French, with Lebanon, as the Levant States from 1920. It is now a presidential republic, independent since 1946. From 1958 to 1961 it formed, with Egypt, the United Arab Republic. Then with Egypt again, and Libya, it formed the Union of Arab Republics created in 1971. It is a "People's Democratic Socialist State" according to the Constitution of 1973, with a People's Council.

Economy: Agricultural production, which employs half the working population, is insufficient for the country's own needs. The main products are cotton, cereals, vines, olives, fruit, tobacco, and beet. Cattle breeding is also important. Skins, hides, wool, and silk and leather goods are produced. Although poor in minerals, mining is developing, especially for iron, chromium ore, manganese, asphalt, and phosphates. Recently oil has been discovered and Syria also receives revenue for the pipelines that cross the country from Iraq to the Mediterranean. The country is moving toward greater industrialization, but the main products

are still those associated with agriculture – textiles, sugar, tobacco, flour, and tanning as well as glassware and cement.

JORDAN (Al Mamlaka al Urdaniya all Hashemiyah)
Area: 37,737 square miles
Population: 2,700,000
Capital: Amman
Language: Arabic
Religion: Islam
Monetary Unit: Jordanian Dinar
History and Government: The country occupies an area that includes the ancient biblical lands of Gilead, Moab, and Edom. It was created in 1921 out of former Turkish territory and became a mandate under Britain as Transjordan. The mandate was revoked in 1946, when the country became independent. In 1949 it became the Hashemite Kingdom of Jordan. The legislature consists of a Senate of 30 members appointed by the king and an elected House of Representatives. According to the 1952 Constitution, the executive power is in the hands of the sovereign. Women do not have the right to vote.

Economy: The loss of the most fertile area in the country, the "West Bank," was a heavy blow to a country where the majority of the population is engaged in agriculture and stock-rearing. Industry is underdeveloped. There is a large trade deficit and heavy dependence on foreign aid. The main agricultural products are cereals, tobacco, legumes, fruit, and vegetables; stock-rearing is especially important, particularly sheep and goats. The only mineral resources are phosphates, but oil deposits have been located. In the industrial field there is an oil refinery and a few cement, beer, and cigarette factories.

LEBANON (Al-Lubnaniya)
Area: 4015 square miles
Population: 2,000,000
Capital: Beirut (Bayrut)
Language: Arabic
Religion: Islam and Christianity
Monetary Unit: Lebanese Pound
History and Government: The area was inhabited by Maronites – a Syrian Christian sect – in the 7th century AD. European powers demanded independence of country under a Christian governor within the Ottoman empire in 1861. The country was taken over by the French as a Levant state in 1920.

Lebanon became an independent republic in 1944. There is a president and single chamber elected by universal adult suffrage. The system is based on an ethnic-political balance, in which the chief public offices are divided between Christians and Moslems. Since the second half of 1975 the Lebanon has been the center of a bloody civil war between the right-wing forces of the predominantly Christian Phalangist Party and the left-wing organizations supported by the Palestinian guerrillas based in the Lebanon. In 1976 the intervention of Arab "deterrent forces," composed mainly of Syrians, tried to restore order, but fighting between Syrians and Phalangist forces has gravely endangered the unity of the country.

Economy: A facade of prosperity covers a state of widespread poverty. There is a vast amount of emigration. Some 47 percent of the working population is employed in agriculture, which contributes a few products for export such as citrus fruits, bananas, and olive oil. The once-famous forests have been denuded by exploitation and the unrestricted grazing of goats. Industry is still underdeveloped and geared mainly to production of consumer goods. There are oil refineries and textile, food, cement, and tobacco factories. There is also a considerable amount of transit trade through the Lebanon, which help the balance of payments, such as duty paid by oil companies transporting crude oil through pipelines across the Lebanon, and maritime freight charges.

ISRAEL (Yisra 'el)
Area: 7992 square miles
Population: 3,500,000
Capital: Jerusalem (Yerushalayim)
Language: Hebrew and Arabic
Religion: Jewish
Monetary Unit: Israel Pound
History and Government: The modern state of Israel was born in May 1948 in the British mandated zone of Palestine. It occupies the old biblical land of Canaan – the land between the Jordan and the Mediterranean. A series of constitutional laws has provided for the establishment of a parliamentary republic, with one chamber, the *Knesset*, which elects the president, who serves five years and is eligible for reelection once. The various wars against neighboring Arab countries – 1948, 1956, 1967, 1973 – led to a considerable extension of Israel's original frontiers, but not all of these have been recognized internationally. It is a highly urbanized society, experienced in the problems of war and economic develop-

Above: Jerusalem, the city holy to Jews, Christians, and Moslems, became the capital of Israel after the Old City was seized from Jordan in 1967.

ment. There is a high rate of immigration into the country – from the establishment of the state until 1975 more than 1,500,000 people from over 100 countries had settled in Israel.

Economy: Enormous development has taken place in all sectors. The country generally is fertile and a wide variety of crops can be grown in the varying climatic conditions. Agriculture supplies many products for export: citrus fruits, legumes, grapes, peanuts, cotton, beet, and tobacco. Stock-rearing is important, especially cattle and poultry. But the main part is played by industry. The oil-wells of occupied Sinai yielded about 6,000,000 tons of crude oil in 1972. The principal manufacturing industries are textiles, clothing, foodstuffs, chemicals, metallurgy, cement. After the 1967 war a big boost was given to engineering in order to ensure a certain self-sufficiency in military equipment. The diamond-cutting and polishing industry is also important and accounts for one third of Israel's exports.

LIBYA (Socialist People's Libyan Arab Jamahirrya)
Area: 810,000 square miles
Population: 2,360,000
Capital: Tripoli (Tarabulus)
Language: Arabic
Religion: Islam
Monetary Unit: Libyan Dinar
History and Government: Libya became a sovereign federal kingdom made up of Tripolitania, Cyrenaica, and Fezzan, in 1951. In 1969, as a result of a coup d'état by young Army officers, Libya was declared a republic. In 1971 the Libyan Arab Socialist Union was created as the nation's sole political

organization. The federal nature of the country was abolished in 1963 and since 1976 the supreme constitutional authority has been the General Secretariat of the General People's Congress.

Economy: Oil is the only source of wealth and Libya has been the most stubborn of the oil-producing countries in its fight to wrest control from foreign companies. Agriculture, limited to two percent of the country, the narrow coastal strip, is not enough for minimum nutritional needs. The chief crop of the oases and the coastal strip is the date palm. In the marginal areas there is some pasture for grazing and some olives, almonds, citrus, and dates are produced. Apart from refineries, industry is confined to the handicrafts such as dying and weaving, leather, and mats. Sponge fishing is important. Most important trading partners are the European countries, including Italy, Libya's former ruler.

ARAB REPUBLIC OF EGYPT
Area: 386,660 square miles

Population: 36,000,000
Capital: Cairo (Al-Qahirà)
Language: Arabic
Religion: Islam
Monetary Unit: Egyptian Pound
History and Government: One of the most ancient states in the world, which by about 3000 BC had developed one of the two early civilizations of the ancient world. Its ancient dynasties came to an end with the conquests of Alexander the Great. Later, it became part of the Roman empire and then the Ottoman empire. British influence ceased when its protectorate was abolished in 1922 and Egypt was declared an independent kingdom. A republic was proclaimed in 1953 a year after a military coup d'état deposed King Farouk. In 1958 Egypt formed with Syria the United Arab Republic, which lasted until 1961 when Syria seceded following a coup d'état. The Constitution proclaimed by President Nasser in 1964 defines Egypt as a "Democratic Socialist State." It is a presidential type regime with a single party, the Arab Socialist Union. The

Below: the modern section of Cairo, looks very like any of the great cities on the northern shores of the Mediterranean.

president is nominated by the National Assembly, which is elected by universal suffrage. In foreign policy, Egypt is moving away from the USSR and concentrating on alliance with the USA and the Western countries.

Economy: The national economy is directed by the state. Predominantly agricultural, it has been blocked by years of meeting the demands of war, which have absorbed a great part of the resources. But since the Yom Kippur war of 1973 Egypt is concentrating on massive foreign investments from the USA, Japan, European countries, Kuwait, and Saudi Arabia for the development of various agricultural sectors and for vast irrigation programs. The reopening and deepening of the Suez Canal, together with the building of the Suez-Alexandria pipeline, should do much to boost the economy. In agriculture, which takes up more than half the labor force, the chief crops are cotton, sugar cane, and cereals; stock-rearing is very little developed. In mineral resources, the focal point is oil, but phosphates, manganese, potassium salts, rock salt, iron, asbestos, and sulfur are also important. The principal industries are textiles and foodstuffs, and, after these, chemicals, electrical engineering, electronics, metallurgy, and cement. Trade is predominantly with the USSR and the two German Republics.

TUNISIA (At-Tunisiya)
Ares: 63,378 square miles
Population: 5,600,000
Capital: Tunis
Language: Arabic and French
Religion: Islam
Monetary Unit: Tunisian Dinar
History and Government: The country was a French Protectorate from 1881 to 1956. In 1957 the constituent assembly deposed the Bey and abolished the monarchy. Now a presidential republic with a single political party – the Neo-Destour Socialist party – and a single trade union. The president and National Assembly are elected simultaneously for five years and the president cannot be reelected more than three times consecutively. In 1975 Bourguiba was elected President for Life. Described as "more Mediterranean than Arab," the Tunisian government practices a cautious reformism at home, while at the international level it aligns itself with the USA.
Economy: There are rich agricultural areas in the northern valleys which produce wheat, barley, and oats, olives, vines, dates, apricots, and other fruits. They also support large flocks and

herds. The rate of industrial development, which employs 30 percent of the labor force, is low, except for the processing of agricultural products. Tunisia is the second largest producer of phosphates in Africa, and there are worthwhile deposits of oil and natural gas. It is becoming an important tourist area.

ALGERIA (El Djazairia)
Area: 855,400 square miles
Population: 17,000,000
Capital: Algeria (El Djazair)
Language: Arabic
Religion: Islam
Monetary Unit: Dinar
History and Government: Known to the Romans as Numidia, and subsequently under the rule of Eastern Roman empire, and of Ottoman empire until 1705, the country finally came under French control 1830-47. Independence was achieved on July 3, 1962, after eight years of armed struggle against France, of which it had been an integral part since 1881. It is a presidential republic. After a coup d'état in 1965 the Constitution was suspended and all the power passed to a revolutionary council of 24 members. Under Colonel Houari Boumedienne the only party recognized is the National Liberation Front (NLF). There are two unions, one of workers and the other of students. The republic has declared itself "revolutionary and socialist" and in it the army carries decisive weight.
Economy: The trend of the regime is toward State socialism, tempered by experiments in self-determination. Economic plans depend on the mineral resources of the country to finance the development phases. Algeria is after Libya and Nigeria, the third greatest oil-producer in Africa and is rich in natural gas, iron, manganese, uranium, platinum, and diamonds. The main industries are textiles, chemicals, iron and steel, and food. Agricultural production has not kept pace with other industries. The most remunerative crops are legumes, fruit, vegetables, and vines. The principal trade partner is France and indirectly the other EEC countries.

MOROCCO (Al-Maghrebia)
Area: 180,000 square miles
Population: 17,000,000
Capital: Rabat
Language: Arabic

Religion: Islam
Monetary Unit: Dirham
History and Government: Once the Roman province of Mauretania, it became an independent kingdom under a Berber dynasty in the 11th century, whose rulers conquered Spain and Portugal. In the early part of the 20th century it was divided between Spain and France as protectorates. It is an absolute monarchy, independent since 1956 after a joint declaration made with France and Spain, and the abolition of the international zone of Tanger (Tangiers). The Constitution granted in 1962 was suspended in 1965 after serious disturbances. A revised Constitution was approved in 1972. It provides for a single chamber, whose members are elected by indirect vote. It also provides for trade unions, chambers of commerce and professional bodies to participate in the representation of the people and the organization of the state. The king appoints the prime minister and other ministers and has the right to dissolve parliament.
Economy: Agriculture and phosphates (of which Morocco is the third highest producer in the world with 15,105,000 tons) are the main sources of wealth. Agriculture employs 70 percent of the labor force, but is still very primitive. The land suffers from drought problems and overgrazing. The principal crops are cereals, potatoes, citrus fruits, dates, and figs; cork, wood pulp, and esparto grass are also produced; livestock farming and fishing are also important. In the industrial sector, Morocco's exports are phosphates and some authracite, manganese, iron ore, lead, and zinc. Foreign capital is encouraged and there is a lively tourist business.

CEUTA AND MELILLA
Area: Ceuta – 7.3 square miles,
Melilla – 4.75 square miles
Population: Ceuta – 79,000,
Melilla – 79,000
Monetary Unit: Peseta
History and Government: These two towns, still under Spanish sovereignty, are all that remains of the former Spanish Morocco. They have been in Spanish hands since 1580. Other Spanish possessions, off the coast, are the islets of Peñon de Velez de la Gomera, Peñon de Alhucemas and the archipelago · of the Chaffarinas, inhabited by a few hundred people.
Economy: Fishing and dock labor are the main activities of the population of the two towns. Melilla exports iron ore mined in the Rif massif, now part of Morocco.

Chapter 5

Northern Asia

The most significant fact about Northern Asia is its immense size. From the western frontier of the USSR in Europe to the Bering Strait in the east is almost 170° of longitude, nearly halfway around the world. From the most southerly part of the Soviet Union in Turkmenskaya (Turkestan) to the Arctic islands of Zemlya Frantsa Iosifa (Franz Joseph Land) is more than 45° of latitude. It is a region whose nearest seas are the frozen Arctic and where only short stretches of coastline border more temperate waters: the almost landlocked Black Sea in the southwest and the Sea of Japan in the east. For the most part it lies north of the great central core of high plateaus and complex mountain ranges that stretch across the continent of Asia and north of the monsoon lands. It is a vast area of plains and rolling plateaus, thinly populated with only ribbons and scattered pockets of closer settlement.

Opposite: the Church of the Intercession of the Virgin, with the characteristic Byzantine architecture of the Russian Orthodox Church, set amid the rolling fertile plains of the heartlands of the USSR.

The Largest Land Mass in the World

The USSR, an unbroken land mass situated in middle and high latitudes, is open to the cold air from the Arctic and the moist air from the Atlantic. It has a very extreme climate, a continental regime, and the "cold pole" of the earth is situated in eastern Siberia, where a temperature of —94°F was once recorded at Verkhoyansk. In winter the cold dry air causes a large high-pressure system to build up, centered in western Mongolia and extending over the whole of northern Asia. The winds that blow out of this anticyclone are both cold and dry, and in west and central Siberia are southerly in direction. The winters are long and hard with almost the whole area – with the exception of the southwest between the Black Sea and the Ozero Balkhash (Lake Balkhash) – having several months of sub-zero temperatures. The summers are short, but hot, with rain. Although nowhere is there more than 20 inches of rain a year, the south and south-west are very dry indeed, producing desert conditions. The northern coast is also dry, with less than five inches annually, mainly in the form of snow. In summer, the snow melts everywhere, even along the Arctic coast where temperatures rarely exceed 50°F.

The most northerly zone, bordering the Arctic Ocean, is tundra. The winters are extremely severe with cold, gale-force winds. Snow covers the ground for eight or nine months of the year and the subsoil, the ground a foot below the surface, is always frozen.

Below: in the arctic conditions that prevail in extreme northerly parts of the USSR, mosses and lichens are the only plants that flourish in the extreme temperatures.

In summer, when the snow melts, a lot of the ground becomes swampy because the water cannot escape by draining through the frozen subsoil. It is a desolate, bleak, mainly flat zone where tree growth is virtually impossible. In summer, mosses and lichens, and some flowering plants, are abundant, but the vegetation is limited in both size and variety, the frozen ground preventing the growth of any long-rooted plants. In the northeast the tundra is grazed by reindeer, and the largest proportion of the USSR's total numbers of this animal are to be found in this particular area between the Kolyma river and the Bering Strait.

The next zone, south of the tundra, is the taiga. Its enormous forests, bordering the inhospitable tundra, are mostly conifers – pines, spruce, fir, Siberian cedar, and larch, together with silver birch. It contains many swampy areas and during the spring much of the land is flooded when the meltwaters from the mountains to the south rush rapidly down the northward-flowing rivers only to be halted when they reach the still-frozen mouths.

Bears, wolves, elks, and other wild animals roam the forests. Fur-bearing animals such as the marten and sable have been hunted almost to extinction in the European part of the Soviet Union and now exist in significant numbers only in Siberia. Like the tundra, the taiga has few inhabitants because the winters are so long and cold. There was once a mixed forest zone between the taiga and the steppe; but because people have lived there for centuries, most of the oaks and other deciduous trees were cut down long ago and the area is now widely, if discontinuously, cultivated.

South of the taiga and this mixed zone are the steppes – the great rolling plains, treeless except along the banks of the rivers. The soil is fertile black earth, or tschernosem, in which many varieties of feather grasses abound. But in most areas it has been plowed for wheat growing. The steppes and the mixed zone define the optimum area of western Siberia for rural and urban settlement, an area served by the Trans-Siberian Railway that is a means of both access and transport. Eastward, on the higher ground, the taiga reappears, although there are pockets of rich agricultural land on some of the lower plateaus and along the river valleys.

Farther south the landscape changes to semidesert. The soil is poorer and the patches of bare ground between the tufts of vegetation get gradually larger. The tufts are smaller and shorter and the sagebrush thrives rather than grass. This in turn gives way to true desert, with shifting sands and salt pans around the Aral'skoye More (Aral Sea) and in the Kyzy-Kum and Kara-Kum and salt basins in the Gobi desert in Mongolia. Fortunately the highest mountains in the USSR are along this southern border. They are the Pamirs and their highest mountain, Pik Kommunizma, reaches 24,590 feet. There are glaciers and snowfields in the Pamirs and the neighboring ranges. Large parts of these melt in the summer months to replenish the lakes and rivers, making possible irrigated agri-

ulture along the foothills and in the enclosed basins
uch as the Fergana.

It was the steppe that was the first habitat of the
vild horse and wild ass before they were driven into
he semidesert areas, probably frightened away from
he traditional watering places by the nomadic herds-
nen and their flocks of sheep. Today the range of the
vild ass has shrunk to a small area of central Mongolia when previously it used to roam as far west as
Kiyev (Kiev), but it has not been seen west of the Volga
or over 200 years. Przewalski's horse has not been
ighted for a number of years and it is feared that the
oreed now exists only in zoos. The wild camel, too, has
ill but disappeared from its traditional homeland in
he Gobi. Some of the most economically important
inimals that do still thrive in this zone are the rodents
hat live in large colonies underground. These
inimals, such as the susliks and bobac marmots,
constantly bring up earth to the surface from the
leeper soil layers. The composition of this lower soil
liffers from that on the surface and helps to diversify
ind enrich the vegetation.

Two large inland seas, the Caspian and the Aral-
skoye More (Aral Sea), are to be found in this great
east-west steppe-cum-desert belt. Like the Black Sea
arther west, they are the vestiges of the former
Tethys Sea of the Cenozoic era. After the Alpine
orogeny, with the formation of the great folded moun-
ains of the Bol'shoy Kavkaz (Caucasus), the Black
Sea became separated from the eastern limb that
ncluded the Caspian and Aral'skoye. These two seas
lave been isolated ever since, gradually becoming less
salty because of the fresh water poured into them by
he Volga river on the one hand and the Amu-Dar'ya
ind Syr-Dar'ya rivers on the other. The Caspian is the
argest body of inland water in the world. It continually shrinks and grows and at the moment it is shrink-
ng and has been doing so for almost a century, probably because less water is reaching it down the Volga as
t is diverted for irrigation needs and power supplies.
The surface of the Caspian is now 92 feet below sea
evel and were it to fall another 20 feet a great deal of
he northern part would become dry land.

West of the Bol'shoy Kavkaz (Caucasus), and south
of the European steppe band, is a warm, damp sub-
ropical region bordering the Black Sea. Almost
rost-free, it has palm trees, eucalyptus, and bamboo,
ind crops like tea and oranges are grown there. All
he ports are ice-free in the winter. The Black Sea is
ich in fauna and vegetable plankton. There are over
70 species of fish in this sea, the best known of which
s the sturgeon, which produces the famous Russian
aviar. In Rumania and Bulgaria, along the Black Sea
coastal areas, deciduous forests have been cleared to
nake agricultural land and where the Danube has
oushed out its delta there are vast reed beds and a
abyrinth of channels.

The Bol'shoy Kavkaz is about 750 miles long, stretching between the Black Sea and Caspian Sea. Its
highest peak, El'brus, rises to 18,481 feet and is an

Above: a farming commune in the Uzbekistan
steppeland. The open undulating grassy plains owe their
origins to the deposits of sandy and sometimes fine clay
soils laid down about 10,000 years ago during the last
glaciation of the ice age.

extinct volcano, as are many of the other peaks in
the range. Along the length of the range are over 1000
glaciers and below the snowline are rich forests of
beech, hornbeam, oak, ash, elm, and lime. In many
parts, especially in the center, the forests have been
denuded by man and his domestic animals, in this case
by sheep. Fortunately, where the forests have disappeared they have been replaced by green meadows.

On the southern limits of the region to the east, the
Tien Shan and other large ranges sprawl out from the
Pamirs, separating the USSR from Mongolia and
China. Mountains and plateaus run in an arc through
eastern Siberia, then bend north along the Pacific
coast. The 400-mile-long Ozero Baykal (Lake Baikal),
the largest freshwater lake in Asia, is set in this arc of
mountains. It is also the deepest lake in the world and
in 1957 scientists measured a depth of 6364 feet at one
point.

South of the lake lies Mongolia, cradled in the
mountain arcs. It was traditionally part of China but
is now settled by peoples who are neither Chinese nor
Russian: the Mongols. The greater part of the country
falls within the Gobi Desert where the nomadic tribes
are eternally on the move looking for new pastures for
their herds of horses, cattle, sheep, and goats. They
have adapted their lives and customs to this type of
existence and have even evolved a portable house, the
yurt, which can be assembled in less than half an hour.
It has a collapsible framework of wooden laths, lashed
together with leather thongs, and over this layers of
felt are tied. On top of the felt a protective canvas can
be placed. The yurt can withstand both strong winds
and rains and provide a warm shelter in winter when
temperatures may drop to −30° F.

Eurasia

113

A pack-train through the Pamirs in Tadzhikistan Republic, USSR. The Pamirs cover a huge region in North Asia, where the Himalaya, Hindu Kush, Kunlun, and Tien Shan mountains meet. Snow covers and blocks the passes for more than half the year.

Natural Resources

All agricultural land in the USSR is owned by the state and the farms that work it are of two kinds. Firstly, the collective farm (kolkhozy), on which the workers use machinery, fertilizers, and seed provided by the state and where production is planned by the state. Instead of a regular wage, workers receive a share of the profits and each household also has a small patch of land, not more than four acres, for private use. Secondly, the state farm (soukhozy) on which the workers are government employees and are paid salaries. They too have their own small patches of land on which they can grow vegetables and fruit for their own families.

Both collective and state farms cover huge tracts of

Above: roses, here grown for the oil used in perfumery, are an important industry in Bulgaria. They are grown in sheltered valleys of the upper Tundzha river. Bulgaria is primarily an agricultural country, with plains and basins suitable for wheat, rye, and tobacco.

land, sometimes up to 100,000 acres. This makes large-scale use of machinery possible and such mechanization cuts farming costs. Although mechanization has been on the increase for some decades, there are still many local difficulties to overcome in the various regions of the USSR, such as the short growing season, especially on the northern boundary of the steppes, irregular and often inadequate rainfall on the marginal zone of the semideserts, the long winter frost period when both ground and water are frozen, and

the great transport deficiencies. In some areas, especially in central Asia, the human element has also presented problems. The peoples, traditionally wanderers, have resented being forced to follow a sedentary life and have resisted the change from nomadic pastoralism to settled agriculture. For instance, the government has not found it worthwhile to change the techniques of the Yakut peoples of northern Siberia, who are pastoralists, herding cows, horses and reindeer, and harvesting the hay in the short summers.

Large areas of the USSR make good farmland especially the fertile steppes with their rich black soils, stretching from Leningrad and Kiyev (Kiev) in the west to Ozero Baykal (Lake Baikal) in the east. The main crops here are wheat, sugar, beet, oats, millet, barley, potatoes, and corn. To the north, in the cooler and wetter mixed zone, the main crops include barley, rye, and hemp. At the same time a lot of land is not suitable for agriculture. Deserts and mountains in the southeast, and the very short, cool summers of the Arctic make farming almost impossible outside the steppes without large-scale expensive projects.

The Soviet government is constantly seeking new ways of increasing food production, however. The ambitious Virgin Lands project in western Siberia and Kazakhstanskaya (Kazakhstan) has involved plowing great tracts of new land for grain growing. Although this region has the disadvantage of a very low annual rainfall – less than 10 inches – the melting snows combined with the spring rain are enough for spring-sown wheat, millet, barley, and flax. The development of the desert and semidesert lands south of the Aral'skoy More (Aral Sea) has been transformed by the harness

ing of the Amu-Dar'ya and Syr-Dar'ya rivers to provide irrigation water. The climate is hot in summer, but, what is more important, the frost-free period lasts for about a third of the year. On the other hand the precipitation is small and the water brought down from the mountains to the south and east was previously lost by evaporation or carried northwestward in the rivers only to disappear into the desert or be emptied into the Aral'skoye. Although irrigation has been used since the Middle Ages, it has been extended greatly in the last half century and now over 24,000 square miles are irrigated. Cotton is the main product, but rice, tobacco, and sugar beet are also grown.

The USSR is the world's largest producer of timber, with forests, mainly conifers, covering one third of the land area. The northern forests of the taiga are the most important. Logs are often floated downstream to Arctic ports such as Arkhangel'sk and Igarka or south down the Volga to the industrial centers. The seas, rivers, and lakes of the USSR provide valuable fishing grounds. Soviet fishing fleets, using modern techniques, operate in all the seas bordering the country, even in the inland seas of the Caspian and Aral'skoye. The USSR has more than 60 factory trawlers, which can process up to 120 tons of fish a day. Large, stern trawlers operate from Vladivostok, Petropavlovsk in Mamchatka, and the ports of Sakhalin, during the summer, and fish in the north Pacific and Bering Sea for salmon and Alaska pollack, a member of the cod family. Whaling fleets also sail from the port of Odessa to the Antarctic every year, and during the last 10 years the Russians have been catching krill in the Southern Ocean. This they have processed into fish paste and marketed it with some success.

Above left: mechanized tea-picking in Georgia, in the extreme southwest of the USSR. Tea and citrus fruits are grown in the warm humid coastlands of the Black Sea and tobacco and grapes are raised in the drier inland valleys. Georgia has large coal and manganese reserves as well as the Soviet Union's largest steelworks.
Above: welding irrigation pipes in the Odessa Region of the Ukraine. This region in the Soviet Union is made up largely of arid steppeland covered with black fertile soil. Irrigation schemes have helped develop the potential of this rich agricultural area.
Below: logs awaiting transportation to the timber mills in the Soviet Union. Much of the northern part of the USSR is forested – some 2300 million acres.

Mining and Industry

The transformation of a sprawling, predominantly agricultural country into the world's second strongest industrial power is one of the most remarkable achievements of the USSR. The more so because industrialization came much later to the Soviet Union than it did to Northwest Europe or the United States.

The beginning was made in 1928 when the Soviet government initiated a series of Five Year Plans for economic development. These plans were prepared by the Gosplan – the State Planning Commission. Each plan set targets for increased agricultural and industrial production and scheduled the opening of new mines and factories. In every plan heavy industry had priority.

in the Asian fields than in the European ones. This partly due to the fact that many of the former hav open-cast workings. There are further rich reserves coal in an area either side of Krasnoyarsk, betwee the Kuzbas and Ozero Baykal (Lake Baikal). In th Arctic regions there is coal around Vorkuta, at th northern end of the Ural'skiy (Urals), and coking co in northeast Siberia, east of Yakutsk. In Mongoli after 20 years of planning, industrial production ha become an economic reality. Coal is now produced and in the Shanryn Gol basin north of the capita Ulan Bator, there are rich reserves.

The Soviet Union now produces more oil from i vast reserves than any other nation. The earlies exploitation was of the reserves in the Europea sector and the large oilfields near the Kavkaz (Cau casus), especially around Baku, and centered o Groznyy and Maikop, farther to the north. The riches European fields are in the area between the centra Volga and the Ural'skiy and in the Saratov regior From these fields oil is piped to East European cour

Below: oil pipes for the Soviet Union's expanding oil industry. Oil production from new fields between the Ural'skiy and the Volga has surpassed the output of the traditional Caucasus and Emba fields in Kazakhstanskay

Underlying economic development is a basic fact of the Soviet system: all natural resources, mines, and factories are owned by the state. There is no private enterprise, there are no large corporations. Each major industry is the responsibility of its own government ministry. The USSR has immense resources, both in variety and scale, but their exploitation does present difficulties because of their inaccessibility and the severe climate over a large part of the country. With more than half the world's reserves, the Soviet Union leads the world in coal production. The major fields are in the Donbas (the Donets basin) in the eastern Ukrainskaya (Ukraine), the Kuzbas basin, between Tomsk and Novokuznetsk in central Siberia, and around Karaganda in Kazakhstanskaya (Kazakhstan).

The production of coal is now much more economic

tries. Oil is also piped from the Russian fields east int Asia to Omsk, Novosibirsk, Krasnoyarsk, and beyonc

A different economic picture has been painted wit the discovery of vast oil reserves in western Siberia in the central Ob valley, which by 1975 was alread producing a quarter of the total Soviet output, mor than that of the Volga-Ural'skiy area. Offshore ex ploration is being carried out, both in the west in th Black Sea, the Azovskoye More (Sea of Azov), th Caspian – where some of the wells are 20 miles offshor – and the Aral'skoye More (Aral Sea), and in the eas in the Okhotskoye More (Sea of Okhotsk). Here, nea the island of Sakhalin, offshore drilling is producin dramatic finds and the Russians have a growing loca need in their increasing home consumption in the eas as well as the tempting market in Japan. There ar also widespread reserves of oil shales in the USSR.

Above: iron ore being loaded at the Lebedinsky ore mine in Kursk. The Soviet Union is rich in mineral deposits and it has been estimated that perhaps 50 percent of the world's resources of iron ore are in its territories.

Some of the world's largest hydroelectric plants are in the USSR and all of them are fully automatic. There are large dams on many rivers, for example, on the Volga above Kuybyshev, on the Dnepr at Dnepropetrovsk, on the Don near Kalachna-Donu, and in eastern Siberia. The world's largest hydroelectric plant is on the Angara at Bratsk. Recently Rumania and Bulgaria have been placing increasing emphasis on hydroelectric power. There is a joint scheme between Rumania and Yugoslavia on the Danube at the Iron Gate and another between Rumania and Bulgaria in the center of their Danubian frontier.

The main center of the Soviet iron and steel industry is still in the Ural'skiy, although the Kuzbas also produces a share, but, as yet, the other centers produce relatively little. The Soviet government is promoting industrial dispersal, partly to bring industries nearer the raw materials and their markets for finished goods, partly because large concentrations of industry are vulnerable targets during a future war. Aluminum smelting and timber processing have been established at Bratsk following the construction of the giant hydroelectric plant; a mining and metallurgical complex has been set up near the Balkhash using locally mined copper; and a new complex is planned for the Tyumen' region of the middle Ob basin where oil has been located. The Ural'skiy and northeast Siberia provide the USSR's richest sources of nonferrous metals. The Ural'skiy contains over 1000 different minerals, many in workable deposits. Northeast Siberia is rich in diamonds – of which it is the main Russian source – tin, and gold. Farther east again, in Kamchatka, there are copper, mercury, gold, and uranium deposits, but the main source of uranium is from the carnotite ores in the Fergana in central Asia.

Below: Zemoavchalskaya hydroelectric power station in the USSR. The Soviet Union uses many low and medium heads of water to power hydroelectric plants.

North Asia

People and Politics

The natural corridor of the western Siberian steppes has been the scene of the movement of peoples since ancient times. The first were the early nomadic tribes. Then came the barbarians – the Goths and Huns who between 600 BC and AD 600 poured westward into Europe and fanned out to all corners of the continent. Later it was the route used by the Mongols in the 13th century as they swept out of Mongolia to conquer a broad expanse of territory that stretched from northwest China to the Black Sea coast and the shores of the Baltic. Since the Middle Ages, however, the movements have been in the reverse direction as the Russians expanded from their center around Moskva (Moscow), and each distinctive area of northern Asia fell into their hands. The Russians pressed eastward relentlessly until they reached the Pacific, establishing posts and settlements and containing the many nomadic groups within defined areas. Although the Russians reached the Pacific by the middle of the 17th century, they did not succeed in conquering the more southerly region, from the Black Sea to the Kavkaz (Caucasus) and the Pamirs, until the 19th century.

The USSR is three times the area of the United States and has a population of about 255 million, made up of many different nationalities. The census for 195_ listed 108 different national groups, but more recent figures put the number as high as 180, of which 60 are fairly large groups. They also distinguish 149 languages. Each major group has its own Republic and there are 15 of these Union Republics in all. The Russians make up more than half the population, most of them living in the western part of the largest Union Republic, the RSFSR (Russian Soviet Federated Socialist Republic), which stretches from Europe right across Asia. The next largest group are the Ukrainians and White Russians living in Ukrainskaya and Belorusskaya. Other groups large enough to have

Above: modern Mongolians, descendants of the peoples of the steppes that swept over their frontiers to conquer an empire that stretched westward as far as the Baltic and Black seas.
Left: impressive military and civilian parades are held in Moscow to celebrate May Day and the October Revolution (November 7). They are centered on the Kremlin, or citadel, once the residence of the former royal family (until 1712), and now the headquarters of government.

their own Republics are the Georgians (in Gruzinskaya), Azerbaydzhanis, and Armenians in the Kavkaz (Caucasus) region; the Turkmenians, Uzbeks, Tadzhiks, Kirgiz, and Kazakhs in central Asia; the Estonians (who are related to the Finns), Latvians, and Lithuanians on the eastern shores of the Baltic; and the Moldavians on the Rumanian frontier. The Karelians of the Kola Poluostrov (Kola peninsula) and along the Finnish border were formerly the 16th Republic but their status was changed to that of an Autonomous Republic within the RSFSR.

Smaller groups, such as the Tartars, who almost 500 years ago halted the Russian advance into Siberia and were not overcome for more than a century, are now scattered throughout the USSR. Others live in "Autonomous Republics" or "Autonomous Regions" and some in "National Areas" within the major Republics. In the far north these are the tribes such as the Yakuts, the largest aboriginal population of Siberia, numbering more than 300,000; the Chukchi, a hunting people who are now being taught to breed reindeer; the Tungus, who are hunters and fishers; and the Voguls, another reindeer herding and hunting people. The Soviet government is gradually settling

Above: these Uzbek children are wearing their national costume. The Soviet government encourages the cultures of the many racial groups within the Soviet Union. While Russian is the official language, national languages, customs, and dress are encouraged.

these nomadic groups in permanent communities. Although Russian is the official language, the national groups are encouraged to preserve their own languages and cultures and they have the option of leading a traditional life if they wish to do so.

The focal point of the Soviet Union is its largest city and capital Moskva (Moscow), which has a population of close on 8 million – a figure swollen daily by a further 1 million commuters and visitors. Leningrad, the second largest city, has a population of almost 4,500,000. More than half the population of the USSR now live in towns and cities. Side by side with the general drift to urban areas is the rapid development of new cities and the remarkable growth of existing settlements, especially in Asiatic USSR. Yakutsk is a good example of such a growth. This town is the ancient capital of the Yakut peoples, who were living in the basins of the Lena, Indigirka, and Kolyma rivers centuries before the Russians arrived in northeast Siberia. Their capital is over 300 years old, with typical Siberian one-story wooden buildings, that are both warm and well adapted to the environment. These are now being destroyed and the inevitable high blocks of flats are being erected in their place. As well as the Russians moving in from the west, the Yakuts themselves are also beginning to drift into the towns, and the capital, Yakutsk, now has a population of 130,000. But the Yakuts, unlike some of their primitive hunter-gatherer northern neighbors, are in positions of power and influence in the Yakut Autonomous Soviet Socialist Republic and their culture continues to flourish.

Women have a special place in Soviet society. They outnumber men by more than 20 million, largely because of the terrible casualties in World War II. Women now form a vital part of the labor force; in 1970 it was as much as 50 percent. The state provides special day nurseries to look after children while their mothers work in occupations that were often formerly male preserves such as heavy work on construction sites, truck driving, and in the merchant marine service, often in command of large tankers.

The government gives education high priority. The majority of the people are now literate. Schooling, which is free and compulsory, may begin with nursery school at the age of three and leads on to the universities, colleges, and technical training institutes. The largest is Moscow State University with about 16,000 students. Most students receive a government grant toward living expenses, but they have to work for two years on a farm or in a factory before they can go to college. Emphasis is on science and technology, but literature and the arts still have an honored place. Religion, though not officially forbidden, is actively discouraged.

In many areas, especially in the former Islamic centers such as Bokhara and Samarkand in central Asia, religious propaganda is actually forbidden as well as the teaching of religion in schools. The government has turned the many religious monuments and

Above: children from a kindergarten in Taganrog, the Rostov Region of the USSR out on a walk.
Right: with children cared for by the state, married women are able to supplement their husband's income and contribute to the economic prosperity of the nation.

houses, such as mosques, into museums or state propaganda halls. The official Communist policy appears on walls and newspapers everywhere – in offices, factories, universities, public buildings, as well as in newspapers such as *Pravda* and *Izvestia*.

In Eastern Europe, the Bulgars are Slavs who crossed the Danube in about the 7th century to mingle with the local peoples. Their relationship to the Russians and Ukrainians is shown in the languages of the three peoples, which have many similarities. They are all Slavonic in origin and have cyrillic alphabets. But Bulgarian has also some words derived from the Greek, Albanian, and Turkish. Rumania, on the other hand, is inhabited by people who arrived directly from the east and because it was a frontier province of the Roman Empire its language has derived much from Latin and is not unlike Italian. Both countries have been ruled by a Communist government for over 30 years and the communist economic system, derived from the USSR, has meant a change from an agricultural population to an industrialized one. The results have been the same as in the Soviet Union, a sharp decline in the rural element and a growth of the towns. Again, women play an important role in the labor force. In Rumania, for example, the workers on the collective farms are predominantly female.

It is in the southeast of the region, in Mongolia, that the most striking changes are to be seen. Historically it formed the nerve center of the great empire of Genghis Khan. Then, as Outer Mongolia, the area became a province of China, but linked geographically with the other divisions of the high plateaus of central Asia, forming a buffer zone between the USSR to the north and China proper to the south. Now it is an independent republic and part of the Soviet orbit. From being a country peopled by nomadic herdsmen it is following the same pattern of change as has been seen throughout Asiatic USSR. The capital, Ulan Bator, has been linked by rail with the Trans-Siberian

Railway at Ulan-Ude and with Pei-p'ing (Peking) in the south.

The Soviet Union, and its Comecon (Council for Mutual Economic Aid) partners, have supplied Mongolia with expert help, guidance, capital, and workers. Illiteracy has almost been wiped out and education and training is being provided in all fields, both cultural and technical. State farms have been established – not an easy task when it involves changing the traditional way of life and outlook of the fiercely independent Mongols. They have shown little interest in crop cultivation, though the Russians have persisted with the emphasis on hay production to provide winter fodder for the various herds. Efforts have been made to improve animal breeding and veterinary stations have been established and the herdsmen encouraged to consult the scientists.

Ulan Bator has grown to over 250,000 from a population of well under 100,000 at the beginnings of the 1950s. This represents about a fifth of the total population of the country. It is the main industrial center, though now other towns, such as Choybalsan, are growing. Industry is mainly concerned with the manufacture of construction materials, food processing, and the processing of the country's animal products such as leather, furs, and woolens.

Its size and population, its resources and development, combined with the relentless political philosophy that drives it, make the Soviet Union one of the world's most powerful countries. It heads the Eastern European Communist bloc of Bulgaria, Czechoslovakia, the German Democratic Republic (DDR), Hungary, Poland, and Rumania. Albania, also a Communist state, has been a faithful follower of Communist China in recent years. Yugoslavia, another Communist country, holds a more independent position between the Communist bloc and the West, but retains close associations with Moskva (Moscow).

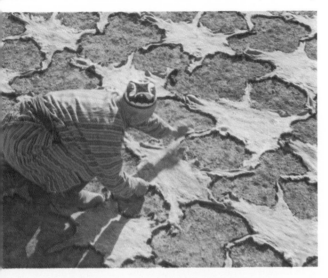

Above: drying astrakan skins in Tadzhikistan by a method that has changed little over the centuries is a far cry from the sophisticated space-age technology required for this intercosmos satellite (above right).

More recently, the Communist countries of Eastern Europe generally have adapted more independent attitudes, and from time to time have openly disagreed with the Soviet Union's policy or attitude.

Communist unity is seen clearly in defense policy and economic development. The Warsaw Pact (Eastern Security Treaty), signed in 1955 by the USSR, Albania, Bulgaria, Czechoslovakia, DDR, Hungary, Poland, and Rumania is virtually the Communist equivalent of the North Atlantic Treaty Organization. Its aim is to ensure the military defense of the countries by the integration of armed forces and the political collaboration of the members. Albania left the pact in 1968. Comecon was established in 1949 to promote the planned development and economic progress of its members, to integrate the economies of Communist countries, and to develop cooperation with all countries. Its members included Albania, Bulgaria, Czechoslovakia, DDR, Hungary, Poland, Rumania, and the USSR. Yugoslavia is an associate, but Albania withdrew in 1961 and Cuba joined in 1962.

In recent years the links between the USSR and China have become strained. Mongolia has occupied the position of buffer state between the two, controlling the direct route to Pei-p'ing (Peking). The USSR has depended upon a friendly Mongolia and to ensure this has given the country economic assistance. Obviously Mongolia has profited from this situation though it has lost the transit trade as a result of the Sino-Soviet quarrel. The Communist agricultural programs, spearheaded by the USSR, are doing much to westernize Asia by changing the land tenure system and establishing collective farms. In Eastern Europe and North Africa the same type of agrarian reforms are resulting in a more profitable use of the land, higher yields, and a better balanced economy.

The Russians have a long tradition of scientific research. This tradition has been continued and enriched by its present-day scientists and technologists. The Russian expertise and "know-how" for working in the frozen Arctic lands – where steel becomes brittle, oil solidifies, and rubber splits at temperatures below $-40°$F, is unparalleled. The Soviets have developed specialized methods and equipment, such as cars and tractors, cold-resistant steel, and lubricating fuels. Such knowledge is of immense value to other countries, such as Canada, the United States, and Norway, which have Arctic environments they are beginning to develop.

These demonstrations of expertise and power are formidable prestige-builders for the Soviet Union. In the United Nations – where the USSR is a permanent member of the Security Council and so has the power of veto – and elsewhere in world affairs, Soviet Russian views and attitudes inevitably command constant attention.

The Countries of Northern Asia

1 Union of Soviet Socialist
  Republics
2 Mongolia
3 Bulgaria
4 Rumania

UNION OF SOVIET SOCIALIST REPUBLICS (USSR) (Soyus Sovyetskikh Sotsialistiches kh Respublik – SSSR)

Area: 8,649,489 square miles
Population: 255,000,000
Capital: Moscow (Moskva)
Language: Russian
Religion: Mainly Eastern (Russian) Orthodox
Monetary Unit: Rouble
History and Government: Formerly the old Russian Empire, whose Moscow princes gradually threw off Tartar domination and united, by conquest, many of the surrounding principalities. It was under the rule of the Romanov Czars from 1613 to 1917, when the monarchy was overthrown and government of soviets was set up. The USSR consists of 15 Union republics within which are 20 autonomous republics, 8 autonomous regions, and 10 national areas. The chief constitutional organ of the USSR is the Supreme Soviet with two chambers (A Council (Soviet) of the Union and a Council (Soviet) of Nationalities) with equal legislative rights and elected for a term of four years. The Council of the Union is elected by citizens of the USSR. The Council of the Nationalities is elected by the union republics, autonomous republics, autonomous regions, and national areas. The Supreme Soviet appoints the presidium, which represents the Supreme Soviet between its twice-yearly sessions. It is chaired by the head of state, and the council of ministers, who are the highest executive power, or government. The Communist Party of the Soviet Union which works through its Congresses (held every four years) and its permanent organs such as the central committees, the politburo, and the secretariat has complete control over all aspects of Soviet life. The top officials of the state, and those responsible for the economic bodies and the trade unions, are all members of the Party.

Economy: In comparison with the other industrialized countries, the process of development in the Soviet Union did not begin until after the 1917 revolution. In a few decades the Soviet Union passed from an underdeveloped, almost feudal country to its present position as the second most important industrial country in the world. Concentrated efforts were made, especially in the field of heavy industry, and now the USSR is the foremost producer in the world of iron, steel, oil, manganese, chromium, magnesite, mercury, and cement; the second largest producer of coal, methane, copper, lead, zinc, tungsten, asbestos, phosphates, basic chemical products, and electric power. The results in agriculture have been slower, but in some areas such as the arid region south of the Aral'skoye (Aral) the results are quite spectacular. The Soviet Union's most important partners are the Comecon countries, the Federal Republic of Germany, Japan, United States, France, India, and Italy.

MONGOLIA (Bugd Nairamdakh Mongol Ard Uls)

Area: 604,246 square miles
Population: 1,500,000
Capital: Ulan Bator
Language: Mongolian
Religion: The state is atheist but part of the population is lamaist.
Monetary Unit: Thgrik
History and Government: Part of a vast territory that was the home of Genghis Khan, founder of the Mongol empire that stretched from China to the Danube, the territory was later split into three areas, Inner Mongolia now part of China, Mongol-Buryat republic, part of the USSR, and Outer Mongolia. For almost all the years between 1691 and 1921, Outer Mongolia was a Chinese province. Its independence was obtained in 1921 but it was not until 1924 that the Mongolian People's Republic was declared. According to the fourth Constitution of 1960, the members of the People's Great *Khurd*, which holds the legislative power, are elected every three years from the lists of the Mongolian People's Revolutionary Communist Party. Mongolia is affected by its strategic position – 2900 miles of frontiers with China and 1695 miles with the USSR – which necessitates a considerable defense effort. It is closely allied, politically and economically, with the USSR and has 60,000 Soviet troops on its frontiers with China.

Economy: The economic plans are concentrated on the industrial sector, which is not highly developed, but the fifth plan for the years 1971-75 gave priority to investments in agriculture. This sector, and especially stock-rearing and its derivatives (milk, wool, furs, and meat), employs a large percentage of the working population. There are good supplies of coal and oil nd the former is now being exploited. he USSR absorbs more than 80 percent f Mongolia's foreign trade.

ULGARIA (Bulgariya)
rea: 42,823 square miles
opulation: 8,800,000
apital: Sofia (Sofiya)
anguage: Bulgarian
eligion: Eastern Orthodox
Ionetary Unit: Lev
listory and Government: Largely ccupying the area that was the old oman province of Lower Moesia, ulgaria was occupied by Slavs and ulgars in the 7th century AD. It came nder Byzantine culture and eventually ecame part, first of the Byzantine mpire (11th century), and later the ttoman empire (14th to 20th century). t has been independent since 1908 first s a principality then as a kingdom. ulgaria joined the Axis powers in 941. A People's Republic was pro-laimed on the abolition of the monar-hy in 1946. According to the new onstitution of 1971 there is a single hamber, the National Assembly, con-isting of 400 deputies, elected from reas of equal population by universal uffrage for a term of five years. The lational Assembly elects the council f state from its members and the chair-an of the council is head of state. hough considered the most submissive f the "satellites" of the USSR, Bul-aria has been pledged since 1973 to ore cordial relations with the West and particularly with the United States.
Economy: About 90 percent of the country's agriculture is run by co-operatives. The agricultural complexes and irrigation schemes have greatly improved yields. The principal crops are wheat, corn, cotton, sunflower seed (for vegetable oils), potatoes, sugar, tobacco and fruit. Stock-rearing consists mainly of sheep, but also in-cludes cattle, goats, pigs, horses, and water buffalo. The exploitation of min-eral resources is increasing (lignite, lead, zinc, uranium) and so is the gener-ation of energy. Oil is being drilled in the northeast and offshore in the Black Sea; an atomic powers station has been built. Investments have been made in the iron and steel industry, engineer-ing, textiles, and cement.

RUMANIA (Republica Socialista Romania)
Area: 91,700 square miles
Population: 21,500,000
Capital: Bucharest (Bucurestl)
Language: Rumanian
Religion: Mainly Eastern (Greek) Orthodox
Monetary Unit: Leu
History and Government: The be-ginning of the present state took place in 1861 when the autonomous Danu-bian provinces of Wallachia and Mol-davia united to form the principality of Rumania. It gained independence from the Ottoman empire and became a kingdom in 1881. Dictator Ion Anto-nescu forced the country to fight on the side of the Axis powers in World War II. A republic was declared in 1947 on the abdication of King Michael. The Grand National Assembly is elected for five years and between sessions the state council of 26 members, led by the presi-dent, has legislative rights. Open-mindedness in foreign policy and cau-tion at home characterizes the Ruman-ian Communist Party, in power since 1952. The constitution was modified in 1974 instituting the office of president of the Republic – a deviation from the usual communist pattern – where the chairman of the council of state is normally head of state. There is also a greater distinction between the state and the party.
Economy: The rich fertile soils of large parts of Rumania make it among the leaders in Europe for the cultivation of wheat, corn, sunflower seeds, flax and hemp, and in sheep-rearing. Cattle, pigs, and poultry are also important. In the mineral sector, Rumania comes second in Europe for oil and is rich in methane, coal, lignite, and iron ore. There is also manganese, bauxite, sul-fur, pyrites, and salt. A large part of the industrial investment is concentrated on iron and steel, but textiles, chemi-cals, petrochemicals, cement, textiles, and light industry are also developing rapidly. Trade is predominantly with the Comecon countries and with China, but the quota with the Western coun-tries is increasing.

Below: Mongol herdsmen, little changed from those described by travelers in the mid-1800s.

127

Chapter 6

Southern Asia and the Far East

South of the USSR, Asia spreads out from Iran through Sinkiang to Mongolia, across the monsoon lands of the south and east and the island fringe beyond. Of the 2000 million people who live in the whole of Asia, over three quarters live in this region. By the outbreak of World War II European expansion into south and east Asia involved the whole of the Indian subcontinent, all Southeast Asia – apart from Thailand, or Siam as it was then called – and many of the trading centers along the Chinese coast were dominated by the Western world. By the end of 1957 the political map of southern Asia was transformed. All the imperialistic powers had been forced out: the British out of the Indian subcontinent, Burma, and Malaya; the Dutch out of the East Indies; the French out of Indochina; and the Americans out of the Philippines. The major areas had achieved independence, but with it came the attendant problems of poverty, illiteracy, and political and social inequalities.

Opposite: soldiers and peasants combine their efforts to till the fields in China. Finding enough food for everyone to eat is an all-consuming task in Southern Asia and the Far East – a task that can often hinder attempts at economic improvement.

Iran and Afghanistan

Iran and Afghanistan lie on the Plateau of Iran, the high massif of folded mountains that forms part of the Alpine system, linking the Kavkaz (Caucasus) with the Himalayas. Because of the extreme aridity and the mountainous terrain, largely composed of limestone rocks, there is little cultivation in either Iran or Afghanistan, except in small irrigated basins and valleys. Only on the southern littoral of the Caspian and the lower slopes of the Alborz (Elburz) is there a luxuriant vegetation, and oranges, date palms, sugar-cane, and cotton can be grown. Elsewhere, the scrub vegetation provides poor grazing land for the nomadic herdsmen.

In western Iran the Persians have practiced a unique form of irrigation for many centuries. They have constructed many hundred of *qanats*, or channels, by tunneling into the permeable rocks along the foothills of the mountains. Through these qanats the water, collected from the melting snows, is carried away to irrigate the more arid areas and gardens that produce vegetables, fruit, and pulses. The sedentary people draw on the qanats for their domestic needs and for their flocks of sheep and goats. The nomadic tribes move between the mountain pastures in summer and the lower areas in winter, using the perennial streams and the qanats to water their herds. They also dig wells in the aquifers – the tilted layers of permeable rock, usually limestone in Iran, that are saturated with water and lie between impermeable layers of rock.

The oil deposits of Iran have been exploited for more than half a century and before World War II Iran and Iraq were the only two countries in the Middle East producing substantial amounts of petroleum. By the end of the war Iranian petroleum production had doubled. By 1976 it supplied 10 percent of the world's total production. The resulting revenue has enabled Iran to improve its transport system, social services, investments, and embark on a program of land reform.

Afghanistan is not as richly endowed as its neighbor Iran. The diversity of its tribes has worked against marked national unity. Only recently has the government begun to exploit the mineral resources and initiate agricultural schemes that make possible the cultivation of fruits and grain with the help of irrigation and a planned crop rotation.

Below: terraced hills and walled villages in the Afghanistan mountains to the southwest of the capital, Kabul. Rainfall precipitated by the high mountains causes high-altitude oases.

Eurasia: Political

Scale:
Miles
0   200   400   600   800   1000   1200   1400   1600
0   200   400   600   800   1000   1200   1400   1600   1800   2000   2200   2400   2600
Kilometres

© Geographical Projects

The Indian Subcontinent

Shut off from the rest of Asia by lofty mountains and deep valleys, the vast subcontinent of India thrusts southward like a giant wedge between the Arabian Sea and the Bay of Bengal. The distance from the mountain barrier in the north to Sri Lanka (Ceylon) in the south is 2000 miles; from Karachi in the west to Assam in the east it is also about 2000 miles. The subcontinent is larger than Europe and it is one of the world's most populous areas. Its three main regions, from south to north, are the Deccan (sometimes called peninsular India), the Indo-Gangetic plain, and the high mountain wall of the Himalayas and associated ranges.

It would be surprising if so vast an area did not have a variety of climates. But although they vary from place to place they have a unity imposed on them by the

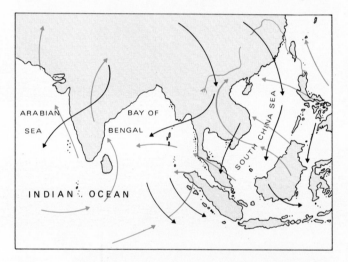

Above: arrows show direction of monsoon winds in the Indian Ocean — black are northeast winds, blue southwest.

monsoons, the system in which the winds completely reverse direction from season to season. There are three seasons: cool, hot and dry, and wet. The first two of these are during the northeast monsoon, the third in the southwest monsoon. From mid-October to February the northeast monsoon blows, bringing the cooler, dry weather. From March to June the winds are still from the north or northeast, but as the sun moves north the temperatures increase rapidly to about 90°F. In the Indo-Gangetic plain they often rise to 105°F and occasional readings of 120°F are recorded in the east in the Thar Desert.

The Deccan is a large plateau sloping down to the southeast from the rugged and well-forested mountain ranges of the Western Ghats and their southern extension, the Nilgiri Hills. There is only a narrow coastal plain between the mountains and the Arabian Sea. In the east, between 50 and 150 miles from the coast, is another range, the Eastern Ghats, cut by a series of broad river valleys into a broken line of hills. These rivers all rise in the Western Ghats and flow eastward across the full width of peninsular India to empty into the Bay of Bengal. In the northwest of the Deccan are vast intrusions of lava that have been eroded into steep-sided, flat-topped hills. These Deccan lavas produce the famous black soils on which cotton is grown. To the northeast and south are the leading areas for the production of peanuts.

The flat, monotonous Indo-Gangetic plain stretches from Pakistan in the west, across the north of the Deccan to Bangladesh and the eastern extension of India in the Naga Hills. Across the western part of the plain the Indus and its tributaries flow southwestward from the Himalaya, through dry lands where farmers have to irrigate with water from the rivers. They take so much water that in places the lower Indus is only a small stream. Houses are made of mud brick and have flat roofs, but farther to the east, near the Ganges where there is more rain, they have straw or bamboo roofs, pitched steeply so that the rainwater runs off. Cotton and wheat are two of the main cash crops, but on the fertile alluvial soils in the wetter parts of the lower Ganges sugar cane is also important. On the borders of India and Bangladesh is the famous jute area, and in the extreme east the great tea plantations of Assam.

The third region, the lofty mountain wall, has many gigantic peaks reaching heights of more than 20,000 feet – Mount Everest, at 29,028 feet, is the highest mountain in the world. The Himalaya is the outer rim of a succession of parallel ranges that include the Karakoram, the Kailas, and the Nyenchentanglha. In winter, these mountains protect the subcontinent from the cold winds of central Asia; in summer they prevent the southwest monsoon from carrying the moist air into central Asia. So winters in northern Pakistan and India are much warmer than those of southern China at comparable latitudes.

In the extreme south is the island of Sri Lanka (Ceylon), which is separated from the southeast tip of India by the Palk Strait and the Gulf of Mannar. Most of the island is undulating plain, but the south has a central mountain core reaching heights of more than 6000 feet. The highest peak is Pidurutalaga, known locally as *Pedro*, and from its summit of 8270 feet the entire coastline of the island can be seen on a clear day. But the most famous peak is Adam's Peak. The natural hollow at its summit, resembling a giant footprint, is said by Buddhists to have been made by Buddha and by the Hindus to be the footprint of Shiva. The Chinese say that it was made by Pan Ku their own first man.

Right: one of the main squares in Calcutta, India. Between 1773 and 1912 the city was the capital of British-ruled India, and with its suburbs is one of the largest cities in Southeast Asia.

China
and
Its Neighbors

The whole of the United States of America could be put into China and there would still be room to spare. China extends across about 50° of longitude and 35° of latitude, from the 6000-mile coastline of eastern China to the edge of the Pamirs in the west, from the island of Hai-nan, south of the Tropic of Cancer, to the Amur river in the north.

Great mountains and high plateaus make up about four fifths of this vast area, but there are broad plains and long rivers flowing from west to east. China generally slopes eastward in three giant, faulted "steps" leading down from the 13,000-foot-high Plateau of Tibet in the southwest to the peripheral seas in the east, between mainland Asia and the arc of islands. The border of the vast Plateau of Tibet is the first of the steps – to the south are the young Tertiary folded mountains of the Himalaya, which turn southeastward through Burma and Southeast Asia to reappear again in the islands of the east Indian archipelago. On the northern rim of the plateau are the Kun-lun Shan, the Altyn Tagh, and Nan Shan, which run eastward from the "knot" of the Pamirs.

The second step, running in an arc around the plateau on the north and east sides, includes the great basins of the Tarim, Dzungaria, and the Red Basin of Szechwan. These basins are separated by the high walls of the Tien Shan and Altay (Altai), the plateaus of Inner Mongolia, the Chin-lin Shan and the Yunnan-Kweichow plateau in south China. The third step includes the broad plains of Manchuria, the Hwang Ho and Ch'ang Chiang (Yangtze Kiang), between which are mosaiclike lower mountain ranges.

Below: the Himalayas seen from Nepal. They extend in a 1500-mile long arc from Kashmir in Western India to Assam in the east and cover most of Nepal, Sikkim, Bhutan and southern Tibet. On the border with Tibet is Mount Everest, the world's highest mountain.

About a third of China is made up of the massive Plateau of Tibet, which has an average height of 15,000 feet. It is sparsely populated. Here, the Tibetans grow buckwheat, highland barley, winter rye, and winter wheat along the valley floors in the short summer months, so increasing their fodder supplies and enabling them to enlarge their herds of sheep, goats, and yaks.

The next step, the basins and plateaus, is also for the most part inhabited by nomadic herdsmen. At the western end, between the Kun-lun Shan and the Tien Shan is the Tarim Basin, a mainly desert area of shifting sand dunes called the Takla Makan. Around the edges of the basin are the ancient oasis towns of Su-fu (Kashgar), Yarkand, and Ho-tien, where the land is more fertile, being watered by the mountain streams. The Turfan depression, on the northeast edge of the basin, is 500 feet below sea level. Here archaeologists have found traces of a civilization nearly 2000 years old: evidence of times when the climate was less arid and the Tarim basin was part of the main east-west corridor along which nomadic peoples moved. On the southeast of the basin is, perhaps, the most desolate basin of all, the Tsaidam.

Above: Chinese "harvesting" bamboo. Before 1950 there was little deliberate cultivation of bamboo. There are now many groves, especially in Kiangsi Province.

The next basin, Dzungaria, is an area where conditions are a little less arid, but east of it, on the plateaus of Inner Mongolia, lies the desolate Gobi Desert, partly sand and partly stone. The Gobi is crossed by ancient trade routes, including the famous "Silk Road" between China and India, and is the home of Mongol nomads, wild horses, wild asses, and wild camels. Near the southern end of this middle step is the third great basin, the Red Basin of Szechwan, immensely fertile, intensively cultivated, and densely populated.

The lowest step of all comprises the plains and lower hills through which the giant rivers of China thread their ways. These rivers – the most famous of which are the Hwang Ho, the Ch'ang Chiang (Yangtze Kiang), and, to a lesser extent, the Hsi-chiang (Sikiang) – have built broad alluvial plains recently in geological history. It is a process that is still going on, with the rivers pushing the coastline out into the seas. The Hwang Ho, for instance, deposits about 14,000 tons of silt every year in the shallow gulf of Po Hai, beyond its mouth.

The loess region, between the southern edge of the Gobi – marked by the Great Wall of China – and the Chin-ling Shan, is one of the most fertile areas in the whole country. Here, too, are some of China's largest

Below: Pei-p'ing's Red Square, like its Moscow counterpart, is the setting for massive parades and demonstrations. In 1928 its name was changed from Peking when Nanking became the capital. Although it is again the capital of China, it retains its new name.

cities such as the capital Pei-p'ing, Yangch'u and Hsi-an (Sian). A giant build-up of fine fertile loam, hundreds of feet deep, has buried most of the older landscape. It was probably deposited about 10,000 to 20,000 years ago, at the end of the last Ice Age, by winds blowing out from the Gobi Desert, in much the same way as they do today during the northwest monsoon. Through this loam – termed loess – the rivers have carved a maze of ravines, and the Hwang Ho flows in a broad, fertile plain bordered by steep-sided bluffs. This river, often called the Yellow river, gets its murky yellowish color from the mud it carries downstream from the loess plateaus. Cultivation of the steep slopes is made possible by terracing. The cliffs are riddled with cave dwellings, many of which have been inhabited continually since the time of early man.

Southern Asia

Scale:
Miles
0   100   200   300   400   500   600   700
0   100 200 300 400 500 600 700 800 900 1000
Kilometres

The Lands of Eastern Asia

By American or Asian standards, Taiwan, North Korea, South Korea, and Japan are all small countries. Taiwan is an island lying off the coast of China and straddling the Tropic of Cancer. Formerly part of the great Chinese nation, it is now a separate political entity, with a government that claims to be the sole representative of pre-Communist China. Korea, a peninsular jutting out toward the Japanese island of Kyushu, is slightly larger than the American state of Kansas. Japan, a country of islands, runs in an arc about 7500 miles long.

In the north, Korea is almost cut off from the rest of Asia by mountains, and rugged hills stretch along its east coast, in some places rising straight out of the sea. Most rivers flow to the west and south, to the Yellow Sea and the Korea Strait. This island-studded strait, 100 miles wide, divides Korea from Japan and

Below: a typical scene in Southeast Asia. Paddy fields in hilly regions have to be divided by low banks into tiny plots. This enables the farmer to keep the same water level in each plot.

Above: Fujiyama, Japan's highest mountain (12,388 feet). The long symmetrical slopes, which have made the mountain world-famous for its beauty, were formed by volcanic action. The summit contains a deep crater.

links the deep Sea of Japan with the shallower East China Sea to the south.

The islands of Taiwan and Japan, on the other hand, form part of the great island arc that marks the boundary of the Pacific and Eurasian plates. The arc forms one of the most unstable areas in the world and is part of the "Ring of Fire" that encircles the Pacific.

Taiwan has a largely tropical climate; there is no cold season. The northeast monsoon winds are warmed a little as they blow over the China seas and the temperatures are always over 60°F, even in the coolest months. There is a summer rainfall with the southwest monsoon, but the high mountains that run the length of the island result in a winter rainfall as well. Even the driest areas have 40 inches of rainfall a year.

Korea, to the north, is still influenced by the monsoons and also by the cold Oya Shio ocean current that flows south from the Bering Sea and has a branch that sweeps down between the island arc and the mainland. This intensifies the cold of the winters when the northeast monsoon blows and temperatures stay around, or below, freezing point for several months. Although there is a little rainfall in winter there is a summer maximum.

Throughout its long history Korea has been subject to a never-ending series of invasions from its more powerful neighbors and at the beginning of this cen-

comes down from the north. Winters are cold and wet with heavy snowfalls on the mountains. Temperatures range from just below freezing point in Hokkaido to over 40°F in the southern islands. In summer, when the winds reverse, the weather is warm and humid and in the south there is a heavy rainfall.

The islands of Japan are the tops of mountains rising seven or eight miles from the floor of the Pacific. On Honshu many peaks rise to over 10,000 feet and Fujiyama, the highest mountain, is 12,388 feet. It is a dormant volcano, perfectly cone-shaped, which last erupted in 1707. There are about 200 other volcanoes on this one island, many still active and many dormant ones with lakes filling their craters. Japan is also subject to earth tremors – some 1500 earthquakes are registered each year. Fortunately most of them do not cause much damage. On the other hand, parts of Japan have often been devastated by tsunami (the "tidal waves" that are caused by undersea earthquakes, thousands of miles away out in the Pacific).

The small lowlands, mostly at the heads of bays or in river valleys, are naturally important in such a mountainous country as Japan. The most notable are along the northern shores of the Seto Naikai (Inland Sea) between Honshu and Shikoku and the largest one in the east, the 5000-square-mile plain at the head of Tokyo Bay. Like the Koreans, the Japanese farmers have terraced the hillsides to use every available bit of land. North of 37°N, in northern Honshu and Hokkaido, the winters are too cold for growing crops all year around but farther south farmers can harvest two crops a year and, in Kyushu, three a year. Two thirds of the country is forested with a variety of broadleaf trees, oak and maple predominating. These forests provide not only timber but charcoal, which is burned as fuel in many Japanese homes. The forests also provide food – nuts, fruits, and bamboo shoots.

tury it became part of the Japanese empire.

After World War II Korea was divided along the 38th parallel between Soviet and American Occupation Forces – a division that was also roughly the dividing line between the industrial north and the agricultural south. In South Korea, irrigation has been developed with a large area of double-cropping and the use of manufactured fertilizers. The intensive cultivation carried out there has resulted in some problems. For instance, deforestation for agricultural land has resulted in soil erosion. Also the failure of the summer rains in some years has meant that South Korea has not produced enough rice for its own growing population, and irrigation canals have become clogged with silt. Industries have been greatly expanded, however, and the country is now independent of outside aid.

Meanwhile North Korea has struggled to maintain independence and to develop without too much interference from its giant Communist neighbors – China and the USSR. Heavy industries have continued to expand, power installations have increased, and land previously used for cotton growing has been given over to grain production.

Japan has four main islands – Honshu, Hokkaido, Kyushu, and Shikoku, in order of size – and hundreds of smaller islands. They extend in an arc from northeast to southwest and are influenced by both the Asian monsoon system and the ocean currents, the warm Kuro Shio the sweeps northward from the Equator along the eastern shores and the cold Oya Shio that

Above: a typical blending of old and new in Japanese life is this modern monorail transport seen against old architectural forms.

139

Southeast Asia

Southeast Asia, a region of mountains, plains, and islands, stretching north and south of the Equator, lies to the east of the Indian subcontinent and south of China. A complex patchwork quilt of countries and landscapes, it includes the peninsula of Indochina and Malaya, the islands of the East Indian archipelago, and the Philippines. Until World War II, with the exception of Thailand, it was a region dominated by Europe and the United States.

Southeast Asia is affected by the Asian monsoon and the maritime influence of the great tracts of water. On the islands the average annual temperature is 80°F and scarcely varies throughout the year, but on the mainland the range is quite considerable. The northeast monsoon – the cold, dry winds that blow out from the continent – causes the temperature to fall as low as 50°F during some winter nights in northern Thailand and Vietnam. It is the rainfall that deter-

mines the seasons however – not the lack of it, but the amount. The whole region is one of the wettest on earth, some parts having well over 80 inches a year. But the rainfall seasons vary from island to island and even from one side of an island to the other.

The Philippines and the mainland north of the Malay Peninsula also lie on the paths of the tropical typhoons. These originate out to sea, about latitude 10°N, then travel westward. Some reach the coast of Vietnam and others curve northward, following virtually the same route as the Kuro Shio current. The Philippines have the misfortune to lie right in the track of the majority of these typhoons.

The rivers of Southeast Asia, particularly those of the mainland, have built huge alluvial plains and are still pushing their deltas out into the sea. These rivers, especially the Mekong, Irrawaddy, and Mae Yom, carry loads of debris down from the mountains and, swollen by the torrential rains, flood easily, depositing silt on the plains. Most of the Indonesian islands also have patches of alluvial plains along the coast and these scattered lowlands support large populations. In Sumatra the lowland is continuous along the northeast-facing coast, but in contrast, Djawa (Java) and Sulawesi (Celebes) have only

Below: the floating market in Thailand's capital, Bangkok. The city is intersected by waterways, canals (klongs), and dikes, but is also well served by modern roads. Bangkok is also the chief port of Thailand.

Above: Mangrove seedlings in swampland around the coasts of many Indonesian Islands. The long arching roots of the mature trees trap soil and extend the land.

scattered lowlands. Mangrove swamps in many of the coast regions are also gradually extending the land at the expense of the sea. The mangrove grows in warm, shallow, coastal water. Its long, arching roots anchor the trees to the sea floor forming an impenetrable barrier that traps soil, sand, and silt.

Burma, to the northwest of Thailand, is potentially a rich land, its peoples concentrated in the central valley of the Irrawaddy and its tributaries. They are, however, of different cultures, some of the most important groups being the Naga of the northwest frontier hills, and the Shan and Karens of the eastern plateaus and mountains.

The British developed the cultivation of rice in the Irrawaddy delta region where conditions of rainfall and the swampy land – which could easily be converted into paddy fields with a regulated flow of water – were ideal. The tropical monsoon forest, full of deciduous trees such as teak, is the natural vegetation of the hillsides of Burma and is regarded as the country's richest resource. Burma is also rich in minerals such as petroleum, tungsten, tin, lead, and silver.

Thailand has always been an independent nation and in many ways has remained isolated from the main shipping lanes and trade routes between Europe and the East. But the advent of the airplane has changed this. The country is now a stopping-off point for air routes from Europe, Africa, the Middle East, and the Indian subcontinent in the west, from Japan and Hong Kong in the northeast, and from Indonesia, Singapore, and Australia in the southeast.

Since World War II Thailand has benefited from American aid and the presence of American troops in the country. Its relatively stable economy meant that, after 1945, it was the main rice producer of Southeast Asia. All the farmers grow rice, both for export and for their own use. Along with many other countries in the region the great problem facing Thailand is the population growth. If it continues at the present rate it will seriously affect the availability of land for cultivation and the rice surplus which is the country's main source of revenue.

Laos, Vietnam, and Cambodia are three independent nations that originally formed French Indochina. Laos borders the middle Mekong and it is this river and its tributaries that in many ways control the economy of the country. They are the major means of transportation, the location of all the large towns, and the providers of water and power. Dams and hydroelectric plants are being constructed to supply both irrigation schemes and power. It is the lowlands bordering the rivers that are irrigated to enable the farmers to grow wet rice. The upland rice, grown on the hillsides, does not require so much water.

Vietnam straggles down the east coast of the peninsula from the lower basin of the Song Nhi Ha (Red) and Song Bo (Black) rivers on the Chinese frontier to the vast Mekong delta at the southern tip. There is an enormous contrast between the north and the south. The delta, in the south, came under French colonial rule in the 1860s and the French developed the area for the production of rice for export. Later,

Below: terraces of rice paddies in the Philippines. Rice is the staple food of many of the countries of Southeast Asia where the climate is generally too wet to grow wheat and corn on a large scale.

Above: natural rubber being tapped from a tree in Malaya. A thin strip of bark is shaved halfway around the trunk and latex oozes from the cut into a cup suspended below. After each tapping, the latex flows for about four hours, providing enough to fill a teacup.

land of the ancient Khmer empire, which was at its height between the 9th and 15th centuries and dominated Southeast Asia. Since then, except for the period of the French protectorate, Cambodia has had a continuous struggle to achieve financial and economic independence. Rice cultivation and fishing are the chief means of livelihood although the French did develop some rubber plantations.

Malaysia is made up of the Malay peninsula and the northwestern part of the island of Borneo, some 600 miles or more to the east across the South China Sea. Within this area lies the independent state of Singapore, occupying the island at the southern tip of the Malay peninsula, and the British dependency of Brunei, on the west coast of Borneo. The peninsula dominates the country. As in the other countries of Southeast Asia, farming is the mainstay of the economy. About 40 percent of the world's natural rubber comes from Malaysia, and tropical fruits, such as pineapples, and tea are also significant. Mining is also important. The large Chinese minority in the country, the diversity of the indigenous ethnic groups, and the contrast between the two main areas of the country, the peninsula, and Borneo, are strong factors against the unification of the country.

Indonesia occupies the 3000-mile-long string of islands that stretches from Sumatra in the west to New Guinea in the east, as well as the more northerly islands of Kalimantan (Indonesian Borneo), Sulawesi (Celebes), Halmahera, and the numerous smaller islands. It is by far the largest nation in Southeast Asia, with a population of over 125 million – of which more than 80 million live on Djawa (Java) – one of the most densely populated countries in the world.

Farming is again the main economic activity and there are two groups of farms: the smallholdings and the former colonial estates that still produce commercial crops. The latter provide the rubber, tea, tobacco, cinchona bark (for quinine), sugar, and other spices. There are also rich supplies of tin, nickel, and bauxite as well as petroleum. The offshore production of oil has been highly developed in southeast Sumatra and in the coastal waters around the islands of Bangka and Belitung (Billitong).

The last of the nations that form Southeast Asia is the Philippines. Its great problem, as in so many other tropical countries, is to relieve the serious social and economic conditions. The cultivation of corn, coconut palms, and sugar cane has been encouraged, mining has been developed, the production of consumer goods and light industries established.

One of the greatest difficulties, however, is language. The local dialects are as diverse as the tribes. Spanish rule, which lasted from the 1500s to the early 1900s introduced the Spanish language; American rule between the early 1900s to the mid-1940s resulted in English becoming the language of the elite groups. Since independence, attempts have been made to develop a modified form of the main language spoken originally in lowland Luzon, the northernmost island.

when they annexed the north they established industries, and accentuated the differences between the two areas. The rich mineral resources of the north are now being worked and the manufacture of consumer goods, especially textiles, expanded, but subsistence farming, augmented by fishing, forms the basis of the Vietnamese economy.

The third former French colony is Cambodia, also sometimes known as Kampuchea, a small lowland country divided unequally into two by the north-south flow of the Mekong river. Cambodia is the home-

The Indian Ocean

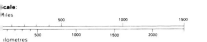

Below: the Indian Ocean is the third largest ocean in the world, covering an area of around 28,400,000 square miles. It stretches from Africa in the west to Australia and the East Indies in the east. To the north lies Asia, to the south, Antarctica. It is separated from the Pacific by the Sunda Islands in Indonesia and touches the Atlantic in the Cape of Good Hope. In one of its arms, the Red Sea, it links with the Mediterranean through the Suez Canal.

Blue thick line   Sea routes
Red thick line   Air routes

People and Produce

In southern Asia and the Far East two out of every three people make their living from agriculture. The best farmlands are the alluvial plains and valleys of the great rivers and these are, for the most part, in the south and east of mainland Asia. Mostly the farmers produce only enough for their own consumption and have nothing left over to sell. The farmers rarely have any modern machinery but plow their fields with wooden plows drawn by bullocks or water buffaloes. The seeds, or rice shoots, are all planted, harvested, dried, sorted, and prepared by hand. Plots are small, and often one family owns a number of tiny scattered plots.

The picture is different in Southeast Asia, where nearly all the world's rice is grown, and where intensive subsistance farming of this one crop supports a large population.

In the lowlands of China and Japan people farm intensively but carefully. Farmers never leave their fields fallow, they use crop rotations and manure their land. Yields of rice per acre are, therefore, high, but not high in terms of yield per agricultural worker. It is in Taiwan (Formosa), however, that the greatest improvements can be seen. There production of rice has risen well above the prewar level due to the land reform movement that gave the farmer the incentive to work his own land. New crops have also been introduced – oranges, apples, pears, tea, soybeans, pineapples, mushrooms, and asparagus. As a result Taiwan is now a major exporter of tinned mushrooms and pineapple.

In India rice occupies a greater area than any other crop, but the yields are low and farming methods less efficient than elsewhere. There is no crop rotation and every year a lot of land is left fallow, often serving as rough pasture for cattle, sheep, and goats. The land has been fragmented so that the peasant farmer has rarely enough ground on which to grow his own food. He is perpetually in debt to the village moneylender-cum-shopkeeper and even in years of good harvests his little profit is mortgaged. In India, too, there is the problem of overstocking and it is estimated that the number of cattle could easily be reduced by 30 percent. But the cow is a sacred animal to the Hindu and used only for draft or for its dairy products.

Europeans brought plantation agriculture to south and east Asia. They cleared large areas of forest, especially in Sri Lanka (Ceylon), Malaysia, and Indonesia, and planted crops such as tea, rubber, and coconut palm. The main object of plantation farming is to produce a crop for export and therefore it must be organized efficiently. The ground is prepared, fertilized, and the crop grown and harvested under strict supervision. Transport facilities must also be developed so that the yield can be delivered to a port as quickly as possible. The Europeans – and in the Philippines the Americans – financed and directed the plantations using the abundant local labor. Some of the most important areas of plantation agriculture are the former British and Dutch territories: for example, the rubber and tea of Sri Lanka, the tea of Assam in India, the rubber and palm oil of the Malay peninsula and the rubber, coffee, sugar, tea, tobacco and spices of Indonesia.

Both India and China grow a lot of wheat. Even though China grows nearly as much wheat as the USA, like India, it still has to import supplies from North America and Australia. Cotton and jute are both important cash crops in this region. Cotton is a cheap fabric for making the light clothing needed in a warm, humid climate and China, India, and Pakistan are all major producers.

Over a great part of the south and east Asia regions religious beliefs prohibit the eating of meat. Hindus will not slaughter the cow, Moslems will not touch anything from the pig, and strict Buddhists will eat neither meat nor fish. Most religions permit the eating of poultry and it is this which furnishes much of the meat in the people's diet. Japan's "meat" is fish. The average Japanese eats about 16 times as much fish as the average American. Japanese fleets fish in nearly all parts of the Pacific Ocean, their whaling boats go

Below: Malaysian farmers drying peppers. The Chinese introduced intensive, small-scale agriculture to the peninsular and were the first to cultivate the pineapples, manioc, gambier, and pepper now grown there. Chinese influence can be seen in the conical hats worn here.

egularly to the Antarctic and their tuna longline fleet has expanded so rapidly since World War II that ts boats are said to be found everywhere where there are tuna. China has a large fishing industry, the second or third largest in the world. Recently, the country has developed deep-sea fisheries using modern techniques, but traditional fishing is in the shallow, coastal waters, the rivers, lakes, and paddy fields. In fact it is the latter kind of fishing that prevails throughout Southeast Asia and does much to augment the diet of the vast population and supply the majority of their protein.

Above and below right: fish is Southeast Asia's main source of protein. The fishing boats near Cochin on the Malabar coast of southwest India belong to one of the many fishing communities along India's coasts.
Below: this Javanese, like many of his countrymen, raises fish in the waters of the paddy fields away from the coast.

Below left: tea harvesting in Sri Lanka. Grown in countries that are both hot and wet, tea plants grow quickly and once mature – after about three years – the new shoots that appear every seven or eight days are ready for picking. When dried, these shoots become the so-called tea "leaves."

Mining and Industry

The mineral wealth of south Asia and the Far East cannot yet be fully assessed because the majority of the countries have not carried out complete geological surveys. At present Iran and Indonesia seem to be the only two countries with vast reserves of oil; China, India, and Japan the only countries that have sufficient coal and iron to develop heavy industry; and Malaysia, Indonesia, and Thailand the countries with rich enough reserves of tin to produce a lucrative trade.

The oil-rich countries of the Third World have an enormous advantage and in south Asia Iran's wealth from petroleum has both stimulated the economic growth of the country and provided for many of the social needs. In Indonesia, the largest oil producer in

Below: a production-line operator in a textile mill in China. As in the Soviet Union and other Communist countries, the state controls the means of production.

Southeast Asia, there has been a recent expansion i[n] production in east Sumatra and further exploitatio[n] is taking place offshore, near the islands of Bangk[a] Belitung (Billitong), and Madura. Considerable ex[-] ploration is also taking place off the coasts o[f] Borneo, Djawa (Java) and western New Guinea. B[y] 1976, Indonesia, China, and Iran together supplie[d] about 15 percent of the total world production. Th[e] remaining fields in Afghanistan, Burma, Japan, an[d] Pakistan together produced only as much as Indonesi[a] alone – not nearly enough for even their local need[s].

South Asia and the Far East have considerable re[-] serves of coal, however, mined in Pakistan, Indi[a] Vietnam, Malaysia, the Philippines, Taiwan, Chin[a] North Korea, South Korea, and Japan. In China th[e] government has realized the importance of a planne[d] industrial development, so with cheap labor availabl[e] and vast coal reserves – which are mainly in the hill[y] areas bordering the Great Plain – there has been [a] steep rise in coal production. Although a very recen[t] development, the annual output is already more tha[n] half that of the USA, and China has become the thir[d] largest producer in the world.

Japan's coal production has also increased rapidly[.] But this increase has been made in order to raise th[e] level of the heavy industries that have undergone [a] massive expansion since 1950. India's richest coal fields are on the northeastern edge of the Deccan in the Damodar valley, less than 200 miles northwes[t] of Calcutta. Here the mines have thick seams and therefore, can be worked easily to provide over 8[0] percent of India's total production of coal.

A great deal of this region is mountainous an[d] potential hydroelectric power is tremendous. In Indi[a] where in the past heavy industry has been dependen[t] on coal, important hydroelectric developments hav[e] taken place in the Western Ghats, to supply power t[o] the industries of Bombay and to the towns in the sout[h] such as Coimbatore, Salem, and Madura. Pakistan ha[s] also made considerable progress and has carried ou[t] several schemes in the Indus valley. But both Indi[a] and Pakistan's hydroelectric potential lies in th[e] great arc of mountains that run from the Sulaiman t[o] the Himalaya. In the latter, India has already com[-] pleted a joint project with Bhutan.

In Japan there are nearly 2000 installations tha[t] supply at least half of the country's electricity need[s.] In China there are a number of giant schemes: i[n] Manchuria, the upper Hwang Ho near Kaolan, th[e] lower Hwang Ho near Lo-yang, the eastern ranges o[f] the Wuyi Shan, and around Kun-ming in the south[-] west. In Indonesia, although again most of the hydro[-] electric potential is untapped, a large multipurpos[e] scheme has been completed south of Djakarta t[o] supply both power and irrigation. Elsewhere, th[e] Thai government has initiated projects; Laos ha[s] completed schemes on the Mekong and its tributar[y] the Ngum; and in North Korea there are several ne[w] installations on the Yalu river. Many of these scheme[s] throughout south and east Asia are multipurpos[e] providing flood control and irrigation as well as power.

China is tremendously rich in minerals. There is abundant iron ore in the hillsides around the Great Plain, the Shantung Peninsula, and the ranges of the Nan Ling and Wuyi Shan. The deposits in the south, near Wu-han, are the richest in the world. China is the world's chief producer of both tungsten and antimony, and has rich reserves of tin in Yunnan in the southwest as well as bauxite, copper, lead, manganese, mercury, silver, and zinc, spread throughout eastern China. Almost half the world's supply of tin comes from Southeast Asia, from Malaysia, Thailand, and Indonesia, where it is found in Bangka, Belitung (Billitong), and the nearby islands. In the Malay Peninsula tin has been mined for centuries, chiefly by imported labor from India and China.

Above: part of Tokyo's space-saving high-level Expressway No. 4, an urban freeway of reinforced concrete on steel pillars.

Above: a scene in a Japanese shipyard. Japan is Asia's most highly industrialized country. Electrical and electronic equipment and other similar types of light industry are being developed.

Below: the Durgapur steel works, one of several situated in an arc around Calcutta. This area of India also has substantial coal deposits – providing over 80 percent of India's needs.

Japan is the only country in the region with what might be called a balanced industrial development. Over 50 percent of the Japanese now live in urban areas and about 60 percent work in nonagricultural jobs, compared with only 30 percent in India and about the same proportion in China. But Japan relies largely on imported raw materials and depends a great deal on the export of manufactured goods, especially to the USA and Europe. For many years Japan led Asia in the production of cheap consumer goods. But now Hong Kong, China, and South Korea are providing strong competition and producing many manufactured goods including textiles, clothes, and shoes.

Overleaf: Kuningan Festival Dancers in Bali. This Indonesian island is one of the smallest in the East Indies and also one of the most beautiful. The great island world of the East Indies contains many peoples and races.

People and Politics

Nearly half of mankind lives in the monsoon lands of Asia, in communities that hug the fertile alluvial land along the coasts and the river valleys. Separated by mountains, plateaus, and deserts, the people in these communities have developed different languages and cultures. From the main language families have come hundred of separate languages and dialects. For example, the 600 million people in India speak 16 major languages. The people of China, Malaysia, Pakistan, the Philippines, and Sri Lanka also have no common tongue. There are several ethnic groups in Asia and many people are a mixture of races – Aetas, Ainu, Bengalis, Burmese, Japanese, Koreans, Malays, Tamils, and Uighurs are only some of the many different groups. Another barrier to national unity in India is the caste system. Although caste discrimination was made illegal in the 1950s, it still prevails among the majority of the population.

Above: a Hindu wedding ceremony. Marriage in India is still largely determined by caste. Endogamy – marriage within the same caste – is the general practice.

In spite of the many racial and language differences within a country, there may be certain common religious beliefs and customs – as in India, where roughly three quarters of the people are Hindus. Racial groups of different nations are linked by common religious beliefs too. Buddhism began in India 2500 years ago. Today people follow this faith in Burma, Cambodia, China, Japan, Laos, Sri Lanka, Tibet, Thailand, and Vietnam. Islam spread into the Far East from Arabia

and now links people in Afghanistan, Iran, India, Indonesia, Malaysia, Pakistan, and the Philippines in particular those living on the island of Mindanao. The Philippines is the only Christian country of the Far East, and, with Japan, the most westernized.

The biggest problem in both Communist and non Communist South and East Asia is rapid population increase, due as much to a falling death rate as an increased birth rate. The area's population goes up by over 80,000 every day. So each year there are millions more to feed and many more to go hungry. India and Japan have birth control programs; in Indonesia priority is given to family planning programs; in Thailand, in the early 1970s, the government recognized the problem and began to make provision in the budget for education and counseling in family planning; and the Chinese government has also taken steps to curb population increase.

Illiteracy is another problem in the region. Japan is the only wholly literate nation. Education has been free and compulsory for those aged between six and 15 years old for over 100 years. But in India at least half the men and over 80 percent of the women cannot read or write. New school and education centers are being built, but the question remains: will building programs ever keep up with population growth?

Asians have a low standard of living compared with Europeans and North Americans. Most of the rural population are subsistence farmers, growing just enough to feed their own families. Farmers use primitive tools and struggle to make a living, hampered by crop diseases and natural disasters such as typhoons and failure of the rains. Scientists have been able to check some widespread diseases that affect man, animals, and crops. Governments are also trying to relieve hardship by importing food supplies and distributing them to famine-stricken areas. But diets still consist mostly of cereal grains such as wheat and rice and people eat little meat or fish, partly because of religious taboos and partly because meat protein is not readily available.

One in three Asians lives in a town or city. There are many cities with populations of more than a million more than 40 million people live in the six cities of Calcutta, Djakarta, Pei-p'ing (Peking), Seoul, Shanghai, and Tokyo. The majority of the large cities are ports, either lying directly on the coast or stretching inland along the river banks. Some cities, such as Manila and Tokyo, have modern development areas; Singapore's public housing program is considered the best in Asia; but Djakarta has little prospect of being able to provide adequate utilities, such as sewage, water, and electricity for its 5 million inhabitants in the foreseeable future.

Japan is the only country in the Far East with a really high standard of living. In the 19th century it adopted Western industrial methods and in less than 100 years had managed to bridge the huge gulf between the feudalism of old Japan and the way of life in the Western world. The change has been spectacular and apid. Japan is now a leader in iron and steel, ship-building, electronics, and other consumer industries. Japanese railroads have crack express trains that any country might envy. Three out of every 100 Japanese has his own car – a higher percentage than in any other Asian country. A network of express highways has been constructed and the main islands are linked by double-decker, undersea highway tunnels. Taiwan is another success story. Due to land reform programs, over 70 percent of the farms are owner-occupied and with a growth rate second only to Japan's, the island has become prosperous since World War II when the Nationalists were driven there from the mainland.

Change in the traditional ways of life in other countries is accompanying agricultural and industrial revolutions. The Chinese call this simultaneous development "advancing on two feet," and developments in their country have been the most far-reaching. For centuries China was backward agriculturally, and hunger and disease were rampant. Now the government is carrying out reforms, the family unit is weakening. The government organizes "communes" where between 20,000 and 70,000 people live. A typical commune, usually including several small villages and a few towns, is an administrative unit that integrates farming with all the affairs of the community. It also pays particular attention to reforestation, water conservation, and road building. Everything is shared: houses, nurseries, dining rooms, laundries.

Above: the Kowloon district of Hong Kong. In spite of extensive building programs, between 10 and 15 percent of the people still live in overcrowded slum conditions.

The commune provides schools, clinics, technical training centers, and homes for old people. The Chinese women also go out to work, in the factories and the fields. Many of them no longer do their own housework: the commune provides cleaners from the personnel service department.

As in China, the majority of India's population depends on agriculture, 80 percent of the people live in more than half a million villages. The government

Below: Shinto priests at Kyoto, the ancient capital of Japan and site of many temples and shrines. Although Shinto (the Way of the Gods) ceased to be the state religion of Japan in 1946, it still has nearly 80 million followers.

is experimenting in community cooperation to try and raise the living standards in rural areas.

Other parts of South and East Asia are also developing agriculture and educating their people. For example, in the Philippines a joint economic assistance program with the USA is helping thousands of farmers, especially in the development and cultivation of new varieties of rice.

But the vast size and population of the region makes the bitter struggle for a better way of life a matter of particular concern to countries all over the world. Asia's foreign exchange reserves are much lower and its trade deficit three times higher than 25 years ago.

In these circumstances it is not surprising that countries once ruled by European nations maintain close relationships with Europe. India, Malaysia, Singapore, and Sri Lanka (Ceylon) are members of the Commonwealth. All the non-Communist Asian countries have joined Australia, Britain, Canada, New Zealand, and the United States in the Colombo Plan, which is a scheme to encourage individual countries to work out their own economic plans by giving them capital, technical training, and equipment. Japan has also joined the Colombo Plan as a donor nation. The largest schemes are major engineering works such as the construction of dams and power stations. The USA has its own plan – the Point Four Program – to help the development of non-Communist countries and the WHO is helping many countries to combat disease, another major problem aggravated by malnutrition.

The Countries of Southern Asia

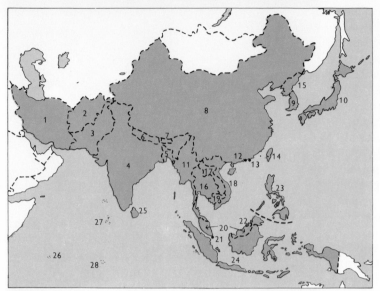

1 Iran	17 Laos
2 Afghanistan	18 Vietnam
3 Pakistan	19 Cambodia
4 India	20 Malaysia
5 Bangladesh	21 Singapore
6 Nepal	22 Brunei
7 Bhutan	23 Philippines
8 China	24 Indonesia
9 South Korea	25 Sri Lanka
10 Japan	26 Seychelles
11 Burma	27 Maldive Islands
12 Macao	28 Chagos Archipelago
13 Hong Kong	
14 Taiwan	
15 North Korea	
16 Thailand	

IRAN (Persia)

Area: 636,293 square miles
Population: 32,000,000
Capital: Teheran (Tehrán)
Language: Persian
Religion: Islam (Shia branch)
Monetary Unit: Rial

History and Government: The country, centered around the Plateau of Iran was the home of the ancient civilizations of Elam, Media, and Persia. It fell to Mongols in the 13th century, and Afghanistan in 1722. Territorial conflicts developed with Russia in the 18th and 19th centuries. The name Iran was officially adopted in 1935. It was a constitutional monarchy until 1979 when the Shah's regime was overthrown and an Islamic Republic declared. Formerly there was a National Assembly (*Majlis*) of 200 and a Senate of 60 members, 30 nominated, 30 elected. The head of state had the right to dissolve either or both houses and was obliged to sign all other legislation. In 1963 a six-point "White Revolution" was instituted to carry out land reform, nationalization of all forest land, sale of government holdings in industry, distribution of factory profits to workers, votes for women, and the creation of a literacy corps. The oil industry was nationalized in 1973. Like all countries in the throes of change there is unrest within the country where there is still considerable poverty among the masses.

Economy: The greatest source of wealth is oil. General development is concentrated in the industrial sector, in particular on the creation of a large petrochemical industry. A large part of the population still lives by agriculture. The principal crops are cereals, and industrial crops such as cotton, sesame, ricinus (castor oil plant), soya, tobacco, dates, and grapes. There is a considerable amount of stock-rearing, particularly sheep, which produce the wool on which the famous carpet industry is based.

AFGHANISTAN

Area: 250,953 square miles
Population: 18,796,000
Capital: Kabul
Language: Pashto and Persian
Religion: Islam (mainly Sunni sect)
Monetary Unit: Afghani

History and Government: Once forming part of the empires of Persia and Alexander, and later the Indian Mongol empire, Afghanistan became an independent country under Ahmad Shah Durrani in the 1700s. He extended the borders to found an empire that included parts of Persia and India. A new line of rulers was established under Nadir Shah in 1919. In 1973 a coup d'état ended the monarchy and proclaimed a republic of the presidential type. The country was ruled by presidential decree until a new constitution was introduced in 1977. On account of its strategic importance and its policy of nonalignment, Afghanistan receives aid from many countries.

Economy: The country is very poor with few industries, most of which are connected with agriculture. There are mainly two crops a year, one of wheat, barley, or lentils, the other of rice, millet and corn. Sheep, including the Kara Kuli, which has a particularly fine fleece, are bred; mineral resources including salt, silver, rubies, lapislazuli, gold, chrome, and talc are waiting to be more fully exploited.

PAKISTAN

Area: 310,401 square miles
Population: 73,000,000
Capital: Islamabad
Language: Urdu and English
Religion: Islam
Monetary Unit: Rupee

History and Government: Pakistan was constituted as a Dominion in 1947 from lands that were formerly part of the British-ruled Indian empire. In 1956 it was proclaimed a republic and in 1972 withdrew from the Commonwealth. The new Constitution of 1973 names the president of the republic as constitutional head and the prime Minister as chief executive. Parliament is composed of National Assembly and Senate. The People's Party is the dominant political force. In December 1971, after a bloody conflict, the eastern province won independence under the name of Bangladesh.

Economy: Pakistan has one of the longest irrigation systems in the world – some 33 million acres. A large part of the population lives by agriculture, the main products of which are wheat, corn, millet, rice, cotton, sesame, tobacco, sugar cane and fodder crops. Stock-rearing is well developed, especially cattle, buffaloes, sheep, and goats. Chromite, coal, and lignite are the chief mineral resources and there are large deposits of rock salt. Manufacturing industries are few, the most advanced being textiles and chemicals.

INDIA (Bharat)
Area: 1,269,338 square miles
Population: 586, 000,000
Capital: New Delhi
Language: Hindi, local languages
Religion: Hinduism and Islam
Monetary Unit: Rupee
History and Government: Formerly part of the British-ruled Indian empire the Indian Union has a long history of civilization and culture brought about by the conquest by or of the surrounding nations, and the assimilation of many peoples in this important geographical area. Since 1950 India has been a republic and a member of the Commonwealth. It is a union composed of 21 states and nine union territories. Each state is administered by a governor, appointed by the president for a five-year term, and each union territory is administered by the president through the appointed administrator. The head of the union, the president, holds office for five years and is eligible for reelection. The central parliament consists of the president, the Council of States and the House of the People. The Council of States does not have more than 250 members and is a permanent body, but one third of the members retire every second year. The House of the People consists of not more than 500 members and serves for five years. In 1971 India supported the secession of Bangladesh from Pakistan.
Economy: The greater part of the working population is engaged in agriculture. The principal crops are rice, wheat, peanuts, and potatoes; there are banana, cotton, tea, and sugar plantations, and silk-worm rearing. Mineral resources are rich – iron ore, manganese, copper, and bauxite – but sources of energy are inadequate and underdeveloped. Engineering and ship-building industries therefore expand slowly and the iron and steel industry is barely adequate. Only the chemical industry has expanded. The most important industry is textiles, using local cotton, and this is expanding.

BANGLADESH
Area: 55,597 square miles
Population: 71,500,000
Capital: Dacca
Language: Bengali
Religion: Islam
Monetary Unit: Taka
History and Government: A republic and a member of the Commonwealth, Bangladesh was formed in December 1971 by separation from Pakistan, of which it was formerly the Eastern Province. The head of state is the president elected by parliament for five years. The president chooses the prime minister. Political life is dominated by the Awami League. The country has been run under martial law since 1975 by a non-political administration.
Economy: Agricultural production is insufficient for the home market and

Below: a field-evaluation officer drives a tractor past the traditional team of plodding oxen it is designed to replace.

massive imports of rice and grain are, therefore, necessary. The principal crops, apart from rice, are jute (Bangladesh is the principal producer of raw jute in the world), cotton, sugar cane, and tea. Cattle-rearing is widespread. The principal industries are jute, cotton, tea, leather, sugar, and paper. Banks, insurance companies, jute, and tea plantations, and the textile industry have all been nationalized.

NEPAL
Area: 54,316 square miles
Population: 13,000,000
Capital: Katmandu
Language: Nepalese
Religion: Hindiusm and Buddhism
Monetary Unit: Rupee
History and Government: The Nepalese peoples represent many races of mixed Mongol origin, the most important of which are the Ghurka people of Hindu origin. Buddha was born in Nepal in 568 BC. Sandwiched between China and India, Nepal occupies a position of strategic importance. In

1953 the king ended direct rule and restored cabinet government. Political parties are not permitted. In 1963 representative bodies were instituted at all levels, from village councils to the National Assembly. Some of these members are elected, some nominated by the king.

Economy: The great majority of the population lives by agriculture and stock-rearing (cattle, sheep, and goats). The chief crops are rice, cereals, potatoes, tobacco, jute, sugar cane. A good quantity of timber is produced; herbs and essences are an excellent source of foreign currency. Industry is of the cottage type, but with Chinese, USA, and USSR aid, investments are being made in jute and sugar mills, leather and chemical works as well as hydroelectric power plants.

BHUTAN (Druk-vul)
Area: 18,146 square miles
Population: 1,000,000
Capital: Thimphu
Language: Dzongkha (a Tibetan-

Below: Buckets attached to this waterwheel raise the water into a flume, or channel, for field-wide distribution by gravity.

Burmese language)
Religion: Mahayana Buddhism
Monetary Unit: Indian currency
History and Government: Bhutanese people are a branch of the Tibetan Mongols. It is an absolute monarchy, a satellite of India which, by treaty, undertakes its defense and guides its government.

Economy: The economy is primitive, based on agriculture, stock-rearing (fur-bearing animals are important), and small industry such as metal working, weaving, and crafts. Chief products are rice, millet, cereals, cardomons, oranges, apples, timber, and yaks. Attempts are being made, through five-year plans financed by India, to exploit forest and mineral wealth more fully.

CHINA (People's Republic of China)
Area: 3,601,386 square miles
Population: 827,000,000
Capital: Peking (Pei-p'ing)
Language: Chinese (Many varieties spoken, one official language, *Putonghua*, or Mandarin)
Religion: Confucianism, Buddhism, Taoism, Islam
Monetary Unit: Renminbi or Yuan

History and Government: Civilization spread throughout China probabl from the Hwang Ho valley, where it ca be traced to as early as 3000 BC. Fro warring tribes, the country graduall became united under the Chi'n dynasty Domination of central Asia lasted unti the end of the Han dynasty around A 220, when the empire was subjected t invasions and migrations. Other rise and falls in China's fortunes followed Opened to western influence in 16t century, it was involved in a series struggles with European powers. Th last of the ruling houses was over thrown in 1912, and their successor the Nationalists were driven out b Communists in 1950. The main politica body and sole legislative authority i the National People's Congress whic is elected for a four-year term. It i composed of deputies elected by pro vinces, autonomous regions, munici palities, the armed forces, and Chines living abroad. It must have at least on session a year. The state council is th executive organ of the Congress, elect the president of the republic and th government, decides on the nationa budget, and on economic planning. I the congresses and public organiza tions, political control is exerted by th Communist Party. The constitutiona order has undergone a series of modifi cations since 1970 as a result of th "cultural revolution," the movemen which, beginning with criticism of th

Above: a steel plant at Anshan (Liaoning province), China's largest steel center. China is the world's sixth largest iron and steel producer.

authorities in power in the cultural sphere, gave the mass of the people control of every sector of activity – political, administrative, and productive.

Economy: Besides cereals, (wheat, barley, corn, millet, rice), legumes, potatoes, peanuts, tobacco, soybeans, sugar, and fruit trees are produced. The production of cotton, tea, hemp, jute, and flax, and silkworm breeding are also important. Livestock, especially pigs, are raised in large numbers. There are deposits of all the main mineral resources such as coal, iron ore, oil, tin, and tungsten. The expansion of industry in iron and steel, chemicals, and engineering has shown a rate of growth even greater than that of the developed countries.

SOUTH KOREA (Korea)
Area: 38,130 square miles
Population: 35,000
Capital: Sŏul (Seoul)
Language: Korean
Religion: Buddhism and Confucianism
Monetary Unit: Won
History and Government: South Korea was settled by tribes closely related to the Yamato tribes of Japan and there appears to have been little contact with the northern kingdom until the 11th century when the peninsula was united as the State of Koryu. Its subsequent history was the same as that of Northern Korea until 1948 when

the south formed its own non-Communist government in that part of the Korean peninsula south of the 38th parallel of latitude. In 1950 the North Koreans crossed the 38th parallel and for two years waged war against the South, who were supported by the UN. Since 1972 South Korea has been negotiating with the North with a view to reunification. A constitutional reform in 1972 limited the number of members of the republic's National Assembly to 250 and stated the president could only be elected for a maximum of three consecutive terms.

Economy: Agriculture employs more than half the working population. The main products are rice, cereals, beans, cotton, and tobacco, and silkworm culture, fishing and timber are important. The mineral resources are coal, iron, graphite, tungsten, gold, silver, but of these only tungsten is found in large quantities. Since 1966 there has been a rapid industrialization of the country.

JAPAN (Nihon koku)
Area: 143,817 square miles
Population: 110,000,000
Capital: Tokyo
Language: Japanese
Religion: Shintoism and Buddhism
Monetary Unit: Yen
History and Government: According to tradition the first emperor ascended the throne of Japan in 660 BC. Written history began in 5th century AD with the adoption of Chinese writing and culture. After a long period of rule by military dictators (1192–1867) the emperors resumed direct rule and adopted Western ideas and civilization. A new

constitution was adopted in 1946 after their defeat in World War II, which invests the emperor with purely representative functions. He is the symbol of state and the unity of the people. The supreme power rests with the Diet, which consists of a House of Representatives (480 members) and a House of Councillors (250 members). Executive power is vested in the Cabinet, which is responsible to the Diet. Japan, closely bound up with American politics, has suffered and overcome the repercussions of different world crises to emerge as one of the major economic powers in the world.

Economy: With an agriculture insufficient to cover its needs and a very small native supply of minerals and energy (except coal and copper), Japan has had to establish a complex foreign trade based on enormous industrial expansion. The most productive sectors are light engineering, electrical engineering, electronic machinery, cameras, textiles, and shipbuilding. Forestry and fishing are especially well developed; tourism is encouraged. Postwar land reform, combined with improved yields from new strains, has resulted in a rice surplus. Other important agricultural products are barley, wheat, soybeans, and many fruits, including mandarin, persimmon, loquat, and peach.

BURMA (Myanma-Nainggan)
Area: 265,263 square miles
Population: 31,000,000
Capital: Rangoon
Language: Burmese
Religion: Buddhism
Monetary Unit: Kyat
History and Government: Settled in 3rd century AD by Hindus, who converted the Mongolian peoples to Buddhism, Burma was first united in the 11th century. The modern Burmese state had its beginnings in the 18th century, when the ruler Alompra and his descendents extended the kingdom until it came into conflict with British interest in India. Eventually it became a province of India under the British. It was granted independence in 1948 and remained a parliamentary democracy until 1962 when power was siezed by a military dictatorship. In 1974 the military rule ended and Burma became a one party socialist republic. The elections to the People's Assembly took place and Une Win became president. Under the new Constitution some scope was once more given to private enterprise and, especially, to foreign capital.
Economy: The majority of the popula-

tion lives by agriculture, especially rice-growing, oil-seeds, corn, millet, cotton, beans, and wheat. Fishing is carried on and forestry is important, in particular teak, rubber, and bamboo. But the greatest efforts to overcome the economic crisis are concentrated on the exploitation of the rich mineral resources – zinc, copper, lead, silver, tin, tungsten, iron, and, particularly, oil. The major oil companies of the world have taken great interest in the oil exploitation.

MACAO (Macau)
Area: 6 square miles
Population: 268,000
Language: Portuguese and Chinese
Monetary Unit: Pataca
History and Government: Macao comprises a peninsula at the mouth of the Hsi-chiang (Sikiang) in south China and two small islands. It has been a Portuguese colony since 1557, and is the oldest European trading outpost in the far East. The population is largely Chinese. After the coup d'état in Portugal in 1974 the question of a return of the colony to China was not forced by the Pei-p'ing authorities (who have a vast influence in Macao).
Economy: The main sources of income are casinos, tourism, and trade in tea, tobacco, oranges, wine, and laquer with China, and textile, and electronic industries.

HONG KONG
Area: 407 square miles
Population: 4,500,000
Capital: Victoria
Monetary Unit: Hong Kong Dollar
History and Government: Hong Kong is a Crown Colony, ceded from China by the Treaty of Nanking in 1842. Administration is in the hands of a governor who presides over a Legislative Council. The colony consists of the island of Hong Kong and the peninsula of Kowloon, the adjacent mainland, and several small islands.
Economy: The population, almost entirely Chinese, lives by trade and industry – only five percent are in agriculture. Main industries are textiles, clothing, foodstuffs, chemicals, and printing. Very heavy trade passes through the free port of Hong Kong, especially for the warehousing and reexport of merchandise from other countries. There is also a considerable tourist trade.

TAIWAN (Formosa)
Area: 13,892 square miles
Population: 16,000,000
Capital: Taipei (T'ai-pei)
Language: Chinese
Religion: Buddhism and Confucianism
Monetary Unit: New Taiwan Dollar
History and Government: Taiwan was ceded by China to Japan in 1895. After World War II it surrendered to General Chiang Kai-Shek in 1945. It is a republic of the presidential type, controlled by the remnants of the Nationalist Government. Taiwan is bound by a treaty of 1954 to the USA, which guarantees its territorial integrity. The Constitution gives extraordinary powers to the president of the republic for the duration of the "civil war" with China.
Economy: American aid has made possible the industrial development of the island. In this way engineering, chemical, textile, and food-manufacturing industries have emerged, largely producing goods for export. There are supplies of oil, methane, and coal. Agriculture, however, is still the main activity of the population. The principal crops are rice, sugar cane, sweet potatoes, soybeans, tobacco, spices, tropical and citrus fruits, peanuts, tea, and coffee.

NORTH KOREA (Chosen Minchu-chui Inmim Konghwa-guk)
Area: 46,539 square miles
Population: 15,000,000
Capital: Pyong Yang
Language: Korean
Religion: Buddhism, Confucianism, and others
Monetary Unit: Won
History and Government: North Korea was the area of the kingdom of Chosen probably as early as the 12th century BC. It was strongly influenced by the Chinese and at times a vassal state of various Chinese emperors. It was united with the rest of the peninsula in the 11th century and was a dependency of Japan from 1910–1945. The People's Democratic Republic was born in 1948 by the efforts of the Korean Workers' Party led by Marshal Kim Il Sung. There is a Supreme People's Assembly elected every four years by universal suffrage, but in practice the country is ruled by the Korean People's Party (the Communist Party), which elects a central committee. The polit-

buro is appointed from this committee. The fierce rivalry with the Seoul government, which exploded into war in 1950–53, did not die down until 1972.
Economy: The North Korean economy is among the most advanced in the Far East. Industrial development is favored by hydroelectric power and the most flourishing industries are iron and steel, heavy engineering, and electrical engineering. But textiles, chemicals, cement, glass, and paper industries are also well developed. Recent plans advocate investments in light industry. Among the mineral resources coal, lignite, iron ore, lead, copper, tungsten, nickel, and graphite are important. The main agricultural products are rice, corn, soybeans, cotton, flax, hemp, tobacco, and ginseng (for use in pharmacy). Animal husbandry, especially cattle and pigs, and fishing are well developed; forests are rich, but at present scarcely exploited.

THAILAND (Muang-Thai)
Area: 198,455 square miles
Population: 42,000,000
Capital: Bangkok (Krung Thap)
Language: Thai
Religion: Mainly Buddhism
Monetary Unit: Baht
History and Government: The Thai people first formed an independent state in 1350. The state was at war several times in the following centuries with Burma and other Asiatic and European countries. It became a constitutional monarchy in 1932, and changed its name between 1939 and 1945 and after 1948 from Siam to Thailand. After student unrest in the capital in 1976 the elected government was replaced by a National Administrative Reform Council composed of senior officers of the three armed services and the police. Later the same year a new cabinet was appointed with the Reform Council in an advisory role to the prime minister.
Economy: Around 76 percent of the labor force is employed in agriculture. The most lucrative crops are rice, coconut palm, peanuts, jute, soybeans, sesame, sugar cane, and cassava. About 60 percent of the land is under forest and the main products are teak and other precious woods, rubber, and resins. Most of these are controlled by British companies. The mineral sector, on the other hand, is mainly controlled by American companies. Thailand is among the biggest producers of tin, manganese, iron ore, lead, tungsten, antimony, and precious stones. Industry is undeveloped, apart from textiles and those connected with agriculture.

LAOS

Area: 91,428 square miles
Population: 3,000,000
Capital: Vientiane
Language: Lao
Religion: Buddhism
Monetary Unit: Kip

History and Government: The kingdom of Laos was founded in the 14th century, but in 1827 accepted suzerainty of Siam. In 1893 it became a French protectorate and in 1949, after World War II, an independent state within the French Union. In 1954 it achieved full independence and became a constitutional monarchy. In conjunction with the Vietnam war on its borders and the increase of North Vietnamese activity in Laos, communist forces gradually occupied most of the strategic areas of Laos. After the conclusion of the Vietnamese war in 1975, Communist Pathet Lao forces took over the country and, following the abdication of the king, established a People's Democratic Republic in December 1975.

Economy: About 78 percent of the working population is engaged in agriculture, although the main product, rice, is not enough even for the home market. Corn, tobacco, cotton, citrus fruits, and tea are also grown. Fishing is important, as are the forests, which cover 63 percent of the territory and provide precious woods such as teak. Tin mining, though not extensive, represents the greater part of the exports. Rich deposits of iron ore have been located recently but, as yet, are not worked.

VIETNAM

Area: 129,000 square miles
Population: 43,700,000
Capital: Hanoi
Language: Annamite
Religion: Buddhism and Taoism
Monetary Unit: Dông

History and Government: Vietnam occupies an area that was partly the early kingdom of Champa, which was formed in the 2nd century AD and existed, though their territory was gradually taken over by the Annamese, until 1822. It became part of French Indochina in the late 1800s. In 1949 the French granted independence to Vietnam (the union of Tonking, Annam, and Cochin-China) under the Emperor Bao Dai, but the northern states aided by Communist China set up their own government. Vietnam remained divided along the 17th parallel for 20 years, but the South finally fell in 1975 after a long fierce war. In 1976 a National Assembly representing the whole of Vietnam was elected, meeting in Hanoi to approve the reunification of the country under the name of the Socialist Republic of Vietnam. The capital, flag, and anthem of North Vietnam were adopted for the whole country and the South Vietnamese capital of Saigon was renamed Ho Chi Minh City.

Economy: At present the majority of the population is employed in agriculture. The chief products are rice, rubber, corn, and tobacco. However, there are rich deposits of anthracite, phosphates, salt, iron ore, zinc, tin, and oil offshore. The industries in the North are textiles, foodstuffs, cement, and chemicals and in the South the traditional manufacture of silk and paper and other light industries.

CAMBODIA (Kampuchea)

Area: 69,897 square miles
Population: 7,900,000
Capital: Phnom Penh
Language: Khmer
Religion: Buddhism
Monetary Unit: Riel

History and Government: The former powerful kingdom and empire of the Khmers, which flourished between the 10th and 14th centuries, it became, as Cambodia, a French protectorate in 1863. In 1954 it was declared independent. In 1970 Prince Sihanouk was deposed as head of state by a vote of the National Assembly and the country became the Khmer Republic. Civil war broke out between government forces supported by America, and Cambodian Khmer Rouge Communists supported by the North Vietnamese. In 1975 the Khmer Rouge captured the capital, and Prince Sihanouk returned to resume his role as head of state. He resigned in 1976 and the head of the Khmer Rouge was elected president of the state presidium. By 1979 the Khmer Rouge had themselves been ousted by an invasion of Vietnamese, Soviet-backed forces.

Economy: Some development of industry had taken place before 1970 but the economy is largely based on agriculture, forestry, and fishing. Two-thirds of the people are employed on the land, the great bulk of these being rice-growing farmers. The industries are fish-canning, sawmills, paper mills, sugar refining, and cotton mills. Rubber is widely exported. There is little mining and little power available, but a scheme – the Mekong Development Project – is underway to use the waters of the Mekong.

MALAYSIA

Area: 130,000 square miles
Population: 11,700,000
Capital: Kuala Lumpur
Language: Malay
Religion: Islam
Monetary Unit: Malaysian Dollar

History and Government: First occupied around 5000 BC by Austro-Melanesoid peoples, then by Indonesians and later mixtures of Chinese, Indian, and some Thais the Malayan Peninsula quickly came under the influence of Indian civilization. From the 12th century onward Buddhism, Hinduism, and the Sanskrit script gave way to Islam and Perso-Arabic Script. British influence on the Peninsula began in 1786 when the island of Penang was rented from the sultan of Kedah. The Federation of Malaya took its present name in 1963 when it was joined by the former British colonies of Sarawak and North Borneo (now Sabah) and the state of Singapore – the latter seceded from the Federation two years later. The Constitution was designed to give a strong federal government and also a large measure of autonomy for the separate state governments. The nine rulers of the Malay states elect one of their number to be supreme head of state. He holds office for five years. The federal parliament consists of two houses, the Senate (*Dewan Negera*) of 58 members, and a House of Representatives (*Dewan Ra'ayat*) of 154 members. The House of Representatives is presided over by a speaker. Though populated chiefly by Malays, the country also has a large Chinese minority as well as other racial minorities including aborigines.

Economy: The main resource is rubber, of which Malaysia is the chief producer in the world, but palm oil, pineapples, bananas, rice, and tropical hardwoods are also important. Malaysia also leads the world for tin ore, the mining of which is largely controlled by foreign capital. There are good deposits of bauxite, iron ore, and oil, the latter in Sarawak. In the manufacturing industries, the foundries produce about half the quantity of tin in the world. The processing of agricultural products is developing and so are chemical, textile, and engineering industries.

SINGAPORE

Area: 224 square miles
Population: 3,000,000

Capital: Singapore
Language: English, Chinese, Malay, and Tamil
Religion: Buddhism, Hinduism, and Islam
Monetary Unit: Singapore Dollar
History and Government: In Sanskrit, the name Singapore means "Lion City" and was an important Malay settlement in the 13th century. It was destroyed by Japanese in the 14th century and refounded by the British in 1819. From being a British colony, Singapore (the main island and its 54 smaller islands) has been independent since 1965, after being part of the Federation of Malaya for two years. It is a member of the Commonwealth and has a parliamentary type constitution. The head of state is the president who heads a presidential council. Parliament has 65 members, one of whom is chosen as Speaker.
Economy: Agriculture is almost non-existent; the economy is based on commerce, the port facilities, and light industries such as refineries, textiles, metallurgical works, and rubber processing. Connected with the port, shipbuilding and repairing are important.

Below: Javanese fishing boats. It is thought that the Javanese reached Australia in their probing expeditions long before the Europeans discovered it in the 16th century.

It is one of the largest ports in the world and is now also an important center for air travel. Tourism and fish production are both increasing.

BRUNEI
Area: 2,225 square miles
Population: 62,000
Capital: Bandar Seri Begawan
Language: English, Malay
Religion: Islam
Monetary Unit: Brunei Dollar
History and Government: In the 16th century the sultanate of Brunei controlled the whole island of Borneo as well as parts of the Philippines and the Sulu Islands. In 1888 it became a British protectorate situated on the northeastern coast of Borneo, bounded by Sarawak. There is a Privy Council and an executive council of ministers, over which the sultan presides, and an elected legislative council. Britain is responsible for the state's external affairs and is under obligation to consult the Brunei government on matters of defense of the state.
Economy: Oil is the main economic resource, but the production of natural gas is also important. These employ seven percent of the population. Rice,

rubber, and coconut palms are the main crops grown.

PHILIPPINES (Republika ng Pilipinas)
Area: 115,830 square miles
Population: 43,000,000
Capital: Manila
Language: Pilipino (a new language based on Tagalog, a Malayan dialect) and English
Religion: Mainly Catholicism
Monetary Unit: Philippine Peso
History and Government: The Spanish settled in the Philippines in 1565. It passed under American control after the Spanish-American war in 1898. The republic of the Philippines has been independent since 1946. It has a presidential form of government based on the United States system. The head of state is elected every four years. In 1973 a new Constitution was ratified, but the president proclaimed a state of martial law and has since ruled by presidential decree while elections for a new National Assembly have been postponed indefinitely. Two guerrilla movements have been active for some years, that of the Moslem minority in the

island of Mindanao and the Sulu archipelago, and that of the Communists in Luzon. There is a very close relationship with the USA.

Economy: The Philippines is a predominantly agricultural country and a large part of the work force is employed in the land. Food production is developing, especially industrial crops such as rice, sugar cane, coconut palms, corn, and coffee. The production of tobacco, timber, manila hemp, and rubber is also important. Government efforts to diversify the economy have led to massive investments in mining: iron ore, zinc, copper, chromite, mercury, molybdenum, and precious minerals, as well as in manufacturing industries, especially textiles, coconut oils, engineering, and petrochemicals.

INDONESIA
Area: 735,000 square miles
Population: 129,000,000
Capital: Djakarta
Language: Bahasa Indonesia
Religion: Islam
Monetary Unit: Rupiah
History and Government: First visited by the Dutch in 1595, by the early part of the 17th century most of the islands of the archipelago were under Dutch rule as the Dutch East Indies. Except for the western end of New Guinea, the Dutch East Indies – as Indonesia – gained independence in 1949 after the withdrawal of the Dutch administration. Dr. Sukarno was elected president of Indonesia until a military coup d'état deprived him of his authority in 1965. An attempted coup d'état by the Communist Party to reinstate President Sukarno resulted in the massacre of 500,000 Communists. In 1966 General Soeharto was elected head of state by the People's Consultative Assembly. The president rules as head of a "Development" cabinet of ministers.

Economy: In spite of heavy foreign investments, the contribution of industry to the national income remains low and 70 percent of the working population is still engaged in agriculture and fishing. Timber is now the second largest foreign exchange earner after oil, and this, with rubber and sugar cane are the chief products, but there are many others including coffee, rice, corn, spices, cassava, sweet potatoes, tea, and tobacco. The greatest resource of all is oil, but other minerals are also being exploited including tin and bauxite. Important industries are shipbuilding, textiles, paper and match factories, glass, caustic soda, and other chemicals.

SRI LANKA (Ceylon)
Area: 25,332 square miles
Population: 12,800,000
Capital: Colombo
Language: Sinhalese and Tamil
Religion: Mainly Buddhism
Monetary Unit: Rupee
History and Government: An important center of Buddhist civilization in the 3rd century BC, Sri Lanka was first settled by Europeans in 1505 and came under British influence in 1796. Independent since 1948 and a member of the Commonwealth, the republic of Sri Lanka (meaning "Resplendent Island") defines itself as "democratic and socialist." The constitutional reform of 1971 reduced parliament to a single chamber, a House of Representatives of 157 members, of whom 151 are elected by universal suffrage for six years and six are nominated. There is a president and a council of ministers, headed by the prime minister. Formerly Ceylon.

Economy: Sri Lanka occupies an intermediate position in the scale of underdevelopment. Some 52 percent of the working population is employed in agriculture, the main products of which are rice, tea, coconuts, cocoa, tobacco, and spices. There are considerable forests and the country is among the foremost producers of rubber. Industry is largely linked with agriculture. Factories have been established for the manufacture or processing of cement and paper, cotton, and oil refining. Graphite is the most important mineral exported, but there are also quartz, kaolin, and precious stones.

SEYCHELLES
Area: 190 square miles
Population: 59,000
Capital: Victoria
Language: English, French, and Creole
Religion: Mainly Protestantism
Monetary Unit: Rupee
History and Government: A British colony since their capture from the French at the end of the 18th century, the Seychelles archipelago (94 islands, many only just above sea level) became independent in 1976.
Economy: Cinnamon bark, copra, vanilla, tortoiseshell, are produced and tourism is thriving. The USA has a satellite telecommunications base on the largest island.

MALDIVE ISLANDS
Area: 115 square miles
Population: 125,000
Capital: Malé
Language: Singalese dialect
Religion: Islam
Monetary Unit: Rupee
History and Government: Resembling Sinhalese in appearance and language, the Maldivians boast of a long tradition of civilization. In the 17th century the sultan placed the islands under Ceylonese protection. In 1953 the islands became a republic but a year later the sultanate was restored. In 1965 the islands were declared independent after having been a British protectorate for almost 80 years, and are now a presidential republic. The president of the republic is elected for four years by direct universal suffrage. He chooses his own cabinet and is responsible to the *Majlis* (House of Representatives) of 54 members elected every five years. The Maldives are made up of around 2000 atolls, only 220 of which are inhabited. The 470-mile-long chain of atolls lies some 400 miles to the southwest of Sri Lanka.
Economy: The population of the archipelago lives mainly by fishing and the cultivation and processing of the coconut palm. Trade, mainly dried fish, which is considered a delicacy, is exported to Sri Lanka. Plans are being made to introduce tourism to one of the uninhabited atolls.

CHAGOS ARCHIPELAGO (British Indian Ocean Territory)
Area: 18 square miles
Population: 2000
Monetary Unit: Rupee
History and Government: The Chagos Archipelago is the British Colony known as the British Indian Ocean Territory, and is made up of some 14 coral atolls, five of which are inhabited. It has a strategic importance because of its central position in the Indian Ocean. The USA has plans to build a military base on Diego Garcia island, the most important of the archipelago, leased from Britain in 1973. The project, however, is being opposed by all the coastal countries – Kenya, Sri Lanka, India, Indonesia, Singapore, and Australia – besides the USSR, because it would be a cause of tension in the Indian Ocean.
Economy: As well as coconut palm plantations producing copra for export, fishing is important.

Chapter 7
Africa and Arabia

To the advanced peoples of the Mediterranean and the Middle East, Africa was an easy and seemingly inexhaustible source of slaves and for more than 200 years furnished the needs of Europe, Arabia, and, later, the Americas. By the end of the 18th century there was still little known of the interior of Africa. The rivers had proved unhelpful in giving access to the heart of the continent. Then, during the 19th century, the objects of exploration became political rather than geographical and as the scramble for Africa gained momentum the continent was gradually partitioned among the European countries. It was not until after World War II that the colonial powers – and the majority of Africans – thought seriously of developing the colonies as independent economic units.

Left: the market in the province of Harar, Ethiopia, is representative of the colorful, lively, outdoor kind of shopping area that is associated with Africa and Arabia. In most of the countries of this region, the populations are largely subsistence farmers who have little demand or opportunity for consumer goods, so the preponderance of foodstuffs is natural.

Climate and Terrain

Africa is often simply described as being a vast, tilted plateau, a rigid ancient Pre-Cambrian shield that slopes down from the southeast to the northwest. Although true in essence, the picture has been greatly complicated by a long history of earth movements, erosion by wind, water, and ice, and the accumulation of many types of rocks, both volcanic and sedimentary. Arabia, on the other hand, can be likened to a subsidiary shield, almost detached from the greater African one.

The African plateau is higher in the south and east where it it everywhere over 3000 feet and, except in Somalia and Mozambique in the east, the coastal lowlands are narrow. In the northern half of the continent the land falls away to about 1000 feet and is divided into a number of smaller plateau surfaces, at different heights and often with abrupt edges. Everywhere this shield is characterized by broad basins, depressions that form areas of inland drainage, and swamp regions such as the Okavango Basin and the Lake Chad area. The ancient crystalline rocks, which underly the whole continent, outcrop on the surface in the Ahaggar, the Air ou Azbine, the highlands of Cameroun and East Africa, and the mountain rim to the south of the Congo mouth. These oldest rocks are intensely folded, eroded, and often masked by a deep layer of weathered material. They sometimes form hills that rise sharply above the surrounding plateau level. In South Africa, through these ancient rocks volcanic lavas have erupted to form extensive beds. They are the gold-bearing rocks of the Rand.

The most striking structural feature of the continent is the Great Rift that stretches from the Jordan valley in the north to the Zambezi in the south. The system contains the Red Sea, most of the great lakes of East Africa and huge volcanoes such as Mount Kenya, Kilimanjaro, and Ngorongoro. In places some of the faulting appears to have taken place in the late Palaeozoic and early Mesozoic eras, in others it is continuing even in present times.

Africa is the most tropical of all continents, it all falls within 35 degrees of the Equator. The same series of climates can be traced northward and southward from the Equator. But because everywhere is over 1000 feet above sea level, rainfall, rather than temperature, is the critical factor. The basic wind direction over the continent is toward the Equator, that is blowing from the northeast in the Northern Hemisphere and from the southeast in the Southern.

Near the Equator, temperatures and humidity are high and constant for most of the year and rainfall is heavy, especially toward the west. The principal rainy areas move north and south of the Equator with the sun – May to October there is more rain to the north, November to April more rain to the south – so that the wide, tree-dotted grassland and scrub region and deserts have alternating wet and dry periods. The mountain areas, such as Ethiopia, have a higher rainfall, but lower temperatures. In the cooler half of the year frost may occur, notably on the tableland in southern Africa, where – as on the Atlas Saharien

Right: Africa in 1950, largely under European control.
Below: the plains of Tanzania, little changed from 1861 when the explorer John Hanning Speke first saw them.

1 British Mandate

2 French Mandate

3 Belgian Mandate of Ruanda Urundi

© Geographical Projects

(Saharan Atlas) in the north – snow is not uncommon. The extreme northwest and southwest of Africa have the typical Mediterranean climate, but the southeast in Natal is mostly warm and moist in contrast to the very dry Horn of Africa in the northeast.

Stretching across North Africa, and continuing into the peninsula of Arabia, is the world's hottest, driest desert. The reason this region is so dry is because the barometric gradient is from north to south throughout the year, that is, the pressure gets lower from north to south. This, in turn, means that throughout the year the winds blow continually from the north and northeast. These are the dry Trade Winds which, as they blow into a region of lower pressure, descend, getting warmer and warmer and, therefore, retaining more and more moisture so that the relative humidity is still further reduced. The climate is too dry to support much if any plant life and this lack of vegetation further accentuates the dryness of the air. Only the mountain fringes of the Yemen in the southwest

corner of the Arabian Peninsula receive any effective rainfall when the southwest monsoon blows during the summer months.

The heat is scorching. Temperatures in summer may reach well over 100°F and noon temperatures often rise to 120°F. The surface of the earth heats up rapidly and may reach 170°F. In winter the temperatures are lower and in the northern Sahara may fall below 70°F. Cloudless skies make the days very hot and night skies clear with a bright moon and sparkling stars. But the ground cools very rapidly after sunset and the nights can also be very cold. There is often frost at dawn, particularly in the mountainous areas.

The Sahara or Arabian deserts are wild, desolate places with little or no vegetation and few people live there. There are many sand dunes, continually shaped and shifted by the wind, vast tracts of bare rock and stony wastes. The rock, where it is swept clean of sand and pebbles, often stands out in unusual shapes, eroded and molded by the abrasive action of the sand-

163

Above: the giant sand dunes of the Sahara sometimes stretch for hundred of miles. These great shifting dunes, many of which reach heights of 700 feet, are formed and shaped by the wind. Because they move and reform as the winds blow, the dunes give the desert a constantly changing landscape.

laden winds. In the Sahara the extensive tracts of sand known as ergs cover about 10 percent of the surface. Here the sand has been sorted, often transported many miles by the wind, and deposited to form a variety of different shapes from the well-known crescent-shaped dunes to the longitudinal dunes. Crescent dunes may reach heights of over 100 feet and the longitudinal dunes often occur in parallel lines, stretching across the landscape for thousands of miles. As the winds continue to blow, so the particles of sand are removed from the windward sides of the dune and accumulate on top or round the sides. The lee slope becomes steeper and steeper until eventually the sand slips down and the dune migrates. In this way the dunes creep forward relentlessly, presenting an ever-changing landscape, often obliterating obstacles in their paths.

The desert is arid and what little rain does fall is normally in the form of short, but violent, thunderstorms. When this happens, the dry channels, or wadis, are suddenly filled with water, which rushes rapidly downhill. As it does so it scours the wadi sides, carrying away the debris. Within a short distance the torrent subsides, choked with debris and the water soaks into the parched ground.

Vegetation is very scarce, or even absent, and what plants there are are especially adapted to withstand prolonged dryness. Some have long roots or fleshy, thick leaves and stems to keep in and store moisture. Seeds may lie dormant for a long time just beneath the surface and then grow and burst into flower immediately the rain has fallen. A traveler will be surprised to return to what he saw as a barren waste when he first passed by, and find it covered with a carpet o short grasses and flowering plants. One rainstorm car create a short-lived field.

There is water in some places even in the desert. The Ahaggar and Tibesti massifs in the Sahara, the Asir mountains of Saudi Arabia, have streams and springs In Libya, for example, the water is retained in porous layers of rock near the surface and people can reach i by digging wells. In other places the water comes naturally to the surface forming small pools, or oases around which date palms cluster. Some are small others are many miles across and have settlements and small fields around the pools and wells. Most desert people live in these large oases, the date palm pro viding the basic necessities – food from the fruit, drink from the sap, shelter from the wood, rope from the fiber and animal fodder from the powdered date stones

The two great oases of this desert region are the long, narrow fertile valley of the Nile and the wide floodplain of the Tigris-Euphrates. Both these valleys were the centers of early civilizations and it was in the Tigris-Euphrates valley that men, using the river water, established one of the earliest drainage and irrigations schemes. The area between these two great rivers has always been known for its beautifu palm groves and produces dates of the highest quality

Since early times the people of the Nile valley have tried to control the river waters. Now the river's dis charge is regulated by a series of dams and storage reservoirs upstream that conserve the floodwaters brought down in summer from the Abyssinian High lands by the Atbara, Bahr el Azraq (Blue Nile), and Sobat. The new Aswan High Dam, in operation since 1968, can hold back enough water in Lake Nasser to both even out the seasonal variations in discharge and conserve water for dry years. The construction of the many new schemes higher up the river has greatly increased the irrigated areas in the Sudan as well as

Above: a man uses a donkey to draw water from a well in M'Zab, Algeria. Most people who live in the Sahara still suffer from great scarcity of water, especially for irrigation.

Above: part of the pipeline connecting Abqaiq, the main oil field of Saudi Arabia, with the large refinery at Ras Tanura. Some desert regions of the world have the richest oil deposits.

the cultivable area downstream in Egypt.

Oil is transforming the economies of the northern Saharan countries of Algeria and Libya – as it has done in the countries of the Arabian peninsula. Apart from Iraq, with its Al Mūsil (Mosul) and Karkūk (Kirkuk) oilfields, and Saudi Arabia, there are the small sheikdoms bordering the Persian Gulf – Bahrain, Kuwait, Qatar, and the Emirates – that have become rich and important. Often the wealth has remained in the hands of a few, but in recent years an increasing amount is being devoted to social services and industrial development. In the small desert countries where the populations are low and where there are not enough local projects in which to invest the money from the oil revenues, the surpluses have been invested in the Western World's financial centers.

South of the Equator are two smaller deserts, the Namib bordering the west coast between the Cunene and Oranje (Orange) rivers, and the Kalahari farther inland. Although these deserts are the counterpart of the Sahara, they are neither so large nor so arid, because the land mass in these latitudes is not so wide and is surrounded by water. The cold, north-flowing Benguela Current to the west means that any air reaching the continent from that direction is cool, therefore rises over the hot land, warms and retains its moisture.

Right: Bushman women roasting some edible roots in glowing embers. Women of this tribe help gather food, scouring the desert for roots they can eat.

Most of the Kalahari is covered with thornbush and acacia, but the lack of surface water combined with the long dry season makes it unsuitable for farming. Only a few European-owned livestock farms are to be found, mainly in the northwestern part. As yet there are no rich mineral resources located comparable to the oil in the northern Sahara, but asbestos and manganese are being mined. The Kalahari, however, is the home of the Bushmen who are often regarded as being some of the original inhabitants of Africa. They now live in the Kalahari Reserve.

Africa and Arabia: Political

The Rain Forests of Central Africa

Dense tropical forests cover much of the Congo basin and stretch along the west coast of Africa, from the Congo mouth to Guinea. In these parts the rainfall is heavy all the year, always exceeding 60 inches and in some coastal areas being as much as 100 inches. There is no dry season. In this warm, humid climate the temperatures never drop below 70°F. Many trees grow to a height of more than 100 feet and under their dense foliage all kinds of forest plants struggle to reach the light. Birds, some with bright plumage, fly above the treetops, monkeys swing and leap from branch to branch, snakes move silently through the forest gloom.

The tropical rain forest, or equatorial forest, is the most imposing section of the plant world. The luxurious evergreen trees include an immense wealth of

region of central Africa is deforestation. Trees have been cleared by cultivators, for either large plantations or smallholdings. This is particularly true round the edge of the Congo basin, and on the slightly higher areas of Cameroun, Gabon, and Angola.

The people of the forest areas of Africa live mainly on the fringes, along the coast of West and central Africa, on the higher ground of the Cameroun mountains, the edge of the Great Rift and along the lower reaches of the Congo. The coastal peoples have been in touch with Europe since the early Portuguese voyagers ventured south toward the Cape, but the people inland had few contacts until the European nations arrived in force at the end of the 19th century – the French, Belgians, Portuguese, and to a lesser extent the Germans and Spanish.

The Europeans did not develop the full potential of the countries they colonized. But in Zaire – or the Belgian Congo as it was formerly called – the Belgians made the Zaire (Congo) river and its tributaries into a major transport system. They developed the country economically, in particular the mineral-rich region of Shaba (then Katanaga) and the rubber, cocoa, and oil palm plantations.

Other countries of central Africa – Cameroun, the Central African Empire, Equatorial Guinea, Gabon, and Congo – have not yet been developed extensively.

Below: lobelias, in a tall shaggy form, have a wide range of distribution throughout the tropics and warm temperate zones. They are especially plentiful and typical of the vegetation in the tropical mountain region of central Africa.

Below: harvesting cacao pods in Ghana, which is the world's biggest producer of this commodity. From the cacao beans come chocolate, cocoa, and cocoa butter, which is used in candies and medicines.

species, valuable tropical hardwoods such as ebony and mahogany, the wild rubber, and the oil palms. Along some of the lagoons of the Gulf of Guinea coast, the Niger delta, and on the floor of the Congo basin, are large low-lying swampy areas often flooded for many months of the year. Here the trees have adapted themselves to life in fresh water. In the coastal areas, the mangrove has colonized the muds, its long arching roots forming an almost impenetrable tangle.

One of the chief problems in the tropical forest

In many areas shifting cultivation is the norm though the numbers of plantations of cocoa, coffee, cotton, sugar cane, and rubber are on the increase. Deforestation is being controlled and exploitation of the mineral wealth has begun – for example the manganese and iron ore of Gabon, the bauxite of Cameroun. But one of the great problems is transportation. Internal transport is difficult, even by water, and construction of either railways or roads is hampered by high costs, natural obstacles, and heavy rainfall.

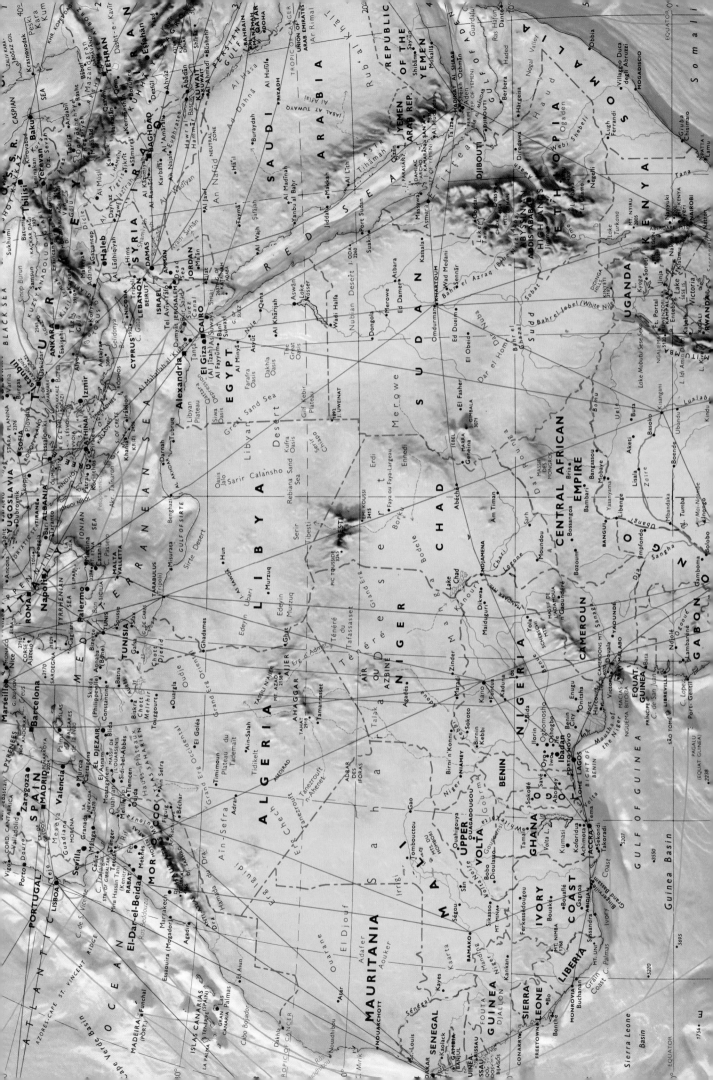

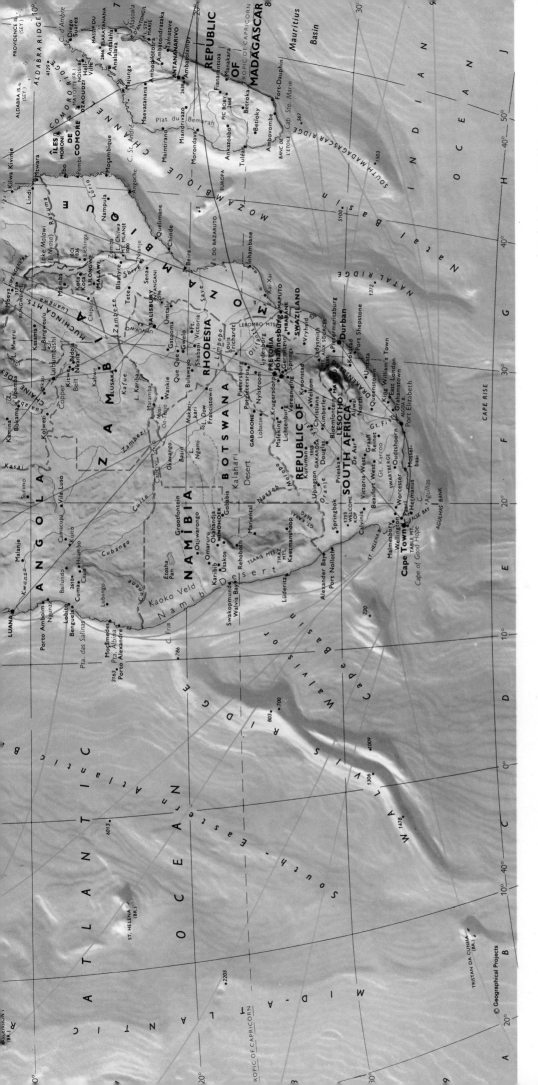

Africa and Arabia

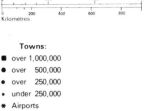

Miles

| 200 | 400 | 600 |

Kilometres

200 400 600 800

Towns:

■ over 1,000,000
● over 500,000
● over 250,000
• under 250,000
✳ Airports

Red thin line	Main roads
Black thin line	Main railways
Blue thick line	Sea routes
Red thick line	Air routes

© Geographical Projects

South of the Sahara

The vegetation belts, like the broad east-west bands of climate, repeat themselves north and south of the Equator. First there are the tropical forests of the equatorial regions; then the dry, tropical grasslands, or savanna, to the north and south of the forests; followed by the arid desert belts, the Sahara in the north and the Namib-Kalahari in the south; and finally the pleasant, more wooded coastal fringes of the northwest and southwest. The only exception to the pattern is the high plateau of East Africa, lying between 5°N and 10°S. This in effect is an equatorial extension of the savanna interrupting the east-west belt of tropical forest. The savanna itself forms the shape of a reversed letter C, extending from the Gambia on the Atlantic coast, across the northern margins of the Congo Basin, south through the plateau country of East Africa, then west through Zambia and Zimbabwe-Rhodesia to southern Angola and Namibia on the Atlantic coast.

The Sahara merges gradually into the savanna in an intermediate zone known as the sahel. The rainfall gradually increases southward, the vegetation becomes more varied and wildlife more prolific. The occasional baobab tree, with its enormous bulbous trunk and bare branches, penetrates the landscape and trees grow in clumps or along the river banks. In the sahel the grass is short and tufty, but farther south in the true savanna, where there is more rain, the grass may be 12 feet high. This "brush" country is the natural home of big game such as elephants, lions, giraffes, zebra, and gazelles.

In Mali much scientific work was done during the 1930s and 1940s, researching into irrigation methods, soils, crops, and marketing possibilities. The emphasis is now on rice cultivation rather than cotton because it is easier for the inexperienced farmers and not necessarily so labor intensive.

Small, local schemes have also proved more successful than large-scale projects, and there have been many of these completed in the neighborhood of the middle Niger, upstream from Tombouctou (Timbuktu). Throughout the region people are engaged in herding in the drier parts and cultivation in the wetter. Cotton, peanuts, and millet are the main crops and in the countries bordering the Atlantic – Mauritania and Senegal – fishing is important.

In this northern belt of the sahel and savanna, the majority of the countries suffer from underpopulation as well as from lack of capital. A great proportion of the people are seminomadic, wandering with their flocks in search of water and pasture. In contrast, the countries bordering the Gulf of Guinea are more heavily

Opposite below: dry grassland supporting acacia trees is the predominant type of savanna landscape in Africa.
Below: lush tropical savanna is typical of the Central African Empire, where up to 30 inches of rainfall permits the growth of palm trees and perennial grasses.

populated and richer. The increased rainfall makes it possible to grow a greater variety of crops including corn, root crops, fruits, sugar cane, coffee, and cocoa palm. The coastal peoples obtain their main source of income from fishing and there are also mineral resources such as gold and diamonds in Ghana and cassiterite (tin ore) around Jos in Nigeria.

The land around Lake Chad is also richer and there are large populations of people and cattle. Wheat is cultivated on the sandy soils, thousands of tons of fish are caught each year in the lake, and from the edges of the lake, as the salty water evaporates, natron is dug and used for cattlelick by both local farmers and those farther afield in Chad and Nigeria.

At the eastern end of the northern savanna belt is the basin of the upper Nile. North from the plateau of East Africa the Bahr el Jebel (White Nile) flows through the Sudan and spreads out through large swamps, where a lot of water is lost by evaporation. Traffic on these waterways has always been hampered by vegetation. The papyrus, various floating weeds, and, more recently, the water hyacinth grow profusely, choking whole stretches. The water hyacinth, in particular, fouls the machinery of the boats and there is a real danger it will spread downstream, blocking irrigation canals and fouling the water pumps.

Engineers are trying to clear the channels to increase the river's flow and attempts are being made to confine the water hyacinth. Work has just begun on the Jonglei Canal, which will draw a quarter of the flow of the Bahr el Jebel (White Nile) at Bur, just north of Juba. This will increase the flow of the Nile as far north as Aswan and also provide extra water for

Above: Masais of Kenya and Tanzania with their cattle. Not indigenous to Africa, cattle were introduced there about 4000 years ago from Asia. Since then, cows have become a symbol of wealth and importance as well as a source of food.

use in the Sudan. But there is, too, some concern that the project may affect the ecology of the swamplands and create a different set of problems.

The core of the plateau of East Africa includes Uganda, Kenya, Tanzania, and the two small countries of Rwanda and Burundi. To the north rise the rugged, massive mountains of the Abyssinian Highlands, fringed by the wide coastal plain of Somalia that bends around the Horn of Africa and skirts the southern shore of the Gulf of Aden. To the south is the basin of the Zambezi. The whole plateau is scored by the huge system of rift valleys. Lakes Turkona (Rudolf), Natron, and Malawi, lie in one huge rift valley stretching from the Jordan to the Zambezi. This deep, steep-sided valley is from 20 to 50 miles wide. To the west of it, Lakes Mobutu Sese Seko (Albert), Idi Amin Dada (Edward), Kivu and Tanganyika, lie in another line of rift valleys. Between these two systems is the plateau and the broad, shallow Lake Victoria, the largest of the African lakes and third largest lake in the world.

Much of the East African plateau is over 4000 feet, shaped like a giant lozenge and bordered by the eastern and western rifts. In the east, the highlands of the rift walls are more discontinuous and the lakes less extensive than in the west. In this belt the altitude modifies the temperature, the rainfall is adequate, and the volcanic soils rich and fertile. In Kenya the crops vary greatly, depending upon altitude, and include such things as wheat, barley, pyrethrum, tea, coffee, and pineapples. In Tanzania sisal is also important. On the plateau itself, occupied by Uganda and Tanzania, the most productive lands are around the shallow Lake Victoria as much of the remainder of the area is dry savanna country infested by tsetse fly. The western rift, the fifth belt, includes the Mitumba Mountains and Ruwenzori massif, as well as the deep trough lakes. Because of its distance from the sea it is,

as yet, less developed than the eastern side of the rift although it is equally fertile and densely populated.

South of the equatorial belt of the Congo basin and the East African plateau, lie the vast plateaus drained by the Zambezi and Limpopo rivers to the east and the Oranje (Orange) river to the west. The Zambezi and its tributaries rise in the western half of the continent and drain the high plateau of Angola, flowing eastward to the southern limit of the Great Rift. But the Zambezi does little to link the countries along its course. The numerous rapids prevent it being used as a highway. On the other hand, the Kariba Dam and

Above: the Kariba Dam on the Zambezi river along the borders of Zambia and Zimbabwe-Rhodesia. A dam like this can power electricity generating stations, distribute water for the irrigation of deserts for agriculture, and use water to offset the effects of periodic droughts.

Below: a salt plant on Lake Magadi, Kenya, where soda ash is refined after extraction from the lake. Although the bulk of soda compounds are synthetically manufactured today, natural soda is still used in the heavy chemical industry. It makes up the chief mineral export of Kenya.

the more recent Cabora Bessa Dam, upstream from Tete, have provided an economic link supplying hydroelectric power to the neighboring countries of Zambia, Zimbabwe-Rhodesia, and Mozambique. Although this whole region of African savanna, between 10°S and 20°S is well endowed with mineral and agricultural resources, few have been developed.

In Angola, mining for managanese, iron ore, and diamonds has developed along the Luanda railway; coffee, cotton, and corn are grown as commercial crops; and off the coast fishing supports an industry for processing fishmeal and provides one of the principal sources of revenue. Zambia has rich mineral resources, especially copper, which largely makes up for the infertile soil of the tsetse-infected savanna. Here the African is being persuaded to change from a shifting cultivation to a more permanent one, growing corn, cassava, and sweet potatoes with the help of irrigation. In contrast, Malawi is predominantly agricultural and remains one of the poorest countries in Africa south of the Equator. Good land is scarce, most of the soils are unproductive and, apart from the highlands in the south where tobacco and tea are important cash crops, the majority of the people practice subsistence cultivation. They grow barely enough for their own needs and exist on a diet of corn and cassava. In Zimbabwe-Rhodesia, as in so many African savanna countries, there is the same contrast between the unhealthy, low-lying areas of the Low Veld, often malarial and tsetse-infected, and the High Veld where the altitude, reliable and adequate rainfall, and fertile soils make the cultivation of commercial crops, especially tobacco, feasible. It is in the High Veld also that the mineral resources can be found – asbestos, gold, and chrome.

Between the southern deserts and the well-forested Drakensberg mountains in the east, is the tropical grassland plateau of the Republic of Africa, the Veld. Because it is farther from the Equator and much of it has an altitude of more than 6000 feet, southern Africa is cooler than the rest of the continent. It is to the Veld that the Dutch farmers (known as Boers) came to escape British rule between 1834 and 1838. Today it is still the Boer who farms the Veld. The yields of corn, other cereals, and potatoes are high, there is good grazing for the pastoral farmer and farther north more tropical plants such as tobacco flourish.

The country also has good agricultural land around the south and east coasts. The southwest, around Cape Town, has a Mediterranean climate, an ideal climate with warm, moist winters when temperatures rarely fall below 50°F, and hot, dry summers with average temperatures of 70°F. Vines, fruits, and wheat are grown. On the more humid eastern coast plains, the citrus fruits, bananas, sugar cane, and other tropical crops grow successfully.

The Republic of South Africa is by far the richest and most powerful state in the continent south of the Sahara. The impact of the European way of life has been stronger in this country than in any other part of the continent, with the possible exception of Algeria. Inland, around Johannesburg, lies the only industrial complex of the continent that is remotely comparable with similar complexes in the great northern industrial belts of North America and Europe. It is a concentration of population based on the presence of raw materials: the goldfields of the Witwatersrand – known as the Rand. Around the two chief ports of Cape Town and Durban, and the smaller ones of Port Elizabeth and East London, as well as round the diamond-mining center of Kimberley, have developed other smaller industrial centers concerned

Above: the excavation known as the Big Hole in Kimberley, South Africa. The Big Hole was dug for the extraction of diamonds, of which South Africa has the richest deposits in the world. Diamonds are formed under great heat and pressure deep down in the earth and rise in a formation of material which is known as kimberlite.

with the manufacture of clothing and textiles, printing, food-processing, and engineering.

The island of Madagascar is off the coast of East Africa. It is almost continental in proportions and geographically transitional between Africa and Asia. It has been separated from the African continent since the Mesozoic era and this long isolation has resulted in a flora and fauna different to those on the mainland. The people, too, appear to have come from both continents, most probably from East Africa and from the East Indies by way of India. The economy of the island is based on agriculture and shows the same combination of African and Asian crops. The cash crops are, as in Africa, coffee, vanilla, and cloves, the staple food is as in Asia, rice.

Natural Resources

Except for palm oil, peanuts, and certain hardwoods, the chief commercial crops of Africa have mostly been introduced from abroad. These include cotton, cacao, tobacco, rubber, vines, pineapples, and tea. Many of the everyday food crops of tropical Africa – bananas, yams, sweet potatoes, cassava, oranges, and corn –

Above: logs being brought into the port town of Sekondi-Takoradi, Ghana. The capital of Ghana's Western Region, Sekondi-Takoradi is served by several railroads, by air, and by road.

were also introduced by Europeans. More than three quarters of the world's supply of cocoa comes from Ghana and western Nigeria where the cacao tree is cultivated on a large scale. A native of northern South America, this small tree is adapted to live under constant moisture in the shade of taller trees. The oil palm, grown mainly in the coastal areas of the Gulf of Guinea, yields a valuable edible oil that now features largely in world trade. The tree bears a crown of huge, feather-shaped compound leaves with glossy, dark-green leaflets. The female flowers, which spring up all the year around, ripen quickly, forming bunches of brown fruits, each holding a hard, brown seed within a layer of thick, oily, yellow pulp. This nutritious pulp can be eaten raw, or processed to extract the oil, which is used either in cooking or to make soap or margarine.

Farther inland in West Africa, where the rainfall is lower and the forest gives way to savanna, the main cash crops are peanuts and cotton. Peanuts are particularly important in Senegal where they were first introduced well over a century ago. At the same time the French improved the port facilities of Dakar, built a railroad inland to Bamako in Mali and developed the processing of peanuts locally. In northern Nigeria also peanuts are an important export crop. Kano is the collecting center, and increasing quantities of nuts are being processed there and the oil taken south by rail. Peanut cake is also processed for export as animal fodder.

A great deal of cotton is grown without irrigation. The crops are harvested in the dry season and some seed reserved for planting. The rest is ginned and transported many miles to the coast, either to the Nigerian ports such as Port Harcourt, or by way of the Ubangi and Zaire rivers to Brazzaville, or to the east coast ports of Kenya and Tanzania, to be sent abroad for processing.

In East Africa, and to a lesser extent in Madagascar, the range of cash crops is greater – cotton, coffee, tea, tobacco, sisal, cloves (especially on the island of Zanzibar), sugar cane, and green vegetables which are air-freighted out to the European markets. There are greater opportunities for specialization in these more fertile, heavily populated areas and the road, rail, and air services are better developed. There are also local markets able to accept agricultural products. One of the most important crops in both Kenya and Tanzania is pyrethrum, a daisy-shaped flower that holds a natural insecticide. The blossoms are har-

Below: a gold smelting plant in South Africa. This precious metal is found in South Africa in abundance, the goldfield at Witwatersrand being the richest on earth. South Africa ranks among the top three producers of gold in the world, with the USSR and the USA.

ested soon after they open and processed to obtain pyrethrin, the active constituent. Tobacco is Zimbabwe-Rhodesia's most important commercial crop. Although after their unilateral declaration of independence, and the subsequent sanctions against the country by other nations, which prevented the export of the crop, farmers diversified into corn, wheat, and cotton as well as the herding and breeding of cattle.

Africa is rich in minerals and power resources. Some minerals have been worked for centuries. The antique ironwork and bronzes from the old kingdom of Benin in Nigeria are among the finest examples of African art. But exploitation of minerals in the modern sense

district. Other mines produce zinc, lead, manganese, and cadmium, silver, and almost the world's total supply of radium. In Zaire large hydroelectric installations have been built to provide the power to treat the ores locally.

The two areas of the Rand and the Copperbelt together produce over 75 percent of the mineral output of Africa, but there are other minerals of importance found elsewhere, for example, tin, bauxite, and oil. Tin is mined in northern Nigeria; bauxite in Ghana and Guinea; Liberia has lead; Sierra Leone has the world's largest reserves of rutile, needed for the manufacture of paint, glass, and titanium metals. In

Below: a Benin statue of a warrior in bronze. The old kingdom of Benin was founded around 1300 and excelled in the use of metals for artistic purposes.

Below: a uranium mine in Gabon helps provide the world with the material necessary for the generation of nuclear energy. Uranium is also used in the steel, ceramic, and glass industries, so the demand for this product is steady and high.

has only developed within the last 100 years and the potential power supplies are only just being exploited.

The discovery of diamonds along the east of the Vaal river, in the Republic of South Africa, led to the founding of Kimberley in 1871. Today this area has some of the world's largest diamond mines. The coastal stretches of Namibia (formerly South West Africa) are an important source of industrial diamonds and these are also mined in Sierra Leone and Zaire. Another South African city, Johannesburg, was founded by the goldminers in 1886 and is now the commercial center of the Rand, the world's greatest goldmining area. Other minerals of the Rand include chromite and iron ore, and around Vereeniging huge steelworks have been in operation since 1951.

The Shaba (Katanga) province of Zaire is another great mineral producer. Here, and across the border in Zambia, are rich but fairly shallow copper mines, the source of the one fifth of the world's copper. As well as copper, the Copperbelt supplies almost two thirds of the world's cobalt, mainly from the Kolwezi

Mauritania, the large mining town of Fort Gouraud has grown up with the development of a very rich find of iron ore.

Generally, Africa is not rich in coal. The Wankie coalfield in Zimbabwe-Rhodesia and fields in Natal and near Johannesburg meet only local needs. But this deficiency in coal is offset by a large hydroelectric potential that is only just being exploited. Examples are the newly completed Volta dam project in Ghana, the Owen Falls dam at Jinja in Uganda, the Kariba and the Cabora Bessa dams on the Zambezi, as well as the numerous installations on the Nile and its tributaries.

Oil has only recently become important and south of the Sahara Nigeria now produces nearly four percent of the world's total and almost half of the total African production. In this country oil has taken over from agriculture and by 1972 accounted for over three quarters of the exports by value. Now pipelines are being built, and terminals at Bonny and Forcados expanded.

North Africa

Peoples and Cultures

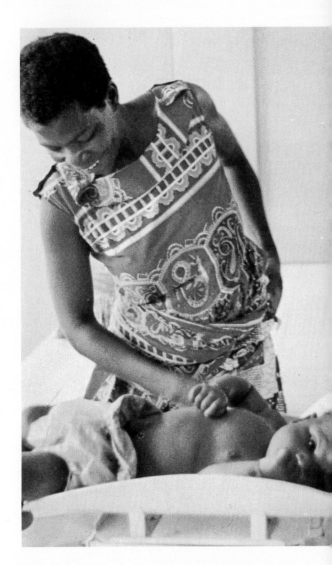

It is the Sahara that forms the great divide between Negro Africa and Caucasoid Africa. Yet during the Pleistocene Glaciation the Sahara was not a desert, and the climate and vegetation resembled that of Europe today. When the ice retreated, the climate changed. It became drier and hotter, the vegetation belts moved north, and left a desert belt stretching across North Africa and into the Arabian Peninsula. For between 5000 and 10,000 years the Sahara was a barrier that impeded and delayed, first the spread south of the discovery of how to produce food by cultivation, then the intermingling of the peoples on the western side of the continent.

The yellow-brown-skinned Bushmen of the Kalahari and the dark-skinned Pygmies of the tropical forests of the Congo are regarded by most experts as being the aboriginal inhabitants. They were driven into their present habitats by the more advanced Negroes who form two main groups: the West African Negroes of the savanna and the coastal forest zone; and the eastern group, the Bantu. The West Africans include the tall, ebony-black Sudanese of the forests and grasslands, the Nilotic tribes like the Dinka and Nuer, the Guinea tribes such as the Ashanti of Ghana and the Yoruba of Nigeria. The Bantu include such tribes as the Kikuyu of Kenya, the Mashona and Matabele of Zimbabwe-Rhodesia, and the Zulu of

Above: a baby getting a checkup in a health clinic. Today Africans themselves staff the clinics that bring modern health care to their people. Doctors, nurses, and social workers often form mobile health teams.

Below: the traditional motifs painted on this house in northern Gulu are more than decorative. The Matabeles believe that they ward off evil spirits and bring good fortune to members of the household. The Matabele belong to the Bantu nation.

Natal. They pushed south down the east side of the continent, and westward across central and southern Africa, interbreeding with the Pygmies and Bushmen. The Hottentots, in the south near the Oranje (Orange) river, are physically akin to the Bushmen, but culturally different.

The paler-skinned Caucasoid people inhabited the north and northeast of Africa and the Arabian Peninsula. They were originally nomadic pastoralists and traders and include the Arabs, with their Semitic language, as well as the Hamitic-speaking peoples. They moved westward along the northern rim of Africa, where such tribes as the Hausa of northern Nigeria and the nomadic Tuaregs resulted from their mixing. In the east, however, they have pushed well south, often mixing with the Bantu peoples. The Masai of Kènya and Tanzania and the Turkona of northern Kenya are considered a mixture of Hamitic and Bantu.

The resulting pattern of all these peoples and their cultures is complicated: there are hundreds of different languages and dialects, customs, traditions, and

liber, meaning free. South Africa became a dominion of the British Commonwealth of Nations in 1910 and, in addition, Southern Rhodesia (now Zimbabwe-Rhodesia) became a self-governing colony in 1923.

After World War II the European powers made plans to develop the colonies as independent economic units, but at the same time the nationalist movements gained momentum. Most countries became independent quite peacefully. But in equatorial Africa there was widespread violence in the Belgian Congo (now Zaire) when it gained independence in 1960 and the United Nations had to intervene. Even this did not pacify the country entirely and it remained at the mercy of ambitious politicians, rival armies, and foreign mercenaries for some years and still has internal conflicts. Algeria, too, was the scene of bitter fighting before it won independence from the French in 1962.

The Federation of Rhodesia and Nyasaland was a shortlived British attempt to make one nation out of Northern and Southern Rhodesia and Nyasaland. This project did not win the support of the African peoples involved, so Northern Rhodesia and Nyasaland became the independent Commonwealth republics of Zambia and Malawi. The future of the third member of the old federation, Zimbabwe-Rhodesia, is still uncertain. The Portuguese territories of Angola, Mozambique, and Portuguese Guinea (now Guinea-Bissau) had become independent by 1975; the Spanish colonies of Rio Muni, Fernando Poo, and Spanish Guinea became Equatorial Guinea, and Rio de Oro merged into Morocco and Mauritania. In 1961 South Africa left the Commonwealth and became a republic.

The 300 million Africans are still distributed un-

ways of life. To complicate even further this pattern there are minority groups of Asians and Europeans. South of the Sahara the Europeans number about four million, which is less than two percent of the total population, but their importance politically and economically cannot be overestimated. They partitioned the continent, cutting across ethnic boundaries and sometimes molding the economic development to suit their own interests. They built railways, often to suit political motives rather than the economy of the African; they provided the administrators, the managers, and the farmers. The diversity of the colonizing nations, superimposed on the complicated pattern of the African peoples, also helps to explain why the African countries are now developing along very different lines.

Before World War I the only independent states in Africa were Ethiopia, Liberia, and the Union (now Republic) of South Africa. Ethiopia, a Christian country since the 4th century AD, is the only state with a long history of self-government. Legend dates it from the meeting of King Solomon and the Queen of Sheba. Liberia was founded in 1822 by freed Negro slaves with the help of America. Monrovia, its capital, was named after President James Monroe of the USA and the name Liberia comes from the Latin word

Below: people on the move in their daily activities near the main gate of the city of San'ā'. The capital of the Yemen Arab Republic, San'ā' has for centuries been a major religious, political, and economic center.

Above: new buildings in Addis Ababa, the capital of Ethiopia. Because Addis Ababa stands about 8000 feet above sea level, its climate is healthy.

evenly over the continent and, considering its size, there are few large cities. Only four – Addis Ababa, Alexandria, Cairo, and Kinshasa – have populations of more than a million and two of these are in the Nile delta. Other cities, such as El Djezair (Algiers), Pretoria, Accra, Lagos, Ibadan, El Giza, Johannesburg, Durban, and Cape Town, are growing fast with more than 500,000 inhabitants. They are closely followed by other towns in the populated areas of the Mediterranean coast, the Nile delta, West Africa, the East African plateau, and South Africa – for example Rabat, Ouahran (Oran), Bur Sa'Id (Port Said), Aswan, Kano, Ogobomosho, Nairobi, and Vereeniging. The Africans are drifting into the towns, but the rapid urban growth has often led to ugly groups of slum shacks on the outskirts of the cities.

Below: television as a teacher in Africa. Developing countries must educate and train people to fill the many work-demands of a modern society.

Even so, Africa is an essentially agricultural continent. Most Africans still make their living from the land, using primitive methods of cultivation; or hunt or fish. Many African governments, however, have economic and social development programs and conditions are gradually improving. In some countries the numbers of cash crops and plantations, introduced by the Europeans, have increased. In others, the Africans have been settled on farms formerly owned by the Europeans. In Kenya, there has been this type of agrarian reform and in many cases it has resulted in the land being used more intensively than before and the production per acre increased. But economic development up to the standard of European or North American countries lies in the distant future.

Although early industries were directly related to readily available raw materials – for example the palm oil processing plants of Nigeria and the cotton mills of Egypt – in many countries total lack of industries meant that the raw materials were exported only to be imported later in the form of manufactured goods. Now the emerging African states are trying to develop both their agricultural and mineral resources and use them to promote industrial growth. They want more industrialization, but have been held up by the lack of capital and technical knowledge. It has not always proved easy to get monetary and technical aid from abroad, especially when the advanced industrial countries find their own investment fields more attractive than low-interest areas in Africa. South Africa is still the only country in the continent with a highly developed industrial complex and the greatest opportunities appear to lie here and, to a lesser extent, in East Africa and the coastlands of West Africa.

One scheme that has been completed in West Africa is the Volta river project and in this case over half of the £82 million spent has been raised within Ghana itself, the remainder coming from the UK, USA, and a World Bank loan. As with other modern hydroelectric installations, the plan has been to utilize the natural features where the Volta river plunges over the plateau edge. A dam has been constructed at Akosombo, forming a lake some 300 miles in length in the river valley on the plateau. The hydroelectric power station has been completed and, at Tema, an aluminum smelter and new port built. There are plans to export electricity to neighboring countries and to construct another plant to process the Ghanaian bauxite.

Lack of good communications is also hampering economic growth in many countries. Transportation is a major problem in a continent where most roads are made of earth and gravel and are often impassable in the rainy season. Rivers are only partially navigable because of the many waterfalls and rapids and there are relatively few natural harbors. South Africa is still the only country in which an extensive railway network has been built. But some governments, with assistance from outside Africa, are working to improve their communication systems. A new railroad

Above: a new housing compound for the blacks of Johannesburg. Under the white national policy of Apartheid, blacks are entirely segregated and often live in hovels on the outskirts of town. Though new, the suburb of tiny prefabricated houses is still cramped.

between Tanzania and Zambia is planned with Chinese and Anglo-Canadian help. The EEC, which provides aid through the European Development Fund, has given grants and loans for road-making schemes in Senegal; road and bridge projects in Niger, Somalia, Togo, and Upper Volta, as well as for the realignment of the Congo-Ocean railway.

Ironically, large schemes, such as have been com-

Above: drilling holes to plant explosives in a South African diamond mine. Blacks from all over the continent work in the mines attracted by relatively high wages.

pleted on the Volta and Zambezi, or agrarian reforms similar to those in Kenya, often accentuate the uneven economic development of Africa. In East Africa, there is now a greater difference between the development of the Baganda people of Uganda around the shores of Lake Victoria, or the Kikuyu on the slopes of Kilimanjaro, and the Acholi of northern Uganda than there was some 50 years ago. On the one hand there is a highly developed and intensive agricultural system producing cash crops, on the other a subsistance agriculture. As such differences develop so too do those between rural and urban areas.

Africa's most complex problem is in South Africa, a country settled by white and black people who arrived at the same time in the area but from different directions. Political power is in the hands of the numerically fewer but technologically more sophisticated whites. A policy of separate development or "apartheid" is practiced in which whites and nonwhites live in different areas of the country. About 13 percent of the country has been earmarked as tribal reserves or "bantustans" in which most of the Bantu people – about two thirds of the total population of over 18 million – will be required to live. The nonwhites, including "coloreds," or those of mixed race parentage, and Indians have only limited political rights in their nonwhite areas. But nonwhites living in white areas have no political rights at all. This arbitrary racial division causes intense dissatisfaction, not only among nonwhite South Africans, but also in the newly independent countries of Africa.

There is much the European powers can do to help African nations. There is still a great need for money, expertise, and experience; for internal trade, which is an important element in a nation's healthy development process.

The Countries of Africa and Arabia

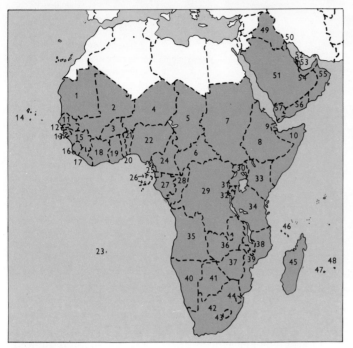

1 Mauritania	30 Uganda
2 Mali	31 Rwanda
3 Upper Volta	32 Burundi
4 Niger	33 Kenya
5 Chad	34 Tanzania
6 Central African Empire	35 Angola
7 Sudan	36 Zambia
8 Ethiopia	37 Zimbabwe-Rhodesia
9 Djibouti	38 Malawi
10 Somalia	39 Mozambique
11 Senegal	40 Namibia
12 Gambia	41 Botswana
13 Guinea-Bissau	42 Republic of South Africa
14 Cape Verde Islands	43 Lesotho
15 Guinea	44 Swaziland
16 Sierra Leone	45 Madagascar
17 Liberia	46 Comoro Islands
18 Ivory Coast	47 Réunion
19 Ghana	48 Mauritius
20 Togo	49 Iraq
21 Benin	50 Kuwait
22 Nigeria	51 Saudi Arabia
23 Saint Helena	52 Bahrain
24 Cameroun	53 Qatar
25 Equatorial Guinea	54 United Arab Emirates
26 São Tomé & Principé	55 Oman
27 Gabon	56 People's Democratic Republic
28 Congo	of the Yemen
29 Zaïre	57 Yemen Arab Republic

MAURITANIA
Area: 419,000 square miles
Population: 1,500,000
Capital: Nouakchott
Language: Arabic and French
Religion: Islam
Monetary Unit: Ouguiya
History and Government: Part of the coastal territory opened by the Portuguese in the 15th century, Mauritania came under French influence in the 19th century. It became independent in 1960, after having been a French protectorate from 1903 to 1920, a colony from 1920 to 1958, and an autonomous republic within the French Community from 1958 to 1960. The republic is administered by a government council of 16 ministers. The National Assembly has 50 members.
Economy: Some 90 percent of the population is engaged in stock-rearing – cattle, sheep, goats, camels – and agriculture. The chief products are cattle, millet, salt, and beans. The exploitation of the rich deposits of iron ore, copper, and salt is developing, and a railway has been especially built between the rich deposits of iron ore around Zouérate, in the north of the country, and the port of Nouadhibou. Fishing is important.

MALI
Area: 478,818 square miles
Population: 6,500,000
Capital: Bamako
Language: French
Religion: Mainly Islam
Monetary Unit: Franc Malien
History and Government: Mali became a republic in the French community in 1958 and became independent in 1960. In 1968 a military coup d'état overthrew the regime and a National Liberation Committee assumed all political functions. In 1974 a referendum was organized to approve a new civil constitution.
Economy: Agriculture is the almost exclusive occupation of the people. Peanuts – raw and processed, and cotton are exported.

UPPER VOLTA (République de Haute Volta)
Area: 105,868 square miles
Population: 6,000,000
Capital: Ouagadougou
Language: French, Mande, and Poular
Religion: Animism and Islam
Monetary Unit: Franc CFA
History and Government: Independent since 1960, the Republic of Upper Volta has been governed by the military since 1966. The restitution of power to the civil authority was promised and full legislative and presidential elections were held in 1978.
Economy: Sheep, goats, cattle, and pigs provide a large part of the produce for export with some fish and peanuts. There is little, if any, industrial development.

NIGER (République du Niger)
Area: 489,188 square miles
Population: 4,500,000
Capital: Niamey
Language: French and Haussa
Religion: Islam
Monetary Unit: Franc CFA
History and Government: As part of the Upper Senegal–Niger colony Niger was a territory of French West Africa from 1904. It became a presidential republic with a single Chamber of National Assembly in 1960. In April 1974 a coup d'état put a military junta at the head of government, which suspended the constitution and dissolved the National Assembly.

Economy: Niger's great resource is its uranium reserves north of Agades. Production there is the third highest in the world, but it is largely exploited with French, German, and Japanese capital. The majority of the population lives by agriculture and stock-rearing. Agricultural production – millet, peanuts, beans, manioc, and rice – is not enough for the home market. The only products exported are peanuts and gum arabic, fish, and the products from stock-rearing. Tin ore and salt are mined.

CHAD (Tchad)
Area: 495,752 square miles
Population: 4,000,000
Capital: Ndjaména (Fort Lamy)
Language: Arabic, French, and Sare
Religion: Animism and Islam
Monetary Unit: Franc CFA
History and Government: The Republic of Chad became independent in 1960 after having been part of French Equatorial Africa and, from 1958, a member of the French Community. In 1962 a new Constitution was adopted with the country ruled by a presidential-type regime. The country has been ruled by a military council after a coup d'état in 1975. It is a country with a large number of ethnic divisions containing the former native kingdoms of Kanem, Wadai, and Baguirmi.
Economy: Besides the traditional crops of millet, sorghum, and manioc, advances are being made in the production of cotton, which now accounts for 80 percent of the exports and supplies a textile industry. Wheat has recently been introduced and is grown for home consumption. A large part of the working population, however, is engaged in stock-rearing. Chad is poor in mineral resources and there is little industry other than textile manufacturing.

CENTRAL AFRICAN EMPIRE
Area: 240,534 square miles
Population: 3,200,000
Capital: Bangui
Language: French and Sango
Religion: Mainly Animism
Monetary Unit: Franc CFA
History and Government: The Central African Empire was part of French Equatorial Africa until 1960 when it changed its name from Ubanghi Shari to the Central African Republic. In 1965 a military coup d'état brought Colonel

Jean Bedel Bokassa to power as president. In 1976 President Bokassa declared himself emperor and a new constitution was adopted turning the government into a parliamentary monarchy.
Economy: Agriculture, especially cotton, coffee, and tobacco, and forestry are the basis of the economy. They employ three quarters of the labor force and provide about half the country's income. Stock-rearing has also become important. The exploitation of mineral resources is limited to diamonds and gold, but there are considerable reserves of iron ore, nickel, manganese, cobalt, tin, copper, mercury, and uranium. The policy of admitting foreign investments has favored the emergence of numerous, though small, industries including foodstuffs, chemicals, textiles, and engineering.

SUDAN
Area: 967,494 square miles
Population: 19,500,000
Capital: Khartoum
Language: Arabic
Religion: Animism and Islam
Monetary Unit: Sudanese pound
History and Government: Ruled by an Anglo-Egyptian Condominium since 1899, the Sudan House of Representatives voted overwhelmingly to become an independent state in 1955. There have been several coups d'état, in 1958, 1964, and 1969. Since May 1969, Sudan has been ruled through a 10-man revolutionary council under the chairmanship of Colonel Jaafar M al Nemery.
Economy: The Sudan is not rich, either in raw materials or in industries. Agriculture employs 80 percent of the labor force, growing mainly cotton, both long and short staple varieties. Next in importance is gum arabic (about 80 percent of the total world production comes from the Sudan), oil seeds, peanuts, sesame, dates, pulses, coffee, tea, and tobacco. Stock-rearing – camels, cattle, and sheep – is important providing hides and skins. Mineral resources are modest and industrial development is barely beginning.

ETHIOPIA
Area: 471,775 square miles
Population: 28,000,000
Capital: Addis Ababa
Language: Amharic
Religion: Coptic Christianity

Monetary Unit: Ethiopian Birr
History and Government: Ethiopia, the "diplomatic capital" of Africa, is the state whose independence dates back furthest in the continent, to centuries before the birth of Christ. In 1936 it was conquered by the Italians, but freed by the Allied forces in 1941. In 1952, Eritrea, the former Italian colony, was handed over to Ethiopia and in 1962 fully integrated with the country. The capital, Addis Ababa, is the seat of the Organization for African Unity (OAU) and gives the country considerable international prestige. The country's internal structure is feudal, authoritarian, and characterized by considerable poverty among the masses. Following years of drought and bad harvests there was military and civil unrest and in 1974 the army seized power, accompanied by student and peasant risings and deposition of the old emperor, Hailé Selassié. In 1977, the military head of state was killed and the old military regime replaced with another equally dictatorial regime.
Economy: The agricultural production provides a very large proportion of the national income. But the primitive organization and techniques are hindering its development. The most lucrative activity is stock-rearing – cattle, sheep, goats, and poultry. The most widespread type of crop is cereals, which are exported despite the starvation level of the local population, then come legumes and industrial crops from which oils and perfumes are produced. Coffee, flax, cotton, sugar cane, and tobacco, are also grown. Proven mineral resources are modest (gold, platinum, salt, and manganese); industries are not very well developed, the chief ones being concerned with foodstuffs and textiles.

DJIBOUTI
Area: 8494 square miles
Population: 99,000
Capital: Djibouti
Monetary Unit: Djibouti Franc
History and Government: Acquired by the French in 1862, it had the status of a colony until 1946 when it became a territory in the French union, as French Somaliland and renamed the French Territory of the Afars and the Issas in 1967. In 1978 it became the independent state of Djibouti.
Economy: It is a poor country and the main activities are stock-rearing, fishing, and forestry. Rock salt is also mined. Djibouti is an important trade center, both as a port and as a terminal of the Djibouti-Addis Ababa railway.

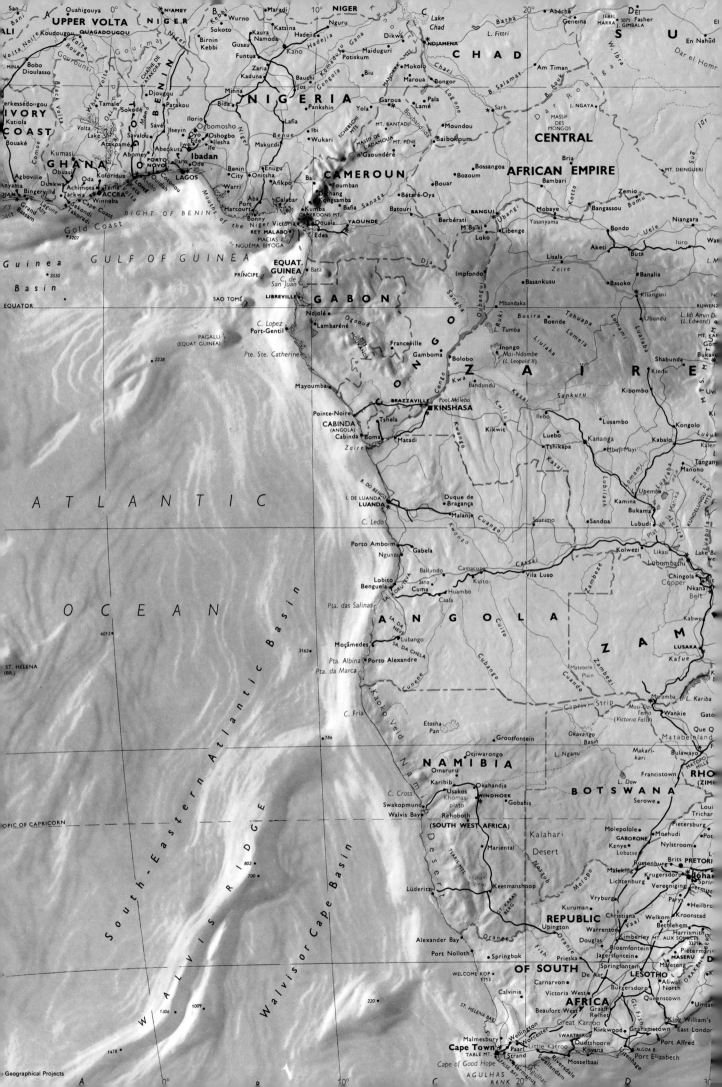

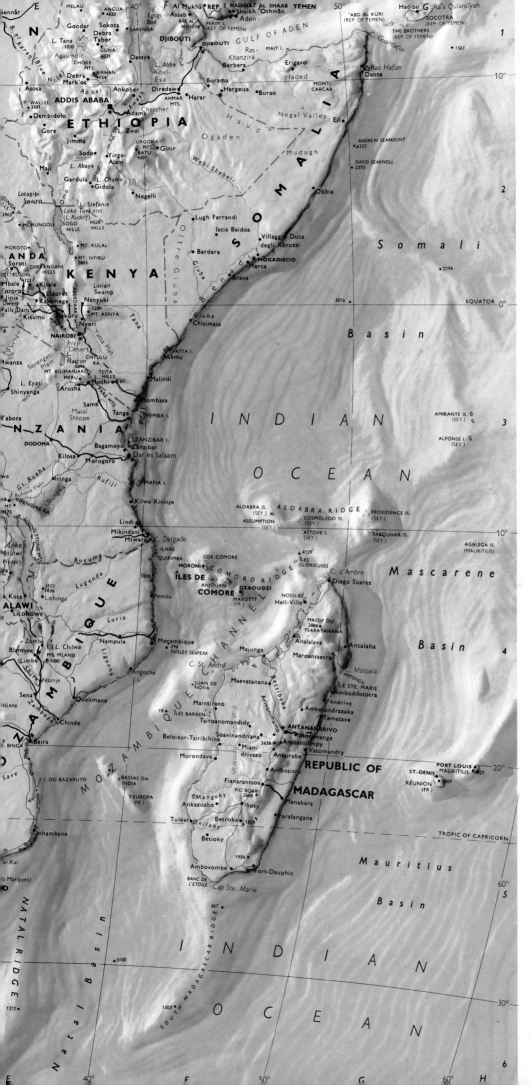

Southern Africa

Towns:
■ over 1,000,000
● over 500,000
● over 250,000
• under 250,000
✱ Airports
Red thin line — Main roads
Black thin line — Main railways
Blue thick line — Sea routes
Red thick line — Air routes

185

SOMALIA (Somali Democratic Republic)

Area: 246,200 square miles
Population: 3,200,000
Capital: Mogadiscio (Mogadishu)
Language: Somali (also Arabic, English, and Italian)
Religion: Sunnite Islam
Monetary Unit: Somali Shilling
History and Government: Incorporating what was once a powerful Arab sultanate in the middle ages, the present republic came into being in 1960 as a result of the merger of the former Italian Somaliland and the British Somaliland Protectorate, which had just achieved its own independence. In 1969, nine years after gaining independence, a military coup d'état overthrew the parliamentary republic and instituted the Democratic Socialist Republic. A supreme revolutionary council was formed, which took over responsibility of legislature. The council appointed 14 civilian secretaries of state. The concept of a national unity was reinforced by the creation of a written language – Somali had only been a spoken language. However, the legacy of two different types of colonization hampers economic development.
Economy: The chief wealth of the country lies in stock-rearing – sheep, goats, camels, and some cattle – the products of which represent more than 50 percent of the exports. Agriculture is practiced only in a limited area in the south. The most lucrative crop is bananas, exported to Italy, then peanuts, cotton, tobacco, sugar cane, and cereals. Mineral resources are poor, but uranium has been discovered. Industrial activity is limited to small firms processing the products of agriculture, stock-rearing, and fishing.

SENEGAL (République du Sénégal)

Area: 75,954 square miles
Population: 5,000,000
Capital: Dakar
Language: French and Wolof
Religion: Mainly Islam
Monetary Unit: Franc CFA
History and Government: Senegal became independent in 1960 after having been a French Territory since as early as 1659 when the town of Saint-Louis was founded on the coast. It is a presidential republic, with a three-party system of liberals, socialists, and marxists. It is administered by a govern-

ment council of 17 ministers and four secretaries of state. The National Assembly has 80 members, elected by universal suffrage every four years.
Economy: The life of Senegal revolves around peanuts, the principal resource of the economy. The production of coffee, cocoa, cotton, rice, coconuts, and the resulting oil is developing. Stock-rearing – mainly sheep, but also goats, cattle, pigs, asses, and horses – and fishing are important. The forests provide precious woods and essences. Even though 80 percent of the population is employed in agriculture, Senegal has one of the longest histories of industrialization in Africa. The industries were set up, and are largely controlled, by the French and revolve around the processing of peanuts for oil and fodder. The mineral resources are mainly phosphates and titanium ore.

GAMBIA

Area: 4003 square miles
Population: 493,000
Capital: Banjul (formerly Bathurst)
Language: English
Religion: Islam
Monetary Unit: Dalasi
History and Government: The state began in 1807 as a settlement on the Gambia river and was controlled from Sierra Leone, but in 1843 it became an independent crown colony. In 1965 it became an independent member of the Commonwealth and in 1970 a republic within the Commonwealth. It has an executive president and a House of Representatives. It is politically conditioned by its attachment to the UK.
Economy: An essentially agricultural country, its chief resource is peanuts, but it depends on imports for its food. With financial help from Britain, it is concentrating on the diversification and rationalization of crops such as rice, the development of the fisheries and the exploitation of the forests. Mineral resources are nonexistent and industry small.

GUINEA-BISSAU

Area: 13,947 square miles
Population: 600,000
Capital: Bissau
Language: Portuguese
Religion: Animism and Islam
Monetary Unit: Escudo

History and Government: Discovered by the Portuguese in 1446, it was active in supplying the slave trade in the 17th and 18th centuries. The boundaries of Portuguese Guinea were established in 1886. In September 1973 after 12 years of struggle against the Portuguese, PAIGC (African Party for the Independence of Guinea and the Cape Verde Islands) proclaimed the independence of the country. This was recognized by the UN. In 1974, Portugal also recognized the new country Guinea-Bissau. A new economic, social, and governmental system was created. The system has already had a measure of success in dealing with the problem of illiteracy.
Economy: Agriculture of a primitive type predominates; the chief products are peanuts, rice, palm oil, and coconuts. Manufacturing and mining are almost nonexistent but there are bauxite deposits in the south.

CAPE VERDE ISLANDS

Area: 1557 square miles
Population: 291,000
Capital: Praia
Language: Portuguese and Creole
Religion: Catholicism
Monetary Unit: Escudo
History and Government: In 1975 after five centuries of Portuguese rule achieved independence after a coup d'état in Portugal. Eventual political union with Guinea-Bissau is desired by both countries.
Economy: The population lives by agriculture (corn, bananas, coffee, etc.), stock-rearing, and fishing, especially for tuna. The only mineral product is salt.

GUINEA (Guinée)

Area: 94,925 square miles
Population: 4,312,000
Capital: Conakry
Language: French
Religion: Animism and Islam
Monetary Unit: Syli
History and Government: Proclaimed a French protectorate in 1860 and after a series of wars with native rulers, became a colony, as French Guinea, in 1893. It was the first country in French West Africa to win independence in 1958. It joined the Sudanese Republic in the Mali Federation in

1959, but withdrew in 1960. It is a presidential republic, the president being elected for a seven-year term and can be reelected. The National Assembly has 75 members from single party, the PDG (Parti Démocratique de Guinée). This party has a political structure based on district and village committees. The president, however, has a strong control over the other authorities.

Economy: Around half the working population is employed in agriculture, a large proportion of the products of which is taken up by the home market. Coffee, peanuts, and bananas are exported. There is a small amount of stock-rearing. Mineral resources, on the other hand, are rich: bauxite, of which Guinea is one of the foremost producers in the world, iron ore, and diamonds. Manufacturing industries are few and mostly connected with the processing of agricultural products. There are plans for development of manufacturing and mining, supported by considerable foreign aid, in particular from the USA, USSR, the FDR, Yugoslavia, and China. China has shares in the extension of the Conakry-Kankan (Mali) railway to Bamako, the capital of Mali.

SIERRA LEONE
Area: 27,699 square miles
Population: 3,000,000
Capital: Freetown
Language: Creole and English
Religion: Mainly Animism
Monetary Unit: Leone
History and Government: The region was first explored by Portuguese in 1462, then raided by slave traders. English philanthropists established settlements for runaway and freed slaves in later 1700s. Became British protectorate in 1896. Independent since 1961, Sierra Leone became a republic within the Commonwealth in 1971. The Constitution of 1971, provides for an executive president. Parliament has 77 elected members, 12 paramount chiefs, and 3 appointed members.
Economy: A large part of the population lives by a very poor type of agriculture; in the west growing cassava, corn, and vegetables for local consumption; in the east, rice, cocoa, and beans. The production of ginger and palm kernels has recently been developed, but the greatest resource remains the mining of diamonds, iron ore, and bauxite. The rapid increase in industrialization and road and transportation communications has meant a shift of population from the land to urban areas.

LIBERIA
Area: 43,000 square miles
Population: 1,669,000
Capital: Monrovia
Language: English
Religion: Animism
Monetary Unit: Liberian Dollar
History and Government: A settlement was formed in 1822 and in 1847 Liberia became a presidential republic modeled on that of the USA, with two houses, a Senate and a House of Representatives. Liberia's political life is conditioned by the rivalry between the descendents of black slaves repatriated from the USA – and who until recently represented the only literate group and governing class – and the aboriginal majority. The influence of the USA is strong in both politics and the economy.
Economy: The USA has a particularly strong control in the production of rubber and iron ore, of which Liberia is the chief producer in Africa. The oil wells, too, are run by foreign companies. Other important mineral resources are diamonds and gold, but there are unexploited deposits of manganese, titanium, graphite, and mercury. Agriculture barely produces enough for food for the local population – the chief crops are rice, cassava, coffee, citrus fruits, and sugar cane. Industries are few and the forests are barely exploited. Liberia's merchant navy is the largest in the world, but the government maintains no control over the ships flying the Liberian flag.

IVORY COAST (République de Côte d'Ivoire)
Area: 127,000 square miles
Population: 6,673,000
Capital: Abidjan
Language: French
Religion: Mainly Animism
Monetary Unit: Franc CFA
History and Government: Ivory Coast became a French protectorate in 1889 after war with the king of Mandingo. It was made a colony in 1893, and became independent in 1960. It is a presidential republic, modeled on the government systems of the USA and the Fifth French Republic. The republic is administered by a government of 17 ministers. The Legislative Assembly has 85 members, all belonging to a single party, Rassemblement Démocratique Africa. All power is in the hands of the president. Despite political and tribal crises, the Ivory Coast maintains a remarkable political stability. The regime is moderate, the economy is based on free trade, and there are opportunities for the investment of foreign capital.

Economy: The country is among the leaders in the production of coffee and cocoa, both cultivated with the help of foreign labor. The tendency is toward diversification of crops such as yams, manioc, corn, bananas, rice, and cotton. There are good mineral resources – diamonds, manganese, gold, tantalum, iron ore. Industrial production is moderate, especially in the fields of textiles, foodstuffs, and the refining of oil.

Below: wood carving of West African drummers. Drums are still used in African folk dance and ceremony.

GHANA
Area: 92,100 square miles
Population: 9,607,000
Capital: Accra
Language: English, Kwa, and Sudanese dialects

Religion: Animism and Christianity
Monetary Unit: Cedi
History and Government: Occupying an area first settled by Portuguese in the 1400s, and later in the hands of various European countries, the Gold Coast and Ashanti colonies, the Northern Territories Protectorate and West Togoland Trust Territory make up what is now called Ghana. It was the first British-ruled black African country to gain independence (1957) and has been a republic within the Commonwealth since 1960. A coup d'état in 1966 put an end to the socialist regime of Dr Nkrumah, and Ghana was ruled until 1969 by the Army and police until a new Constitution was brought into effect in 1969. After a coup d'état by the army, a National Redemption Council (NRC) was established to administer the country and its chairman is head of state. Rule is by decree.
Economy: Ghana is the biggest cocoa producer in the world and in recent years has increased the yield and introduced improved varieties. Other crops are also grown: palm oil, tobacco, rubber, cereals, and fruits. Ghana grows most of her own food – peanuts, rice, corn, millet, yams, and cassava. Other important resources are timber, gold, manganese, bauxite, and industrial diamonds. A modern industrial complex has been set up in the Accra-Tema area. Fishing supplies 80 percent of home demand and the industry is growing.

TOGO
Area: 21,000 square miles
Population: 2,000,000
Capital: Lomé
Language: French
Religion: Mainly Animism
Monetary Unit: Franc CFA
History and Government: Togo, or Togoland, was a German protectorate from 1894 to 1914, then a mandate of the League of Nations and a British and French trusteeship territory under the UN. British Togoland was incorporated into the independent state of Ghana, French Togo became the independent Republic of Togo in 1960. After two coups d'état the military suspended the Constitution, dissolved parliament and the old political parties, and created a single party.
Economy: Around 80 percent of the people live by agriculture. The most important crops are cocoa, cotton, coffee, peanuts, palm oil, and cassava. Unemployment is endemic, resulting in considerable seasonal emigration. There are textile, food, and chemical industries. Exports of agricultural pro-

ducts have been superceded by those of phosphates. There are also reserves of bauxite that are being exploited. Iron ore has also been located.

BENIN
Area: 47,000 square miles
Population: 3,000,000
Capital: Porto Novo
Language: French
Religion: Mainly Animism
Monetary Unit: Franc CFA
History and Government: Formerly a native kingdom that arose in the 17th century and had its capital at the town of Abomey, captured by French, who deposed the ruler in 1892. It was, as Dahomey, part of French West Africa. Now known as Benin, it has been independent since 1960. After various experiments, including a three-man presidency, the army seized power in 1972. The causes of the unrest are the conflicts between ethnic groups that result in tension between the north and the

south, and serious economic difficulties.
Economy: Agriculture is in a backward state and the reason is a lack of industry. Because Benin also lacks good mineral resources, it has to depend on French aid, though it also receives aid from the USA. Kernels and oil (from the oil palm), coffee, coconuts, and cotton provide the main exports. Corn, wheat, peanuts are grown for home consumption. There are some forests and stock-rearing is little developed. There are small deposits of iron ore, chromite, and marble.

NIGERIA (Federation of Nigeria)
Area: 356,666 square miles
Population: 80,000,000
Capital: Lagos
Language: English, Hausa, Ibo, and Yoruba
Religion: Animism, Christianity, Islam
Monetary Unit: Naira
History and Government: Nigeria occupies a region of diverse ethnic,

eligious, and social groups including he former medieval negro empire of he Songhai, the Fulah empire under Berber and Arab influence, the highly organized native kingdom of Benin, and the former Islamic sultanate of Bornu. It came under increasing British influence in 19th century eventually becoming the colony and protectorate of Nigeria in 1914, and a Dominion in 1960. Nigeria became a republic within the Commonwealth in 1963. It is a federation comprising a number of areas formerly under separate administration. In 1967-70 the balance of the various ethnic groups was upset by the war of secession of the Eastern Province, Biafra, the site of the largest oil deposits. The country is now ruled by a federal military government with military governors administering the 19 states.

Below: people of Dogondoutchi, southwestern Nigeria, preparing their grain surplus for storage in the town granaries. Food surpluses are highly prized in an area of famine. Dogondoutchi's granaries on stilts are therefore the equivalent of city banks.

Economy: The predominant activity is agriculture and there is great variety of tropical crops – peanuts, soybeans, cotton in the north; cocoa, oil palm, rubber in the wetter south. The main resource however is oil, of which Nigeria is one of the largest producers in the world. Since 1974 Nigeria has had direct control of its oil industry. There are also rich deposits of other minerals, including tin, columbite, coal, gold, tantalite, as well as natural gas. The textile industry and the processing of agricultural products are well developed and there are industries dealing with peanuts, oil, canned fruits, plywood, and treatment of hides.

SAINT HELENA
Area: 121 square miles
Population: 6000
Chief Town: Jamestown
Language: English
Religion: Mostly Protestantism
Monetary Unit: Saint Helena Pound
History and Government: A British dependency famous as the deathplace of the exiled Napoleon Bonaparte in 1821. It includes its own dependencies of the islands of Ascension and Tristan da Cunha (which includes Gouch Island). Saint Helena is administered by a governor with the aid of a Legislative Council.
Economy: In Saint Helena potato-growing and stock-rearing are the chief occupations; in Tristan da Cunha fishing, and in Ascension turtle-hunting. In 1961, the volcano of Tristan erupted and the whole population had to be evacuated and did not return until 1963.

CAMEROUN
Area: 183,568 square miles
Population: 5,836,000
Capital: Yaoundé
Language: English and French
Religion: Animism
Monetary Unit: Franc CFA
History and Government: The German colony of Kamerun founded in 1884 was divided between Britain and France after World War I. The portion under French Trusteeship became independent in 1960, and was joined by the former British-administered trusteeship of Southern Cameroons in 1961. After a period as a federal republic, the quest for national unity overcame the geographical, ethnic, and social differences, and a referendum in

Above: a Buduma woman from Lake Chad. The Buduma inhabit some 70 islands in Lake Chad.

1972 modified the Constitution and proclaimed the United Republic of Cameroun.
Economy: Agriculture occupies some 85 percent of the working population. Among the crops that are most highly developed for export are cocoa, coffee, cotton, bananas, and timber. The problem of the government is to rationalize industry, exploit the mineral resources, which include large reserves of bauxite and iron ore, and develop the manufacturing industries. Foreign investment is encouraged.

EQUATORIAL GUINEA (Guinée Equatorial)
Area: 10,830 square miles
Population: 305,000
Capital: Malabo (formerly Santa Isabel)
Language: Spanish
Religion: Mainly Catholicism
Monetary Unit: Ekuele
History and Government: Equatorial Guinea has been an independent republic since 1968. It was formerly a Spanish colony and consists of Rio Muni on the mainland, the islands of Macias Nguema Biyoga (formerly Fernando Póo), Pigalu (formerly Annobón) and the Corisco Islands. The republic is administered by a president with an assembly elected for a five-year period. The first president was elected for life in 1972. The first years of independence were marked by severe disorders resulting in the evacuation of the large numbers of resident Spanish and Nigerian workers – on whom the cocoa production mainly depended. The economy depends upon aid from Cuba, China, and other communist countries.

Economy: The chief wealth is from agriculture – cocoa, palm oil, bananas, pineapples, coffee, and coconuts. A large proportion of the exports consist of cocoa and precious woods, but agriculture, and the plantations in particular, are suffering since the departure of the Spanish managers. Industries are few, and only of the cottage type, except in Macias Nguema Biyoga where fish processing is being developed. Communications are inadequate.

SÃO TOMÉ E PRÍNCIPE
Area: 372 square miles
Population: 74,000
Capital: São Tomé
Language: Creole and Portuguese
Religion: Catholicism
Monetary Unit: Escudo
History and Government: Discovered by the Portuguese in the 1470s, the islands played a part in the slave trade at one time. In 1951 they were made an overseas province. Portugal granted independence to the islands on July 12, 1975.
Economy: The principal activity is the production of cocoa. There is also cultivation of coffee, coconuts, palm oil and bananas. Industries are fish canning, palm-oil processing and soap manufacturing.

GABON
Area: 103,346 square miles
Population: 520,000
Capital: Libreville
Language: Bantu (Fang), and French
Religion: Animism and Catholicism
Monetary Unit: Franc CFA
History and Government: Gabon became an independent republic in 1960 after having been a part of French Equatorial Africa since 1910, though it had been settled by the French since 1841 and a colony since 1903. After a period of conflict which was cut short in 1964 by a demand for French military assistance, Gabon has experienced a long period of stability and·one of the fastest economic growth rates in Africa. The regime is of a presidential republic with a single party pledged to the development of the economy.
Economy: The greatest source of wealth is oil, of which Gabon is the fourth largest producer in Africa. Forests cover 85 percent of the country and provide the okome wood that is exported all over the world. In agriculture food

crops predominate and plantations of bananas, coffee, and cocoa are developing. Special attention is concentrated on the rich mineral resources of uranium, manganese, iron ore, and other minerals. There is little manufacturing industry but an oil refinery is in operation at Port-Gentil.

CONGO
Area: 132,040 square miles
Population: 1,300,000
Capital: Brazzaville
Language: French, Kikongo, Lingale
Religion: Mainly Animism
Monetary Unit: Franc CFA
History and Government: As Middle Congo, the Republic of Congo was formerly part of French Equatorial Africa. It became independent in 1960 and was proclaimed a People's Republic in December, 1969, after the rise to power of the "Marxist" movement of Marien Ngouabi. After Ngouabi's assassination in 1977 the military took over the leadership of the state.
Economy: Agriculture employs most of the population, but does not provide enough for the country's needs. Cocoa, coffee, peanuts, lead, zinc, hides, butter, ivory, and beeswax are exported. It is also an important producer of cotton, diamonds, and gold.

Above: Africans fishing in the swiftly running rapids of the Congo river. The fish are caught in trawl-shaped baskets hung from pierlike structures of tree trunks built out over the water

ZAIRE
Area: 905,360 square miles
Population: 24,500,000
Capital: Kinshasa (formerly Leopoldville)
Language: French, Kikongo, Lingala, Swahili
Religion: Animism and Christianity
Monetary Unit: Zaire
History and Government: The territory was developed under the auspices of King Leopold II of Belgium from 187? and became Congo Free State in 188? and was annexed to Belgium as Belgian Congo in 1908. It became independen? in 1960 under the name Congo Republic later changing its name to Zaire in 1971 Colonial intervention and tribal an? political strife marked the first five years of independence of the republic which were finally ended by the rise of General Joseph Mobutu in 1965. The present regime gives a large part of the power to the president of the republic parliament has only consultative functions. Candidates for the presidency and for parliament are designated by the Mouvement Populaire de la Révo

ution (MPR), whose president is President Mobutu.

Economy: Development programs are concentrated on the great hydroelectric power stations of Inga on the Zaire River, potentially capable of supplying the whole continent. It is the mineral resources that provide the key to the country's development, however. Zaire is among the foremost in the world for copper, the first for cobalt, and is the biggest exporter of diamonds. It also has considerable deposits of zinc, manganese, tin, silver, uranium, radium, germanium, coal, and methane. These are, for the most part, in Shaba. The manufacturing industries are developing, especially in the production of foodstuffs, textiles, chemicals, metallurgy, and engineering. Agriculture with stock-rearing and fishing, employs the majority of the population. The cultivation of palm oil is widespread; the next most important products are cotton, coffee, rubber, rice, cocoa, peanuts, and sugar cane. The rich forests have scarcely been exploited.

Below: pouring slag from a copper mine at Chingola, Zambia. Copper is Zambia's chief industry and copper ores are to be found over a vast area.

UGANDA
Area: 91,451 square miles
Population: 11,500,000
Capital: Kampala
Language: English and Swahili
Religion: Animism, Christianity, and Islam

Monetary Unit: Uganda Shilling
History and Government: In 1962 Uganda became a fully independent member of the Commonwealth after having been a protectorate since 1849. Troubled by serious tribal conflicts, the republic was governed between 1971–79 by General Idi Amin, who overthrew the president, dissolved parliament, and suspended the Constitution. In 1979 the country was invaded by Ugandan exiles backed by neighboring Tanzanian forces. After fierce fighting, General Amin's forces were overthrown and the former dictator fled the country. A provisional government was set up under a retired university professor, Dr Yusuf Lule, until normal political life could be resumed in the country.

Economy: Coffee and cotton are the basic products of the economy and represent about 75 percent of the exports. Programs of diversification of the crops have developed the production of sugar cane, tea, peanuts, sesame, and various other food products such as green vegetables. There is a considerable amount of stock-rearing. Copper has been exploited and there is also some tantalum, tin, and tungsten.

RWANDA
Area: 10,169 square miles
Population: 4,000,000
Capital: Kigali
Language: French and Kinyarwanda
Religion: Mainly Catholicism
Monetary Unit: Rwanda Franc
History and Government: The Tutri kingdom was established in the 16th century and in 1890 was incorporated in German East Africa. From 1919 Rwanda (as part of Ruanda-Burundi) was a Belgian mandate. Independence was granted in 1962 and after a referendum against the retention of the monarchy, it became a presidential republic. In 1973, after bloody tribal clashes, a coup d'état brought to power a committee of generals.
Economy: It is one of the most densely populated countries in Africa, but subsistence agriculture is almost the exclusive activity of the people. The cereal crop is not sufficient for internal needs and there are chronic famine conditions. The main product exported is coffee. Cattle are of importance traditionally and efforts are being made to improve their value. The minerals mined are tin, cassiterites, and natural gas. Hydroelectric power is abundant, but manufacturing industry is non-existent. The rate of migration is high and the people find work in other countries in East Africa.

BURUNDI
Area: 10,746 square miles
Population: 4,000,000
Capital: Bujumbura (Usumbura)
Language: French, Kirundi, and Swahili
Religion: Animism and Catholicism
Monetary Unit: Burundi Franc
History and Government: Burundi has had a similar history to that of its neighbor Rwanda and gained its independence in 1962 as a constitutional monarchy. In 1966 the monarchy was overthrown by General Micombero, who proclaimed a republic and dissolved parliament. In 1972, he dissolved the council of ministers and took full power, until he himself was ousted in 1976 and supplanted by a supreme revolutionary council.
Economy: Like Rwanda, Burundi has one of the densest populations in the world. It is a very poor country, struggling with the endemic problem of famine. The population is engaged in subsistence agriculture – beans, cassava, sweet potatoes, peanuts, and bananas. Products for export are mainly coffee and cotton. There are good prospects for stock-rearing and also fishing, in Lake Tanganyika. There are no industries. The mineral resources are cassiterites, basthennaesite (which contains europium, used in the French color television system), kaolin, and gold.

KENYA
Area: 224,960 square miles
Population: 13,000,000
Capital: Nairobi
Language: English and Swahili
Religion: Christianity and Islam
Monetary Unit: Kenya Shilling
History and Government: Kenya originally was a British colony and mainland protectorate of the dominion of the sultan of Zanzibar. Now a republic within the Commonwealth, it became independent in 1963 after a six-month period of internal self government. The National Assembly consists of a single House of Representatives. The country had a long period of stable government, due to the prestige of its first president, Mzee Jomo Kenyatta who died in 1978. The only party represented in parliament is KANU (Kenya African National Union).
Economy: Agriculture dominates Kenya's economy, providing 35 percent of the national income. A partial

form of socialism based on the develop
ment of the country regions rather than
on industrialization with the help of
foreign investments.

Economy: The economy is essentially
agricultural. The principal crops are
sisal (Tanzania is among the foremost
producers in the world of sisal), cotton
and pyrethrum. Plans for diversifying
the crops have been speeded up and
now tea, sugar cane, tobacco, carda-
moms, beans, coconuts, and corn are
all grown. Different types of farming
are also on the increase, particularly
animal husbandry and forestry. Mineral resources have scarcely been exploited but there are rich deposits of
diamonds, gold, tin, magnesite, and
salt. Industry is not very extensive
but has a high rate of development in
foodstuffs, textiles, chemicals, cements
metallurgy and engineering. In 196
the banks were nationalized, and short-
ly afterward the foreign companies as
well. The first branch of the Tanzan
railroad, linking Dar es Salaam with
Kipiri Mposhi in Zambia, is now in
operation. This was financed and buil
by the Chinese. Dar es Salaam, with its
six deep-water berths, is the main port
and it also has an international airport

ANGOLA
Area: 481,351 square miles
Population: 6,000,000
Capital: Luanda
Language: Bantu languages and
Portuguese
Religion: Mainly Animism
Monetary Unit: Escudo
History and Government: Settled
originally by Portuguese in 16th century, this, the richest of the former
Portuguese overseas territories, was
involved in an anti-colonial war from
1961 to 1975 when the country won
political independence. Its mineral
wealth and strategic position in Africa
have given Angola a crucial role to
play in the future of the continent and
have also made the country a theater
of international armed conflict.
Economy: The majority of the population is engaged in agriculture, in the
coffee plantations (among the most
important in the world), and in cotton
tobacco, sisal, corn, sugar cane, and
palm oil cultivation. Forced labor was
used in the past. The main resource is
oil, of which there are enormous reserves, especially in Cabinda (the detached part of Angola to the north of
the mouth of the Congo). Also important are deposits of diamonds, iron ore
and other minerals. Industry is poorly
developed.

Above: Endo warriors from Kenya.
Although Kenya's tribes retain their
own dialects, they have a common
root in Bantu, the great African
language spoken by many peoples in
Africa. Many Bantu tribes were once
fierce warriors – as well as being
skilled in pottery and weaving.

agrarian reform has been carried out.
Crops are sufficiently varied – coffee,
tea, peanuts, corn, sisal, wheat, pyrethrum, sugar cane. There is also a wide
variety of fruits and vegetables. The
livestock industry is also important
producing canned beef, butter, hides,
and skins. There are large areas of
forests which provide both hard and
softwoods. Principal minerals produced
are soda ash, gold, and salt. There has
been a rapid growth of industry, especially in the sectors of food, metallurgy, cement, fertilizers, and oil refining. Great efforts are being made to
develop tourism and this is rapidly
becoming one of the principal sources
of revenue.

TANZANIA
Area: 361,847 square miles
Population: 12,000,000
Capital: Dodoma
Language: English and Swahili
Religion: Mainly Animism
Monetary Unit: Tanzanian Shilling
History and Government: With
Ruanda-Urundi it formed German East
Africa, which was eventually placed
under the protection of the German
empire in 1891. After 1919 the part
known as Tanganyika became a British
mandate. The federal republic of Tanzania was founded in 1964 with the
union of Tanganyika and Zanzibar
(which had been independent since
1963). The republic is of the presidential
type, with a president who is both head
of state and head of government. Tanzania is a single-party state and a member of the Commonwealth. Economically, the country is moving toward a

ZAMBIA

Area: 288,128 square miles
Population: 5,000,000
Capital: Lusaka
Language: Bantu languages and English
Religion: Animism
Monetary Unit: Kwacha
History and Government: Administered by the British South Africa Company between 1889 to 1923, and a crown colony from 1923 to 1953 Northern Rhodesia was for a short period part of the Federation of Rhodesia and Nyasaland. As Zambia it has been independent since 1964. It is a republic within the Commonwealth and had a multiparty constitution until the Constitution of 1972 changed to single party rule.
Economy: The greatest resource is copper, of which Zambia is the second highest producer in the world. It represents 95 percent of the exports. Since Zambia closed its frontier with Rhodesia, the outlet for its copper exports is now through the newly constructed Tanzam railroad, which links Zambia with Tanzania. There are also deposits of iron ore, cobalt, manganese, lead, and zinc. The chief agricultural products are corn, peanuts, tobacco, cotton, and sugar cane. There are attempts to diversify the economy by developing new industries and initiating programs of education and the establishment of training schemes.

ZIMBABWE-RHODESIA

Area: 150,819 square miles
Population: 6,000,000
Capital: Salisbury
Language: Bantu languages and English
Religion: Animism and Christianity
Monetary Unit: Dollar
History and Government: Like Northern Rhodesia, Southern Rhodesia was administered by the British South Africa Company until 1923 when it became a self-governing colony. After dissolution of the Federation of Rhodesia and Nyasaland it reverted to the status of a self-governing colony within the Commonwealth. Legally this is still the position. In fact it proclaimed its Unilateral Declaration of Independence (UDI) in 1965 and left the Commonwealth a year later. In 1970 it constituted itself a republic, and in 1979 the white citizens voted to modify the Constitution allowing for "safe-

guarded" black majority rule. The country's name was changed to Zimbabwe-Rhodesia. The country has a Legislative Assembly of 66 members and a cabinet of 14 members. There is considerable guerrilla warfare by nationalist party forces backed by bordering states.
Economy: The traditional basis of the economy is tobacco of which Rhodesia is the foremost producer in Africa. Other important crops are cotton, corn, sugar cane, peanuts, tea, and citrus fruits. The Africans practice subsistence agriculture growing grains, rice, and cassava. Minerals are also important exports – gold, chromite, nickel, amianthus, rock salt, coal, iron ore, and copper. Manufacturing industry is developing rapidly, especially metallurgy, foodstuffs, cement, chemicals and petrochemicals, and electrical engineering. The economy, however, is suffering from the sanctions imposed by member-nations of the UN.

MALAWI

Area: 45,746 square miles
Population: 5,000,000
Capital: Lilongwe
Language: English
Religion: Mainly Animism
Monetary Unit: Kwacha
History and Government: From 1893 to 1907 Malawi was known as the British Central Africa Protectorate, after which it was known as Nyasaland. After a short period in the Federation of Rhodesia and Nyasaland, it became in 1963 a self-governing country, and in 1964 an independent member of the Commonwealth under the new name Malawi. In 1966 it became a republic within the Commonwealth. The president is head of government and for all practical purposes there is only one party. Malawi's position in the OAU (Organization for African Unity) is sometimes controversial as it cooperates with South Africa, from whom it accepts financial and technical aid. Africanization has proceeded only slowly since independence; public offices are still largely held by Europeans, who also control industry and commerce.
Economy: Unlike its neighbor, Zambia, Malawi has few mineral resources and industries. Its only proven deposits are bauxite, which have been discovered recently. Agriculture provides over half of the national income and three quarters of the exports. However, owing to the rapid growth of the population, production is not enough to supply local needs and consequently many people are leaving the country. The crops that are developed commercially

are tea, cotton, peanuts, and tobacco. Corn is the chief subsistence crop.

Below: an Arab dhow on Lake Malawi, shows influences of a one-time Arab slave trade in the area.

MOZAMBIQUE (Moçambique)

Area: 308,640 square miles
Population: 10,000,000
Capital: Maputo (formerly Lourenço Marques)
Language: Bantu and Portuguese
Religion: Animism
Monetary Unit: Escudo
History and Government: Discovered by Vasco da Gama in 1498 and colonized by Portugal in 1505, Mozambique achieved independence in 1975. Power was handed to the Marxist liberation movement, Frelimo, and the constitution of 1975 made the head of Frelimo head of state. Rule is through a 210-member People's Assembly.
Economy: Collectivized agriculture is the basis of the economy, as laid down by the new government. Exports are of several crops – sugar cane, cotton, peanuts, sisal, coconuts, cashew nuts, and tea. Mineral resources are small but there are deposits of iron ore, gold, beryl, and bauxite. Industries are few.

Namibia's sovereignty is in dispute; no single flag.

NAMIBIA (South West Africa)

Area: 318,259 square miles
Population: 750,000
Capital: Windhoek
Language: Afrikaans, Bantu
Religion: Mainly Animism
Monetary Unit: South African currency
History and Government: A former

German colony, South West Africa became a South African mandate in 1919. In 1971 the International Court of Justice at The Hague ruled that the continued presence of South African administration in Namibia was illegal. In 1975 constitutional talks were begun in Windhoek and it was agreed that it would be granted independence in the late 1970s.

Economy: In this country are the biggest diamond (industrial) and uranium mines as well as copper, zinc, lead, manganese, and salt deposits. It is essentially a stock-rearing country, cattle being kept in the north and sheep and goats in the south. The production of the Karakul (sheep) pelts for export is gaining importance. Fishing is also important.

BOTSWANA
Area: 220,000 square miles
Population: 720,000
Capital: Gaberone
Language: English and Setswaha
Religion: Animism
Monetary Unit: Pula
History and Government: Botswana was the former British protectorate of Bechuanaland. In 1966 it became the independent republic of Botswana and a member of the Commonwealth. The president, Sir Seretse Khama, the former Paramount Chief, is responsible to

Below: a dried-up salt pan in the Kalahari Desert, the wasteland area in Botswana and Namibia.

Above: a Namaqua woman of Namibia carrying firewood. The Namaqua are members of the Hottentot people.

the National Assembly. There is also a House of Chiefs to advise the government.

Economy: Botswana is predominantly a pastoral country with the majority of the population engaged in cattle-rearing and dairying. There is a Tribal Land Grazing Program to encourage modern ranching techniques. There is some British aid toward stabilizing the economy, which is thrown out of balance by the massive imports of food. Good deposits of copper, nickel, coal,

and diamonds are being developed and have become a major source of income

REPUBLIC OF SOUTH AFRICA
(Republiek van Suid-Afrika)
Area: 455,616 square miles
Population: 22,500,000
Capital: Pretoria
Language: Afrikaans, Bantu language, and English
Religion: Animism and Christianity
Monetary Unit: Rand
History and Government: The Union of South Africa, comprising Cape of Good Hope, Natal, the Transvaal, and Orange Free State, elected to become a republic in 1961 when it left the Commonwealth. Its connection with the British went back to 1814 when Dutch settlers gave up their Cape settlement and trekked overland to found Orange Free State and Transvaal. The British gradually annexed large areas of South Africa ending in a federation of British and Boer states. The head of the South African Republic is a president, elected for seven years. Legislative power is vested in a parliament consisting of the president, a Senate and House of Assembly. The president has the power to dissolve either or both. A senator, or a member of the House of Assembly, must be a South African citizen of white descent. South Africa is a center of attraction for international capital; it is rich in minerals, and is strategically important. Politics and economy are both controlled by the white minority (19 percent of the population) which has imposed the regime of apartheid, or separate development on the country. The dominant political force and originator of apartheid is the Nationalist Party. There is an act to provide a system of Bantu tribal, regional, and territorial authorities, which will become self-governing units, eventually achieving political autonomy.

Economy: There is a wealth of raw materials making South Africa the economic giant of the continent. Gold represents 80 percent of world production; diamond deposits are second only to those of Zaire, the production of uranium is surpassed only by Canada, and that of platinum is half the world total. South Africa also produces 90 percent of African coal, leads all other countries for amianthus and has large reserves of iron ore. Much of this wealth is controlled by multinational companies. Industrialization is rapid, particularly the production of food-stuffs, textiles, chemicals, metal, and engineering products. A decisive factor for the future is the possibility of exploiting the hydroelectric power sta-

tions at Cabora Bessa on the Zambezi in Mozambique, as well as the Orange River Project. Agricultural resources are varied – corn, vines, citrus fruits, sugar cane. The country is also among the foremost exporters of wool and has a large fishing industry.

LESOTHO

Area: 11,720 square miles
Population: 1,200,000
Capital: Maseru
Language: English and Sesotho
Religion: Animism and Christianity
Monetary Unit: South African currency

History and Government: The British colony of Basutoland became the independent constitutional monarchy of Lesotho within the Commonwealth in 1966. Parliament consists of a National Assembly of 60 and a Senate of 33 members. The country is divided into nine administrative units, each with an administrator who coordinates government activity in the area. The country cooperates closely with South Africa – a policy that is partly dictated by the peculiar geographical situation of Lesotho, which is surrounded by South African territory.

Economy: It is a poor country, stock-rearing and agriculture being the main occupations. The chief crops are wheat, corn, beans, and peas. There are few industries and the country depends upon imports for all consumer goods. There is large-scale emigration of the population to South Africa to work in the mines on the Rand. The money they send back to their families, together with aid from the UK, help to offset some of the deficit in the balance of payments. Hopes of improvement in the economy depend upon the exploitation of a recently discovered source of diamonds and the building of a hydro-electric power station on the Oranje (Orange) river.

SWAZILAND (Ngwane)

Area: 6703 square miles
Population: 495,000
Capital: Mbabane
Language: English and Siswati
Religion: Animism and Christianity
Monetary Unit: Lilangeni
History and Government: The independence of the Swazis was guaranteed

in 1884. In 1894 the South African government was given powers of protection and in 1903 the country was administered by the governor of the Transvaal until it became independent in 1968. Swaziland is now a monarchy within the Commonwealth. Parliament has a House of Assembly of 30 members (six nominated) and a Senate of 12 members, six of whom are elected and six appointed by the king. The modern institutions have been superimposed on a tribal structure which remains, for the most part, intact. In 1973, in response to a motion passed by both houses of parliament, King Sobhuza II assumed supreme power. The country is on good terms with South Africa, which almost completely surrounds it.

Economy: In comparison with Botswana and Lesotho, Swaziland appears a rich country. It has large deposits of amianthus, iron ore, and coal. Stock-rearing is important, and the chief agricultural crop is sugar cane. The cultivation of rice and citrus fruits under irrigation as well as cotton, corn, tobacco, and pineapples, are all well developed. The eucalyptus and coniferous forests provide valuable exports.

MADAGASCAR

Area: 266,656 square miles
Population: 8,000,000
Capital: Antananarivo (Tananarive)
Language: French and Malagasy
Religion: Christianity
Monetary Unit: Franc Malgache
History and Government: The queen of Madagascar finally accepted the protection of France after two wars with the superior European power and Madagascar became a French colony in 1896. The republic of Malagasy was proclaimed in 1958 and had for 12 years an inactive government that did nothing to alleviate the poverty of the country. In 1972 a referendum suspended the Constitution and gave power to a military government, under General Ramanantsoa, which pledged itself to a program of development. Because of its strategic importance, French, British, and American bases are maintained on the island. It recently reverted to the name of Republic of Madagascar.

Economy: Rice growing employs 40 percent of the working population and, together with manioc, provides the basic food of the country. The exports are sugar cane and coffee and also cotton, tobacco, raffia, vanilla, cloves, and pepper which are of less importance. Animal husbandry and forestry are important. Industry, which was

formerly confined to the processing of agricultural products, is now developing further and includes such things as vehicle assembly plants, plastics, and paint. Mineral resources are scarcely exploited, but there are rich deposits of chromite (the country should become one of the largest producers of this mineral) and graphite. There is also hope that oil will be found and prospecting has been carried out.

COMORO ISLANDS (Îles de Comore)

Area: 800 square miles
Population: 275,000
Capital: Moroni
Language: Bantu dialects and French
Religion: Islam
Monetary Unit: Franc CFA
History and Government: The archipelago, a French possession since 1886, gained independence in 1975 after the population of all the islands, except Mayotte, voted in favor in a reverendum. Mayotte remains a French possession.

Economy: Though very popular with tourists, the islands are poor. The economy is based on the export of vanilla, sisal, coffee, and oils of citronella, lemon-grass and others. Sugar cane was formerly of importance, but this has declined. Stock-rearing and fishing are also carried on.

REUNION (La Réunion)

Area: 969 square miles
Population: 490,000
Capital: Saint-Denis
Language: French
Monetary Unit: French currency
History and Government: Reunion, which as the Ile de Bourbon had been annexed to France in 1643, is an overseas department of the French Republic. The department is under a prefect and an elected general council of 36 members. In the National Assembly in France it is represented by three deputies and in the Senate by two senators.
Economy: The most widespread crop is sugar cane, which determines the export of rum and sugar. Fragrant plants are important, supplying oils and essence for industry. Vanilla, tobacco, and tea are also grown. Stock-rearing and fishing are carried out and the products used in the home market.

MAURITIUS

Area: 805 square miles
Population: 870,000
Capital: Port Louis
Language: Creole, English, and French
Religion: Christianity, Hinduism, and Islam
Monetary Unit: Rupee
History and Government: Mauritius was occupied by the Dutch between 1598 and 1710 (the island was named for Prince Maurice of Nassau) and held by the French in the 18th century, then by the British to whom it was formally ceded in 1814. It became independent in 1968 and a member of the Commonwealth. The British monarch is the head of state. The cabinet is presided over by the prime minister and there is a Legislative Assembly.
Economy: The relative prosperity is counterbalanced by the rapid growth in population – it has one of the highest densities in the world – and the risks attached to the reliance on the single crop system – sugar cane. Sugar cane, in the form of sugar or molasses, represents 90 percent of the exports. Attempts are being made to develop the plantations of tea, tobacco, pineapples, and vegetables and to speed up industrialization, which at present is very limited. Tourism is increasing in importance, but unemployment remains high.

IRAQ

Area: 167,924 square miles
Population: 10,413,000
Capital: Baghdad
Language: Arabic
Religion: Islam
Monetary Unit: Iraq Dinar
History and Government: Established as a kingdom in 1921 out of former Turkish territory, the Iraq republic was proclaimed in 1958 after a coup d'état by army officers and the assassination of King Faisal II and members of the royal family. There followed further coups d'état in 1963. The country is governed by the National Council of the Revolutionary Command. The Ba'ath Party of Major General Ahmed Hassan Bakr has put the larger income created by the increase in the price of oil, to social uses, such as the increase of wages, reduction of taxes, and free education. In 1974 the government granted autonomy to Kurdistan, where for 10 years there had

been guerrilla warfare on the part of the Kurd minority.
Economy: It is one of the biggest oil producers in the Middle East and the industry has been nationalized. A large part of the population is still employed in agriculture, however, but this is inadequate for home needs. The principal crops are wheat and barley in winter, rice in summer, dates, cotton, tobacco, sesame, opium, and flax. Stock-rearing – sheep and goats – is mainly nomadic and wool is an important export. The development of industry is just beginning and new plants established with Soviet aid – both technical and monetary – include textiles, tobacco, beer, cement, asbestos, cigarettes. These are all nationalized.

KUWAIT

Area: 6880 square miles
Population: 1,000,000
Capital: Kuwait
Language: Arabic
Religion: Islam
Monetary Unit: Kuwaiti Dinar
History and Government: Kuwait is a sheikdom, ruled by descendents of a dynasty founded in the 18th century. It was under British protection from 1914 and independent since 1961. The Neutral Zone, to the west, is jointly owned and administered by Kuwait and Saudi Arabia. There are no political parties. Executive power is in the hands of the Sheik and his family and legislative power rests with the National Assembly of 50 members.
Economy: Oil has made Kuwait a very rich country, capable of financing the Arab countries. The manufacturing industry consists primarily of oil refining plants with a few chemical, cement, and brick works. Other economic activities include trading in wool, pearls, and horses; agriculture is limited to one oasis.

SAUDI ARABIA (Al Mamlaka al 'Arabiya as-Sa'udiyah)

Area: 831,338 square miles
Population: 8,700,000
Capital: Riyadh (Raid)
Language: Arabic
Religion: Sunnite Islam
Monetary Unit: Riyal
History and Government: In 1927, a treaty between the UK and Ibn Sa'ud, signed at Jiddah, recognized the inde-

Above: a Bedouin tribesman on his camel. The nomadic, tribal Bedouins inhabit the deserts of Arabia, Syria, and northern Africa.

pendence of Ibn Sa'ud's dual kingdom of the Nejd and Hejaz. In 1932, the kingdom was united as the Saudi Arabia Kingdom. From 1962 effective power has been held by the president of the council of ministers. There is a Consultative Assembly whose members are nominated or approved by the king. The Islamic laws are the common law of the land.
Economy: The great and only resource is oil, of which Saudi Arabia is among the largest producers in the world. Agriculture, which occupies 60 percent of the work force, is limited to the oases and is insufficient for home needs. There are major projects underway for reclamation of the desert and irrigation schemes. Dates, honey, and fruit are the main crops. Nomadic tribes live by stock-rearing, producing wool, hides, and clarified butter. Manufacturing industry is almost nonexistent.

BAHRAIN (Bahrein)

Area: 240 square miles
Population: 250,000
Capital: Al-Manamah
Language: Arabic
Religion: Islam

Monetary Unit: Dinar

History and Government: Bahrain is a hereditary monarchy, a British protectorate from 1882 and independent since 1971, There is a National Assembly, the members of which serve a four-year term. The country is administered by a cabinet but all power is in effect in the hands of the emir.

Economy: The principal economic resource is oil, but in recent years a few industries have emerged. Of these an aluminum smelter is of importance and there are minor industries such as boat building and weaving. The agricultural products are dates, rice, and vegetables. Fishing is important but the pearl fishing is declining. The island has been a trading post since 2000 BC.

QATAR

Area: 4247 square miles
Population: 89,000
Capital: Doha
Language: Arabic
Religion: Islam
Monetary Unit: Qatar Riyal

History and Government: Qatar is a hereditary monarchy, independent since 1971 and formerly a British protectorate from 1916.

Economy: It is one of the big oil producers and has practically no other economic activity. Now, however, the income from oil is being used to establish an agricultural development program. There are many gardens and farms near the capital.

Above: these Arabs listening to a news broadcast keep abreast of international affairs. The modern Arab world – those peoples who use the Arabic language and identify themselves with Arab culture – embraces peoples from North Africa to India.

UNITED ARAB EMIRATES

Area: 38,278 square miles
Population: 656,000
Chief Town: Dubayy (Dubai), Abú Dhabi
Language: Arabic
Religion: Islam
Monetary Unit: Dirham

History and Government: The country is composed of seven emirates, Abu Dhabi, Ajman, Dubai, Fujeirah, Ras al Khaimah, Sharjah, and Umm al Qaiwain, that were formerly British protectorates.

Economy: The principal source of wealth is oil. Agriculture is limited to the oases, in particular one fertile oasis near Abu Dhabi. An agricultural school and research station has been set up and has resulted in an increase of the area under cultivation and the variety of crops grown. Other activities are fishing, including pearl fishing, stock-rearing, and crafts.

OMAN

Area: 120,000 square miles
Population: 743,000
Capital: Muscat (Masqat)
Language: Arabic
Religion: Islam
Monetary Unit: Rial Omani

History and Government: Oman is an independent sultanate known until 1970 as Muscat and Oman. Although Muscat is the original capital the new port at Matran, three miles away, has led to the transfer of government offices to this new commercial center. The country is divided historically and physically into north and south separated by a large desert area.

Economy: The main economic resource is oil. The population, however, is chiefly engaged in agriculture, in particular, the cultivation of the date palm, which has reached a high level, citrus fruits, coconuts, and tobacco. Stock-rearing – sheep, goats, and camels – and fishing are also important.

PEOPLE'S DEMOCRATIC REPUBLIC OF THE YEMEN

Area: 180,000 square miles
Population: 1,590,000
Capital: Madinaat al Shaab

Language: Arabic and English
Religion: Islam
Monetary Unit: Yemeni Dinar

History and Government: Famous as a port in Roman times, ruled by the sultan of Şan'ā' in the 17th century, Aden was for over a century under British rule. In 1967 it became independent as the Republic of South Yemen. In 1970 the name was changed to the People's Democratic Republic of the Yemen. The regime declares itself Marxist and is led by a presidential council of five members. In 1972 an agreement was reached for eventual unification with the Yemen Arab Republic.

Economy: Agriculture employs almost two thirds of the working population and is mainly of a subsistence type. The chief products are cotton, dates, cereals, resin, and incense. Stock-rearing is also practiced, and fishing supplies one of the major exports. The industries are concentrated around the trading port of Aden where there are some factories and large oil refinery.

YEMEN ARAB REPUBLIC

Area: 75,000 square miles
Population: 6,500,000
Capital: Şan'ā'
Language: Arabic
Religion: Islam
Monetary Unit: Riyal

History and Government: Part of the Arabia Felix of the ancients, Yemen has a long history of foreign conquest – from Egyptians in 1600 BC, Romans, Ethiopians, Turkey, and by Ibn Sa'ud in 1934. The monarchy was overthrown in 1962 and the Arab Republic of the Yemen was proclaimed. Until 1967 there was a civil war, the republicans being supported by Egypt and the royalists by Saudi Arabia. In 1967 the foreign troops withdrew. In 1974 a military coup d'état dissolved parliament and suspended the Constitution, which was restored provisionally later that year. The Yemen is a feudal country, economically and politically dependent on Saudi Arabia and is influenced by the numerous international interests present in the Arabian Peninsula.

Economy: The Yemen is one of the few countries in the Middle East where oil has not yet been found. It is very poor country with an essentially agricultural economy employing three quarters of the working population. The chief products are coffee, cereals, cotton, fruit, and qat, of which a drug is made. Fishing and stock-rearing are also practiced. Industry has hardly been developed.

Chapter 8

North America

North America, a region of incredible contrasts, is the third largest continent after Asia and Africa. Every kind of natural challenge, from icy waste and mountain barrier to burning desert and steaming swamp, faced the pioneers and frontiersmen who built these two great and growing nations. To the first explorers America was indeed a "new world." The great continent stretched before them, unknown, mysterious, seemingly endless. In its vastness were hidden deserts and snow-capped mountains, great rivers and rolling plains. There were furs for the trader, land for the farmer, and adventures for the intrepid.

Although the European legacy of religion, language, culture, and political structure is still strong in North America, there is scarcely a nation in the world, let alone Europe, that is not represented there.

Opposite: a modern United States cowboy shows his skill at tackling a young steer in a rodeo exhibition. Such daredevil skills, a commonplace necessity in the pioneer days of the first settlers in North America, are still a widely admired part of the cultural tradition of the large cattle producing regions.

North America

Miles
0   200   400   600   800

0 200 400 600 800 1,000 1,200
Kilometres

Towns:
- ■ over 1,000,000
- ● over 500,000
- ● over 250,000
- · under 250,000

Red thin line	Main roads
Black thin line	Main railways
Blue thick line	Sea routes
Red thick line	Air routes

North America's Eastern Seaboard

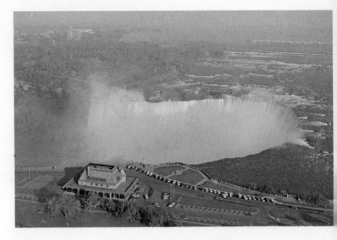

Above: Niagara Falls, the Canadian Horseshoe Falls, are widely known as a tourist attraction. The hydroelectric power they provide has played a major part in attracting industry to the area.

The Canadian maritime provinces and the six small New England states lie along the northeast coast of North America. They occupy the northern extension of the great Appalachians, which stretch south for about 1400 miles, from Newfoundland and the mouth of the St Lawrence in the north to Alabama in the south. South of New England the coastal plain of the eastern United States widens out as it spreads southward to Florida. This northeast coast was one of the first areas in the New World to be settled by Europeans and in the early days of settlement the people stayed close to the sea. The Appalachians, though not high compared with the Rockies – the highest peaks are little over 6000 feet – proved an impenetrable barrier between the first coastal colonies and the interior.

From east to west the Appalachians form four regions. First the undulating upland of the Piedmont, over which the streams flow easily, but tumble at the Fall Line – a succession of rapids that mark the junction between the coastal plain and the mountains. Along this line grew up such towns as Trenton on the Delaware river, Philadelphia, Baltimore, and Washington. The second region takes in the mountains of New England and the Blue Ridge, which stretches for 600 miles from the Potomac river to northern Georgia. This region is heavily forested. Together these first two regions contain the roots of the earlier mountain system of the Older Appalachian.

To the west are the younger ranges forming the third and fourth regions. In the first of these regions narrow, flat-topped, wooded ridges alternate with fertile valleys. The rivers, such as the Susquehanna, swing from one side of the valley to the other and sometimes cut through the ridges, but it is only the St Lawrence and the Hudson that provide the natural routeways through the Appalachians. West again, the fourth region is made up of rugged plateaus that rise to between 5000 and 3000 feet. These are the Catskills, the Allegheny, and Cumberland plateaus. The rocks here are almost horizontal and in the north the headstreams of the Ohio score the landscape. The Appalachian coalfield lies under one of these plateaus where the rivers have made deep cuts, exposing the four-feet thick, horizontal coal seams.

In the extreme north of the Appalachian system the land rises from the rocky, indented, island-strewn coasts of southeastern Canada to the mountains massed overlooking the Gulf of St Lawrence. During the Ice Age the whole of the region, as far south as Philadelphia and the Ohio river, was covered by ice. The retreating ice left behind low morainic ridges that dammed the meltwaters. These waters spread out behind the ridges forming a huge lake, which in places covered part of the Laurentian Shield to the north. Today the remnants of this lake – Lakes Superior, Michigan, Huron, Erie, and Ontario – form the world's largest group of inland lakes. In fact the whole landscape is marked by numerous lakes and abandoned channels where the rivers were forced to cut new valleys after the ice retreated.

The three isolated maritime provinces of Canada – New Brunswick, Nova Scotia, and Prince Edward Island – and the islands of Newfoundland and Anticosti are relatively undeveloped. This can partially be attributed to their isolated geographical position with only the natural corridor of the St Lawrence leading into the more attractive lands around the Great Lakes.

The provinces are rich in natural resources, however. Belle Island, off the northern tip of Newfoundland, has large iron ore deposits, while copper, lead, and zinc are to be found on Newfoundland itself. New Brunswick has coal, gypsum, and other minerals and near Sydney on Cape Breton Island, Nova Scotia, are some of the largest coal deposits in Canada, which extend out under the sea. Besides these mineral resources that provide industrial raw materials, the provinces also have tremendous hydroelectric power potential.

Most towns in the maritime provinces are near the coast yet two thirds of the people live in country districts, poorly served by road and rail transport. Farmers depend on a short growing season, from May to October, and this, together with thin, poor soils, means that the scope of agriculture is limited.

The provinces are nevertheless well known for their apples – especially from the Annapolis valley in Nova Scotia, and their seed potatoes, grown in New Brunswick and Prince Edward Island.

Fishing is one of the original occupations of these people. The Grand Banks, to the southeast of New-

Above: Canadian lumberjacks floating logs in Quebec. Forestry is a major industry in Canada, with over 1,600,000 square miles of forests – roughly 40 percent of the country's total area.

foundland, have been a rich fishing ground for boats coming from both sides of the Atlantic for a long time and European ships fished in these waters long before settlers established the first permanent colonies on the North American mainland. Many kinds of fish are caught including cod, haddock, hake, plaice, and halibut. In the Gulf of St Lawrence, the Bay of Fundy,

Below: Canadian fishermen landing a catch of cod in the North Atlantic. The rich fishing grounds off Canada's eastern coasts attract fishing fleets from many nations.

and other coastal waters are shellfish, herring, and mackeral. The introduction of quick freezing methods has given a boost to the fishing industry, though salting and canning are still carried on.

There is good farmland in the fertile lowlands of the province of Quebec bordering the St Lawrence where long, straggling villages lie close to the river and narrow fields stretch back to the forest edge. In spite of the severe winters with temperatures well below freezing, short summers, and a surface strewn with glacial debris, there is a ribbon of intensive agriculture along the valley only 80 miles across at its widest. The summers are warm enough for farmers to grow oats, hay, and root crops, and keep livestock such as cattle and pigs. Dairying is also highly developed.

The St Lawrence valley is the site of many of Canada's pulp and paper mills. A large proportion of these mills are situated at the junction of the Laurentian Shield and the valley that marks the southern edge of the forest zone. Here there is power available from the rivers, which flow southward from the Shield, and the navigable St Lawrence provides an easy means of transport. Quebec, the provincial capital, and Montreal, one of Canada's most important industrial towns, are both situated in the St Lawrence valley. Ocean ships can navigate the St Lawrence 1000 miles upstream, as far as Montreal. It had long been the dream of Canadians to make this natural gateway to the heart of the continent a continuous navigable waterway, and with the opening of the St Lawrence Seaway in 1959 this dream was realized. Ocean-going ships can now sail to Chicago, on the southern shores of Lake Michigan, or to Duluth, at the western end of Lake Superior.

Since the Seaway was completed it has proved valuable to the economy of both Canada and the USA

Above: an aerial view of New York City – the largest city in the United States of America.

and traffic has increased annually. The associated hydroelectric power developments are, of course, also of immense value, in particular those on the Niagara river. But some doubt that the enormous costs of the Seaway project will ever be recouped. A great handicap is that the St Lawrence freezes over for between four and five months every year and from December to April, Halifax in Nova Scotia is the only Canadian port in the east that stays ice-free.

In the six New England states – Maine, Vermont, New Hampshire, Massachusetts, Connecticut, and Rhode Island – the landscape is similar to that of the Canadian maritime provinces: rocky coasts, forests, and minimal good farmland. The great bays, such as Massachusetts Bay, at the head of which stands Boston, are ideal for shipping and stay open all year. Most of the American ships operate either from these New England harbors or from those to the south, such as New York, Philadelphia, and Baltimore.

The United States' first manufacturing centers were set up along New England's short, swift-flowing rivers, using the water power to drive machinery. Textile mills, tanneries, foundries, and boot and shoe factories grew up and prospered with the opening of the interior. Factories drew a lot of their raw materials, such as wool and hides, from the surrounding countryside. This early emphasis on manufacturing was the basis of New England's prosperity. Unlike the Canadian maritime provinces, however, the New England states have no coal or iron ore and few other minerals. So when coal became the primary power source, many factories moved to the southwest nearer the Pennsylvanian coalfield. Nevertheless, New England remains a major manufacturing and commercial center and has many more large towns than the isolated Canadian provinces of New Brunswick, Nova Scotia, and Prince Edward Island.

Similarly, the developments of large-scale agriculture to the west, on the great plains, made some farm products cheaper to produce there and the New England farmers could not meet the competition. Now they specialize in dairying and crops such as cranberries and sweet corn for canning. The forested hills support a paper and pulp industry and are rapidly proving to be a tourist attraction. As in Canada, fishing is still of importance and large fleets sail regularly from Boston.

West and south of New England the industrial northeast of North America stretches from the Richelieu-Hudson valleys west to Chicago and south to Baltimore. About two fifths of the people of the USA and one fourth of the Canadians live in this region. But it is not continuously built up like the great industrial areas of northwest Europe. New York, the

commercial and financial capital of the USA, stands at the eastern edge of the region, at the junction of the rocky New England coast and the sandy coastal lowlands of the eastern seaboard. Manhattan, the heart of the city, is built on a rocky island at the mouth of the Hudson river, while Brooklyn stands on the western tip of Long Island. New York also has a fine natural harbor and is the world's largest port. On the plain south of New York are other large cities such as Philadelphia, Wilmington, Baltimore, and Washington, DC. The fertile farmlands of this coastal plain supply many of the needs of these large urban markets on their doorstep.

In the early days of settlement people stayed close to the sea and ever since fishing, boat building, and maritime industries have flourished along the eastern coast from the St Lawrence to Chesapeake Bay. Apart from the St Lawrence itself, the easiest, although not the most direct, way through the Appalachians from the east coast to the interior was along the Hudson and Mohawk valleys. The result is a line of manufacturing towns dotted along this busy route, such as Albany, Glovesville, and Utica, which make all kinds of goods from electric generators to dominoes. The discovery of coal and anthracite to the west fostered the growth of industry in the valleys of the Appalachians. It also justified the great expense necessary to construct the Baltimore-Ohio Railroad and the Penn-

sylvania Turnpike to cross the mountains and the Pennsylvania Railroad to link with the Great Lakes. Many of the coal mining valleys converge on Pittsburgh and in these valleys conditions for mechanical cutting and loading are ideal and consequently output per mine is one of the highest in the world.

Many of the cities around the shores of the Great Lakes owe much of their importance to the trade on the lakes and to the industrial region of the northeast. Detroit, on the Detroit river, which links Lake Huron with Lake Erie, is one of the world's most important manufacturing cities as well as a gateway between the eastern and western ports of the lakes. Buffalo, though it originally developed before the building of the Welland Canal as the eastern terminus for the four upper Great Lakes, grew in importance after the canal was completed and the railroads were constructed. It became a point for transshipment of wheat, coal, and iron ore. Cleveland, on the southern shore of Lake Erie, became a point of transshipment for the iron ore from Duluth for the Pittsburgh iron and steel industry and for the despatch of the coal from the Pennsylvanian coalfields. Toronto, on the Ontario peninsula, is Canada's fourth largest port and also serves the area as a route and commercial center. Almost half of Canada's manufacturing capacity is situated in this small peninsula and a large proportion of the population of the country lives there.

The Middle West

The great plains, which lie in the center of the North American Continent, extend from the Laurentian Shield in the north to the Gulf of Mexico in the south; from the Appalachians in the east as far as the Rocky Mountains in the west. They are drained by one of the longest rivers in the world, the Mississippi, and its tributaries. East of the Appalachians, from Washington southward the coastal plain sweeps southwestward to link with the central plains. From this arc the arm of the Florida peninsula juts south toward the line of islands forming the Greater Antilles.

Much of the coastal plain is sandy and infertile with a cover of pine forest. The peninsula of Florida is entirely composed of limestone, parts of which are covered by sand. There are numerous sinks and lakes and in the south the large ill-drained areas of Lake Okechobee and the swamps of the Everglades.

During the Ice Age the ice sheet extended south to the Ohio and Missouri rivers. To the north of the central plains the ice was mainly eroding, but to the south of the Great Lakes the ice sheet deposited debris, filling in the hollows until a smooth surface was formed. It dammed the north-flowing rivers, so the water accumulated and rose until it could escape, either across the morainic ridges to the south or along the edges of the ice sheet. The fore-runners of the Great Lakes and the Manitoba lakes, Lake Algonquin and Lake Agassiz, at various times overflowed into the Hudson, the Ohio, the Mississippi, and its tributaries

upstream of St Louis and the Missouri. The silt deposited by these giant lakes, together with the glacial deposits, provide some of the best farmlands in the world. At the same time as deposition was taking place, winds picked up some of the very fine material and scattered it over Kansas and Nebraska. Today the Middle West includes the Dairying, Spring Wheat, and Corn Belts. South of the glaciated area, the Mississippi has been, and still is, building huge alluvial plains in its lower valley and a great delta at its mouth that thrusts out into the Gulf of Mexico.

In the interior of any continental mass there are great temperature differences and the central plains from Lake Winnipeg to St Louis are no exception. In winter the winds from the north and northwest bring the bitterly cold polar air southward. Temperatures fall below freezing point and precipitation is in the form of snow. Farther south are warmer, moister winds from the southeast and the Gulf of Mexico; the temperatures here are higher and vary from 44°F to 60°F in winter. In summer, pressure over the continent is lower and the warm air sweeps in from the south and southeast.

The rainfall decreases northwestward from Florida, from almost 100 inches at the southern tip of the peninsula to 60 inches along the coasts and less than 25 inches in the northwest in North Dakota and southern Saskatchewan and Manitoba. There is no dry period, but a summer maximum. As in Southeast Asia at similar latitudes, tropical cyclones originate out to sea – in this case in the Atlantic at about 10°N. They travel westward through the Caribbean, or the West Indies, then turn northward to continue their journey, either along the eastern coast of the United States or across the gulf coast into the lower Mississippi. They occur most frequently in late summer and early autumn and the damage caused by these hurricanes can be immense in terms of human life, the destruction of property, and the devastation of crops.

The Great Plains form the drier, higher western

Left: a Saskatchewan wheatfield, the chemical plant in the background provides on-the-spot fertilizers that make the abundant harvests possible.
Below: the southern United States provides the bulk of the world's cotton crop to be turned into durable fabrics.

part of the interior plains. Here is the Spring Wheat Belt and the western part of the Hay and Dairying Belt that stretches as far as Lake Huron. But with the exploitation of oil and natural gas in the region, especially around Edmonton, the economy no longer depends solely on agriculture. Grasslands once covered the whole of the interior plains of the Middle West and in the east, where there is more rain the grasses grew up to 10 feet high. But most of the ground has been plowed and planted with corn and other cereal crops although sheep and cattle still graze here.

As well as being a grazing and livestock area, the Middle West is also a manufacturing region. It has the mineral resources – coal, iron ore, oil, and salt – as well as the route to the ocean by way of the Great Lakes and the St Lawrence Seaway. The main indus-trial areas are at the southern end of Lake Michigan, from Milwaukee to Chicago, in the Indianapolis-Cincinatti-Columbus triangle, around Minneapolis-St Paul, St Louis, and near the Wisconsin river. Most of these areas have heavy industry such as aircraft and agricultural machinery works, and industries based on agriculture and oil refining.

To the south of the interior plains is the Cotton Belt, although cotton is now grown only in the areas of richer soils in Texas, along the lower Mississippi, the Tennessee valley, and along the Piedmont. Elsewhere, poultry and cattle had been introduced to great advantage and sheep graze on the drier areas of western Texas where cultivation is impossible.

Along the coasts and in the near-tropical peninsula of Florida, sugar cane, rice, and citrus fruits are grown with tobacco in the more northerly areas of Virginia. Off the gulf coast, as well as inland in Texas, Oklahoma, and Arkansas, oil has transformed the economic scene. The large towns of Dallas, Houston, Galveston, Baton Rouge, and New Orleans have grown rich on oil and oil refining.

Below: part of a vast tract of marshland in southern Florida known as the Everglades. The soil and weather in Florida are ideal for fruit growing, especially oranges, grapefruit, and pineapple. There is much fishing, too, off the coast.

The United States

The Rocky Mountains

From the western edge of the central plains the land begins to rise steeply into a system of mountain ranges towering over 10,000 feet. These are the young fold mountains, like the Alps and the Himalaya, crumpled, fractured, and pushed up by the earth movements to form the Rocky Mountain system. Since then erosive agents have been at work, exposing the ancient crystalline beds.

The system falls into three north-south belts: the Rocky Mountains, the plateaus, and the Pacific coast mountains. The Rocky Mountains, the easternmost chain of the system, stretch almost without interruption from Alaska to Mexico. These bold, rugged mountains are often snow-capped and their lower slopes are covered with forests. The highest peak is Mount Robson in Canada, which reaches 12,972 feet. There are two breaks in the Rockies: in the extreme north of Canada, immediately south of Brook Range, and farther south in the USA, the Wyoming Basin.

The tract of plateaus and basin country lies between the Rockies and the Pacific coast ranges, extending from the central uplands of Alaska, between Brooks Range and the Alaska Range, south to Mexico. South of Alaska and the areas drained by the Yukon and its tributaries in British Columbia is the narrowest part of the plateau belt drained by the Stikine, Fraser, and Columbia rivers. These plateaus are vast areas of basaltic lava that welled up through fissures and spread out across the surface. Farther south again, the Great Basin occupies the widest part of the middle belt and is made up of a series of north–south ridges, separated by numerous depressions and basins. It is a region that has undergone servere faulting and the ridges are, in fact, the edges of upturned blocks. The whole area can be likened to a series of steps that descend from the Rockies as far down as Death Valley, 282 feet below sea level.

The Great Basin, centered on Nevada is for the most part a desert region encircled by mountains which block off the flow of most of the rivers. It is essentially an area of inland drainage and only the streams in the extreme north and south drain down to the sea. The remainder dry up or flow into lakes. The water in these lakes, such as the Great Salt Lake, is extremely salty, much more so than the ocean. The dried up lake beds provide raw materials, in the form of salt and potash, for the chemical industry. To the southeast of the Great Basin lies the Colorado plateau, which consists of horizontally laid beds. The Colorado

river and its tributaries have cut into the plateau' horizontal rocks to form canyons like the 5000-foot deep Grand Canyon.

The third belt, the Pacific coast mountains, i really two chains separated by a trough. The easter chain runs south from the Alaska Range – which ha the highest peak in North America, Mount McKinle 20,320 feet – through the Coast Mountains of Britis Columbia, the Cascade Range of the Sierra Nevada, t the Sierra Madre Occidental of Mexico. The Hecat Strait and Georgia Strait, Willamette river valley central valley of California, and the Gulf of Californi make up the central trough.

The Rockies also divide the climate of Nort America. They form a formidable barrier to the ai masses moving in from the Pacific in winter and th complexity of the numerous ranges and basins create many varied climatic conditions inland. The easter slopes of the Rockies, on the other hand, like th

Above: the snow-clad rocky tundra and coniferous forest of the Canadian Rockies.

Above: the Grand Canyon, the mile-deep gorge carved in the Colorado Plateau by the Colorado river. The Plateau lies some 6500 to 10,000 feet in the southern Rockies. The highest point in the United States section of the Rockies is also in Colorado – Mount Elbert, 14,431 feet.

central plains, are affected by the cold polar air from the north and the warm, moist air moving into the continent from the Gulf of Mexico. The rainfall increases steadily from the 10 inches around Los Angeles to over 200 inches in the mountains of British Columbia. Rainfall is highest in winter everywhere west of the Rockies.

In the extreme north of the Rockies is Alaska, the 49th state of the USA, twice as large as Texas but with a population of little over a quarter of a million. Both Alaska and the neighboring Canadian province of the Yukon owed their original importance to gold, and it was the news of the Klondike finds that first attracted settlers to the region. Now fishing is of equal importance with mining and the Alaskan fisheries provide over 60 percent of the salmon catch of the USA.

Because of the effects of the North Pacific Current, the coastal plain around the Gulf of Alaska experiences mild winters with temperatures rarely falling below freezing point. This means that it is possible for farmers to grow apples and potatoes along the sides of the sheltered fiords. Recently, however, three factors have played an important part in the economic importance of the region. The building of the Alaska Highway and the increase in air travel have provided a link with the United States and done much to attract tourists, while the discovery of oil around the Kenai peninsula and along the Arctic coast is providing a rich source of revenue.

Southward in British Columbia, although the mining of lead and zinc is important, forestry and fishing are the main economic activities. About half the total population depends directly or indirectly upon the forests of Douglas fir and red cedar and is engaged in logging, pulping, paper production, and other operations. British Columbia, however, has suffered because of its position on the periphery of a continent, away from the main markets of eastern Canada and facing an ocean across which there has been little trade with the Asian seaboard.

The northwest Pacific states of the USA have also been similarly affected in the past and due to their isolation and distance from the larger markets, industries were not established in them until after World War I. Here again the mountains bordering the ocean are covered with giant redwoods and the hydro-electric power potential is tremendous. Today the whole area has begun to develop this potential and industries are well established.

South again is the 400-mile long central valley of California, only 50 miles wide and almost entirely surrounded by mountains. The central valley is extremely fertile, but in some places it has to be drained and in others, because of the summer droughts, irrigated. Farmers can grow subtropical fruits such as oranges, apricots, peaches, dates, and figs as well as vines and cotton. To the south of the valley of California the coastal ranges rise almost straight out of the sea and there is little lowland until one reaches the vicinity of Los Angeles. This flat area is important both agriculturally and industrially. Citrus fruits are grown on the encircling slopes, and alfalfa and barley on the more level ground. The latter are used in the dairying industry.

In the USA almost 1000 miles separate the eastern side of the Rocky Mountains from the Pacific coastal

Above: these orange groves in California are irrigated with water from melting snow on the San Bernadino Mountains in the background.

ranges. People once thought this mountain and plateau region was impassable, but with the discovery of gold in California and the 1849 Gold Rush thousands of prospectors crossed the Rockies. With the gold they sometimes found other minerals such as silver, lead zinc, and copper. But as the rich gold veins became exhausted, the miners deserted the shanty towns. Today most of the gold is worked out and it is doubtful if the intermountain region of basins and plateaus will ever become densely populated, although irriga- tion will make possible more pockets of intensive farming.

Below: prospectors washing gold from the Calaveras river, California at the start of the "Gold Rush."

North and Central America: Political

The Frozen North

Above: purple saxifrage (top) and perennial mountain avens (above) are typical flowering plants found in the tundra areas of North America and Greenland.

The whole of the northeastern quadrant of North America is occupied by the Laurentian, or Canadian, Shield. The shield protrudes into the United States south of Lake Superior and in the Adirondack Mountains that lie between Lake Ontario and the Richelieu-Hudson valleys. Wedged between the eastern band of the Rocky Mountain system and the shield the interior plains extend northward along the valleys of the Peace and Mackenzie rivers to the shores of the Arctic Ocean.

For much of the Palaeozoic and Mesozoic eras the Laurentian Shield was covered by the sea and sediments were deposited. Then, during the Pleistocene Glaciation the whole area was covered by ice which is estimated to have attained a thickness of some 10,000 feet in the central part of the sheet. As the ice melted, the land began to rise, relieved of its great burden. This isostatic readjustment is still continuing and in some areas, for example round the shores of James Bay, the marks of former beach lines can be seen about 500 feet above the present shoreline. The shield today is a region of low relief, rarely higher than 1000 feet, broken by countless hollows, the majority of which are water filled.

Long, cold winters dominate this northern part of North America. Temperatures everywhere fall well below freezing point and more than two thirds of Canada has temperatures of 0°F in January. Snow covers the ground for nearly half the year, the rivers and lakes are frozen over, and the Arctic coasts icebound. In Hudson Bay the build up of ice begins as early as October and by midwinter the whole bay is frozen solid. The ice does not begin to break up again until the following June or July. The summers are short and cool with temperatures rarely rising above 60°F, except along the southern edge of the shield.

The extreme northern belt bordering the Arctic seas, the islands and the coast of Greenland is tundra. The subsoil is permanently frozen and in summer water lies on the ground in stagnant pools. The frozen subsoil and intense winter cold make tree growth impossible. In summer, mosses and lichens appear in abundance, grasses and sedges spring up and there is often a covering of short, brightly colored flowers such as the Arctic poppy. Southward the tundra gradually merges into the taiga – the subarctic coniferous forest of spruce, larch, and fir, which stretches in a huge arc from the Yukon, southeastward to the Great Lakes then eastward to the Labrador coast. It covers almost half of the country, extending south in places almost to the Canadian-United States border.

At the southern margins of the forest the timber industry and hydroelectric installations have developed. As the rivers cross the edge of the shield they drop down, forming waterfalls that power the generators. In contrast to British Columbia, where lumbering is carried on throughout the year, on the shield it is a winter occupation only. Today Canadian forests provide more than one third of the world's supply of wood pulp for newsprint.

The Laurentian Shield has great mineral reserves too. The importance of these has been enhanced by the exhaustion of the high grade iron ore deposits around the southern shores of Lake Superior. Recently new deposits have been discovered in the forested wilderness of Labrador, 300 miles north of the St

Lawrence. This new field, near Schefferville, probably has reserves of about 400 million tons. In contrast to lumbering, the ore can only be mined and transported in summer. Iron ore has also been found north of Lobstick Lake in a belt stretching as far as the western shores of Ungava Bay. On Baffin Island also prospectors have found 150 million tons of ore with an iron content of 69 percent – the highest in the world. The shield also supplies a large part of the world's gold, silver, nickel, platinum, copper, lead, zinc, radium, and uranium.

Northern Canada is really too cold to grow many crops. Oats, rye, and hay can grow as far north as the

Below: this view over the Canadian tundra reveals an enormous patchwork of lakes and rivers. They are created often as a result of poor drainage due to the underlying permafrost. Much of Canada has long cold winters with average January temperatures below 0°F.

Mackenzie lowlands or on the clay belts formed by the beds of the former glacial lakes, especially the belt midway between Hudson Bay and the Great Lakes in the neighborhood of Lake Abitibi. But elsewhere poor soils, short growing seasons, and isolation from large markets handicap the northern farmers.

Settlement in Canada crowds close to the United States border. Most Canadian cities are south of latitude 50°N and few people live north of this parallel. In the same latitude in Europe, there are 10 capital cities and a dense concentration of people – London, the Low Countries, the Ruhr, Berlin, and Warszawa (Warsaw) all lie north of 50°N. Canada, however, does not have a Gulf Stream to influence its climate as does Northwest Europe. Its climate and land are inhospitable and more comparable with similar latitudes in central and east Asia around Ozero Baykal (Lake Baikal) and along the Trans-Siberian Railway.

Canada and Greenland

Natural Resources

Although in the past 30 years North American agriculture has gradually become more diversified, single crops still dominate large areas. North America grows all the crops it needs except for tropical products such as coffee, cocoa, bananas, rubber, and palm oil. Farm layouts are very different from those in Western Europe. In the east of the continent they reflect to a large extent the rural pattern of the early colonists. In the west they are determined by the early system of land survey.

In eastern Canada there are two main patterns: the French-Canadian and the English. In the former, large blocks of land along the natural corridor of the St Lawrence were granted to landlords – seigneurs – who undertook to build a church, a mill, and provide the nucleus of a village for settlers. These villages were on the rivers and their lands ran back at right angles to the river, giving rise to long, narrow farms. The English, on the other hand, brought with them a more irregular pattern that persists in the Canadian maritime provinces of Ontario, New England, and also along the Atlantic seaboard as far south as Chesapeake Bay.

In the Prairies and the Middle West there is a completely different pattern. The general flatness of the land and the grassy open-type vegetation lend themselves to a geometric layout. Government surveyors, working along the great transcontinental railroads, divided the land into sections composed of standard units. Each unit was 1 square mile, or 640 acres. Quarter sections of 160 acres were made available as farms and the early homesteads were based on this unit.

Canada and the United States produce almost one quarter of the world's wheat crop. Both countries have a large surplus, especially Canada which has only a small home market. The wheat lands of North America lie between latitudes 35-N and 55-N and are centered along longitude 100-W. In the Prairie provinces of Canada and the adjoining states of the USA, spring-sown wheat matures in about 100 days and needs 15–20 inches of rainfall. The exact time of sowing depends upon the locality and weather conditions, and care must be taken to sow after the end of the frosts. In Canada, although wheat is grown all over the Prairies, it is the most important crop in the central areas around the South Saskatchewan river. The Winter Wheat Belt lies farther to the south in the USA in Nebraska, Kansas, and Oklahoma. Here the wheat is sown in autumn and the growing season is between 150–200 days, longer than that of spring wheat.

Corn is the United States' most important crop in acreage and three times as much corn is grown as is wheat. The fertile Corn Belt, between the Spring and Winter Wheat Belts and to the east of them, runs through Iowa, Illinois, Indiana, and Ohio. Corn requires a growing season of not less than 150 days,

Below: extremely fertile soil and an abundant water supply help to make Iowa a leading farm state. Its great fertility is due largely to the action of the four great glaciers that moved over the area during the Ice Age grinding down the hills to fill the valleys with fine rich soil.

Above: a United States fishing boat hauling in a catch of tuna off the coast of Ecuador. The method of catching tuna is by seining – in which a long net is drawn in a circle around the school of fish being pursued. The Pacific fishing grounds off Central and South America are particularly rich in tuna.

with daytime temperatures of over 70-F and night-time temperatures that must not fall below 58-F, and more than 20 inches of rainfall. It is the heaviest yielding of all grains, but any drop in night-time temperatures checks growth and yields are reduced if there are not at least four inches of rain in July.

Truck farming and dairying are to be found near most of the towns. But immediately west, south, and east of the Great Lakes, and north of the Corn Belt, is a band of mixed farming that runs astride the Canadian-United States border. Here farmers grow hay and oats and keep dairy cattle for milk, butter, and cheese. Nearer the lake, where the water has an ameliorating effect on the climate, fruit can be grown.

Cotton and corn are the dominant crops in the southern section of the USA, in Texas, Louisiana, Arkansas, Mississippi, Tennessee, Alabama, Georgia, and South Carolina. They are now limited to special tracts where conditions are most favorable, and they are also grown in rotation with fodder crops and soybeans, which are used for cattle food.

North American fishing fleets work mostly in the oceans around the continent, the Atlantic and the Pacific. Their catch includes sardines, tuna, halibut, mackerel, herring, haddock, cod, and salmon. The Grand Banks of Newfoundland are the most important fishing grounds where the trawlers fish for cod, and the majority of the sardines come from the Pacific waters. The salmon fisheries of the Pacific coast are famous. There are five different species of salmon of which the Bristol Bay Sockeye, the Columbia River Chinock, and the humpback are the most important. They all have different migration patterns and live in the ocean for between one and four years, then return to their home waters to spawn. The fishermen know the directions of salmon "runs" and the various spawning grounds. Most of the catch is canned, but production is now declining and steps have been taken to regulate salmon fishing and conserve the stocks. A great number of menhaden are caught off the American east coasts. This fish, which forms the bulk of the total United States' catch, is used mainly for oil, fertilizer, and as meal for poultry and livestock.

Above: potatoes being harvested in Missouri. The potatoes will be sent to a packing station. The cultivation of vegetables and fruits for the crowded industrial areas is known as "truck farming" in the United States.

Mineral Reserves

The mineral resources of North America are rich and varied – copper and salt from the Rockies, bauxite from Canada, sulfur from Louisiana, phosphates from Florida and deposits of gold, silver, lead, zinc, iron ore, uranium, and nickel in both countries. The United States produces about one seventh of the world's coal, most of it from the Appalachian field that extends for some 800 miles from Pennsylvania to Alabama. The best coal comes mainly from Pennsylvania, West Virginia, and Alabama, around the town of Birmingham.

As well as the smaller fields in Wyoming and Colorado, there are two other coalfields to the west: the central coalfield in Illinois and the western interior coalfield that stretches from Iowa to northeast Oklahoma. Canada also has giant reserves of coal in Cape

first tapped in western Pennsylvania 100 years ago and prospectors first struck oil in California in the 1880s and southwest of the central plains in 1901. Today the leading petroleum states are Texas, with one third of the total production of the USA, Louisiana with a fourth, California with one tenth and Oklahoma with a little less. Long pipelines carry oil and natural gas from the fields to all parts of the country, but in spite of these immense resources oil is still imported to supply the never-ending needs. Oil was discovered in Canada only in 1914, but in the last two decades production has boomed in the whole region between Calgary and Edmonton, as well as in southern Saskatchewan.

Nearly all Canada's electricity and one fifth of the United States' is water generated. The potential supplies of hydroelectric power for Canada are tremendous and are concentrated in two areas: the mountains of British Columbia and the southern edge of the Laurentian Shield where the rivers tumble over the marked break of slope formed by the steep faults. It is the latter area that is the most developed, the lakes on the shield forming the reservoirs and the hydroelectric power stations being built along the northern rim of the Great Lakes and the St Lawrence valley. The United States' sources, tapped and potential, are the mountains of the west, the rivers of the Mississippi

Above: a West Virginia aluminum sheet rolling mill and (right) a fractional tower at a petroleum refinery in Baytown, Texas, represent the enormous mineral wealth of North America.

Breton Island and Alberta, but in the past has found it cheaper to import coal from the United States rather than develop the remote fields. This is because the United States is the only country producing coal economically, although in recent years it has found increasing competition from other fuels. The numbers of miners has decreased but this is in part due to increased mechanization.

The USA was until recently both the largest producer and the largest consumer of petroleum. Oil was

Above: part of a giant nickel mine near Ontario, Canada. Nickel is a hard tough metal with many of the properties of iron. It is used in alloys to withstand high temperatures, which makes it an invaluable material in the aerospace industry and in the construction of furnaces.

basin and the New England rivers. Mammoth installations have been built such as the Grand Coulee Dam on the Columbia and the Hoover Dam on the Colorado.

Like coal, low-grade iron ore deposits were centered on a single area south of Lake Superior in northern Minnesota and Wisconsin. In the Mesabi Range the ore is actually obtained by opencast mining methods, but elsewhere underground mining is necessary. The ore is taken by rail to the ports on the Great Lakes then shipped across the lakes to Chicago, Cleveland, and Buffalo, for use in the local steel centers or for onward shipment by rail to Pittsburgh. More and more high-grade iron ore is now coming from the newly developed Canadian fields in western Labrador and the Ungava Peninsula. Around Birmingham, at the southern end of the Appalachian coalfield, there are low-grade iron ore deposits, which, together with the coal, form the basis of a steel industry.

The United States probably produces over half the total of the world's manufactured goods. Its range of manufacturing activity is immense. The first industrial centers were dependent upon local supplies of power: the New England factories used the water power from the local rivers; Cleveland, Pittsburgh, and Birmingham grew up close to the Appalachian coalfield; the Canadian towns developed along the edge of the St Lawrence valley where the hydroelectric power was available; and recently spectacular de-

velopments of industry have occurred all along the Texas and Louisiana coast, around Corpus Christi, Houston, Beaumont, and Port Arthur. This most recent development is due to the presence of oil and natural gas that can be used as a source of power. As the early centers grew, specialist industries became concentrated in certain areas. The automobile industry is in southern Michigan and Ontario, around Detroit. The electrochemical and metallurgical industries are around Buffalo, Niagara, and Toronto. Chemical industries are along the Gulf coast and the modern aircraft industry is in Seattle and Los Angeles.

The west coast and the southwest of the plains are not alone in the development of new industries, however. Factories as far apart as Texas, Ontario, and New England make electrical equipment, drugs, and plastics. Factories all over North America are producing thousands of different kinds of goods every day.

The assets of industrial organizations are the large size of the units and mechanization. Most industries in North America are dominated by a few large corporations that have a tendency to spread between Canada and the USA, irrespective of the frontier. Transport is also vital to healthy industrial development and good transport systems are available in much of North America. Many bulky materials such as coal, iron ore, timber, wheat, and cotton are shipped on inland waterways and, in particular, on the Great Lakes where traffic is mainly freight. Railroads are still an important means of transport especially for heavy merchandise although many other goods are being increasingly carried by road, especially in the east.

The People of North America

The fact that Alaska is separated from Siberia by a shallow strait is only one of the many reasons for believing that long ago people of Asia crossed into the New World by the Bering Strait. Also, the absence, so far, of any early Palaeolithic finds such as tools strongly suggests that the first Americans learned to make their primitive tools before they arrived on the continent.

Most probably some time between 10,000 and 20,000 years ago, during an interglacial phase of the Pleistocene Glaciation, there was a trickle of people of Mongoloid type across to Alaska. They were hunters who probably brought dogs with them, but no other domestic animals and no seeds. At the end of the Ice Age, when this land bridge once more disappeared under the sea, these early peoples, the "Amerinds," spread over the continent and came across a wide range of environments, from Arctic tundra to grassland, from the deserts of the southern Rockies to the tropical swamplands of southern Florida.

In the north the Eskimos, who were probably the latecomers, spread across from Alaska to Greenland. Their mode of life kept them to the seashores and their food, clothes, shelter, and means of transport on land and sea all depended to a great extent on the animal life of the tundra and Arctic waters.

The Indians who remained to live and hunt in the forests of Canada and northern USA were also nomadic peoples. Tribes such as the Beaver, the Cree, and the Algonquin were hunters and fishers, obtaining food and clothing from the caribou, the fur-bearing animals, the lakes, and the rivers. The forest Indians of eastern USA were able to augment their diet with fruits from the trees and grow some crops in the clearings. The Plains Indians, such as the Comanche, the Sioux, and the Apache, hunted the bison; the Indians of the southern Rockies, such as the Pueblo and Hopu, lived in permanent homes and grew crops of corn, beans, and pumpkins. All over the continent their cultural advance followed the pattern of their forerunners in Asia: hunters eventually began to sow seasonal crops until finally their economy was based on agriculture.

Irish monks reached the southern tip of Greenland toward the end of the ninth century and a century later the Norsemen set up colonies there. It was only a short time before they ventured farther west and discovered a new land. But the Vikings' hopes of settling in Vinland (New England), Markland (Newfoundland), or at any other of their landfalls on the eastern coast of Canada were destroyed by the Indians. Within a few years America had been forgotten by the rest of the world.

It was to be almost four centuries before the Europeans once again found the continent of North America. This time, however, favorable reports of the new continent attracted settlers from across the Atlantic. The Spanish in the Caribbean pushing northward from the Mexican border; the French traveling along the natural corridor of the St Lawrence; and the English thrusting into the Hudson Bay from the north and also settling the eastern coast of the USA farther south. Each of these peoples brought different customs, religions, languages, and other cultural features. These variations are still apparent today in the peoples of North America.

Today there are over 236 million people living in the

Right: Chinatown in San Francisco. The sizeable Chinese population of the USA preserves many traditions of its homeland.
Below: Eskimos inhabit the icebound areas and islands of North America.

Above: part of a rush-hour crowd in New York. Nearly every nation in the world is represented among the peoples that make up the USA. The indigenous peoples represent only a tiny percentage of the total population.

USA and Canada – with scarcely a nation in the world that is not represented in these two countries, for all these people, with the exception of the Indians and Eskimos, are descended from immigrants.

In Canada nearly half the population is of British descent. The other main group is made up of the peoples descended from the French. Four out of five of these French-Canadians speak French and in Quebec province a law has been passed making French the normal business language. English, however, remains the language used in federal business.

Two thirds of Americans live in or near cities and recently the majority of the immigrants have chosen to settle in just a few large cities, with the result that the "million" cities are composed of more than 65 percent foreign-born people. For example, New York

Above: automobiles are the chief means of passenger transportation in Canada and the United States and account for the largest proportion of all miles traveled by North Americans. Industrialized societies generally are dependent on comprehensive networks of road and rail transportation.

has more Irish than Dublin, more Italians than Rome, and more Greeks than Athens. Los Angeles has more than 100,000 Japanese and Chinese.

North Americans have made formidable progress in the 400 years or so since they set foot on the continent. They have opened up the whole land, drained it, irrigated it, and cultivated it. They have exploited the mineral resources, developed and powered industries, built a vast web of railways and roads. American farms and factories produce huge quantities of goods cheaply and efficiently, using labor-saving machinery. Much of the wheat crop is gathered by combines; cars roll off assembly lines; computers simplify office work. About 33 out of every 100 employed North Americans work in manufacturing and construction and 8 out of 100 work in farming, fishing, forestry, and mining.

There is a great amount of trade between the United States and Canada and the USA is certainly Canada's chief trading partner. The high productivity in both countries means that the people have a high standard of living and more leisure time. The American industrial worker spends on average less than 38 hours a week at his job compared with the 40 hours or more of the European. The average American buys more food, clothes, and household goods than any other people. Six out of every 10 own their own homes and nearly every family has at least one car, a refrigerator, television set, washing machine, and an air conditioning unit for their house. Americans have more than half the telephones in the world, almost half the motor vehicles, and a large proportion of the private air planes.

North America has taken enormous strides in medicine and education. They have done much to promote public health programs and have made great advances in medical research. Elementary and secondary education is free; 9 out of 10 children go to primary school and there are more high schools in North America than in any other area. Higher education is not neglected either and over half a million graduate from college every year.

Canada and the United States of America share similar institutions of democratically elected governments, legal processes, and religious beliefs. Both are federal states, where the central government is responsible for defense and foreign affairs. The individual provinces or states make their own laws governing education, transport, marriage, gambling, and so on. But Canada is the only monarchy in North America, in fact in the New World, as well as being the only country that operates a parliamentary system. The governor general acts on behalf of the monarch who resides in the United Kingdom, and the prime minister is head of the government. This is the significant difference between Canada and the USA where the President is both head of state and head of government.

North America and the World

By comparison, the United States, from the time of the Declaration of Independence in 1776, followed a policy of abstention from European affairs. It discouraged further attempts at colonial expansion and opposed the infiltration of the European nations into Latin America. It was not until the end of the 19th century that the USA escaped from its isolation to push into the Pacific, to the Hawaiian Islands, Samoa, and the Philippines; to take over Puerto Rico from the Spanish; to construct the Panama Canal; and eventually to intervene in the final stages of World War I. But in 1919 it returned again to its policy of isolation and devoted its energies to becoming a great economic power.

Between the two world wars, the United States established a great industrial system based on steel and its own wealthy resources of power – coal, electricity, natural gas, and oil. It built up a countrywide communications system and entered into the field of international commerce. This caused a reversal of the flow of capital which, for centuries, had been from Europe into North America. Now it was North America that invested in European concerns. The nation survived the trauma of the Great Depression and closed its doors to the persecuted who had been hounded out of Europe. Then, with the attack on Pearl Harbor, in 1941, the USA suddenly found itself no longer able to turn its back on Europe and the rest of the world.

Because of its position as a Dominion within the Commonwealth, Canada has always retained a special relationship and close ties with the United Kingdom. Up to 1931 people of British origin formed more than half the total population. Since then, however, the proportion has been getting smaller as greater numbers of people arrive from other European countries as well as from Asia. The French element of the population, which in the earliest years was the largest, is now only about a fourth of the total – although because of its historic cultural links, its allegiance to France, and the French language, it has remained a very powerful element.

Below: the White House, Washington, DC, the official residence of the President of the United States. Because of its position it inevitably exerts tremendous political and economic influence over other countries.

Above: the lunar module being inspected for damage by astronaut Edward Aldrin. United States technological ability has contributed greatly to man's knowledge.

In the decades following World War II, the USA organized the North Atlantic Treaty Organization (NATO) and the South East Asia Treaty Organization (SEATO), the military pacts in Europe and Asia; the Australia, New Zealand, United States pact (ANZUS) in the Pacific, and the Central Treaty Organization (CENTO) in the Middle East. It established with the Latin-American countries the Organization of American States (OAS) and also concluded numerous military alliances with Japan, the Philippines, and some of the Southeast Asian and Middle East countries.

At the same time the USA became the leading industrial country in the world and the growth of manufacturing industry in its North American neighbor, Canada, has been one of the most remarkable features of the postwar years. Together they produce well over half the world's manufactured goods. The people of North America not only have a high standard of living themselves but also provide substantial aid and technical assistance to countries in Asia, Latin America, and Africa. This aid has done a lot to lessen the gap between the "have" and "have not" nations. It has been given in a variety of forms, from direct gifts to loans or investments in industrial concerns, from technical manpower to the establishment of research centers.

The USA alone provides more than half the foreign aid in the world and, together with Canada, distributes large stocks of surplus agricultural products to the developing countries under its Food for Peace program. The American Peace Corps and Canadian University Service Overseas, both youth organizations, send volunteers to work in 47 countries, assisting in educational and technical development projects. Both countries are members of the Colombo Plan, which helps economic progress in Southeast Asia.

North American contributions to the arts have received worldwide recognition. American writing has influenced the development of new literary forms. The West has inspired its own ballads, as distinctly American as jazz, and both have influenced modern classical music. Artists and architects have helped develop contemporary design trends.

The telephone and electric light are part of a long American tradition of invention and technological development. Plastics, synthetic fibers, computers, automation, and mass production techniques – all these affect the way the rest of the world lives and works. Almost 500,000 scientists, backed by an increasing research program, are finding new cures for disease, discovering more about the structure of the atom and the chemistry of heredity and working closely with other countries in oceanographical and radio astronomy studies. Basic genetics research in the USA has greatly increased the world's supply of food, developing new strains of hybrid corn and rice. Their space probes have added to knowledge about the earth and the universe. Relay satellites have revolutionized worldwide coverage of radio and television communications.

North Americans, with their vigor and vast economic resources, political influence and concern for the people of other countries, are taking their full share of responsibility for the future welfare of the world.

The Countries of North America

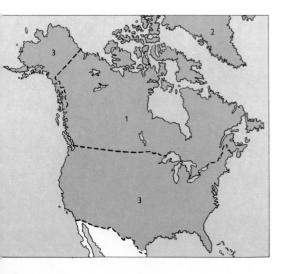

1 Canada
2 Greenland
3 United States of America

CANADA
Area: 3,851,785 square miles
Population: 23,000,000
Capital: Ottawa
Language: English and French
Religion: Catholicism and Protestantism
Monetary Unit: Dollar
History and Government: Discovered first by Norsemen around AD 1000 Canada was rediscovered at the end of the 15th century by explorers in search of a northwest route to Asia. It was the scene of rivalry between the British and French during the 17th and 18th centuries, eventually falling to the British crown in 1763. Canada is a federal state of 12 provinces and territories and is a member of the Commonwealth. The British sovereign is represented by a Governor-General. The Senate consists of 104 senators, with representatives from each province, and all nominated by the Governor-General. The House of Commons has 264 members and is elected by the people to serve for five years. The federal government is responsible for the maintenance of the armed forces, criminal law, banking, etc. Provincial powers are, however, considerable, especially in the social, education, and administrative fields. French-speaking Quebec's agitation in favor of independence for the province has come to the fore in recent years.
Economy: Canada is among the leading suppliers in the world for many minerals: nickel, platinum, zinc, silver, radium, amianthus, uranium, gold, lead, copper, potash, and methane. Almost half the area of the country is covered with forests, exploitation of which place it among the world's biggest producers of timber, cellulose, and various wood manufactures. Canada is the second largest exporter of wheat in the world, after the USA. It also exports beef, butter, and other dairy products. Deep-sea and fresh-water fishing is carried on and the salmon fishing off British Columbia is of great value. The manufacturing industries occupy about a quarter of the labor force, the most industrialized province being Ontario. Canada is also one of the leading producers of aluminum.

GREENLAND (Grølland)
Area: 840,000 square miles; ice-free portion 132,000 square miles.
Population: 52,000
Capital: Godthab
Monetary Unit: Danish currency
History and Government: Greenland was discovered and settled by Norsemen in the 10th century AD. It was made a crown colony by Denmark in 1924, annexed by Norway in 1931, and returned to Denmark in 1933. Until 1979 it was an integral part and a province of Denmark, sending two deputies to the Danish parliament. It was administered by a governor and a democratically elected council. In January 1979 Greenland voted for independence and its own parliament, retaining its representation in the Danish parliament. A treaty in 1951 conceded the use of air bases to the USA.
Economy: Hunting and fishing are the main economic activities together with the associated fish-processing industries. Cryolite, a valuable mineral, is mined at Ivigtut. A great interest is now being shown in the possibility of oil being obtained both in Greenland and offshore.

UNITED STATES OF AMERICA
Area: 3,615,102 square miles
Population: 216,000,000
Capital: Washington D.C.
Language: English
Religion: Catholicism and Protestantism
Monetary Unit: Dollar
History and Government: The United States is a federal republic consisting of 50 states and one federal district. The first permanent settlement of Europeans was by the Spanish at St. Augustine, Florida, in 1565. English settlements were made in Virginia in 1607. English forces defeated the French in the French and Indian war of 1754-63 and began a period of colonial rule that lasted until the War of Independence from 1775 to 1783. The country retains its original Constitution of 1787. This is based on the political and administrative preeminence of the president, controlled by a Congress, which has the legislative power. The Congress consists of the Senate of 100 members, two for each state, and a lower chamber, the House of Representatives, of 435 members. The president serves for a four-year term and is eligible for reelection once only. The political system is based on two parties, Democrats and Republicans, with ample scope for administrative autonomy in the various states.
Economy: Agriculture has the greatest productive capacity in the world, largely due to the vast extent of cultivable land and a high degree of mechanization and chemical aids for soil fertility. The industrial potential is also enormous. The country is first in the world for electric power, basic chemical products, paper, motor vehicles, and tires; second for cement, steel, cast iron, iron alloys, radio and television equipment. The USA is at the head of an economic system of worldwide proportions. Through the great multinational corporations dealing in oil, iron and steel, engineering, chemicals, and electronics (10 of the 12 greatest industrial companies in the world are American) the USA has organized a world market for the supply of raw materials and a market for industrial products abroad. These they finance by the export of large amounts of capital.

227

Chapter 9

Central America and the Caribbean

The first Spanish emigrants to the West Indies were hardy adventurers. They had need to be, for the early colonies on the Caribbean islands afforded little but hard work and disease. In time, however, the search for gold and glory led the Spanish west from the islands to the American mainland. Here, first in Mexico and later in Peru, they found the treasures they had sought. In Mexico they also found two mighty empires: the Maya, a people whose civilization was in the final stages of decay, and the flourishing empire of the Aztec, a warrior people who continually sought to widen their rule from their capital, Tenochtitlán. Within a few years these early Spanish adventurers – the conquistadors – had destroyed these two civilizations and founded new empires under the distant control of Spain. They had paved the way for 300 years of Spanish colonial rule in the lands embracing the Caribbean Sea and the Bahia de Campeche (Bay of Campeche).

Opposite: statues of the Virgin Mary and saints being carried through the streets of a town in Guatemala during a religious festival. After the religious duties are over, such festivals, or *fiestas*, are celebrated with dancing and feasting. The Church's influence is strong in Central and South America, particularly among the poorer population.

229

The Gulf of Mexico

This region of high plateaus and small swampy plains, where much of the land is still uncultivated, lies mostly in the tropics. It is an area of hurricanes and palm trees, legends and oil derricks, which includes Mexico, the Central American land bridge, and the island arcs of the West Indies. It is one of the world's most crowded areas, supporting over three percent of all the people on earth on less than two percent of the total cultivated area of our planet.

Much of Mexico is taken up by a high plateau that varies from 3000 feet near the United States border to over 8000 feet in the south. The plateau is bordered by the Sierra Madre Oriental to the east and the Sierra Madre Occidental and the mountains of Baja California (Lower California) to the west. In south Mexico the two ranges of the Sierra Madre join together in a tangle of volcanic ranges from which rise the famous volcanic peaks of Popocatapetl, 17,887 feet, and Citaltepec, 18,701 feet. Bordering the south coast is the Sierra del Sur, separated from the volcanic peaks by the valley of the Rio de les Balsas. East of this chaotic area of peaks and basins, the mountains trend west–east rather than north–south.

The climate of the whole region of Central America and the Caribbean is greatly influenced by the presence of the waters of the Gulf of Mexico and Caribbean Sea, which are warmed by the North Equatorial Current. The prevailing winds are the trade winds that blow from the east throughout the year. As a result the Caribbean islands and the coastal lowlands are all uniformly hot and humid. The temperatures are consistently high and rarely fall below 70°F. The rainfall is distributed throughout the year, though it reaches a maximum in summer, and on the Pacific coast lowlands a more marked dry season. Much of the mainland plains and islands receive well over 60 inches of rain and on the tropical lowlands of Mexico, bordering the Bahia de Campeche (Bay of Campeche) there are more than 100 inches annually.

Over much of Mexico altitude determines the climate. There is a greater range of temperatures and the nights are far colder on the plateau where frost is not unknown. In winter it is not unusual for the cold north winds that sweep down from the Arctic across the central plains of the United States to reach as far south as the northeast and eastern coast of Mexico. When this happens, the temperatures will suddenly drop between 10° and 15°F for a few days. The plateau is also much drier than the rest of Mexico and the rainfall decreases toward the northwest where the arid desert areas receive less than two inches a year.

More than half of the land in Mexico lies at about 5000 feet and has an inadequate rainfall. There are also the other disadvantages of steep slopes and periodic flooding, which impose severe limitations on agriculture. In the past the people have been subsistence farmers, growing corn and beans. But this one-crop system has, over the years, reduced the fertility of the soil. At the same time there has been continuing deforestation as the people cleared more and more land for cultivation. This in turn has caused soil erosion which has been further aggravated by the overgrazing of cattle and goats. The outcome today is that agricultural opportunities are very limited and unless more

Above: a giant saguaro cactus grows in the semiarid state of Sonora, northwestern Mexico. It is part of a region of rough dry land that stretches northward into Arizona and New Mexico, USA.

irrigation and reclamation schemes are introduced, production of food will fall even lower.

Farther south, in Central America, the higher ground is more productive. The plentiful rainfall and rich volcanic soils make possible the cultivation of a wide variety of crops such as coffee, corn, beans, and staple foodstuffs and, higher up the slopes, the more temperate fruits, wheat, and barley. The more valuable commercial crops, such as sugar cane, bananas, coconuts, and tropical fruits can be grown in the wet, humid lowlands.

Although the country is still the leading producer of silver in the world, the emphasis on mining has shifted from precious metals to lead, zinc, copper, sulfur, and, more recently, oil, all of which are more

of the fuel. Nicaragua is the only other country with mineral resources, and gold used to form one of its major exports until exceeded by commercial crops such as coffee and cotton. The main manufacturing area is around the capital, Mexico, and Puebla, where textiles and the clothing industry are important. In the north, Monterrey is the center of the iron and steel and engineering industries.

Mexico is fortunate to have both coal and hydroelectric power, but the smaller Central American states have as yet few power installations. It is this lack of power that has been the main drawback to their industrial expansion, although projects are now underway in Nicaragua and El Salvador. All these countries, however, are heavily dependent on the

Above: Trinidad, the most southerly of the West Indies islands. Most of the larger West Indies islands were settled by the Spanish in the 1500s.

lucrative. This change has also meant a shift in the traditional mining areas from the southern belt of volcanic peaks and basins to the plateau, the Sierra Madre Occidental and the coastal plains of the Gulf of Mexico where the largest oilfield lies to the south of Tampico. So far oil has not been found farther south along the Caribbean coast except in Costa Rica where interest has been awakened recently by the discovery

USA, both as a market for their raw materials and goods and a supplier of their imports. This in turn means that any variation in the economy of the USA is soon reflected in the trade of the Central American nations.

The dependence of the countries of this region upon the United States has not lessened in recent years, except in the case of Mexico; there the expanding economy has increased international confidence in the country and enabled it to increase its trade with Europe and Japan.

231

Central America and the Caribbean

Scale:
Miles
0   100   200   300   400
Kilometres
0   100   200   300   400   500   600   700

PACIFIC OCEAN

Guatemala Basin

ALBATROS PLATEAU

Clipperton Fracture Zone

ISLAS REVILLA GIGEDO (MEXICO)

UNITED STATES

MEXICO

GULF OF

BAHÍA DE CAMPECHE

GOLFO DE TEHUANTEPEC

SIERRA MADRE OCCIDENTAL

SIERRA MADRE ORIENTAL

SIERRA MADRE DEL SUR

BAJA CALIFORNIA

TROPIC OF CANCER

The Islands of the Caribbean

The West Indies consist of three groups of islands: the Bahamas, the Greater Antilles, and the Lesser Antilles. The Greater Antilles – Cuba, Hispaniola, Puerto Rico, and Jamaica – are a partially submerged chain of fold mountains that extends eastward from Honduras for some 1500 miles. The Bahama Islands, to the north of them, are made of coral that has been built on an ancient platform, now submerged.

The Lesser Antilles fall into two sections, those lying along a huge arc enclosing the eastern end of the Caribbean and the west–east line of islands that lie close to the northern shores of South America. The latter mark an extension of the fold mountains of the Andes system on the mainland of South America. The islands lying along the north–south arc are more complex. They are for the most part volcanic, typical conical peaks rising out of the sea, with their fringing aprons of gently sloping land. The outer islets of the arc, Antigua, Barbuda, and Anguilla and others, are the remnants of uplifted, folded rocks that have been worn away leaving a series of low-lying islands.

These apparently idyllic islands have three great hazards: earthquakes, volcanoes, and hurricanes. The first two of these are only to be expected in this region of instability. They are part of the "Ring of Fire" that encircles the Pacific marking the junction of two large plates – the North American and the South American – and several smaller plates. There is almost continual evidence of movement and earth tremors in the mountains of both the mainland chain, which curves between the Rockies and the Andes, bordering the Guatemala Trench, and the highlands of the Greater Antilles, bordered by the deep sea trenches of the Cayman Islands and Puerto Rico. These mountains all appear to be continually shifting, settling, and fracturing. In recent years the most serious earthquakes have been not on the islands, but in Central America, in Guatemala and Costa Rica.

Volcanic activity is greatest in the central area of Mexico and the curve of islands forming the Lesser Antilles. Here volcanoes, often considered dormant or extinct, have suddenly erupted causing untold damage and havoc. In 1943, in Mexico, a whole mountain, Paricutin, suddenly came into being. A farmer plowing his fields heard rumblings beneath the ground. As they grew louder the earth cracked open and clouds of smoke poured out. For days streams of

Below: Mexicans digging out a car buried by the 130-mile-an-hour winds and driving rain of a tropical hurricane. The Atlantic Coasts of Mexico, Central America, and the West Indies are particularly vulnerable to hurricanes.

burning lava and ash spurted out and piled up into a dome-shaped mountain. Where once there had been corn fields there now stands a mountain, 9101 feet high.

The third hazard, the hurricane, is perhaps the greatest and most unpredictable. These tropical storms originate out to the east in the center of the

Above: harvesting sugar cane in Jamaica. Its peoples are the descendants of slaves brought from Africa.

Above right: bananas being loaded onto a flat-bottomed craft to be taken out to ships in deep water. Many small Caribbean islands do not have deep-water harbors.

Atlantic in an area where the air is hot and moist and the pressure is falling. If the fall in pressure suddenly becomes more rapid over a small area, the winds blow in from all sides, then, influenced by the earth's rotation, they form a whirl around the center of the low pressure area. This center, known as the eye, is usually very small, about 20 miles across. Outside the eye, the winds revolve quicker and quicker and the whole system moves westward.

The hurricane destroys everything that happens to be in its path. Winds, reaching over 150 miles an hour, uproot trees, flatten crops, lift whole buildings, and scatter the debris over a wide area. Torrential rains cause flooding, landslides, and wash away the crops in the fields or plantations. Within a relatively short time, sometimes only two or three hours, the hurricane has moved on leaving behind a tale of destruction.

Until recently the people of the West Indies had been able to cultivate sufficient land to grow enough food for their own needs. But with the steadily rising growth of population the smaller islands are finding

it more and more difficult to support their people. Many of these islands have little level land and often the leeward sides lack sufficient water for more intensive cultivation. The people are drifting into the towns where the slow growth of industries means that there are not enough jobs available for them.

The main cash crops, as in the other tropical countries, are those demanded by the people of the temperate areas of the world – sugar, tobacco, coffee, bananas, and spices. For a long time sugar cane has been the dominant cash crop of the majority of the islands, grown in plantations run by the European colonists and relying on the local labor or the slaves brought across from Africa. But its place is now being challenged by the production of sugar beet in the cooler latitudes.

In some of the islands other cash crops have been introduced or extended. In Cuba tobacco is important and the island is world-famous for its Havana cigars. Coffee is also well established in Cuba, Hispaniola, Puerto Rico, and Jamaica. Some of the small islands have specialized in the cultivation of individual crops: Grenada grows the nutmeg tree for nutmegs and mace; St Vincent produces arrowroot; Aruba the bitter aloe; Dominica limes; and Curaçao the divi-divi tree, whose pods are used in the leather industry.

As elsewhere in the world towns have attracted many of the rural dwellers. Each of the small islands has its chief town, usually built on the leeward side of the island, nestling around a harbor at the foot of the steep mountain slopes and sheltered from the full force of any hurricane. But the disadvantage of these towns today, as with many on the larger islands, is that there is not enough room for them to expand, confined as they are between ocean and mountain.

Natural Resources

One of the least exploited resources in the Gulf of Mexico and the Caribbean is the sea. Great efforts have been made in recent years to take more advantage of the rich seafood, particularly shrimps, that the area offers. Several large, ambitious projects have been launched in an attempt to make the islands not only self-sufficient in fisheries' products, but also have enough supplies to promote an export trade.

Cuba has already shown how this can be done. In 1958 the Cuban fish catch was a little over 20,000 tons a year; 20 years later it is well over 100,000 tons. Headed by the Instituto de la Pesca, the Cuban fleet is divided into five sections: The Caribbean Shrimp Fleet consists of several hundred trawlers that operate in the Gulf of Mexico and over the Caribbean. Most of these vessels have refrigeration and process the shrimp catch on board. The Southern Shrimp Fleet has over 1000 vessels of which one-third catch shrimps and the remainder fish, whereas the smaller Gulf Fleet has less than 100 wooden vessels. The Cuban Fishing Fleet operates from a Soviet-built base

Below: fishermen on Lake Pátzcuaro, Michoacán state, southwestern Mexico. Efforts are being made throughout Mexico and the Central American and Caribbean area to exploit the fishing grounds.

and fishes all over the world. It includes factory ships, side trawlers, tuna longliners, refrigerated ships, and supply ships. The fifth group, the Coastal Fleet, has over 100 vessels operating on the continental shelf around the Cuban coast for rock lobster, spiny lobster (crayfish), sardines, and sponges.

The UN Development Fund and the FAO (Food and Agricultural Organization) is assisting some 15 Caribbean countries in a research project to develop deepwater fishing for sea trout, grouper, and snapper. Vessels owned by the FAO have explored various areas of the Caribbean around Jamaica, Trinidad, and Barbados for suitable fishing grounds. Fishermen have been trained in modern techniques. It is hoped that a fleet of some 400, entirely Caribbean-owned, trawlers will eventually operate from the various islands.

Haiti is also investigating the possibility of large-scale fishing for bonito, tuna, and albacore in the bay north of Port-au-Prince. In Mexico the government is trying to promote the consumption of fish, but the country needs improved freezing facilities if it is to realize the full potential of the shrimp grounds to the east, and the Pacific tuna and sardine to the west.

The vast continental shelf of the Gulf of Mexico and the Caribbean is also the most productive offshore oil and gas area in the world. In fact, the coastal waters off Texas and Louisiana and Lake Maracaibo in Venezuela were the cradle of the offshore oil industry, which started in the 1920s. The drilling is now being extended to areas offshore near the mouth of the Rio Grande, Tampico, and the Dutch Antilles as well as various points in the Gulf of California, especially around the island of Tiburon.

On shore the prospects for greater oil production are also promising in Mexico and Costa Rica. Farther

Above: the Guri Dam in northeastern Venezuela harnesses the Orinoco-Caroni river system for hydroelectric power. Venezuela also has large resources of petroleum and natural gas north of the Orinoco.

east, Trinidad, too, has large reserves of oil, both onshore and offshore, and these have been exploited with beneficial results for the economy. Trinidad also has one of the world's largest supplies of asphalt that occur in Pitch Lake, in the southwest of the island.

All the countries of the Central American mainland have rich hydroelectric power potential. It is not developed to any great extent, however, except in the central states of Mexico, around the capital, where industrialization is greatest. A recent project is the construction of a dam across the Grijalva river, which, although principally intended for flood control, will also serve to generate electricity for the El Limon area in southeast Mexico near the Guatemala border. Since 1949 El Salvador has actually harnessed the greatest proportion of the hydroelectric power potential in the whole region although Costa Rica has constructed the largest installations.

The area of land under forest in the Caribbean and Central America is very large and trees cover more than half of the total area of these countries, providing mahogany, rosewood, and other cabinet woods. There are valuable pine forests in the Sierra Madre Occidental and the central volcanic highlands as well as tropical forests on the slopes of the Sierra del Sur and Sierra Madre bordering the south coast. All these are now being exploited more economically and pulp and

paper mills operate in the northwest near Chihuahua. In Honduras, timber from the pine forests is the third most important export after coffee and bananas, and schemes have already been put forward to produce pulp wood from the pine forests of Guatemala, to develop the paper industry in Nicaragua, and to build a large-scale timber and pulp plant in eastern Honduras.

Above: part of a large harvest of corn near Acapulco. Corn is one of Mexico's principal crops and the rich soil and plentiful rainfall of the central plateau area also help produce other cereal crops, coffee, sugar cane, and fruits in abundance. Mexico is also rich in mineral deposits.

The People of Central America

Whatever their origins, the peoples of the New World took thousands of years establishing themselves over the two continents. By the time the Europeans arrived in the West Indies, there were groups in various degrees of development between the pure hunters and established farming peoples – and on the mainland two advanced cultures, the Mayan and the Aztec civilizations.

The Mayan culture flourished in the jungle region of Honduras about the time of the Roman Empire. They learned controlled agriculture, they were pyramid builders, astronomers, calendar makers, and they developed their own form of written language. Their "pyramids" were astonishing achievements for a simple farming people living in a tropical environment of forest and swamp and using only stone tools. Their decline and sudden collapse is still a mystery, but the empire lingered on until it was finally crushed by the Spanish invaders.

It is thought that the founders of the other great central American culture, the Aztecs, wandered southward across the Mexican plateau to settle finally on the high, fertile, and well-watered lands of the volcanic highlands. There they achieved wealth, built

Above: Aztecs being massacred in 1520 by the Spanish under Pedro de Alvarado. It happened during a religious festival when the Aztecs were unarmed and was typical of the brutality of the conquistadors toward the Indians.

heir pyramid temples for sacrifices, developed irrigation, constructed aqueducts and viaducts, produced a form of writing, and gained a knowledge of astronomy and calendar making. The impact of the white man was so sudden and ruthless that the Aztec civilization was swept away within a few years.

The people who spread southward from the Bering Strait turned eastward to wander along the northern shores of South America or down the valley of the Orinoco. As they reached the tip of the Peninsula de Paria some sailed north to the islands, then, using the islands as stepping stones, gradually spread through the Lesser Antilles to the Greater Antilles and the Bahamas. Some of these peoples had advanced cultures. They were farmers and fishermen and had a little knowledge of metallurgy. Others were clever sailors as well as being particularly skillful in their cultivation and preparation of bitter cassava and cotton. But in the islands, as on the mainland of Central America, the story is the same. Few local

Above right: the site of the 1968 Olympic Games in Mexico City.
Left: Religious festivals play an important part in the lives of the peoples of Mexico and Central America.
Below: the famous floating gardens of Xochimilco, south of Mexico City.

peoples survived the invasions from Western Europe.

Spanish settlers made the greatest impact in this region. The colonists arrived first in Cuba where major cities were founded and land distributed to the settlers. The land was farmed and used for stock-rearing to provide salt beef for the towns and the ships that stopped off on their way to Mexico, and horses for the armies on the mainland. The influence of Spain has remained throughout the region and today Mexico is the most populous Spanish-speaking country in the world. The cultivation of the sugar cane with its dependence on a large labor force, gave rise to a period of importation of slaves between 1750 and 1850. Today, although the white-skinned peoples are

more numerous on the mainland and the three larger islands of Cuba, Hispaniola, and Puerto Rico, the African Negro forms the overwhelming majority on all the other islands. In the middle of the last century more than 250,000 Indians were brought into the area from Asia, many of them settling on Trinidad, where they now form a large racial group.

This whole region, which together with South America is termed Latin America, is considered to form part of the Third World. The countries all depend to a large extent on the United States, Western Europe, and Japan for trade, technology, and capital. Of these, the United States is by far the largest participant. As with other Third World countries, the region exports basically agricultural and mineral products and imports machinery and manufactured goods. Yet in contrast to other Third World countries, the nations of Central America and the Caribbean have been politically independent for a longer time.

Already Mexico has experienced the results of the growing international confidence in its ability to expand its economy. The country has acted host to such international meetings as the International Women's Year (IWY), the 1968 Olympics, and the 1970 World Football Cup. Elsewhere in Central America plans are afoot to improve communications, develop some of the lowland areas, and exploit the hydroelectric power resources. In the West Indies, Cuba is no longer considered an appendage of the USA and since 1959 has turned to the USSR for technical aid and machinery. In Puerto Rico an industrialization program has been devised with the assistance of the USA and has proved successful in providing both employment and training schemes. The example of Puerto Rico has since been copied by some of the other islands including Trinidad and Jamaica and many smaller islands. At the same time tourism is being encouraged and efforts made to persuade people to return to the land and agriculture in order to produce some of the essential foodstuffs.

The Countries of Central America

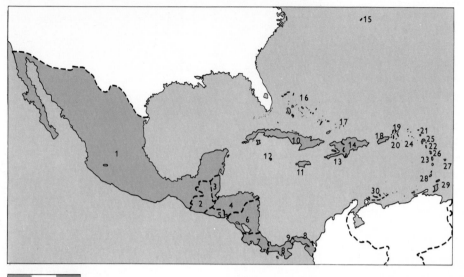

1 Mexico
2 Guatemala
3 Belize
4 Honduras
5 El Salvador
6 Nicaragua
7 Costa Rica
8 Panama
9 Panama Canal Zone
10 Cuba
11 Jamaica
12 Cayman Islands
13 Haiti
14 Dominican Republic
15 Bermuda
16 Bahamas
17 Turks & Caicos Islands
18 Puerto Rico
19 Virgin Islands (British)
20 Virgin Islands (USA)
21 Associated States of the Caribbean
22 Dominica
23 St Lucia
24 Montserrat
25 Guadeloupe
26 Martinique
27 Barbados
28 Grenada
29 Trinidad & Tobago
30 Netherlands Antilles

MEXICO (Estados Unidos Mexicanos)
Area: 761,600 square miles
Population: 54,000,000
Capital: Mexico City (Mexico)
Language: Spanish
Religion: Catholicism
Monetary Unit: Peso

History and Government: Three of the great Pre-Columbian cultures originated in Mexico – the Toltecs, the Aztecs, and the Mayas. The Spanish arrived in 1517 and in 1535 the colony became the viceroyalty of New Spain, which lasted until 1821, when independence was declared and the state of Mexico came into existence. The social revolution of 1920–21 resulted in a new Constitution that was subsequently amended many times. It is now a federal republic of the presidential type and is unique in Latin America because of its relative political stability. The president is elected by direct popular vote, serves six years and cannot be re-elected. There is a Congress that consists of a Senate and a Chamber of Deputies. There are four political parties the largest of which, Parti do Revolucionario Institucional (PRI), has formed the government of the country for many years.

Economy: Agriculture, which employs nearly half the labor force, is distinguished by a few crops of world-wide importance such as cotton, coffee, and henequen, though the most widespread crops are cereals. Also important are fruit-growing, stock-rearing, and fishing. There are rich mineral resources. As well as silver and sulfur, of which Mexico is among the foremost producers in the world, gold, iron ore, lead, zinc, copper, and mercury are also mined. The oil industry is expanding and in the future the country should be self-supporting. Various sectors of manufacturing industry are developing considerably in the fields of food and textiles, chemicals and pharmaceuticals, iron and steel, and engineering. A primary objective is to find new markets in order to reduce dependence on the USA, which today absorbs about half the trade. Contacts have recently been made with the USSR, China, and the EEC countries to try to correct this imbalance.

GUATEMALA
Area: 42,024 square miles
Population: 5,500,000
Capital: Guatemala
Language: Spanish
Religion: Catholicism
Monetary Unit: Quetzal

History and Government: From 1524–1821 the country was included in the Spanish captaincy general of Guatemala – which then included much of Central America, with its capital at Antigua. It became independent in 1821, from 1821 to 1839 was part of the Confederation of Central America and is now a presidential republic. A new constitution of 1965 established a council of state under the chairmanship of the vice-president and for the reduction of the presidential term from six to four years. Congress was elected in 1966 Administration is by the cabinet under the president.

Economy: The main economic activity is agriculture and coffee is the principal crop. Banana plantations together with cotton provide a large part of the exports. From the forests come chicle gum, exported to the USA for the manufacture of chewing gum. Industry is almost nonexistent but there are some electrical and plastic factories dependent mainly upon massive amounts of foreign capital. In the mineral sector zinc and lead are exported and nickel is being developed. The country is subject to violent earthquakes that cause whole-scale destruction and loss of life

BELIZE
Area: 8867 square miles
Population: 140,000
Capital: Belmopan
Monetary Unit: Belize Dollar

History and Government: Originally part of the Maya civilization but, uncolonized by the Spanish, it was left to the British to colonize in the mid-17th century. As a British colony it was known as British Honduras. Belize has been internally self-governing since 1964. The governor appoints a premier from the majority party in the House of Representatives, the lower house in the General Assembly. The Upper House is a senate of eight members appointed by the governor and premier.

Economy: The principal economic resources are timber, sugar cane, and citrus fruits, particularly grapefruit, which are largely exported. Fish is also important, especially lobster tails, shrimps, and dried fish, all of which are exported. Mahogany, cedar, and chicle (for chewing gum), pine, and rosewood are grown.

HONDURAS
Area: 43,377 square miles
Population: 2,700,000
Capital: Tegucigalpa
Language: Spanish
Religion: Catholicism
Monetary Unit: Lempira
History and Government: Christopher Columbus visited Honduras on his fourth voyage in 1502. Later it was part of the captaincy general of Guatemala. It gained its independence from Spain in 1821 and in 1826 it became a member of the Federation of Central America. Honduras became an independent sovereign state. In 1972, after a coup d'état, Congress was suspended. Since then Honduras has been dominated by the army and has a Constitution of the presidential type. A further coup in April 1975 followed allegations of corruption and bribes from foreign banana companies. This led to the setting up of a Honduran Banana Corporation to control all operations concerning bananas.
Economy: Bananas are the main economic resource and represent half the exports. Other important products are coffee and timber as well as tobacco, beans, corn, rice, cotton, and sugar. Cattle raising and frozen meat exports are also important. Industry is little developed. The country is rich in gold, silver, lead, zinc, and mercury.

EL SALVADOR
Area: 8250 square miles
Population: 4,250,000
Capital: San Salvador
Language: Spanish
Religion: Catholicism
Monetary Unit: Colón
History and Government: Throughout the period of Spanish rule El Salvador was part of the captaincy general of Guatemala. It became independent in 1821, then part of the Central American Federation (San Salvador was the capital). It became an independent republic in 1841. The republic is of the presidential type. Under the constitution of 1950 the president is elected for

six years and the legislature for two. For years the presidency of the republic has been in the hands of the military, while political life is controlled by the National Conciliation Party (PCN) (Partido de Conciliación Nacional).
Economy: It is essentially agricultural based on plantations of coffee and cotton, which represent more than half the exports. Food productions, including rice, corn, sugar cane, is less than sufficient for internal needs. Forests supply the world's principal source of the medicinal gum from the balsam trees. Industry is modest; the most important are textiles and foodstuffs. Mining is almost nonexistent though attempts are being made to exploit newly discovered deposits of silver.

NICARAGUA
Area: 53,668 square miles
Population: 2,400,000
Capital: Managua
Language: Spanish and Chibcha
Religion: Catholicism
Monetary Unit: Córdoba
History and Government: The region that is now Nicaragua was at one time included in the Spanish captaincy general of Guatemala until 1821 when it became independent. Later it joined the Central American Federation. Nicaragua became independent in 1838, but part of it, "Mosquitia," remained a separate kingdom under British control until 1860. It is now a democratic representative republic, with legislative power vested in a Senate of 30 members and the ex-president, and a chamber of 70 Deputies.
Economy: Over half the working population is employed in agriculture. The chief products are coffee and cotton which are largely exported, sugar, sesame, and bananas. Beef is also exported. For home consumption, pineapples, sweet potatoes, and yucca are grown together with corn, rice, and sugar cane. Among the mineral resources are gold and silver and, recently, oil has been discovered offshore. The foodstuff and textile industries are of local importance. The Atlantic fisheries are valuable and shrimps are processed for export. The forests are not yet fully exploited.

COSTA RICA
Area: 19,652 square miles
Population: 2,000,000
Capital: San José

Language: Spanish
Religion: Catholicism
Monetary Unit: Colón
History and Government: Costa Rica – meaning "Rich Coast" – was allegedly given its name by Christopher Columbus in 1502. It was conquered in 1563 and brought under the captaincy general of Guatemala. It has been independent since 1821 but formed part of the Federation of Central America from 1824 to 1838. It is one of the "banana republics" ruled by a legislative Assembly. The president is elected for four years. He has the power to appoint and remove members of his cabinet. In December 1948 the army was abolished, the then president declaring that it was unnecessary, as the country loved peace.
Economy: The principal resources are bananas and a particularly high quality coffee. Important also are cocoa, rubber, abaca, and dairy products which are largely exported. There are few industries and mining is little developed though there is some gold and a recent source of haematite has been located. Costa Rica is the seat of the Inter-American Institute of Agricultural Sciences. It has the highest literacy rate in Latin America.

PANAMA (Panamá)
Area: 29,208 square miles excluding the Canal Zone.
Population: 1,800,000
Capital: Panama City
Language: Spanish
Religion: Catholicism
Monetary Unit: Balboa
History and Government: Occupying what was once the route by which the treasures of the Inca empire went to Spain, Panama was incorporated into first the viceroyalty of Peru, then the viceroyalty of New Granada. After the overthrow of Spanish rule Panama joined the Republic of Great Colombia, but broke away in 1903. It is a presidential republic. The president is elected every four years, but since the coup d'état of 1968 the power has been in the hands of the military. In 1972 a new Constitution was approved. In September 1977 President Carter of the USA and General Torrijoa, for Panama, signed a treaty giving Panama control of the Canal in the year 2000.
Economy: A large part of the population lives by agriculture, which, however, does not supply sufficient food for internal needs. Nearly half the land is uncultivated. Bananas are the chief product; sugar, coffee, and cocoa are also exported. Stock-rearing and fishing, mainly for shrimps, are practiced.

Industry is scarcely developed and although deposits of copper have been discovered they are not yet worked. The greatest source of income is the rent paid by the USA for the lease of the Canal Zone. Tax exemptions and lenient labor laws make the merchant navy one of the largest in the world.

PANAMA CANAL ZONE
Area: 647 square miles
Population: 45,000
Chief Town: Balboa Heights
Monetary Unit: United States currency
History and Government: A treaty of 1903 gave the United States the rights to build a canal and occupy and control "in perpetuo" this enclave in the interior of the state of Panama. In return, the USA guaranteed the independence of the republic of Panama. The canal, built by the USA was opened to traffic in 1914. In the military bases, "green berets" from various countries are trained.

CUBA
Area: 44,178 square miles
Population: 8,800,000
Capital: Havana (La Habana)
Language: Spanish
Religion: Catholicism
Monetary Unit: Peso
History and Government: From 1492 to 1898 Cuba was a Spanish possession, except for a brief spell under British rule in the second half of the 18th century. Its first independent government was formed in 1902. In 1959 a "socialist" revolution led by the Marxist-Leninist Fidel Castro overthrew the dictatorship of General Batista. In 1965 the Communist Party of Cuba was formed to succeed the United Party of the Revolution as the only authorized political party. Elections are no longer held. Land and urban reform have been carried out together with the nationalization of the means of production.
Economy: Sugar is still the mainstay of the economy although attempts have been made to diversify into other crops such as tobacco, tropical fruits, coffee, and henequen. A policy of reforestation and development of the fishing industry have both proved successful. Attempts to develop industry have suffered from insufficient availability of power sources. The considerable iron ore deposits have not yet been fully exploited.

JAMAICA
Area: 4411 square miles
Population: 2,100,000
Capital: Kingston
Language: English
Religion: Mainly Protestant
Monetary Unit: Jamaican Dollar
History and Government: Jamaica was a Spanish possession between 1509 and 1655, when it became a British colony. It was an important center of the slave trade, and later as a producer of sugar. Jamaica gained its independence in 1962. A governor-general represents the crown. Government is of the parliamentary type, with two chambers, House of Representatives of 60 members and a Senate of 21 nominated members.
Economy: The island is supported by two resources, sugar cane and bauxite. Other crops grown for export are bananas, cocoa, coffee, and citrus fruits. The most important industries are those producing aluminum, sugar, rum, and cigarettes. There is also a native-developed breed of dairy cattle, Jamaica Hope and a beef breed, Jamaica Black. Tourism is also important.

CAYMAN ISLANDS
Area: 100 square miles
Population: 11,000
Capital: Georgetown (on the Grand Cayman)
Monetary Unit: Cayman Islands Dollar
History and Government: The Cayman Islands were discovered by Columbus in 1503 but remained uncolonized until the British arrived around 1734. It was a dependency of Jamaica until 1962 when the islands became a British crown colony. The constitution provides for a governor, a Legislative Assembly, and an Executive Council. They consist of three islands – Grand Cayman, Little Cayman, and Cayman Brac.
Economy: The people live mainly by fishing – turtles and sharks – and tourism.

HAITI (République d'Haiti)
Area: 10,700 square miles
Population: 4,800,000

Capital: Port-au-Prince
Language: Creole and French
Religion: Catholicism
Monetary Unit: Gourde
History and Government: Haiti was first a Spanish colony, then ceded to France in 1697. The country finally declared its independence in 1804. At one time in the 19th century Haiti was united with the rest of the island – known as Hispaniola – then, from 1915 to 1934, was under the occupation of the USA. In 1957 Dr Duvalier was elected President for Life and was succeeded on his death in 1971 by his son.
Economy: It is the poorest country in the subcontinent, with an essentially agricultural economy, although now only one third of its land is arable. The chief product is coffee, followed by sisal, sugar cane, bananas, cocoa, cotton, and ricinus. Mining is modest there is some bauxite and copper. Manufacturing is almost nonexistent but the assembly and finishing of goods is expanding. Tourism is also developing.

BERMUDA
Area: 20 square miles
Population: 53,000
Capital: Hamilton
Monetary Unit: Bermuda Dollar
History and Government: Although the Bermudas, or Somers Islands, were originally discovered by the Spanish this archipelago of some 150 islands was settled by the British in 1609. The archipelago became a Colony in 1684. The governor is appointed by the crown and there is a Legislative Council and a House of Assembly. There is internal self-government, introduced in 1968.
Economy: The principal industry is tourism and over 500,000 visitors are catered for each year. Cotton, tobacco, coffee, are also grown together with some foodstuffs.

DOMINICAN REPUBLIC
(República Dominicana)
Area: 19,322 square miles
Population: 4,250,000
Capital: Santo Domingo (de Guzman)
Language: Spanish
Religion: Catholicism
Monetary Unit: Peso
History and Government: Discovered by Christopher Columbus in 1492, Santo Domingo was the Western part of the island of Hispaniola; the

eastern part (later Haiti) was ceded to France as Saint Domingue in the 17th century. Subjugated by neighboring Haitians in 1822, until 1844 when Dominican republic was proclaimed. The Americans occupied the country between 1916–24. After over 30 years' dictatorship, a coup d'état and a civil war, peace was finally restored and Joaquin Balaguer elected president in 1966. The president is elected for four years by direct vote.

Economy: The chief resource is sugar cane, which also provides the leading industry. Coffee, cocoa, tobacco, and bananas are also exported. The mineral resources are scarcely exploited, although there are quantities of calcium sulfates, rock salt, iron ore, and, most important, bauxite.

BAHAMAS (Commonwealth of)
Area: 5352 square miles
Population: 198,000
Capital: Nassau (on island of New Providence)
Language: Creole and English
Religion: Protestantism
Monetary Unit: Bahamian Dollar
History and Government: Settled originally by British subjects (although assigned to Spain by papal grant) the ownership of the islands was taken over again by Spain in 1782, and restored to the British crown in 1883. The former British colony is made up of over 700 islands (only 30 of which are inhabited) and many more cays. It has been independent since 1973 and is a member of the Commonwealth. A governor-general represents the crown. There is a Senate of 16 members (nine appointed by the Governor-General on the advice of the premier, four on the advice of the Leader of the Opposition, and three at the discretion of the Governor-General) and a House of Assembly of 38 elected members.

Economy: Tourism is the main resource and more than 1,000,000 people visit the island annually. There is also the cultivation of sugar cane and pineapples. Fishing for shellfish, turtles, and sponges is important. There are a few industries and cement, petroleum products, crayfish, and salt are exported.

TURKS AND CAICOS ISLANDS
Area: 192 square miles
Population: 7000
Capital: Grand Turk
Monetary Unit: United States currency
History and Government: The first permanent settlement on the islands was made in 1781. They were originally under the Bahamas government but transferred to Jamaica in 1848. In 1962 they became a British crown colony. There are two groups of islands consisting of some 30 cays of which eight are inhabited. Geographically they are an extension of the Bahamas. There is a governor and an Executive Council and a Legislative Council of elected members.

Economy: The islanders live mainly by the extraction of sea-salt and fishing. Tourism is increasing with over 8000 visitors annually.

PUERTO RICO
(Commonwealth of)
Area: 3426 square miles
Population: 3,250,000
Capital: San Juan
Language: English, Spanish
Religion: Catholicism
Monetary Unit: United States currency
History and Government: Puerto Rico was ceded by the Spanish to the USA in 1899. Its constitution was determined by the United States Congress in 1917 and was in force until 1952 when the present constitution of the Commonwealth of Puerto Rico was adopted.

Below: part of the Haitian city of Port-au-Prince in 1963 after a hurricane had devastated five of the island's cities and left thousands dead.

There is a governor elected every four years, a Senate of 27 members and a House of Representatives of 51 members. The country sends a Resident Commissioner to the US Congress who is elected for a four-year term but is not allowed to vote.

Economy: Predominantly agricultural the country is gradually becoming industrialized, mainly the processing of agricultural products, heavy industry, and manufactured goods. The principal crops grown are sugar cane, bananas, tobacco, coffee, and also the citrus fruits, pineapples, and cereals which are widely cultivated. Tourism is important.

VIRGIN ISLANDS (BRITISH)
Area: 59 square miles
Population: 10,000
Capital: Road Town (on Tortola)
Monetary Unit: United States currency
History and Government: The islands were acquired by England in 1666. There are about 36 islands of which 16 are inhabited and Tortola is the largest. They are a British dependency, ruled by a governor. The Executive Council consists of the governor and five members. There is a Legislative Council.
Economy: The main activities of the population are fishing, stock-rearing, and the cultivation of sugar cane and vegetables. There are a few rum distilleries.

VIRGIN ISLANDS (USA)
Area: 133 square miles
Population: 90,000
Capital: Charlotte Amalie
Monetary Unit: United States currency
History and Government: The Virgin Islands, made up of St. Thomas, St. Croix, St. John, and some 50 small islands, were, as the Danish West Indies, purchased by the USA from Denmark in 1917. Their value is purely strategic. Virgin Islanders are citizens of the United States. In 1970 the islanders elected their own governor for the first time. There is a single chamber legislature of 15 senators, popularly elected.
Economy: Tourism, fishing, and the production of sugar and rum are the chief resources of the economy.

Member states of the Association each have their own flag.

ASSOCIATED STATES OF THE CARIBBEAN
(Antigua, St Kitts-Nevis-Anguilla, St. Vincent)
Area: 390 square miles (all the islands)
Population: 320,000
Language: English and French Dialect
Monetary Unit: East Caribbean Dollar
History and Government: The Islands of Antigua, Dominica, Grenada, St Lucia, St Kitts-Nevis-Anguilla became self-governing states associated with Britain in 1967, and St Vincent (which includes half the Grenadines) became an associated state in 1969. Grenada, Dominica, and St Lucia later became independent. Britain has responsibility for external affairs and defense.
Economy: The principal economic activity is agriculture. The most widespread crop is sugar cane, which supplies rum distilleries and sugar refineries. Also important are bananas, cotton, coconuts, cocoa, and coffee. Tourism is well developed.

SAINT LUCIA
Area: 238 square miles
Population: 11,000
Capital: Castries
Monetary Unit: East Caribbean Dollar

History and Government: The island was discovered around 1500 and settled by Europeans in 1650. The island passed from French to British control in 1814. Until February 1979 it was part of the Associated States of the Caribbean. It is now an independent state within the Commonwealth.
Economy: the main activity of the island is agriculture, with bananas accounting for 80 percent of production. Coconuts, cocoa, citrus, and spices are also produced.

DOMINICA
Area: 290 square miles
Population: 70,500
Capital: Roseau
Monetary Unit: East Caribbean Dollar
History and Government: The island was discovered and named by Christopher Columbus, and was colonized by the French in the 17th century. It became a British possession in 1805. Between 1967 and 1978 it was an Associated State of the United Kingdom. It is now a fully independent member of the Commonwealth.
Economy: Agriculture is the main activity of the island, with bananas the chief exports. Citrus and fruit juices are also important products.

Below: a procession of dancers and musicians wends its way through a village in Mexico during a festival. The procession stops before certain houses along the route to salute the statues of the saints set up there.

MONTSERRAT
Area: 39 square miles
Population: 13,000
Capital: Plymouth
Monetary Unit: East Caribbean Dollar
History and Government: Settled by Irishmen, conquered by the French, and assigned to Britain in 1783, Montserrat has had cabinet-style government since 1960. The governor of the island represents the Crown. There is an Executive Council of four elected and two appointed members and an 11-member Legislative Council.
Economy: The island exports cotton, bananas, and vegetables.

GUADELOUPE
Area: 687 square miles
Population: 337,000
Capital: Pointe à Pitre
Monetary Unit: French currency
History and Government: Guadeloupe consists of two island and five dependencies (smaller islands). It is an overseas department of the French Republic and has been a French possession since 1675. It is administered by a Prefect and sends three deputies to the National Assembly and two to the French Senate.
Economy: Sugar cane is the main economic resource, supplying the industries of sugar refining and rum distilling. Bananas, coffee, cocoa, pineapples, oranges, and vanilla are widely cultivated.

MARTINIQUE
Area: 425 square miles
Population: 344,000
Capital: Forte de France
Monetary Unit: French currency
History and Government: A French possession since 1635 except between 1762 to 1763, 1794 to 1802, and 1809 to 1815 when it was British, Martinique is now an overseas department of the French republic. It is administered by a Prefect and is represented by three deputies in the National Assembly and two in the Senate. It was the birthplace of the Empress Josephine, wife of Napoleon I of France.
Economy: The chief resource is sugar

cane, which supplies sugar refineries and rum distilleries. The cultivation of pineapples and bananas is also widespread.

BARBADOS
Area: 166 square miles
Population: 251,000
Capital: Bridgetown
Language: English
Religion: Protestantism
Monetary Unit: Barbados Dollar
History and Government: A British colony since 1605, and seat of government for Windward Islands between 1833 and 1855, Barbados became an independent state within the Commonwealth in 1966. The governor-general appoints the privy council and there are two chambers, a Senate of 21 members and House of Assembly of 24 members.
Economy: The economy depends mainly upon sugar cane, sugar refineries, and rum distilleries. Stock-rearing and fishing are also carried on. Tourism is expanding.

GRENADA
Area: 133 square miles
Population: 104,000
Capital: St. George's
Language: Creole and English
Religion: Christianity
Monetary Unit: East Caribbean Dollar
History and Government: Named Concepción by Columbus, who discovered it, Grenada became a possession of French crown in 1674 before passing into the hands of the British in the late 1700s. Grenada has been an independent nation within the Commonwealth since 1974. Half the chain of small islands known as the Grenadines also come under its jurisdiction. A governor-general represents the crown. There is a two-tier legislature of a Senate and House of Representatives. Britain administers foreign policy and defense.
Economy: Agriculture, stock-rearing, and fishing are the main activities of the people. Bananas, cocoa, nutmegs, citrus fruits, sugar cane, and coconuts are important. The few existing industries process agricultural products.

TRINIDAD & TOBAGO
Area: 1980 square miles

Population: 1,250,000
Capital: Port of Spain
Language: English and Spanish
Religion: Mainly Christianity
Monetary Unit: Trinidad and Tobago Dollar
History and Government: Formerly Spanish, Trinidad was ceded to Britain in 1802 and in 1889 was joined with Tobago. The country – the two islands – has been independent since 1962 and a member of the Commonwealth. There is a Senate and a House of Representatives. The former has 24 appointed members and the latter 36 elected members. In 1976 legislation was passed making Trinidad and Tobago a Republic with a president as head of state.
Economy: Rapid industrialization has taken place, but this has accentuated the dependence of the country on the multinational companies. The most important agricultural crop is sugar, with diversification into other crops. Oil, asphalt, and tourism are the principal resources. Foreign investments have developed numerous industries such as the oil refineries, chemical and petrochemical plants, sugar refineries, and rum distilleries.

NETHERLANDS ANTILLES
(Nederlandse Antillen)
Area: 394 square miles
Population: 235,000
Capital: Willemstad
Language: Dutch, English, and Spanish
Religion: Catholicism
Monetary Unit: Netherlands Antilles Guilder
History and Government: There are six islands: the Leeward Islands of Curaçao, Aruba, and Bonaire (often termed the ABC islands) and the Windward Islands, east of Puerto Rico, of St. Maarten, St. Eustatius, and Saba. They were captured from the Spanish by the Dutch West India company in 1634 and held by the British for a short time before reverting to the Netherlands in 1815. The capital was seized briefly by Venezuelan revolutionaries in 1929. The islands have full autonomy in their domestic affairs. Administration is by a governor nominated by the Dutch sovereign, who, together with a council of ministers forms the government. There is a single chamber.
Economy: The islands of Curaçao and Aruba have large oil refineries and the former also has petrochemical works and phosphate mines. Agriculture largely produces for home consumption, the most important crops being oranges, the peel of which is used for manufacture of the liqueur Curaçao.

Chapter 10

South America

South America is in every way a continent of extremes, extremes of landscape, climate, development, and peoples. The towering Andes run down the west side of the continent, forming a giant barrier. To the west the narrow coastal plain changes from tropical forest to desert to temperate grassland and finally to coniferous forest as it stretches from just north of the Equator to 55°S latitude. To the east lie the vast tropical forests of the Amazon Basin, flanked on the north and south by the savanna-covered Guiana and Brazilian Highlands. Southward are the drier regions of the Gran Chaco and the Pampas that give way finally to the scrublands of Patagonia. Although it was the first continent to be colonized, it has remained isolated from the Western World. It has seen its North American neighbor take the lead in modern economic development and political strategy, and has become regarded as part of the Third World.

Opposite: an oil derrick in Colombia, symbol of the increasingly important petroleum industry located in a wide area from Colombia, Peru, Ecuador, Argentina, Chile, and Venezuela to Mexico and Trinidad. South America, largely still under-developed, is a continent of enormous resources and potential whose importance as a future powerful new trading bloc is being taken seriously by the industrial nations of the world.

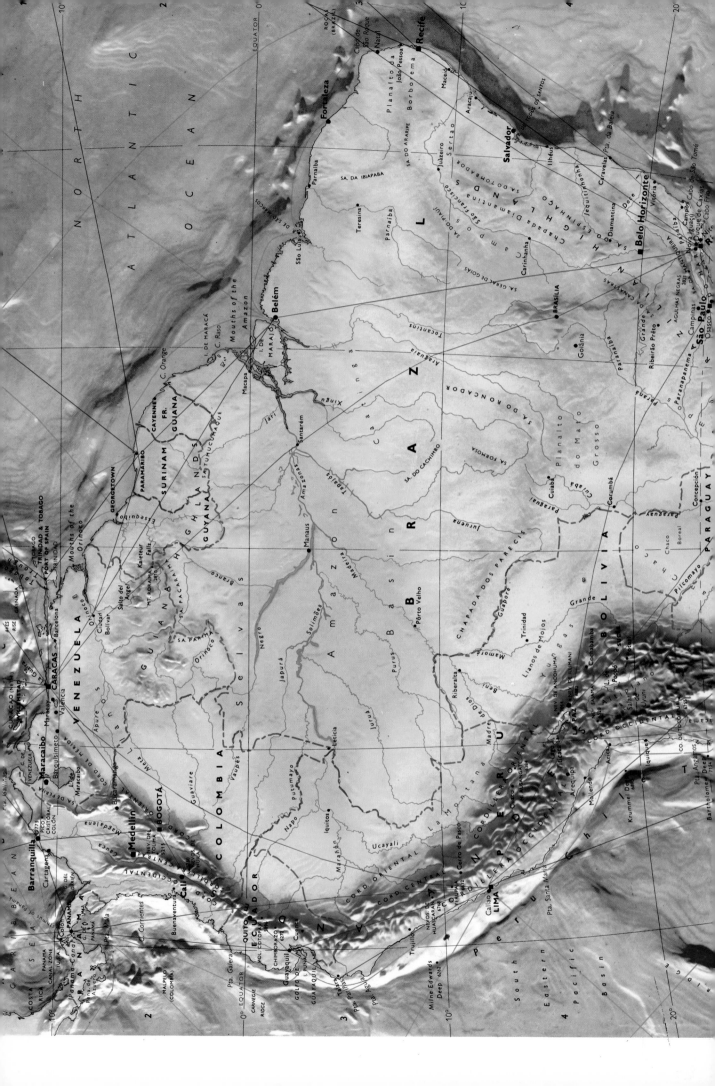

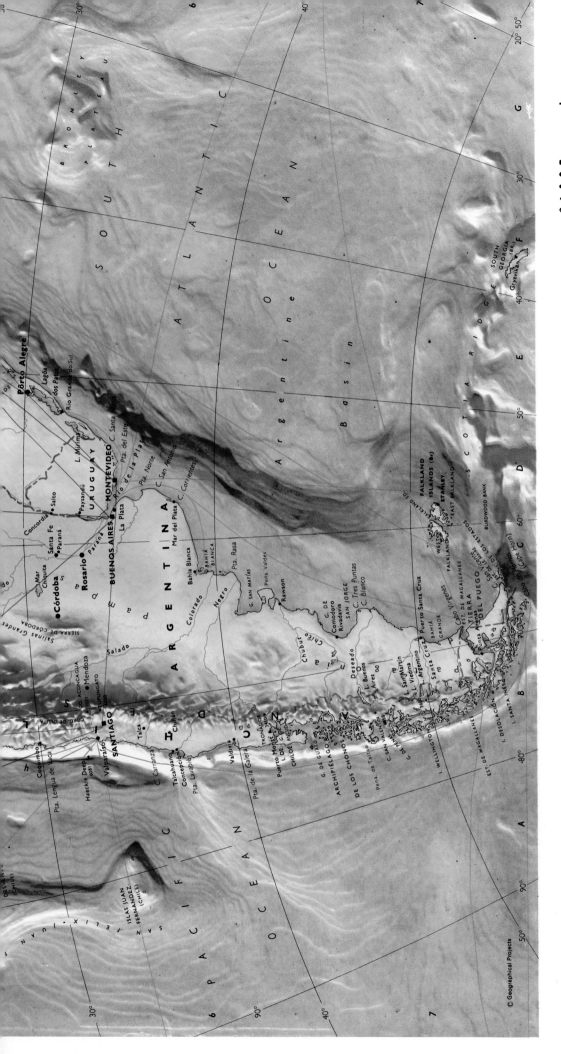

South America

SOUTH ATLANTIC OCEAN

Argentine Basin

SCOTIA RIDGE

SOUTH GEORGIA (Br.)

Grytviken

Pôrto Alegre

Lagôa dos Patos

Rio Grande do Sul

L. Mirim

C. Santa María

Pta. del Este

URUGUAY

MONTEVIDEO

Paysandú

Salto

Concordia

Santa Fe

Paraná

BUENOS AIRES

La Plata

Río de la Plata

Pta. Norte

C. San Antonio

C. Corrientes

Mar del Plata

ARGENTINA

Rosario

Mar Chiquita

Córdoba

SIERRA DE CÓRDOBA

Salinas Grandes

SIERRA GRANDES

Bahía Blanca

BAHÍA BLANCA

Colorado

Negro

Pta. Rasa

G. SAN MATÍAS

Pta. Valdés

Rawson

Chubut

Chico

Deseado

G. DE Comodoro Rivadavia

SAN JORGE

C. Tres Puntas

C. Blanco

L. Buenos Aires

Salado

Mendoza

UPUNGATO

CO. ACONCAGUA

CORD. DE OLIVA

SANTIAGO

Valparaíso

Talca

Chillán

Concepción

Talcahuano

Pta. Lavapié

C. Carranza

Coquimbo

Pta. Lengua de Vaca

Haeckle Deep

Valdivia

Puerto Montt

I. DE CHILOÉ

CHILOÉ

TRONADOR

ARCHIPIÉLAGO DE LOS CHONOS

G. DE GUAFO

G. DE PENAS

Pena. de Taitao

C. SAN VALENTÍN

Pta. de la Galera

FALKLAND ISLANDS (Br.)

STANLEY

WEST FALKLAND

EAST FALKLAND

FALKLAND SD.

BURDWOOD BANK

San Martín

L. Viedma

Santa Cruz

L. Argentino

Puerto Santa Cruz

Cabo Vírgenes

EST. DE MAGALLANES

Punta Arenas

TIERRA DEL FUEGO

GRANDE

Cabo de Hornos (Cape Horn)

EST. DE MAGALLANES

I. SANTA INÉS

I. DESOLACIÓN

ISLAS JUAN FERNÁNDEZ (CHILE)

DESVENTURADAS (CHILE)

PACIFIC OCEAN

From the Andes to the Amazon

The Andes mountain system, the South American equivalent of the Rockies, molds the western coast of the continent, from the Isthmus of Panama to Tierra del Fuego. These mountains were formed at the same time, and in the same way, as the Rockies, though they are much narrower and much higher, with many peaks over 20,000 feet. The Andes are extremely complex and form part of the Pacific "Ring of Fire." They are still subject to volcanic activity and massive earthquakes such as occurred in Chile in 1960 and Peru in 1970.

Throughout the whole of the Andean chain altitude rather than latitude has the greatest effect on climate and vegetation. The highest parts have a perpetual Arctic climate, even at the Equator. There are rugged, snow-capped mountains with glaciers sliding slowly down their sides, icefields occupying the highest basins between the peaks and large areas that are permanently snow covered. In contrast, on the narrow coastal plain to the west, between the mountains and the Pacific, it is latitude that determines the climate. The Andes, however, form a meteorological barrier, cutting off the trade winds that blow eastward from the Pacific from the winds that blow across the continent from the Atlantic. In this way they affect the climate of the western coastal strip as well as of the lands to the east.

The Andes can be divided into three major sections: the north, the central, and the southern. In the northern section, extending from the Caribbean to about 5°S, are the usual zones of climate and vegetation from sea level to the higher altitudes. Throughout this northern section of the Andes there is a remarkable uniformity of weather day by day, but a great range of temperature between day and night. The rainfall is heavy everywhere, varying from 80 inches along the northwest coast of Colombia to 40 inches farther inland and to the south around the Gulf of Guayaquil.

At the northern extremity of the Andes the mountains fan out into three prongs, divided by the north-flowing Cauca and Magdalena rivers which provide a passage from the Caribbean to the heart of the cordilleras and the Gulf of Maracaibo. The western prong curves around to form the snakelike backbone of Central America; the central one disappears in the northern tip of the Peninsula de Guajira; and the eastern prong curves in a great arc ending at Trinidad, then reappears again in some of the islands of the Lesser Antilles. The largest towns – such as Bogotá, capital of Colombia, Quito, capital of Ecuador, Medellín, and Cali – all lie in the valleys in the mountains, where the heat is not so stifling and the nightly fall in temperature results in a varied sequence of daily weather.

The central section of the Andes, from 5°S to 30°S, is a wide plateau between bordering mountain chains. Here, in Peru and Bolivia, the climate is much drier and there is a marked wet season in summer, from November to March, when the sun is overhead. The central, coastal strip, between the Pacific and the Andes, contrasts markedly with the coastal lowlands nearer the Equator. It is dominated by the southwest

Above: llamas grazing high on the windswept grasslands in the Peruvian Andes. This 4000-mile-long mountain range is the longest in the world.
Above right: the dense canopy of the Amazon rain forest occupies the drainage basin of the Amazon river.
Right: Gauchos, of mixed Spanish and Indian blood, are the cowboys of the South American pampas.

trade winds that blow from the high pressure area of the southern Pacific. These dry winds are cooled as they pass over the cold waters of the Peru (Humboldt) Current and their humidity is reduced even further on reaching the warm land. The Andes block off the moist winds from the east and the result is that the whole coastal plain is arid and receives less than 10 inches of rainfall. The only short rivers are those fed by the melting snows and rains on the high western cordilleras. In this coastal strip is the Atacama desert, which lies south of the bend in the coast at Arica.

The third, southern section, south of latitude 30°S, has a much more varied climate. There is a small area of coastal plain, near Valparaiso, which has a Mediterranean type climate with mild winters and dry summers. Farther south the rainfall increases rapidly and some of the lowland and western slopes of the Andes receive as much as 100 inches or more a year.

The continent of South America has the widest area of land in the neighborhood of the Equator and to the east of the Andes is the vast area of the Amazonian jungle, or selvas, occupying the whole of the drainage basin of that great river, and the less extensive flood plain of the Orinoco. These basins are covered with

thick alluvial deposits, debris brought down over thousands of years from the Andes and the ancient highland areas of Guiana and Brazil by the Amazon and its tributaries. The climate throughout the region is equatorial, hot, and humid. The northeast trade winds blow in from the Atlantic to the equatorial low pressure area and are then forced to ascend when they reach the Andes barrier. There they cool and exceptionally heavy rainfall develops over a large area.

The Amazon rises in the Peruvian Andes and winds a tortuous course right across the continent to the Atlantic, a distance of more than 3000 miles. The river continually builds a large delta out to sea, discharging the silt-laden water and carrying fresh water as far as 200 miles out.

South America: Political

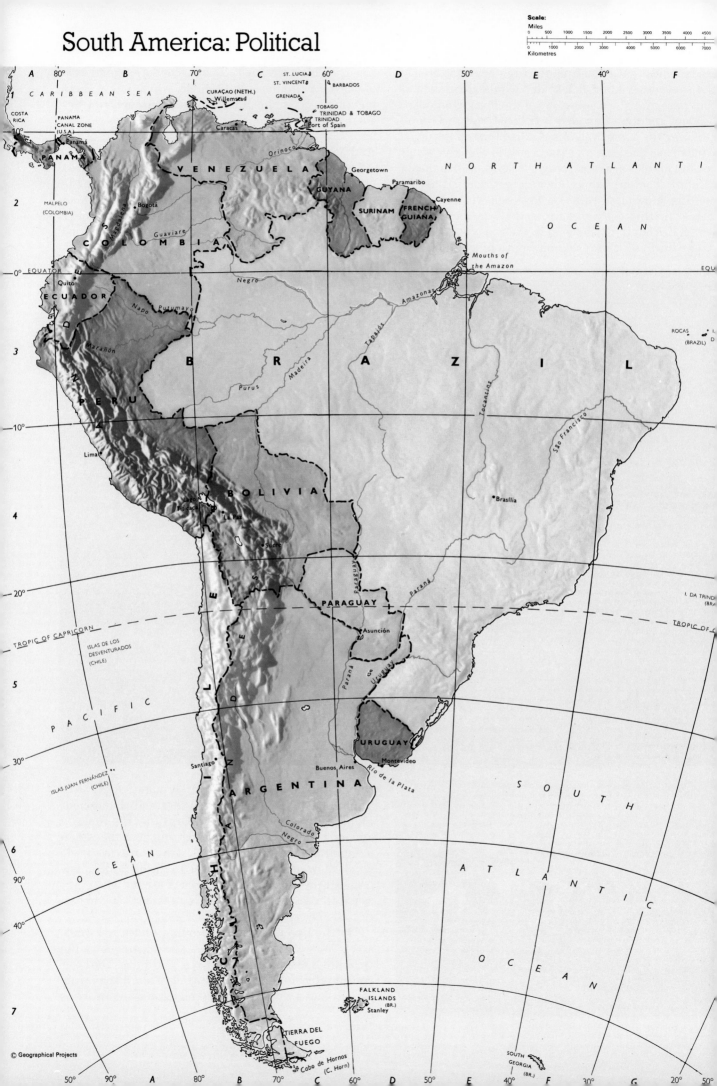

Scale:
Miles
0 500 1000 1500 2000 2500 3000 3500 4000 4500
Kilometres
0 1000 2000 3000 4000 5000 6000 7000

CARIBBEAN SEA

COSTA RICA
PANAMA CANAL ZONE (U.S.)
PANAMA
Panamá

MALPELO (COLOMBIA)

ST. LUCIA
ST. VINCENT
CURAÇAO (NETH.)
Willemstad
GRENADA
TOBAGO
TRINIDAD & TOBAGO
TRINIDAD
Port of Spain
BARBADOS

Caracas
Orinoco
VENEZUELA
Bogotá
GUYANA
Georgetown
Paramaribo
SURINAM
FRENCH GUIANA
Cayenne

COLOMBIA
Guaviare

EQUATOR
Quito
ECUADOR
Napo
Putumayo
Negro

NORTH ATLANTIC OCEAN

Mouths of the Amazon

ROCAS (BRAZIL)

Marañón
Amazonas

PERU
Purus
Madeira
Tapajós
B R A Z I L
São Francisco
Tocantins

Lima

BOLIVIA
Lago Titicaca
La Paz
Sucre
Brasília

PARAGUAY
Paraguay
Paraná

TROPIC OF CAPRICORN
ISLAS DE LOS DESVENTURADOS (CHILE)
Asunción

Paraná
Uruguay

I. DA TRINDADE (BRA.)

TROPIC OF C

PACIFIC
ISLAS JUAN FERNÁNDEZ (CHILE)

URUGUAY
Montevideo
Buenos Aires
Río de la Plata

Santiago
Colorado
Negro
ARGENTINA

SOUTH ATLANTIC OCEAN

OCEAN

FALKLAND ISLANDS (BR.)
Stanley

TIERRA DEL FUEGO
Cabo de Hornos (C. Horn)

SOUTH GEORGIA (BR.)

Highlands and Plateaus

There is a third type of terrain found in South America – an extensive outcrop of crystalline rocks in the Brazilian Highlands and, in smaller areas, in the Guiana Highlands, in the Pampas, and the plateaus of Patagonia. Between the Andes and these exposed rocks are sedimentary rocks and alluvial deposits of the great rivers, Orinoco and Amazon in the north, Paraná-Paraguay in the south.

The Brazilian Highlands rise to over 9000 feet along the Atlantic coast where the escarpment facing the ocean is steepest in the Serra do Mar and bordering the Planalto do Borborema. The remainder of the Brazilian plateau area is gently undulating, low ranges alternating with the north-flowing Amazon tributaries.

From being a predominantly sugar colony, Brazil became also a gold mining colony in the 18th century. Then came a demand for food for the laborers and transport for the products, which led to ranching on the lands bordering the cane fields and the mining areas. As the area under cultivation increased, so cattle ranching was pushed farther inland. It was only

after Brazil became independent in the early 19th century that coffee became the dominant cash crop. Small quantities had been grown north of Rio de Janeiro, but there was little demand for it until the middle of that century when it became a popular drink in Europe and North America. Transport has been improved with the building of the new capital, Brasilia, and the interior is now linked by a road and rail network with the coast. This has given a great boost to the agricultural development.

South of the Rio de la Plata are the Pampas and Patagonia. The latter is one of the coldest areas of the continent due to the high latitude and average altitude of 2000 feet. In winter temperatures are between 35° and 45°F, in summer they range from 75° on the Pampas to 55°F near the Estracho de Magallanes (Strait of Magellan). The largest part of this southern tip lies in the rain shadow of the Andes, which cut off the prevailing westerlies. Consequently rainfall is less than 10 inches a year except on some of the eastern slopes where it can be up to 80 inches.

The Gran Chaco, west of the Paraná, is partly forested, partly scrubland. Cotton is cultivated in the deforested areas and cattle are raised before being fattened on the richer grasslands to the south. These grasslands of the Pampas, with from 20–40 inches of rainfall a year, are one of the world's largest meat producing areas.

In southern Argentina, the Patagonian plateaus form tablelands that end in steep cliffs along the Atlantic seaboard. From the sea they rise like giant steps, the highest one over 5000 feet above sea level. These cool tablelands, windswept and crossed by deep west–east canyons, form one of the world's largest sheep grazing areas. The sheep somehow survive on the sparse grass and in arid conditions.

Below: Chilean pines grow in southern Chile. Cool oceanic air brings moisture to these mountain slopes.

Natural Resources

South and Central America have a large variety of minerals, other than the gold that drew the Spanish conquistadors. These are unevenly distributed, but forming one of the continent's principal assets. Much of this wealth lies untouched, however, either because it is too remote or there is a lack of capital to exploit it.

South America has very little reserves of traditional fuel. There are small coal deposits in many places, including Brazil, Chile, and Colombia. Of these, Chile is the largest producer, the coal coming mainly from mines south of Concepción. In Colombia, mines to the north of Bogotá are expected to produce enough coal to supply the country's needs and an iron and steel industry.

As if to offset this lack, many countries have deposits of petroleum and enormous hydroelectric power potential. Petroleum is found near the Andean fold mountains, especially in the north where the eastern arm swings toward Trinidad. Oil has made Venezuela's fortune. It occurs in three major areas: Lake Maracaibo, the llanos around the Apure river, and north of the Orinoco delta. The government has recently established a corporation to produce, refine, and distribute petroleum products, enlarged the port of Maracaibo to take large tankers, and built refineries. It has also stated that no new concessions will be granted. This means that once the present ones expire – which for many foreign companies is in 1983 – they will pass to the nationalized industry.

Chile is rapidly exploiting her oil deposits near the Estracha de Magallanes (Strait of Magellan) and now produces half its needs. Argentina has large reserves in Patagonia and the northwest, but despite greatly increased production still has to import oil for home consumption. Other countries, particularly Brazil, Colombia, Ecuador, Peru, and Trinidad also have oil reserves they exploit.

Above: building a dam in Brazil. Its many large rivers give Brazil one of the world's largest potential sources of hydroelectric power.

Below: erecting an oil derrick in Colombia. As well as oil, Colombia is rich in coal, gold, silver, iron ore, and the only platinum mined in South America.

Many South American countries are now developing their hydroelectric power potential. In Brazil, the development of power installations near the Serra do Mar escarpment is one of the factors that accounts for São Paulo's position as the greatest industrial and manufacturing center in the continent. In Argentina a new project has just been completed on the Limay, near Neuquen, with aid from the World Bank. Local cheap hydroelectricity has been one of the main reasons for the growth of Córdoba as the only inland industrial center in the country. In Venezuela, an immense power station and dam is being built at Guri on the Caroni, which flows northward to the Orinoco. This will be one of the world's largest plants and will supply low-cost electricity to both eastern Venezuela and to the Guyana industrial complex for iron smelting, steel, and aluminum works. Farther east, installations have been built on the Surinam river.

Like the Rockies, the Andes are a rich source of a wide variety of nonferrous minerals such as silver, lead, copper, zinc, platinum, and tin. The world's demand for copper outstrips supply, so Chile's reserves are highly valuable, supplying almost two-thirds of the country's exports income. In the past the Bolivian economy depended primarily upon tin, and although the country is still heavily dependent upon its tin exports, silver, lead, copper, and antimony are now also exported. Recently aid has been given to Bolivia by the USA and the Federal Republic of Germany for

and by a phenomenon known as upwelling. This occurs when the combined effects of the drag on the sea surface of the southeast trade winds and the rotation of the earth drive layers of surface water away from the coast. Deeper water rises to take the place of the surface water bringing with it nutrients that have accumulated in the deeper water from dead organic material that has sunk to the lower layers. In the surface layers these nutrients act as fertilizers, encouraging plant plankton to multiply and provide food for millions of fish. Of all the species, it is the

Above: a sugar barge at Maceió, northeastern Brazil. Sugar, together with coffee and soy beans, are leading exports in Brazil.

the modernization of the tin plants and exploration surveys for new, richer deposits.

Bauxite, the mineral used to make aluminum, is also a valuable resource. In Guyana it is found under an overburden of sand and clay, a little way inland up the Demerara and Berbice rivers. Surinam also has rich reserves and there is a large complex at Paranam that combines mining, refining, and smelting. Both these bauxite processing plants rely heavily on hydroelectric power and Guyana will benefit from the new Venezuelan plant. The iron and steel industry is growing in Chile, Peru, Colombia, and Brazil. The latter has some of the richest reserves of iron ore in the world, south and east of Belo Horizonte where the ores have an exceptionally high iron content, in southern Mato Grosso, in the Serra do Plaui and inland from Fortaleza. Chile has rich deposits in the Atacama desert from which nitrates are produced.

The ocean along the Chilean and Peruvian coasts supports a fishery that makes Peru the greatest fishing nation in the world. Over 500 species are found in the area, all supported by the north-flowing Peru Current

tiny anchovita that is of greatest importance. Peru has a fleet of some 200 boats, equipped with every modern aid. The catch all goes to processing factories where it is converted into fishmeal or animal food for export to the USA and western Europe. The fish also provide food for the birds that live on the offshore islands and whose droppings provide a rich source of guano, which is also used as a fertilizer. Off Argentina is the largest single area of continental shelf in the Southern Hemisphere where herring and other species similar to those in the North Sea abound. As yet these reserves are barely exploited, but a start has been made.

In spite of the great mineral and sea wealth, more than half the people of South America make their living from agriculture. There is abundant land, though a great deal of it is exhausted and soil erosion has become a constant problem. In many countries there is an urgent need for land reform, for raising productivity through mechanization and improvement of strains, for a good communications network, and for improved marketing systems.

255

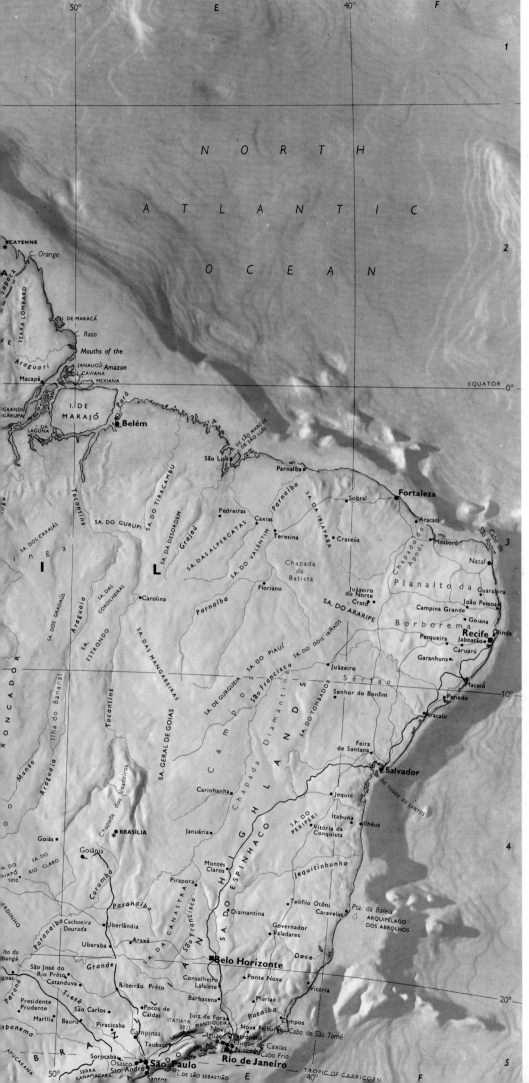

Northern
South America

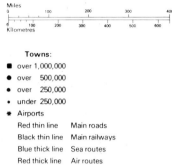

Miles
0 100 200 300 400
0 100 200 300 400 500 600
Kilometres

Towns:
■ over 1,000,000
● over 500,000
● over 250,000
• under 250,000
✳ Airports

Red thin line	Main roads
Black thin line	Main railways
Blue thick line	Sea routes
Red thick line	Air routes

257

The Peoples of South America

The population of South America contains three main streams: Amerind (American Indian), Iberian (Spanish or Portuguese) and African Negro. Many people are of mixed descent. The Amerinds must have reached Peru around 9000 BC, and by 1000 BC the people on the coast had some form of agriculture. On the high upland basins of the Andes – known as punas – the Amerinds established themselves about the beginning of the first millennium BC. Gradually, over the years, they developed physical characteristics that enabled them to cope with the high altitude and traces of permanent habitation have been found at over 17,000 feet.

It was in this central Andean area that the great empire of the Incas developed. The Incas developed intensive agriculture in and near the high river valleys devising an elaborate system of irrigation and terracing. But their tools were nothing more elaborate than the digging stick, hoe, and clodbreaker. The importance of water for irrigation united the people of each valley and led to a strong centralized state. While peoples in the valleys were engaged in agriculture those living on the grassy uplands tended valuable herds of llamas and alpacas – much in the same way they do today. All the central Andean people

Above: a Brazilian Indian girl of the primitive Karajà tribe that lives on the banks of the Araguaia river of the rain forest of Brazil. She is painting a tribal dancer with the traditional dyes of the region made from forest plants.

were skilled in weaving, the making of beautiful pottery – without the help of the potter's wheel – metalwork, and the working of the local materials such as wood, stone, rushes, and precious metals.

The Inca empire was at its peak when the Spaniards arrived. Within a short time they conquered the Incas and ruled from the Caribbean coasts and islands down the western side of the continent. They destroyed the Indians except for the few who retired deeper and deeper into the western cordilleras of the Andes.

To the south, in central Chile, and spreading eastward, lived the Araucanians in the dense forest regions. They were a tough people, never conquered by the Incas and were not overcome by the Spanish for more than a century. In the east the continent was only sparsely populated when the Europeans arrived. Isolated Indian tribes, many nomadic, inhabited the plateaus and grasslands and a few existed in the heart of the Amazon jungle. For the most part they were hunters and primitive cultivators, struggling for survival, fiercely and bitterly resentful of the Europeans. Along the Caribbean and northeast coast it was the British and Dutch, and later the French, who arrived to search for gold and settle the coastal areas, establishing plantations for the cultivation of sugar cane. In the east it was the Portuguese who colonized the coastal areas of what is now Brazil. But the Indian population was unwilling to work for them so the Europeans brought in slave labor from the Guinea coast of Africa to work the plantations. At later stages, after the emancipation of the Negroes,

Left: a young Amerindian on a Reserve uses an outboard motor to assist a traditional fishing trip.
Right: Argentinian Gauchos. The country's wealth is based on its great cattle industry.

Above: Indian women from the highlands of the Andes mountains. Andean Indians can work hard in the rarified high-altitude air. some even living semipermanently above 20,000 feet in spite of the severe lack of oxygen.

Chinese, and Indians were brought to the continent. Later still, between 1850 and 1920, there was a wave of immigration from western Europe to Argentina, Uruguay, and southern Brazil.

In the end Spain lost all her hard-won territories, but not before it and Portugal had impressed on all the continent the spirit of their homelands. Part of that spirit was the readiness to mix both physically and intellectually with other races. Today South America is the classic example of the successful mixing of races on any large scale.

Today South America has a pure native Amerind population of less than 20 million, most of them living in Bolivia, Ecuador, and Peru. White people form the majority of the population of Argentina, Brazil, and Uruguay. The distribution of the Negro population mainly reflects the pattern of the gold mining area of Colombia and Venezuela, and the plantations in Guyana and Brazil. But by far the largest population group is the mestizos, the people of mixed Amerind and Iberian descent. In countries such as Chile they form the greatest percentage of the total population. Mulattoes are people of Iberian-African descent and people of Amerindian-African descent are called zambos or cafusos. Many of the peoples speak Spanish and Portuguese and some speak French, but a lot of the Amerinds speak only the language or dialect of their own tribe.

The drift of populations to the towns is an ever-present problem in South America. The attractions of the city are obvious. There is also the ease with which the farmworker can move by bus, especially since World War II and the subsequent growth of roads, and the continual bombardment of information and propaganda from the transistor radio, both of which persuade the peasant to uproot himself. Yet despite the many newly created industries there is still great unemployment in the cities, in many cases over 10 percent or as high as 25 percent. Another problem is illiteracy. In theory all countries provide free schooling, in practice there is a shortage of both schools and teachers. In Bolivia only 40 percent of the people can read and write, in Argentina and Uruguay 80 percent are literate. In many areas there is the added difficulty that parents expect their children to work and help support the family, rather than go to school. This is especially true among the rural and village dwellers.

Economic Growth and World Trade

South America sprawls across a wide range of latitude. It is a producer and exporter of primary products: agricultural produce of tropical and temperate climates such as coffee, bananas, sugar, cocoa, linseed, sunflower seeds, meat, wheat, and wool; and a wide variety of minerals such as gold, copper, silver, tin, and petroleum. The agricultural products are mainly foodstuffs, largely from the tropics. Even though the process of industrialization and urbanization has gone several stages further in South America than in other Third-World areas, agriculture is still the dominant factor in the economies of the countries. In fact, many national economies, until recently, depended on a single cash crop with the consequent risks if the crop failed or there was a glut on the world market.

The Latin Americans have been obtaining expert advice from the Food and Agricultural Organization (FAO) and major Western nations concerning agricultural programs and the possibilities of expanding both agricultural land and output. In Mexico, the International Maize [Corn] and Wheat Improvement Center, developed high yielding, dwarf wheats for subtropical regions some 20 years ago. Since then progress has been made using this preliminary research in developing varieties in Colombia, Chile, Peru, and Uruguay and in producing varieties of high yielding rice in Brazil. Now work of a similar kind is being undertaken on corn, which it is hoped will improve its protein quality. As corn is the most important single cereal in South America, these results should have far-reaching effects.

Research and experiments carried out in the field of animal breeding have been notably successful. Efforts have been made to improve the herds and eliminate the inferior stock, especially the native criollo breed. A Zebu strain has been introduced into the Hereford herds to help improve the animals' resistance to fly-borne diseases. This has proved successful. The European strain ensures good milk yields, the Indian provides the necessary stamina and resistance for tropical grassland conditions. Similar upgradings are also being carried out with another important part of animal husbandry – that of the sheep flocks.

In their trade with one another the Latin American nations have tried to reduce their tariff barriers and form economic alliances in efforts to benefit their development. Apart from the Central American Common Market (CACM) formed in 1960, which included all the Central American countries except Panama, the Latin American Free Trade Association (LAFTA) was created. The latter eventually included Mexico and all South American countries with the exception of the three Guyanas. In 1968, the Caribbean Free Trade Association (CARIFTA) was established by

Left: a boy selects seed corn for next year's planting in Bolivia. Corn and potatoes form a major part of the people's diet.

11 British Commonwealth of Nations members.

Unfortunately, the largest of these alliances, LAFTA, was unable to solve the problems of its economically weaker members or provide markets for its dominant members, Argentina, Brazil, and Mexico. In an effort to overcome the problems, the Andean Common Market (ANCOM) came into being in 1969. ANCOM now includes the countries of Bolivia, Chile, Colombia, Ecuador, Peru, and Venezuela, that is the weaker members of LAFTA with the exception of democracy for the first time since they became independent. If it succeeds, it will transform the whole economy of the region. The great gulf between rich and poor and the absence of a middle class has, in the past, meant that only the rich had enough education and power to rule. Now, as the creeping tide of new democracy begins to spread, a middle class is emerging, providing rulers who are both closer to the poor and able to transform industrial and agricultural development. Today, South America is no longer iso-

Above: a strain of specially bred Nelori cattle in Brazil. They are a very hardy breed and used for beef. They are also sometimes interbred with exotic breeds.

Above: building a petrochemical plant in Brazil.
Below: construction work on a hydroelectric plant at Paulo Alfonso on the São Franciso river, Brazil.

Uruguay. The resources of this bloc – mineral, energy, and agricultural – are tremendous. But the industrial and manufactured products are negligible and it is in this direction that cooperative programs lie. Already ANCOM has assigned responsibility for the manufacture of specific products to different countries to avoid duplication and consequent competition between its own members. All tariffs and trade restrictions between the members are to be removed and an overland transport provided between them.

Private North American and European companies have developed many mining and manufacturing industries. But the capital investments and the resulting large profits that go abroad do not benefit the local communities. As a result, a limitation has been imposed on foreign-owned companies and they have to hand over 51 percent of their share of capital to the country concerned within a specified period. Countries in the Andean bloc have also negotiated individual contracts with the USSR, as well as the bloc exchanging official trade delegations.

Many Latin American countries are showing signs of being on the verge of a determined drive toward real

lated and it can no longer maintain its position on the periphery of the world. The revolution in modern communications, as well as the awareness of the people of the South American nations, have ensured that they take their place in international affairs.

The Countries of South America

1 Colombia
2 Guyana
3 Venezuela
4 French Guiana
5 Surinam
6 Ecuador
7 Peru
8 Bolivia
9 Paraguay
10 Brazil
11 Chile
12 Argentina
13 Uruguay
14 Falkland Islands

COLOMBIA

Area: 439 square miles
Population: 23,500,000
Capital: Bogotá
Language: Spanish
Religion: Catholicism
Monetary Unit: Peso

History and Government: Colombia was colonized after the Spanish had defeated the highly civilized Indian nation of the Chibchas, 1536–38. It became part of the viceroyalty of New Granada – which included also Panama, Venezuela, and Ecuador – from 1740 until it became independent of Spain in 1819. In 1830 Colombia and Panama separated from New Granada and became the republic of New Granada and in 1859 the Confederation of Granadina. In 1863 it finally took the name Colombia, becoming a republic in 1886. (Panama threw off Colombian rule in 1903). Legislative power rests with a Congress of two houses, the Senate (106 members) and House of Representatives (204 members), both elected for four years. The president is elected for four years and cannot immediately be reelected.

Economy: Very little land is under cultivation, but the soil is fertile and due to the climate and altitude an extraordinary range of crops can be grown. Principal crops are coffee, of which Colombia is the second largest producer in the world, sugar cane, cotton, tobacco, bananas, and cocoa. Exploitation of rich deposits of oil and coal has been accelerated by the high demand for oil. There are rich reserves of copper, lead, mercury, iron ore, gold, silver, platinum, and emeralds.

GUYANA

Area: 83,000 square miles
Population: 774,000
Capital: Georgetown
Language: English
Religion: Mainly Protestantism
Monetary Unit: Guyana Dollar

History and Government: Discovered by the Spanish in 1499–1500 and part of a larger region that included French Guiana and Surinam, this area was originally settled by the Dutch in 1620, but captured by the English in 1796 and as British Guiana ceded to the United Kingdom in 1814. It has been an independent republic since 1970 and is a member of the Commonwealth. There is a National Assembly of 53 elected members who serve a five-year term. The country is inhabited mainly by peoples of Amerind origin and by the descendants of African slaves.

Economy: This poor, thinly populated territory has as its chief resource bauxite of which it is an important producer. There are also gold and diamond mines. Important agricultural products are rice, sugar cane, coconuts, coffee, cocoa. Rum is exported.

VENEZUELA

Area: 352,142 square miles
Population: 12,000,000
Capital: Caracas
Language: Spanish
Religion: Catholicism
Monetary Unit: Bolivar

History and Government: Settled by the Spanish in 1520 it became, with Colombia, part of the viceroyalty of New Granada in 1718; became independent from Spain in 1821. Separated from Colombia in 1830, and subsequently lost territory to British Guiana (Guyana), Brazil, and Colombia. The Constitution of 1958 provides for a president to serve a five-year term and a Congress of a Senate and Chamber of Deputies. The president has the power to veto.

Economy: The chief crop is coffee. The country can be divided into three zones: the agricultural zone, which includes, as well as coffee, cocoa, sugar cane, corn, rice, wheat, tobacco, and cotton; the pastoral zone, where cattle and horse breeding predominate; and the forest zone, which supplies such products as divi divi, vanilla, and balatá. The basis of the economy is oil which is controlled by multinational companies.

FRENCH GUIANA (Guyane Française)
Area: 35,136 square miles
Population: 48,000
Capital: Cayenne
Monetary Unit: Franc CFA
History and Government: Settled by French at Cayenne in 1604 and occupied briefly by British from 1809 to 1815, the country has been a French overseas department since 1946, administered by a Prefect and has an elected council of 16 members. It sends a deputy to the National Assembly and one to the Senate. The Iles du Salut (St. Joseph, Ile Royal, and the once-notorious penal settlement of Devil's Island, or Ile du Diable) are under its administration.
Economy: The main resources are the forests and gold mines. Bauxite deposits have been located also. Little land is under cultivation but the most important agricultural products are sugar cane, corn, manioc, rice, and bananas. Fishing is of growing importance.

SURINAM
Area: 63,036 square miles
Population: 480,000
Capital: Paramaribo
Language: Carib, Creole, Dutch
Religion: Catholicism, Hinduism, and Islam
Monetary Unit: Guilder
History and Government: In 1667, at the peace of Breda, between Netherlands and the UK, Surinam was assigned to the Netherlands in exchange for the colony of the New Netherlands in North America. Since then it has twice been a British possession – 1799 to 1802 and 1806 to 1816. It became independent in 1975. The republic is disturbed by conflict between the Creole community, the descendents of the African slaves, and the Asiatic Hindustanis and Javanese.
Economy: The population is employed predominantly in agriculture – sugar cane, cocoa, bananas, rice, coffee, etc. – which is restricted to the coastal areas. The greatest wealth is bauxite, of which it is one of the foremost pro-

ducers. There are also industries producing aluminum, sugar, and rum.

ECUADOR
Area: 226,000 square miles
Population: 7,000,000
Capital: Quito
Language: Spanish
Religion: Catholicism
Monetary Unit: Sucre
History and Government: Pizarro's conquests for Spain in the 16th century led to the inclusion of Ecuador in the viceroyalty of Peru. The Spanish were overthrown in 1822. In 1830 the presidency of Quito became the republic of Ecuador. Since 1976, this largest of the "banana republics" has been a military dictatorship. Ecuador is claiming from Peru a vast tract of land in the Amazon Basin.
Economy: Over half the working population is employed in agriculture. The chief product is bananas, of which Ecuador is the largest exporter in the world, then comes coffee and cocoa, all of which are grown on the tropical lowlands. The forests and mineral resources are little exploited but there are rich oil deposits.

PERU
Area: 531,000 square miles
Population: 14,000,000
Capital: Lima
Language: Aymará, Quechua, Spanish
Religion: Catholicism
Monetary Unit: Gold Sol
History and Government: Once the seat of the Inca empire, established around 1230, which included Ecuador and parts of Bolivia and Chile, Peru was conquered by the Spanish in 1533. It became a viceroyalty of Spain in 1542. Peru declared its independence in 1821. The constitution provides for the election of a president for a term of six years and for a two-chamber Congress of Senate and Chamber of Deputies. A military junta, which overthrew the last president in 1968 has ruled the country since then. The government pursues a policy of reducing the influence of the USA and forming closer relationships with the Communist countries.
Economy: The chief agricultural products are cotton, sugar cane, cereals, and other food products, but these are insufficient for home needs. Sheep grazing is important and there are also

cattle and goats that supply hides and wool. Fishing is of greatest importance. There are vast mineral resources: copper, of greatest value, then iron ore, silver, lead, gold, zinc, and many others, most of which are exported in their crude state. Oil is now being exploited.

BOLIVIA
Area: 424,162 square miles
Population: 4,700,000
Capital: Seat of Government – Sucre
Administrative capital – La Paz
Language: Spanish
Religion: Catholicism
Monetary Unit: Peso
History and Government: Originally the home of the highly civilized Aymara Indians who were conquered by the Incas, Bolivia was brought under the rule of Spain in 1538. After being part of the Spanish viceroyalty of Peru, Bolivia became independent in 1825. Since 1969 there have been several military coups d'état, and since 1974 political parties have been banned with no elections promised until 1980.
Economy: It is one of the poorest countries in South America. Since 1952 sugar cane, rice, and cotton have been cultivated east of the Andes with some success. Coffee, corn, and potatoes, are also grown. There is some cattle rearing and exploitation of the forest. Bolivia is the first in the world for tin, tungsten, and antimony.

PARAGUAY
Area: 157,046 square miles
Capital: Asunción
Language: Guarani and Spanish
Religion: Catholicism
Monetary Unit: Guarani
History and Government: A Spanish possession from 1538, when Asunción was founded, Paraguay was part of the viceroyalty of Buenes Aires until it revolted against Spanish rule in 1811. Under the 1967 Constitution Paraguay is a presidential republic, with a two-chamber parliament – a 30-member Senate and a 60-member Chamber of Deputies. The president is elected for five years and can be reelected. He has very wide powers.
Economy: The Paraguayan economy is based on agriculture and stock-rearing but dominated by land-owners. The production of cereals and soybeans is not enough to feed the population, but the cultivation for export of cotton, tobacco, sugar cane, coffee and tropical

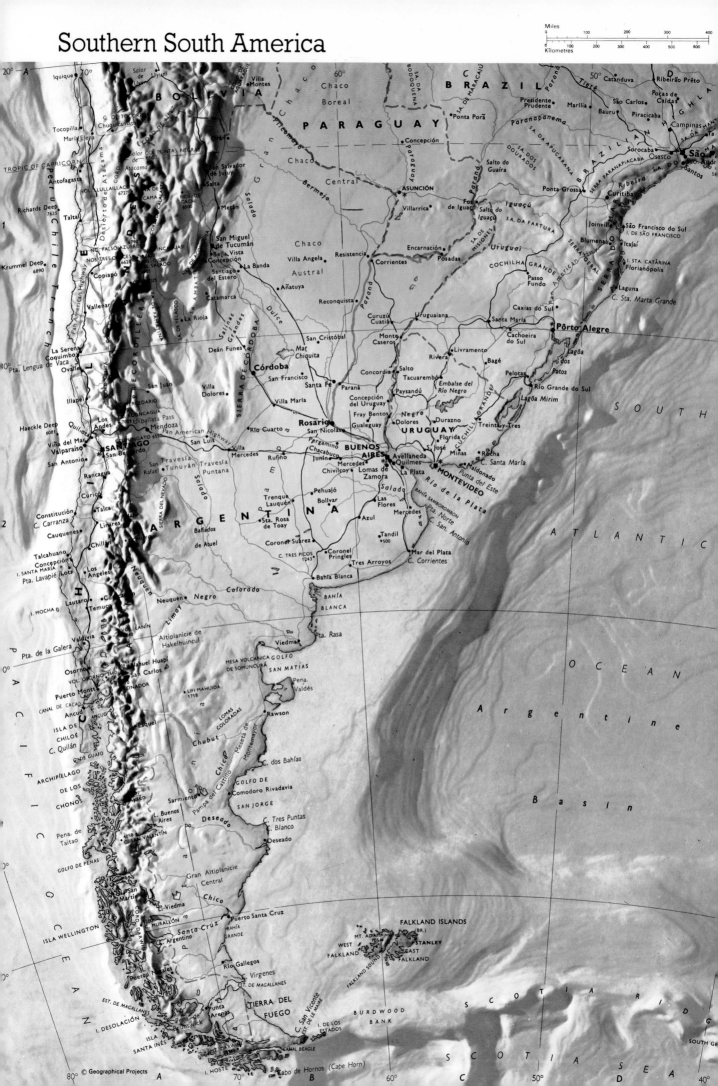

Southern South America

fruits is well developed. The products of stock-rearing, from cattle, horses, pigs, and sheep, together with timber, are exported in quantity.

BRAZIL
Area: 3,286,470 square miles
Population: 107,000,000
Capital: Brasilia
Language: Portuguese
Religion: Catholicism
Monetary Unit: Cruzeiro
History and Government: Brazil was made a viceroyalty of Portugal in 1640. In 1815 the colony was declared a separate kingdom and its independence was proclaimed in 1822 under Emperor Pedro I. In 1889 it became a republic. The Constitution of 1967 provides for a two-tier parliament of a Senate, elected for eight years and a Chamber of Deputies elected for four years. There are indirect elections for a president and vice-president, who serve a five-year term. In 1969 Congress amended the Constitution to provide for the election of the president by an electoral college composed of 66 senators, 310 Deputies and 127 delegates from the state legislature.
Economy: The products are very varied: corn, rice, legumes, potatoes, citrus fruits, peanuts, cocoa, jute, and flax, etc. Coffee above all is the source of the country's wealth, together with plantations of cotton, sugar cane, coconuts, oranges, and tobacco. The wealth of the forests is immense – precious woods and rubber. Fishing and stock-rearing (horses, pigs, and cattle) are also important. There are very abundant mineral resources. The largest industries are textiles, in particular weaving of cotton, silk, and man-made fibers.

CHILE
Area: 292,133 square miles
Population: 10,000,000
Capital: Santiago
Language: Spanish
Religion: Catholicism
Monetary Unit: New Peso
History and Government: In 1541 the first Spanish settlement was established, and until 1778 when it became a separate captaincy-general, it was part of the vice-royalty of Peru. Chile eventually gained its independence from Spain in 1818, after eight years of struggle. There is a National Congress consisting of a Senate of 50 members and Chamber of Deputies. The president is elected for six years and is not eligible for reelection. In 1970 the Marxist Dr Salvador Allende was elected president by a narrow margin. Following industrial unrest, widespread violent incidents, and a vote of censure against the government by Congress, the leaders of the armed forces and police overthrew the government, annulled the Constitution, outlawed political parties and trade unions, and assumed wide-ranging civil powers.
Economy: The principal crops are wheat, corn, barley, oats, beans, lentils, vines, tobacco, hemp, chili pepper, potatoes, melons. Stock-rearing, mainly sheep, is very important and accounts for almost half of the total value of the agricultural production. The most important forest product is the pine wood. Good wines are produced for export. However, the basis of Chile's economy is its mineral resources, copper (Chilean reserves are 40 percent of those of the whole world), then sodium nitrate, iron ore, coal, oil, gold, silver, and uranium. The manufacturing industries are among the most advanced in South America.

ARGENTINA
Area: 1,073,393 square miles
Population: 25,000,000
Capital: Buenos Aires
Language: Spanish
Religion: Catholicism
Monetary Unit: Peso
History and Government: The Rio de la Plata was discovered by the Spanish in 1515 and in 1534 a city was founded on the site of the present Buenos Aires. It was attached to the viceroyalty of Peru in 1620. In 1810 the people rose against the Spanish and independence was proclaimed in 1816. However the country did not have a stable government until 1853. It is now a federal republic with a president. The National Congress has a Senate with 46 seats and a House of Deputies with 192 seats. The government of President Maria Estela Peron was overthrown by a bloodless coup d'état in 1976 when the army intervened and seized power.
Economy: The country's wealth is based on agriculture and livestock. Agriculture was traditionally based on cereals, but now other crops such as cotton, sugar cane, flax, vines, citrus fruits, olives, and rice have been introduced with some success. Stock-rearing still plays an important part and meat is one of the main exports. Mineral wealth – mainly gold, iron ore, copper, zinc, tungsten, manganese, and silver – is modest, but the production of oil and natural gas is increasing.

URUGUAY
Area: 72,172 square miles
Population: 2,800,000
Capital: Montevideo
Language: Spanish
Religion: Catholicism
Monetary Unit: Peso
History and Government: Formerly part of the Spanish viceroyalty of Rio de la Plata, then a province of Brazil, Uruguay became independent in 1825. It is a presidential republic. There is a two-tier Congress consisting of a Senate of 30 members and a Chamber of Deputies of 99 members. The vice-president presides over Congress.
Economy: The production of wool, meat, and skins is considerable and animals and animal products make up over 70 percent of the exports. Wheat, barley, corn, linseed, sunflower seed, rice, sugar beet, and citrus fruits are the most widespread crops. The mineral resources are scant, although iron is now being quarried. The textile industry and the processing and preserving of meat, cheese, and condensed milk are particularly advanced. The economy is influenced a great deal by the USA.

FALKLAND ISLANDS (Islas Malvinas)
Area: 4618 square miles
Population: 2000
Capital: Stanley
Language: English
Religion: Protestantism
Monetary Unit: Pound Sterling
History and Government: The Falkland Islands is a British crown colony and includes the dependency of South Georgia (1450 square miles), South Sandwich Islands, South Shetland Islands, and South Orkney Islands. The colony is administered by a governor assisted by an Executive Council and Legislative Council. The colony is claimed by Argentina.
Economy: Sheep farming is almost the only occupation and wool, hides, and sheepskins are exported. South Georgia was originally a whaling and sealing station; now it is occupied by 22 members of the British Antarctic Survey (BAS).

Chapter 11

Australia and Oceania

It was the ancients who put Australia on the map long before any European explorers discovered it. They argued that such a land mass was necessary to offset the weight of the continents in the Northern Hemisphere and to balance the earth on its axis. They called it Terra Australis Incognito, the unknown southern land.

Even so, it was not until after Magellan's famous voyage in the first half of the 16th century that European interest really centered on the Pacific and the search for the southern land. European settlement in Australasia has an even shorter history. It is less than 200 years since the first British ships sailed into Botany Bay; less than 100 years since people moved into the interior; less than 50 years since many of what are today large industrial towns were established. The modern continent of Australia displays all the features of European culture, with cities of European design, and a modern transportation network.

Opposite: a typical Australian landscape. Much of the island continent of Australia consists of vast plains of desert or semiarid lands. But in the north and east and southeast areas adequate rainfall provides pasturelands for the vast sheep-farming industry for which Australia is famous.

The Smallest Continent

Australia is the smallest continent and the only continent not divided into more than one country. Most of the continent is rolling plains or low plateaus, broken in the northwest and center by more rugged country. Running down the east coast, behind the narrow coastal plains, is the Great Dividing Range, a chain of tablelands and mountains culminating in the Australian Alps with Mount Kosciusko, at 7316 feet, Australia's highest peak. These mountains reappear in the island of Tasmania, which lies to the south of the southeastern corner of the continent.

The whole continent falls into three main sections: the shield area of west Australia, the eastern highland rim, and the central lowland basin region that lies between the Gulf of Carpentaria in the north and Spencer Gulf in the south. The shield is made up of the ancient Pre-Cambrian rocks such as granites, schists, and gneisses. But for the most part the western two-thirds of Australia is an area of vast, featureless plains, broken only occasionally by low ranges of hills where the igneous rocks appear above the surface.

The three more rugged areas of the Kimberley Plateau, Hamersley Range, and the central mountains of the Musgrave and Macdonnell Ranges are masses of sandstones and quartzites that have been folded and faulted. They stand out above the general level of the shield, highly dissected, with narrow valleys and steep gorges. The Great Dividing Range divides the short rivers that flow eastward into the Tasman Sea and the longer rivers that flow westward into the basins. The lowlands are a trough of recently deposited clays, sandstones, and limestones. To the north is the Great Australian Basin, the largest artesian basin in the world, to the south the Murray Basin. An artesian basin is formed when a saucer-shaped layer of permeable rock, such as sandstone, is sandwiched between two impermeable layers. As rain falls on the outcrops of the sandstone, at the higher edges of the saucer, the water seeps through and collects in the lowest part of the layer, the bottom of the saucer. If a well is sunk into this lowest part – which may be over 1000 feet below the ground – and the source of the water at the outcrop is sufficiently high, then the water in the well will rise above ground level.

Off the northeast coast of Australia is the natural breakwater of the Great Barrier Reef, the greatest coral structure in the world. It is a complex system of reefs that stretches for over 1200 miles along the edge of the continental shelf, from New Guinea in the north to just south of the Tropic of Capricorn.

Below: a blue haze, caused by the aromatic oils exuded by the eucalyptus trees, hangs over the forested slope of the Great Dividing Range of southeastern Australia.

Australasia: Political

Scale:
Miles
Kilometres

Above: a sheep auction in Australia. Some 46 percent of the total Australian farming area is accounted for by the sheep industry. One breed of sheep that is particularly well suited to the extremes of the Australian climate is the Merino sheep.
Below: Aborigines perform a totemic dance. Many of these original inhabitants live on reservations and follow the same primitive way of life as that led by their ancestors. Some work on large farms and ranches in the Outback, and others in city factories and offices.

In many ways Australia is comparable to North Africa, where in similar latitudes the Sahara lies. The northern third of Australia lies in the tropics, in one of the driest belts on earth. About 35 percent of the country has less than 10 inches of rain a year and only seven percent has more than 40 inches. The wetter areas are along the northern coast, east of Darwin, along the east and southeast coasts, and in the southwest. There is no contrast in temperatures between the west and east coasts of the continent as in South America and Africa and no marked cool current offshore to make its effect. Apart from Tasmania and the extreme southeast, summer temperatures everywhere are over 68°F and in winter, only in the area inland from Perth, New South Wales, Victoria, and Tasmania do temperatures fall below 50°F.

Geologists think that Australia was once part of a much larger land mass. About 50 million years ago the land bridge between Australia and Asia disappeared. This had the effect of cutting off all forms of life – animal, plant, and human – which subsequently developed independently of the other continents. These forms of life also learned to tolerate extremely arid conditions.

Nobody is certain when man reached this farthest outpost, nor exactly from where he came. It is thought that the Tasmanians – extinct since the middle of the last century – were the firstcomers. They were probably driven southward by the next peoples, the Aborigines, who settled principally around the fringes of the continent and along the rivers of the central basins. Like the Tasmanians, they were hunters and gatherers, but had a wider range of weapons and also the semidomesticated dingo. They also had knowledge of fire, but not of agriculture.

When the Europeans arrived they found simple, nomadic people but little evidence of their culture. It is thought that at that time the indigenous people numbered only some 300,000, but they roamed the whole of the continent. Even since the arrival of these first colonists the population of Australia has remained comparatively small. Today it is a little over 13 million and more than half live in five state capitals: Sydney, capital of New South Wales and Australia's largest city; Melbourne, capital of Victoria; and Brisbane, Adelaide, and Perth.

Most Australians are of British origin, although since World War II about one million other Europeans have migrated there. Over the years the culture of the Aborigines has been allowed to collapse and their numbers severely reduced. Today, some live in reserves, some work on the large farms, but a great number have migrated to the cities.

More than a quarter of the world's wool comes from Australia, which is also a major producer of wheat, beef and dairy cattle, sugar cane, and fruits. The best pastures and farmlands are in the warm, moist southeast where the Murray river, with the Darling, Murrumbidgee, and other tributaries, forms Australia's chief river basin. But vast areas rely on artesian well water. In some places dams and irrigation schemes have helped solve water problems.

Below: an industrial site at Newcastle, southeastern Australia. Large industries have been built all along the coasts making Australia one of the most highly industrialized nations in the world.

The most heavily populated and intensively cultivated land is the areas around the coasts – with the exception of central south coast; the cultivated grasslands on the slopes of the mountains on the east and southwest; and the drier pastoral lands farther inland. It is the pastoral lands that have spread in recent years, due partly to the demand for wool and beef and partly to the sowing of more palatable and nutritious grasses and the sinking of artesian wells.

The development of mining and the exploitation of the mineral resources has probably had the greatest impact on Australia, both visually and economically. There are large reserves of gold, lead, silver, zinc, iron ore, nickel, copper, coal, uranium, and bauxite as well as petroleum. A great many of these minerals were first discovered on the surface and mined by opencast methods. Only when the shallow holes were worked out did large companies take over deep mining with all the attendant expensive outlay.

Australia is one of the most industrialized, as well as one of the most urbanized, countries in the world. Industrialization began early in Australia. It started first in the settlements that had been established around the coasts, especially those in the southeast. The goods produced were the basic needs of the settlers – bricks, wooden furniture, beer, flour, and other foodstuffs. Then followed machinery for the agricultural settlements in the hinterland, for the opencast mines and power plants. Today the majority of Australian industry is still heavily concentrated around the periphery of the continent. It manufactures over 80 percent of all Australia's needs and attracts investments from Britain and North America.

Australia

273

New Guinea and New Zealand

New Guinea consists of a series of northwest-southeast parallel folds, formed recently in Tertiary times. The outer fold appears as a chain of islands offshore, including the Admiralty Islands and the Bismarck Archipelago; the second fold is made up of the coastal ranges of north Irian Djawa and Papua New Guinea, which reappear in the Trobriand Islands; the third, and greatest fold, is the lofty mountainous spine of the island, stretching from the Sneeuw Gerbergte to the Owen Stanley Range. On either side of this central chain are the lowland plains of the Sepik river to the north and the Digul and Fly to the south.

This large island – the second largest in the world – has a varied climate due to its great length and high mountainous spine, which stretches for over 1500 miles and in places rises to over 16,000 feet. The western end of the island has a true equatorial climate with a heavy rainfall. The remainder has high temperatures throughout the year, rarely falling below 78°F in the cooler months, but with a marked seasonal rainfall.

The indigenous peoples of New Guinea are the first peoples who ventured into the Pacific from Asia. They

Above: an old New Guinea warrior gives a boy an arrow-shooting lesson. The mountain tribesmen of New Guinea are the remnants of an early migration from southern Asia.

have survived as the Papuans who live mainly in the inaccessible interior. Many have a primitive culture and lead nomadic lives as hunters and gatherers. Later, people of Melanesian and Polynesian descent arrived and settled around the coast and on the lowland areas.

The majority of the island is covered by dense tropical forest and only in a few areas, where rainfall is low or shifting cultivation has resulted in deforestation and erosion, are there tracks of savanna country. Higher up the mountainsides, the tropical forest gives way to coniferous trees, then beech forests, and finally Alpine scrub, just below the snowline. Much of the island is still unexplored and unknown. Even so, many resources have already been found: oil in the Vogelkop peninsula, gold in the extreme southeast of Papua New Guinea, and natural gas in the west of the coun-

Left: a tribesman cultivates a sweet-potato garden high among the mountains that extend from northwest to southeast of the island.

try. The resources of the vast forests and the hydro-electric power potential are, as yet, little exploited.

Agriculture is the most productive economic activity, although plantation crops have not been of great importance due to transport difficulties, inaccessible capital, and lack of training facilities for the local peoples. Coconut palm is one of the most important plantation crops in Papua New Guinea, with rubber in the south and cocoa and timber in the north of the country. In Irian Djawa, on the other hand, there is little commercial agricultural development and oil is the only significant export.

New Zealand is, from the structural point of view, a most interesting country. Almost every geological period is represented in the two islands. In South Island, the Southern Alps have been subject to two epochs of mountain building. The first was in the

south it rarely drops below 50°F.

New Zealand was peopled by the Polynesian Maoris, who must have settled there before 1400 AD. By the time the English colonists arrived in 1800 they numbered some 200,000. For the next century due to warfare and disease, their numbers declined rapidly. Now their numbers are once more over the 200,000 mark. They are accepted as equal to New Zealanders of European descent, although there are problems with the Maori farmers who, in the past, were allocated the poorer farming land.

Below left: Corriedale sheep on a New Zeland farm. Corriedales are cross-breeds between two successful breeds, one yielding first-class wool, the other good meat.
Below right: underground hot springs at Wairakei, New Zealand are tapped to drive turbines for the production of electricity.

Mesozoic era when the ancient rocks were uplifted, crumpled, then eroded. Then followed a time when the whole of New Zealand was under the sea while sandstones and limestones were deposited. During the Alpine building period, when the Alps and Himalaya were being formed, the rocks were pushed up again, some of the older ones breaking through the new sediments. In South Island the ancient rocks broke into blocks and formed a most spectacular feature, the Alpine Fault. This is a giant wall of rock on the western side of the Southern Alps, which rises to more than 3000 feet and extends for over 300 miles. At the same time in North Island, large areas were covered by lava, which welled up and poured over the landscape. It formed the plateau around Lake Taupo and where it was ejected violently, volcanoes were built up such as Ruapehu, 9175 feet, and Mount Egmont, 8260 feet.

Although New Zealand is in the same latitude as Italy, the extremes of heat and cold are less. To the north the temperature rarely exceeds 85°F and in the

Broadly speaking North Island is the dairying region and the cooler, wetter South Island the sheep-rearing and wheat-growing region. However, there are four main ranching regions, two on each island, where the vegetation is not rich enough to fatten stock. These are the central area of South Island, the eastern slopes of the Southern Alps bordering the Canterbury Plains and, in North Island, the area between North Taranaki Bight and Lake Taupo and the eastern coast. In these regions sheep are reared for their wool and cattle raised to be fattened elsewhere.

New Zealand lacks the minerals and fuels needed for heavy industry, but on the other hand has an abundant supply of water-power and many large hydroelectric plants are in operation. The country has developed the industries based on the primary products, the production of leather goods, canning, fertilizers, wood pulp, and paper making and, more recently, oil refining. Recently there has been an important discovery of iron ore in the black sands that may lead to the development of some heavy industry.

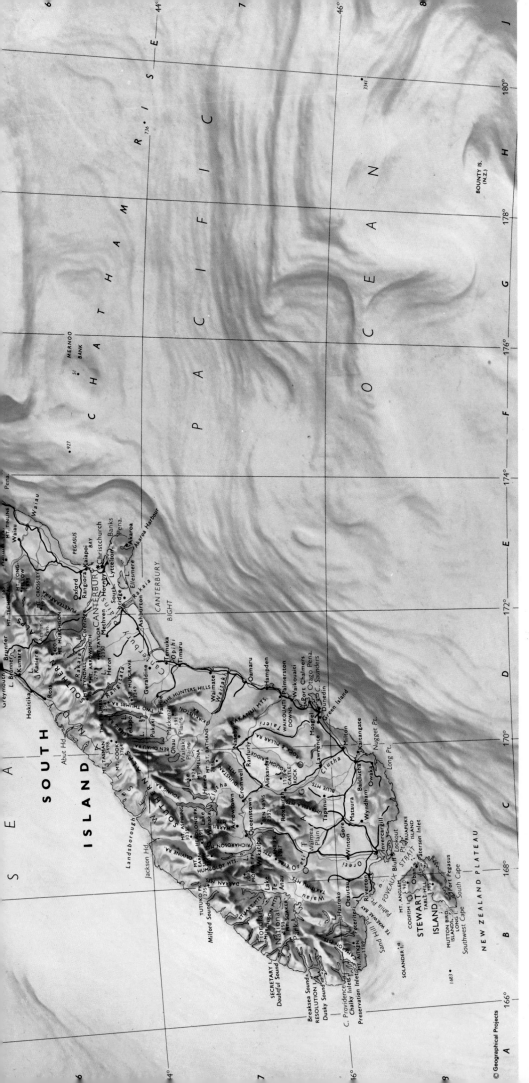

New Zealand

277

© Geographical Projects

Pacific Islands

The Pacific – the largest and deepest ocean, covering over a third of the world's surface – is studded with countless islands. There are more than 30,000 of them, mostly tropical and most of them in the southwestern part. Many of these islands are grouped in archipelagos. Some are the tips of isolated volcanic peaks rising from the ocean floor. Some islands are coral atolls, low and sandy, encircling beautiful blue lagoons. Others are mountainous, often covered by fertile soil and fringed by white sands and coral reefs.

The Pacific can be divided into two major sectors. The eastern half of the ocean is well defined by the young fold mountains of North and South America and the ocean bed is only interrupted by a few scattered submarine ridges and volcanoes. These oceanic islands are scattered and, for the most part, small. Hawaii is the only large one. The islands are the summits of underwater mountains, mainly volcanic in origin.

In the second sector, the western Pacific, the ocean bed has been folded and contorted in a complex manner. The area marks the junction between the Pacific, Eurasian, and Australian plates. Where the folds break the surface they appear as islands. The most westerly fold are the large islands of Japan, the Philippines, New Guinea, New Caledonia, and New Zealand. Other areas of these folds include the Marianas, Palau Islands, Bismarck Archipelago, Solomon Islands, and New Hebrides and again in Fiji, Tonga, and the Kermadec Islands. These islands all vary. Some are volcanic like Tonga, some are metamorphic rocks, and yet others are small coral banks built up on a suboceanic ridge like the Gilbert Islands.

Since they are mostly within the tropics, all the islands have a warm climate. The temperature hardly varies between summer and winter, averaging 75°F, rarely rising above 90°F or falling below 60°F. Most islands lie within the belt of the northeast or southeast trade winds. The islands of the eastern sector have regular rainfall. The heaviest rainfall occurs in the mountainous high islands, such as Hawaii, where the windward side may receive as much as 300 inches a year, but the leeward side less than 30 inches. Such islands are covered with lush vegetation. Tropical forests often spread right up the mountain sides. In the western sector, however, there is a seasonal reversal of the winds and many islands have a low and irregular rainfall.

It is most probable that man first began to populate the Pacific Islands toward the end of the Ice Age when some of the Melanesian islands were still joined to Asia. The first peoples were short, dark-skinned, and reached New Guinea and south to Tasmania. They were followed by another group of Negroid peoples who spread through Australia (the Aborigines) and Melanesia. It was not until some 8000-9000 years ago that the next wave of migrants moved into the Pacific. This time it was a Caucasoid people with a more advanced culture and some knowledge of agriculture. They mingled with the original inhabitants and today the Melanesians are descended from this fusion.

Very much later, most probably between 3000 and 1000 BC, yet another group of peoples entered the Pacific. These were the Polynesians, a people highly skilled in boat building, seamanship and navigation. It is not known for certain in which direction they spread throughout the islands of the Polynesian triangle, but by the end of the 14th century they had settled all the islands. In some islands, on the borders of Melanesia, they mingled with the earlier peoples. Micronesia is inhabited by still later migrations of a more Mongoloid people.

In some Pacific islands comparative newcomers have become prominent. Fiji, for example, now has more Indians than Fijians. Many Japanese, Filipinos, and Chinese live in Hawaiian Islands, whose capital, Honolulu, is the only large city in Oceania.

Below: the mountainous island of Raiatea in French Polynesia, now fringed with coral, is one of the many islands pushed up in the Pacific by volcanic action.

Subsistence farming is widely practiced throughout the islands and the people grow their own food crops including yams, taros, breadfruit, sweet potatoes, bananas, and cassava. Some islands produce foods on a commercial scale. Hawaii is known for its sugar cane and pineapples. Both are also grown on Fiji along with rice and coconut palm. New Caledonia has large coffee plantations and Western Samoa exports cocoa. The coconut palm grows everywhere and on some of the atolls is the only form of vegetation. Mineral resources are limited and unevenly distributed. Throughout Polynesia and Micronesia phosphate rocks are the only known mineral. New Caledonia has the richest resources of all with nickel, chrome, iron ore, and other minerals. Fiji has deposits of both gold and silver.

All the islands supply sufficient seafoods for their own consumption and fishing has been put on a commercial basis in the New Hebrides, American Samoa, and Fiji.

The growth of tourism has increased the demand for quick transport and resulted in the construction of airports capable of handling large jets. Hawaii, Fiji, and Tahiti have large airfields and many small islands are able to take small aircraft and thus be linked with the larger airports.

Since World War II there has been a great influx of people into the area – the Koreans, Japanese, Chinese, and Filipinos to the Hawaiian Islands, the Chinese to Melanesia and parts of Polynesia, the Indians to Fiji, the Americans and Puerto Ricans to the Hawaiian Islands and all have brought new ideas and skills.

Above: a Satawal fishing canoe off the Caroline Islands in the western Pacific. Two of these fragile vessels made a 1100-mile trip to the Marianas Islands in 1974.

Australasia

TARAWA
GILBERT
ISLANDS
(BR.)

EQUATOR 0°

NAURU

OCEAN I.
(BR.)

PACIFIC OCEAN

MELANESIA

M PELAGO

ELAND

Planet
Deep
9140

BOUGAINVILLE I.

CHOISEUL I.

SOLOMON

SANTA ISABEL I.

OMON

Trench

OR
IS.

WOODLARK I.

NEW GEORGIA
GROUP

THE SLOT

MALAITA I.

TUVALU

FUNAFUTI

STEAUX IS.

Solomons GUADALCANAL I.

HONIARA

Basin

SAN CRISTOBAL I.

RENNELL RIDGE

10°

LOUISIADE ARCHO.

S. Cristobal Tr.

Santa Cruz
6061

ROTUMA I.

SANTA CRUZ IS.
(BR.)

MELANESIAN BORDER PLATEAU

899

Coral Sea Basin

LOUISIADE RIDGE

Basin

New Hebrides

BANKS IS.

North Fiji Basin

ORAL

HRISE

OU REEF

SEA

Basin ESPIRITU SANTO I.

MALEKULA

NEW

HEBRIDES
(BR. & FR.)

VANUA LEVU

FIJI

ÎLES CHESTERFIELD
(FR.)

MARION REEF

EFATE

VILA

Nandi
VITI LEVU
SUVA

SAUMAREZ REEF

BELLONA PLATEAU

NEW
CALEDONIA
(FR.)

IS. LOYAUTÉ
(FR.)

CONWAY REEF

20°
180°

N CHAN.

NOUMÉA

MATTHEW
HUNTER

HUNTER ISLAND RIDGE

andy Cape

FRASER OR GT. SANDY I.

WALPOLE

TROPIC OF CAPRICORN

BRISBANE

C. Byron

South Fiji Basin

4

LORD HOWE I.
(AUSTRALIA)

NORFOLK ISLAND RIDGE

NORFOLK I.
(AUSTRALIA)

KERMADEC IS.
(N.Z.)

on Deep 5944

30°

LORD HOWE RISE

LORD HOWE TROUGH

Norfolk Island Trough

Three
Kings
Basin

NORTH CAPE RISE

COLVILLE RIDGE

KERMADEC RIDGE

GALATHEA
DEPTH
9994

HAVRE TROUGH

Kermadec Trench

C. Maria
van Diemen

North Cape

5

TASMAN SEA

Auckland

NORTH
ISLAND

BAY OF
PLENTY

East Cape

L. Taupo

MT. EGMONT
2518

RUAPEHU VOLC.
2797

Gisborne

HAWKE BAY

Napier

C. Farewell

Wanganui

TASMAN BAY

Nelson

NEW
ZEALAND

SOUTH
ISLAND

WELLINGTON

COOK STR.

40°
170°

SOUTHERN ALPS

MT. COOK
3764

Christchurch

Timaru

CHATHAM RISE

C. Providence

FOVEAUX STRAIT

STEWART I.

Dunedin

CHATHAM IS.
(N.Z.)

Invercargill

NEW ZEALAND
PLATEAU

160°   50°   170°   180°   170°

The Countries of Australasia and the Pacific

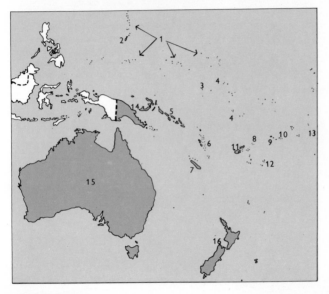

1 Caroline Islands, Marianas, Marshall Islands
2 Guam
3 Nauru
4 Gilbert Islands, Tuvalu (Ellice Islands)
5 Solomon Islands
6 New Hebrides
7 New Caledonia
8 Wallis & Futuna
9 Western Samoa
10 American Samoa
11 Fiji
12 Tonga
13 French Polynesia
14 Papua New Guinea
15 Australia
16 New Zealand

CAROLINE ISLANDS, MARIANAS ISLANDS, MARSHALL ISLANDS

Area: 687 square miles
Population: 107,000
Chief Town: Saipan (Marianas Islands)
Monetary Unit: United States currency
History and Government: In 1919 Japan took over the mandate of the former German possession in the Pacific north of the Equator. In 1946, the USA agreed to administer these islands – the Caroline Islands (which include Palau Islands, Ponape, Truk, and Yap), Marianas Islands (excluding Guam) and Marshall Islands – as a Trusteeship for the United Nations. They are termed Trust Territory of the Pacific Islands and are made up of more than 2100 islands and atolls. The Bicameral Congress of Micronesia, established in 1965, is the legislative body and consists of a Senate and House of Representatives. Nine individual languages are spoken in the territory.
Economy: The exports from the islands are principally bauxite and copra. Fishing is also important.

GUAM
Area: 212 square miles
Population: 105,000
Capital: Agaña
Monetary Unit: United States currency
History and Government: Guam is the largest and most southerly island of the Marianas archipelago and was ceded to the USA by Spain in 1898. In World War II it was in Japanese hands from December 1941 to August 1944, when the USA regained possession. It is termed an unincorporated territory of the United States and a non-voting delegate is elected to serve in the United States House of Representatives. The island is of great strategic importance.
Economy: The numerous military bases constitute practically the only important activity in the island, even from the economic point of view. Fishing has some importance and some food crops are grown – corn, sweet potatoes, taro, cassava, bananas, citrus fruits, coconuts, and sugar cane. Cattle and pigs are kept. Tourism is now being developed.

NAURU
Area: 8.2 square miles
Population: 6970
Capital: Makwa
Language: English and Nautuan
Religion: Protestantism
Monetary Unit: Australian currency
History and Government: Nauru was discovered in 1798, annexed by Germany in 1888 and surrendered to the Australian forces in 1914. It was a mandate of the British empire from 1920 to 1947, then a trusteeship administered jointly by Australia, New Zealand, and the UK. It has been an independent republic within the Commonwealth since 1968. There is an 18-member Legislative Assembly.
Economy: The wealth of the island comes from the rich deposits of phosphates.

GILBERT ISLANDS, TUVALU
Area: 342 square miles
Population: 59,000
Capital: Tarawa (Gilbert Islands), Funafuti (Tuvalu)
Religion: Protestantism
Monetary Unit: Australian currency
History and Government: The Gilbert and Ellice Islands were a protectorate of the UK from 1892 to 1916 when they became a colony, at the request of the native governments. In 1975, the Ellice Islands became a separate colony and changed their name to Tuvalu. Then in 1978 they gained their independence. The Gilbert Islands remain a colony, which includes Ocean Island, Phoenix Islands, and Line Islands. It has been internally self-governing since 1977 with an elected House of Assembly.
Economy: The chief agricultural product is coconuts, and copra is exported. On Ocean Island there are large phosphate deposits.

SOLOMON ISLANDS
Area: 10,983 square miles

Population: 196,000
Capital: Honiara
Monetary Unit: Solomon Islands Dollar

History and Government: The Solomon Islands were placed under British protection in 1893 and by 1898 the British Solomon Islands Protectorate

Pacific Ocean

Scale:
Miles
0   500   1000   1500
Kilometres
0   500   1000   1500   2000   2500

Blue thick line   Sea routes
Red thick line   Air routes

Below: the Pacific ("peaceful") Ocean, covering more than a third of the world's surface, is not always peaceful. The crust beneath its waters gives rise to earthquakes and volcanoes, while the surface is the birthplace of some of the most destructive storms on earth.

included, as well as the main islands of the group (excluding Bougainville) Duff, Florida, Reef, Russell, Santa Cruz, and Tikopia groups, Shortland, Mono, Vella Lavella, Kolombangara, Ranongga, Gizo, Rendova, Rennell, Ballona, Lord Howe islands. There is a Legislative Assembly and the islands are largely self-governing.

Economy: The principal agricultural products are coconuts, rice, pineapples, sweet potatoes, chillies, and the cultivation of the oil palm is being developed. Timber has some importance and there is fishing, chiefly for skipjack.

NEW HEBRIDES (Nouvelles Hebrides)
Area: 5700 square miles
Population: 90,000
Capital: Vila
Monetary Unit: New Hebrides Franc and Australian Dollar
History and Government: The islands were discovered by the Portuguese in 1606 but not visited and explored by Europeans until the 1700s. The group has been an Anglo-French condominium since 1906. It is administered jointly for some purposes and unilaterally for others.
Economy: The principal economic activities are the production of copra, fishing, and the mining of a manganese deposit. Coffee is grown as a commercial crop and yams, manioc, and bananas for local consumption. There is a forestry industry and the kauri pine is exported. There is also a plant for freezing tuna and bonito.

NEW CALEDONIA (Nouvelle Caledonie)
Area: 7358 square miles
Population: 117,000
Capital: Noumea
Monetary Unit: Franc CFP
History and Government: The archipelago, New Caledonia and its Dependencies were annexed by France in 1853. It is an overseas territory of France, administered by a governor and represented in the National Assembly by one deputy and in the Senate by one senator. There is a Territorial Assembly of 35 members.
Economy: The island is rich in deposits of nickel – of which it is one of the biggest producers in the world – chrome, iron ore, cobalt, manganese, and other minerals. Agriculture is enough to supply the home market with corn, fruits,

and vegetables. Coffee and copra are exported. The manufacturing industry includes some metallurgical works and food factories as well as sawmills.

WALLIS AND FUTUNA
Area: 77 square miles
Population: 10,000
Capital: Mata Utu
Monetary Unit: French currency
History and Government: After being dependencies of New Caledonia, these islands became an overseas territory of the French republic in 1961. They send a representative to the National Assembly in France.
Economy: Copra is exported.

WESTERN SAMOA (Samoa i Sisifo)
Area: 1097 square miles
Population: 155,000
Capital: Apia
Language: English and Samoan
Religion: Christianity
Monetary Unit: Tala
History and Government: Formerly a kingdom and for centuries a cradle of Polynesian settlement, all the Samoan islands were jointly administered by Britain, the United States, and Germany between 1889 and 1899. The islands were assigned to Germany as a protectorate from 1900. After World War I Western Samoa was given as a mandated territory to New Zealand and in 1962 became independent and in 1970 a member of the Commonwealth. The regime is monarchical and the present head of state was elected for life, but his successors will be elected for five years by the Legislative Assembly. The sovereign holds the executive power. The Legislative Assembly has 45 members.
Economy: The main activities are the cultivation of coconut palms, cocoa, bananas, and rubber. There is some stock-rearing and fishing.

AMERICAN SAMOA
Area: 76 square miles
Population: 31,000
Capital: Pago Pago
Monetary Unit: United States currency
History and Government: In 1889

the Samoan Islands were proclaimed neutral territory by a treaty between Germany, the UK, and the USA. In 1899, Germany and the UK renounced all rights to the islands of the group east of 171°w and these islands were ceded to the USA in 1900 and 1904 by the high chiefs. Congress accepted the islands in 1929 after the USA had annexed Swains Island in 1925. The latter is northeast of the group and is administered as part of the group. American Samoa is an "unorganized, unincorporated territory of the United States" administered under the Department of the Interior. Most of the Samoans are United States citizens. The government consists of an executive and a two-chamber legislature.
Economy: The majority of the population is employed in fishing and on the coconut and banana plantations. The food crops grown are taro, bread-fruit, bananas, oranges, and papayas. Poultry, pigs, and cattle are also kept.

FIJI
Area: 7054 square miles
Population: 90,000
Capital: Suva
Language: English and Fijian
Religion: Protestantism
Monetary Unit: Fiji Dollar
History and Government: There are more than 800 islands and atolls, most of which are uninhabited. Fiji was offered to the UK in 1874 by a native ruler after a period of tribal wars. It remained a British colony until 1971 when it gained its independence. It is a member of the Commonwealth and a governor-general represents the crown. There is a Senate of 22 members and a lower house of 52 members.
Economy: The most widespread activity is agriculture, the principal crops being sugar cane, coconuts, and bananas as well as pineapples, rice, corn and tobacco, which are grown for home consumption. Mineral resources are gold and manganese. There are sugar mills, food industries, as well as textile factories, cement works, and plants for the processing of copra.

TONGA (Friendly Islands)
Area: 270 square miles
Population: 94,000
Capital: Nuku'alofa
Language: English and Tongan
Religion: Protestantism

Monetary Unit: Pa'anga
History and Government: Up to 1899 the kingdom of Tonga was a neutral region, but from that date the Tonga Islands were under the protection of the UK. They became independent within the Commonwealth in 1970. The group is made up of over 150 islands. The Constitution provides for a monarch and a Legislative Assembly of 22 members under a speaker and includes the Ministers of the Crown, Governors of the Nobles and the People, elected every three years.
Economy: Copra, manioc, bananas and sweet potatoes are the chief commercial crops of these islands.

FRENCH POLYNESIA
(Polynesie Française)
Area: 2500 square miles
Population: 127,000
Capital: Papeete
Monetary Unit: Franc CFP
History and Government: These islands were formerly known as French Settlements in Oceania. In 1958 they opted to become an overseas territory within the French Community. They are administered by a governor, a government council of five members and a Territorial Assembly of 30. The country is represented in the National Assembly by 1 deputy and in the Senate by 1 senator and the Economic and Social Council by 1 councillor. French Polynesia include the Society Islands, Tuamotu group, Illes Tubuai (Asutral Islands) and the Marquesas. The island of Clipperton in the eastern Pacific is annexed to French Polynesia.
Economy: Processed copra, coffee, vanilla, fishing for pearls and mother-of-pearl, and tourism are the principal economic resources. The deposits of phosphates have been exhausted. The few industries produce rum, sugar, copra oil, and mother-of-pearl.

PAPUA NEW GUINEA
Area: 178,259 square miles
Population: 2,800,000
Capital: Port Moresby
Language: English and Pidgin English
Religion: Christianity and Animism
Monetary Unit: Kina
History and Government: In 1884 a British Protectorate was proclaimed over the southern part of eastern New Guinea and in 1888 it was annexed and named British New Guinea. In 1901 it came under Australian control and in 1906 it was renamed Territory of Papua. The northern part of eastern New Guinea was a UN-Australian Trust Territory 1949-72 and administered with the Territory of Papua, having been under the mandate of Australia between the two world wars. Finally despite certain opposition from the local government, which was anxious about the extreme backwardness and the ethnic diversity of the territory, independence was gained for the whole of eastern New Guinea in September 1975. The final decision was made by the Australian government. The country of Papua New Guinea now includes the whole of the eastern half of New Guinea, Louisiade Archipelago, New Britain, New Ireland, Bismarck Archipelago, and Bougainville. There is a House of Assembly of 100 members and a governor-general represents the crown. Australia retains some reserve powers over defense and foreign affairs.
Economy: The only economic resource of note is the deposit of copper, one of the largest in the world, discovered in the island of Bougainville. At present coffee, copra, cocoa, tea, rubber, and peanuts are exported together with oil from the oil palm. The beef cattle industry is being developed. There is some gold and silver which is not fully exploited.

AUSTRALIA
Area: 2,966,136 square miles
Population: 13,496,000
Capital: Canberra
Language: English
Religion: Mainly Protestantism
Monetary Unit: Australian Dollar
History and Government: The island continent was first sighted by the Spanish in the 16th century. First Europeans to land were the Dutch in 1606, and settled by the British in 1788. The whole continent was claimed by Britain in 1829. Self government through the Australian Colonies government Act of 1850. The Australian Federation was founded in 1901 when the colonies changed their names to states – New South Wales, Victoria, Queensland, South Australia, Western Australia, and Tasmania. The Northern Territory was transferred by South Australia to the Commonwealth as a territory in 1911. In 1911 also, Australia acquired from New South Wales the site for Canberra, the capital, and in 1915 another area at Jervis Bay. Australia is a member of the Commonwealth. The Crown is represented by a governor-general. There is a bicameral parliament consisting of a Senate and House of Representatives. The former has 60 seats the latter about 120 members, their numbers being proportional to population, but not less than five per state. Australia's external territories include Norfolk Islands, Cocos (Keeling) Islands, and Christmas Island.
Economy: Besides precious minerals (gold, tungsten, manganese, molybdenum) and strategic ones (zircon, tantalum, cobalt, and uranium), the country is among the foremost suppliers of lead, bauxite, and iron ore. There are also oil and methane deposits. Agriculture, which occupies only eight percent of the work force as opposed to 37 percent in industry (1970), is very advanced and makes a strong contribution to exports. The principal crops are sugar cane and cereal. In animal husbandry, Australia leads the world for its number of sheep and for wool production.

NEW ZEALAND
Area: 103,735 square miles
Population: 3,120,000
Capital: Wellington
Language: English
Religion: Mainly Protestantism
Monetary Unit: New Zealand Dollar
History and Government: New Zealand was discovered in 1642 by the Dutch explorer Abel Tasman. Colonization by British began in 1840 when in the same year the Maori chiefs ceded the sovereignty of New Zealand to the British crown and it became a British colony. It has been independent within the Commonwealth since 1931. Parliament consists of a House of Representatives of 87 members, including four Maoris. The governor-general represents the Crown and is chairman of the Executive Council. Political life is essentially two-party. A number of other islands are also included within the boundaries of New Zealand: the 14 Cook Islands, which have their own government and High Commissioner. Niue, which is administered separately and has its own government; Tokelau islands, which have been part of New Zealand since 1948; and the Pitcairn Islands, whose governor is the British High Commissioner in New Zealand.
Economy: The chief source of wealth is stock-rearing, especially sheep farming. Meat and wool, together with dairy produce, are the main exports. Fishing is highly developed. The most important industries are those connected with stock-rearing – frozen meat, wool, hides, dairy products – and those producing consumer goods.

Chapter 12

The Polar Lands

The extreme north and extreme south of the earth are covered by an ocean and by a continent where the ice lies deep winter and summer alike and the cold is always intense. There are situated the ends of the earth's axis, the North and South Poles.

The Arctic Ocean is the heart of the Arctic. Most years it is covered with pack ice, while the lands around its shores enjoy only the briefest of growing season. Yet man cannot ignore this region. There are important mineral resources, deposits of coal and oil, civil air routes criss-cross it, and it is also an area of high strategic importance.

By contrast, Antarctica is a vast continent, half as large again as the United States. It is covered by an ice cap that contains 90 percent of the earth's ice.

It, too, contains minerals, but conditions make it unlikely that they will ever be economically workable. Antarctica is not owned by any one country and here, at least, man has learned that peaceful coexistence between nations is possible.

Left: a lone figure in the vast expanse of ice and snow that is northwest Greenland – this is typical of the Arctic at the northernmost tip of the earth. Bleak and forbidding, but with a kind of austere beauty all its own, the North Pole region is one of the most barren places in the world. In this it is like the Antarctic at the opposite end of the globe, though the South Pole region is even worse for cold and wind. Life, where it exists at all, is a constant struggle.

The Arctic Lands

From the North Pole the Arctic region extends beyond the Arctic Circle, 66° 30′N, to the tree line where the forest growth begins. This means that the Arctic area includes land along the northern coasts of Eurasia and North America, most of Greenland, and the islands in the Arctic Ocean. All around the Arctic Ocean there is a general absence of high land, but four of the longest rivers in the world drain into it – the Ob, Yenisey, Lena, and Mackenzie.

The major part of the North Polar lands were covered by ice during the Pleistocene Glaciation. But it is remarkable that some of the islands of the Canadian Arctic, the lower Yukon and much of Siberia escaped glaciation. Recent work in the USSR, however, has suggested that Soviet geologists have found evidence of a more widespread distribution of the ice in the valleys of the Lena and Kolyma.

The Arctic is the smallest ocean in the world and yet less is known about it than all the others. The whole area is in darkness for nearly half the year, it is always cold, and winds constantly blow at near gale force. Yet the North Pole is not the coldest place in the Northern Hemisphere; the "cold pole" is in northeastern Siberia. Over the Arctic Ocean, in summer, there is a constant high pressure area, but in winter this retreats to the area bounded by Alaska, the Bering Strait, northeastern Siberia and the 90°E–90°W longitude. This allows the low pressure systems of the North Atlantic to penetrate through the open end of the ocean and pass north of Svalbard (Spitzbergen) and Zemlya Frantsa Iosifa.

Most of the coastal regions have a July temperature of 45°F or just below, inland the temperature rises to 50°F at the Arctic Circle and 60°F around the 60°N latitude. But over the pack ice it rarely rises above 35°F. In January, the whole region is below −10°F except for the southern coasts of Greenland, Iceland and northern Scandinavia, all of which are affected by the warm waters of the Gulf Stream. Over the pack ice the temperature falls to below −30°F.

The heart of the region is the Arctic Ocean itself, most of which is covered all year around with pack ice. The permanent pack, which is not navigable at

Below: pack ice off the northern coast of Greenland glowing in the light of summer. There are only six months of the year in which the Arctic has any daylight.

Arctic Ocean

Scale:
Miles
Blue thick line   Sea routes
Red thick line   Air routes

Below: the Arctic Ocean is at the top of the world – an icy expanse that keeps its geographical secrets in the deep freeze. In fact, the whole of the Arctic region is locked in snow and ice, although its brief summer sees the sudden flowering of many plants, and some hardy animals live there.

any time, covers the deep basin at the enclosed end of the ocean, between northeastern Siberia, Alaska, northwestern Canada, and northern Greenland. The pack ice is usually at least 12 feet thick. In winter it extends to the surrounding coasts, into the northern half of the Bering Sea, the whole of Hudson Bay, Baffin Bay, south along the coast of Labrador to eastern Newfoundland and the Gulf of St Lawrence, and down the east coast of Greenland. The only coasts that are ice-free are those affected by the Gulf Stream, the extreme southwest of Greenland and Scandinavia. This pack ice is only navigable by heavy icebreakers. In summer, the pack ice retreats leaving the coasts in open water with the exception of some of the smaller islands in the Canadian Arctic, northwest Greenland, and the north coasts of the islands of Severnaya Zemlya.

An ice cap covers about seven-eighths of Greenland and is the second largest extent of ice in the world.

For centuries Greenland has been regarded as the largest island in the world, but now it is known that it is the ice cap that makes it so large. Beneath the ice scientists have so far distinguished the shape of the bedrock in the form of a hollow oval enclosing an enormous inland sea, over 900 miles long, which would have only one narrow outlet to the ocean, just south of the Disko island. Much of the ice is thought to be over 14,000 feet thick and in places probably goes down as much as 5000 feet below sea level. It is only around the edges of the ice cap that mountain peaks poke through the ice forming what are known as nunataks. In the north, the ice cap extends right down to the edge of the sea, but in the remainder of the country it is bordered by a mountainous rim, broken by innumerable fjords.

Only in local fjords does glacier ice, which is formed on the land in contrast to sea ice which is formed by the freezing of sea water, actually get pushed out to cover the water. As the end of the glacier, the snout,

Above: an aerial view of a lead, which is a channel of water that opens in the pack ice. Leads provide valuable breathing holes for sea mammals, especially whales, and their passage up and down the watery lanes helps to keep the leads free of ice. Leads present a hazard to explorers, however, often opening suddenly and causing falls.

moves into the sea pieces break off to form icebergs in a process known as calving. Active calving glaciers are found in Greenland, Svalbard (Spitzbergen) and in the Canadian Arctic in Devon and Ellesmere islands.

The Arctic has hardly any trees, because the permanently frozen subsoil prevents long roots; also, the short growing season is cool and the winds are too strong. Only small, low evergreen shrubs such as bilberry can survive in the acid soils of the tundra, with sedges, cotton grass, and moss in the wet and peaty grounds and lichens in the drier, rockier areas. In the short summer the landscape is full of color and movement. But in the long winter, with its almost perpetual night, life slows down to a complete standstill.

Reindeer (the wild reindeer in North America is known as the caribou), Arctic foxes, Arctic wolf, musk oxen, lemmings, and other migratory animals live in the Arctic. Many of them, as do plants, show striking adaptations to the extreme cold and long periods of snow cover. For example, the seasonal changes in color of the Arctic hare, from brown to white, makes it difficult to distinguish from the snowy background; the extensive hoof of the caribou and moose enables them to walk on boggy ground and in the snow; and

Above: the Arctic hare is one of three species of hare that has adapted to life in the harsh Arctic. Its chances of survival are reduced by the fact that the Arctic fox preys on it.

the accumulation of a fat reserve in many of the mammals, birds, and fish enables them to withstand extreme cold.

The most productive part of the North Pole region is the sea. The economy of the Eskimo is, after all, based upon the life in Arctic waters not upon the life on land. As in the waters of the Southern Ocean, the Arctic is rich in plankton, which in its turn supports other forms of life. The Arctic and sub-Arctic fisheries are one of the planet's greatest food resources. Attempts are being made to market types of fish that have not previously been generally eaten, such as the Greenland cod. There are also seals and whales, but the killing of them is now strictly supervised. In fact, whales are almost extinct after three centuries of continuous hunting.

The Arctic has important mineral resources also. There are large, but scattered, deposits of coal; iron ore has been found in the Canadian Arctic; Greenland

has deposits of lead and silver, and in the south, Ivigtut is the world's only known source of natural cryolite, used in the production of aluminum, in enamel and glassware industries, and in insecticides.

Exploratory drilling for petroleum has already been carried out in the Davis Strait, the Chukchi Sea, the Beaufort Sea off the coast of Alaska, and around some of the islands of the Canadian Arctic. The USSR has also drilled off the Siberian coast. It is the finds north of Alaska, however, which have so far proved the most valuable economically. Scientists are considering taking oil below the ice in a supertanker submarine. The idea for this stems from the subpolar trips

Below: the ringed seal is one of the most common of the Arctic seals and lives as far north as the pole itself. This small seal does not migrate during the winter, managing to live under the ice by using the leads as breathing holes. Eskimos use the ringed and other seals for food, clothing, and lighting oil. Its natural enemy is the polar bear.

by the nuclear submarine, *Nautilus*, and other vessels. If it proves practical it will open up vast new possibilities for subsea transport of other bulk commodities. Merchant nuclear submarines, making a transpolar journey from Japan to Europe, could save about 5000 miles over the traditional sea route.

It is perhaps through man's discovery of oil that our knowledge of the hostile Arctic Ocean is now increasing at a tremendous rate. Far more has been learned about the movements of sea ice, ice thickness, winds, waves, and currents in the Arctic Ocean in the past 15 years than over the preceding century. Before too long it is hoped this knowledge will be put to use to make the Arctic Ocean as much utilized as the Atlantic Ocean.

Antarctica

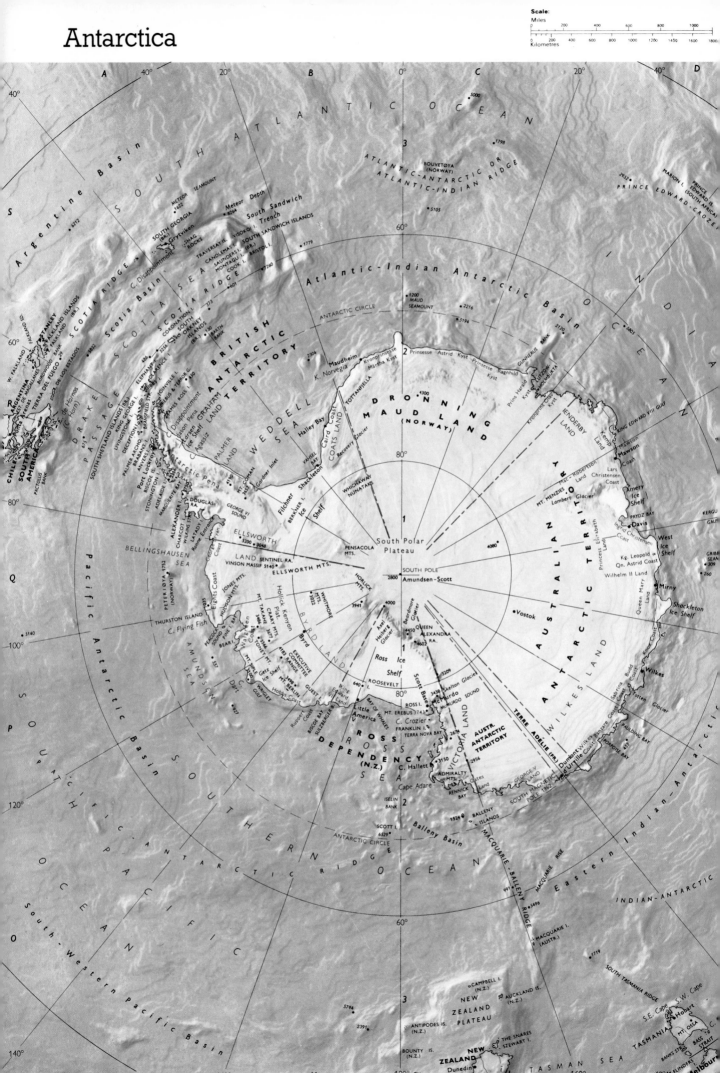

The Antarctic Continent

From the South Pole the Antarctic region extends to beyond the Antarctic Circle, 66° 30′S, to include the islands of the Southern Ocean and the southern Scotia Sea. But in contrast to the Arctic, the heart of the Antarctic is a huge continent, half as large again as the United States. It is a perfect example of an ice age in full swing. There is no life at all on this barren land except for mosses and lichens and a few minute insects that manage to survive in spite of being frozen for most of the year. The chief features of the region are wind and cold. It has truly been called the "home of the blizzard."

The sea around the continent teems with life. Small marine life supports the many whales, seals, and penguins that inhabit the belt of drifting pack ice surrounding this vast and inhospitable continent.

It is only during the last 20 years that geologists have been able to utilize sophisticated scientific methods and begin to have a more detailed knowledge of the formation of this continent. It is now known that there is a marked structural contrast between what is termed East and West Antarctic. The former, defined as the area east of a line through Vassel Bay – Pensacola Mountains – Horlick Mountains – mountains of the eastern margin of the Ross Ice Shelf (often termed Transantarctic Mountains), is a true continental shield composed of ancient Pre-Cambrian rocks. The latter, the West, which includes Graham Land, Ellsworth Land, and Marie Byrd Land, is much younger and has been continually subject to massive earth movements. It is thought that the rocks there were folded, faulted, and formed at the same time as the Andean mountain system. There has also been intense volcanic activity. The twin active volcanoes of Mount Erebus, 12,474 feet (which is in continuous eruption) and Mount Terror, on Ross Island, have been a familiar landmark to explorers and scientists since they were discovered in 1840.

Antarctica has not always been covered by ice. It was first glaciated for a long period some 300 million years ago in the Palaeozoic era, during the Permian and Carboniferous periods. Then the climate slowly changed until, by the middle of the Mesozoic era, desert conditions had entirely replaced the glacial climate. For a second time, the climate became colder and local ice caps began to form again on the high mountains. As it got colder and colder, the ice cover

Below: the telltale flat top of this Antarctic iceberg, tinted by the midnight sun, identifies it as a piece broken off one of the ice shelves. Icebergs of over 80 miles in length have been recorded.

Above: Mount Erebus is an active volcano, one of the two volcanoes on Antarctica. Its heights were first scaled by the 1908 expedition under Ernest Shackleton.

increased and eventually by the time of the Pleistocene Glaciation Antarctica was once again shrouded in ice.

The Antarctic ice sheet covers 99 percent of the surface, broken in places only by steep mountain peaks. It is in fact one vast accumulation of ice that is slowly, but continuously, working its way toward the coast and discharging into the sea. Some areas move quicker than others because of the shape of the rocks underneath or because they lead from areas of great accumulation. These form streams of ice, or glaciers, moving through the surrounding ice sheet. In other places, the ice forms a shelf on the sea and the front of the shelf gradually moves forward. For example, the Ross Ice Shelf is between 600 and 1200 feet thick over much of its area and floats on sea water that has a depth of some 100 feet. This ice shelf covers an area almost as large as France.

Along the coast massive sections of ice break off and float away as huge flat-topped icebergs. These spread over a wide area of ocean reaching far up the east coast of South America in the Atlantic and almost as far as the Cape of Good Hope. They are of a formidable size, dwarfing their Arctic counterparts and having a characteristic perpendicular sided, table-top shape. Bergs of 300 feet in height above the waterline and 80 miles long have been recorded: a ship sailing along one of these at a speed of 15 knots would, assuming the iceberg to be motionless, take five hours to pass it.

Like the Arctic, Antarctica is in darkness for six months of the year. This and its height make the continent much colder than the North Pole region. The surrounding Southern Ocean, mostly covered by pack ice and swept by bitter winds, is the stormiest part of the world. It is desolate except for a few islands such as those stretching out from the Antarctic Peninsula, Bouvet Island, Heard Island, Balleny Islands, Scott Island, and Peter I Øya (island). It is not until almost as far north as 50°S that the sea temperatures rise above freezing point.

Summer temperatures in Antarctica are always below freezing point, except occasionally in some ice-free area near the coast when the air is still and the temperatures may rise to 66°F for a short period when the sun shines. Average winter temperatures are the world's lowest, often less than −70°F. In 1960, Vostok, a Russian base in East Antarctica near the summit of the ice cap, recorded the lowest ever temperature of −127°F.

It is almost impossible to measure snowfall in Antarctica because it is impossible to distinguish between the snow that is actually due to local precipitation and that which has been blown there from a distance. The annual average accumulation of snow in the coastal regions is generally considered to be between 8 and 10 inches a year and over the ice sheet probably as little as 4 inches a year. There is a weather condition known as "whiteout," which comes about when the sky is overcast from horizon to horizon and the surface is entirely snow covered. When this happens and there are no dark objects to see, no shadows cast by the sun, differences between land and sky are

indistinguishable. Under these conditions people have been known to ski right over the edge of a cliff. If it is also snowing at the same time, the terrifying conditions can well be imagined.

Most of the research on the plant life of the Antarctic has been done in Graham Land and the offshore islands such as the South Shetlands and South Orkneys groups. Outside these regions, the richest area so far discovered has been the nunataks in King Edward VII Land, part of Marie Byrd Land, where almost 1000 species have been identified, the great majority of them lichens. In East Antarctica only a few lichens and mosses have been reported from some of the scientific stations. These plants must not only be able to withstand long periods of temperatures well below freezing point, but must also be able to withstand the sudden increases in temperature that occur on the rock faces when the winds cease and the skies clear. In these short periods the plant must absorb and manufacture food as well as grow and reproduce.

The seas are rich in plankton. This includes krill, the small shrimps on which whales, seals, and birds feed. The krill themselves feed directly on the minute plankton plants that flourish in the surface waters of the Southern Ocean. These plants require light and nutrient salts, particularly nitrates and phosphates,

Above: the shrimplike krill is plentiful in the Antarctic seas, feeding on the plant plankton in which the waters are so rich. In turn, the krill is the main food for larger animals such as whales, seals, and penguins.

Left: Adélie penguins breed on Antarctica's shores in October.

which are brought to the surface layers by the deep and relatively warmer waters. Here the Antarctic Convergence, which marks the boundary at the surface where the cold Antarctic surface water sinks and the warm, deep water rises, is of great biological significance. Many species of fish, birds, and plants, found in abundance on one side of the boundary are rarely seen on the other. Krill are almost entirely south of the Antarctic Convergence where the rich nutrients are being brought up from the lower layers.

Natural Resources

In the past the great resource of the Antarctic has been the seemingly endless supply of the economically important whales, and, to a lesser extent, seals. The whaling industry began in the Southern Ocean at the beginning of the century with the establishment of a land station on South Georgia. In 1926–27 factory ships were introduced, each of which was capable of hauling an entire whale carcass up a slipway and onto the deck. The impact of these ships was tremendous. In the 1930–31 season 41 vessels operated with 200 catcher boats. They established a record catch of 37,465 whales of which no fewer than 28,325 were blue whales. If whale catching had continued like this it would soon have led to the extinction of the main species. Fortunately, having saturated the market with whale products, the industry made voluntary restrictions and scientists imposed further ones, including a total ban on the taking of gray and right whales as from 1946.

In 1972 the United Nations Conference on the Human Environment resulted in the total protection of blue and humpback whales and established catch quotas for other species. Until stocks of large Antarctic whales have built up sufficiently for them to be able to be culled, Soviet factory ships have turned to experimenting with methods of catching and processing krill to make a type of fish paste with a high protein content.

Above: the Pribilof fur seal lives in the northern Pacific Ocean, coming to the same breeding ground each year. Mature bulls have harems of about 50 cows.

Below: slaughtered sperm whales tied to the side of a whaling vessel. Overhunting has endangered the species.

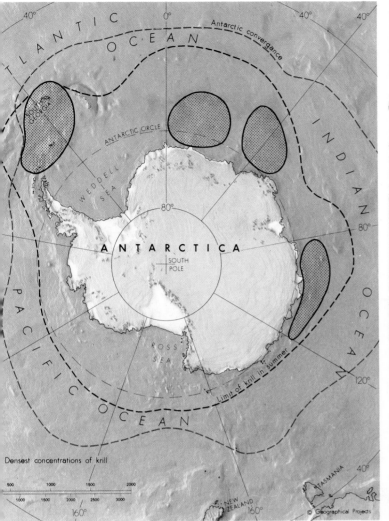

Above: this map shows the concentration of krill in the seas surrounding Antarctica. If it were not for krill and other plankton, no animal life could survive.

Above: Antarctica is never free of pack ice, but during the slightly warmer weather of the brief summer high winds and warmer weather break up the ice, filling the surrounding ocean with icebergs and larger chunks of ice.

Fantastic as it may sound, Antarctic icebergs are now being examined closely as a way of solving water shortages in places as far away from Antarctica as California. Scientists have suggested lassoing icebergs, towing them to California, or wherever they are needed, and melting them. They would be towed slowly, several linked together like a train, and each berg wrapped in a double sheet of plastic film, separated by water, to prevent erosion by sea water. It is estimated a berg would lose only a tenth of its water content during the 10-month voyage and the cost would be some two and a half times cheaper than southern California pays for some of its water supplies at the present time. The Saudi Arabian government has also expressed great interest in this scheme.

There have been suggestions that Antarctica might be used as a huge, natural refrigerator for surplus food storage, and also as a dump for the world's radioactive wastes. As far as dumping radioactive waste, it was argued that the containers, when dumped on the ice surface, would use the heat generated by the radioactive wastes to melt their way through the ice until

they rested on the bedrock. In this way the waste could be isolated for up to 250,000 years. The idea has been rejected. Too little is known about the behavior of the ice at the base of a giant ice sheet and the results of the heat produced by the wastes.

Long term studies in the Antarctic region have been undertaken since 1904, but only with the International Geophysical Year (IGY) 1957-58 did 12 countries undertake to maintain 44 stations around the edge and in the interior of the continent. Today there are 27 stations manned continually. But the IGY did provide the impetus and led to the signing of the Antarctic Treaty in 1961. This treaty, signed by 12 nations – Argentina, Australia, Belgium, Chile, France, Japan, New Zealand, Norway, South Africa, UK, USA, and USSR – perpetuated the use of Antarctica for research.

This means that Antarctica is free from political disputes. The work already undertaken in this vast continent and the surrounding ocean has proved a great stimulus to scientific explorations and research in meteorology, aurorae, the ionosphere, magnetism, earthquakes, and other fields.

International Organizations

The United Nations (UN) and its related agencies

The attempt to create a universal organization to save humanity from war found political expression immediately after the end of World War I with the formation of the League of Nations in 1919, then after World War II with the United Nations Organizations (UNO) in 1945.

The peacemaking efforts of the League of Nations failed tragically. The instruments and methods used by its successor proved to be inadequate in many instances. Because the United Nations Organization (or UN as it is now termed) has no real political power, and depends on the economic and military resources of the richer countries, its interventions in search of a peaceful solution to conflicts between states have not proved entirely successful. Apart from these limitations, the political role of the UN is still very important insofar as the General Assembly brings together the representatives of almost every state in the world. For the countries of the Third World especially, the General Assembly can prove a source of clarification and political understanding amid the economic and strategic complications that inevitably occur in the course of debates.

In addition, the specific interventions and the work of documentation of some associated bodies are of great importance. In the main they succeed in working with real autonomy and are not dominated by the major powers.

Origins: The United Nations Charter, drawn up by the representatives of 50 Allied Nations at the United Nations Conference on International Organizations, which met at San Francisco from April 25–June 26, 1945, came into force on October 24, 1945.

Member States: There are 149 Member States of the UN, which includes all the independent states in the world except Switzerland, Rhodesia, Taiwan, and North and South Korea.

Aims: The main purpose of the UN is to maintain international peace and security. To this end, friendly relations are fostered between the states and, wherever possible, cooperation is advocated in order to solve problems whether economic, social, or cultural. On the basis of the principle that all states are equal and sovereign, any controversies that arise should be re- solved by peaceful means, excluding forms of violence against the independence of any state.

Main Organs: The Main Organs of the UN are:

1. *General Assembly*, which is made up of representatives of all the Member States of the UN, each Member being entitled to five representatives, but having only one vote. The General Assembly holds an ordinary session every year in September and can be convened for a special session by a majority of Members or by the Security Council. It is the main deliberative organ of the UN and can make recommendation on any matter concerning peace, economic, cultural, and social matters, etc. It elects the Members of the other UN bodies, except for the five permanent Members of the Security Council. Its work is carried on by seven Main Committees on each of which every Member has a right to be represented.

2. *Security Council*, which is made up of five permanent Members – China, France, UK, USA, and USSR and ten members elected for a two-year term of office. It bears the prime responsibility for the maintenance of peace and security. As a deliberative body it makes recommendations, among the most serious of which is the advice to apply sanctions against a nation that threatens peace. In every case its decisions are valid only when they have the majority vote of nine members including all five of the permanent Members, who thus have the right of veto. The only exception is if one of the five is a party to a dispute, when it may refrain from voting.

3. *Economic and Social Council (ECO- SOC)*, which is composed of 54 Members of whom 18 are elected each year for a three-year term. It directs the economic, cultural, educational, and social activity of the UN, coordinating its work with that of any associated bodies. It has many standing committees, commissions, and other subsidiary bodies. For example there are standing committees on Non-Governmental Organizations (NGOs) and Natural Resources; the commissions include the Commission on Human Rights and the Commission on the Status of Women; and the other bodies include the regional economic commissions.

4. *Trusteeship Council*, is composed of the permanent Members of the Security Council, countries administering Trust Territories, and one other country elected by the General Assembly for a three-year term. Its work is entirely concerned with all aspects of the Trust Territories. However, as countries administering such territories have decreased so the Council has grown smaller and is now only composed of the USA, the only administering country, and the other four permanent Members of the Security Council.

5. *International Court of Justice*, is a court of 15 judges elected for nine years, with not more than one from the same Member State. It is the principal Judicial body of the UN and acts as consultant when an opinion is required by other organs of UN. Its seat is at The Hague (Netherlands).

6. *The Secretariat*, services the other organs of the UN and administers the programs and policies. The Secretary-General is appointed by the General Assembly, on the recommendation of the Security Council, and remains in office for five years.

Subsidiary Organs: In order to carry out the UN Programs many permanent organs have been set up by the General Assembly and these organs report both to the General Assembly and ECOSOC. They are:

1. *United Nations Conference on Trade and Development (UNCTAD)*, which was set up in 1964 to act on behalf of the underdeveloped countries as economic consultant in the field of commerce.

2. *United Nations Development Program (UNDP)*, is for the purpose of financing technical projects and giving assistance to the low-income countries.

3. *United Nations Industrial Development Organization (UNIDO)*, was set up in 1967 to act as economic consultant and to promote the industrialization of the developing countries.

4. *United Nations Institute of Training and Research (UNITAR)*, was established in 1965 to help train national officials and foreign service officers of all grades for work in international cooperation.

5. *United Nations University (UNU)*. It opened in 1975 in Tokyo. It has no degree students of its own, no central faculty, no main campus. Its object is the advancement of knowledge and it works through a worldwide network of associated institutions.

6. *World Food Council*, is the organ of the UN charged with the responsibility for implementing the resolutions of the UN World Food Conference first held in 1974.

7. *United Nations Environment Program (UNEP)*, was created in 1972 and has its headquarters in Nairobi – the first UN agency to be based in a developing country. It is concerned with pollution and other menaces to the world.

8. *United Nations Children's Fund (UNICEF)*, was established in 1946 to help developing countries improve the conditions of life for children. It embraces all aspects of child welfare.

9. *Office of the United Nations High Commissioner for Refugees (UNHCR)*, was set up in 1951. It provides legal protection and if requested, material assistance, for refugees.

10. *United Nations Relief and Works Agency for Palestine Refugees in the Near East (UNRWA)*, is a subsidiary and temporary organ of the General Assembly, established in 1949 to help the refugees who had left their homes in the territory that became Israel.

11. *United Nations Special Fund*, helps when disasters such as earthquakes, floods, and other catastrophes strike.

12. *Joint UN/FAO World Food Program*, seeks to stimulate economic and social development through food aid.

Related Agencies: These are separate, autonomous organizations related to the UN by special agreements. They work with the UN and each other through the coordinating machinery of ECOSOC and report annually. There are 14 such specialized agencies:

1. *Food and Agriculture Organization (FAO)* was established in 1945, with headquarters in Rome. It works to improve agricultural production, the level of nutrition, and the distribution of food products.

2. *International Bank for Reconstruction and Development (IBRD)* is better known as the World Bank. It was also established in 1945 to promote the development of investments and international trade.

3. *International Civil Aviation Organization (ICAO)*, established in 1947 it promotes the adoption of common regulations and standards in the field of civil aviation and studies the associated problems.

4. *International Development Association (IDA)*, established in 1960, is an affiliate of the World Bank. Its purpose is to promote economic development and increase productivity, especially in the less well developed areas.

5. *International Finance Corporation (IFC)* established in 1956 is closely associated with the World Bank. Its aim is to help the less developed Member countries by promoting the private sector of their economies.

6. *International Labor Organization (ILO)* was established in 1919, and in 1946 became the first specialized agency associated with the UN. It works for improvements in economic and social conditions especially in the field of labor and the productivity of industrial enterprises.

7. *Inter-Governmental Maritime Consultative Organization (IMCO)* was constituted in 1948 but did not come into effect until 1958. It seeks a solution of problems of sea transport and navigation and exchanges information.

8. *International Monetary Fund (FUND)* or *(IMF)* established in 1945 to promote international monetary cooperation and expansion of international trade and also concerns itself with maintaining the stability of exchange.

9. *International Telecommunication Union (ITU)* was founded in Paris in 1865 and the present title adopted in 1934; in 1947 it entered into an agreement with the UN. It promotes cooperation in the field of telecommunication of every type and establishes regulations.

10. *United Nations Educational, Scientific, and Cultural Organization (UNESCO)* was established in 1946 and aims to develop collaboration in the cultural and scientific field promoting respect for the basic rights and liberties of man.

11. *Universal Postal Union (UPU)* established in 1874 and became associated with the UN in 1947. It ensures the organization and improvement of the postal services of the world.

12. *World Health Organization (WHO)* came into being in 1948 and works for the development of the means of prevention and cure of disease, promotion of medical health, and attainment of a high level of health.

13. *World Intellectual Property Organization (WIPO)* was established in 1967 to promote the protection of intellectual property and ensure the cooperation of states in the enforcements of agreements on such matters as trademarks, industrial designs, etc.

14. *World Meteorological Organization (WMO)* came into force in 1950 to facilitate the establishment of a network of stations, promote the rapid exchange of weather information, and further aspects of meteorology.

In addition to these 14 agencies there are two others of a slightly different nature that work with the UN, which are:

1. *International Atomic Energy Agency (IAEA)*, which came into existence in 1957 and reports directly to the General Assembly. Its aims are to accelerate and enlarge the contribution of atomic energy to peace, health, and prosperity and to ensure that it is not used to further any military purpose.

2. *General Agreement on Tariffs and Trade (GATT)* has been in force since January 1948. It lays down a code of conduct for international trade, aims at the progressive reduction of customs barriers and other obstacles to the expansion of international trade, and assists the developing countries in the promotion of their export trade.

ECONOMIC AND POLITICAL ORGANIZATIONS

It is in the economic field, and specifically in the sector of trade and customs, that attempts at international integration have begun to develop. This has been due to a great extent to the need for expansion of the world markets, which have tended to eliminate the traditional customs barriers within certain areas. The most advanced experiment in international integration is the European Economic Community (EEC), though certain obstacles have slowed down the process of integration of the EEC. These include the conflicting interests of some of the European partners and the resistance of some countries outside Europe, such as the USA. Outside Europe there has been some anxiety lest the EEC gain considerable economic and political weight and finally emerges as a new world super-power.

The EEC is opposed by the COMECON, which is closely bound up with the political and economic policies of the USSR. Other large international organizations are the Organization for African Unity (OAU), particularly committed to supporting the emerging African states, and the Arab League, which maintains a marked military as well as economic and political character. On the other hand, intercontinental organizations that depend almost entirely on United States directives are the Colombo Plan, the Alliance for Progress, and the Organization for Economic Cooperation and Development (OECD).

Andean Development Corporation (ADC) constituted 1967.
Member States: Chile, Colombia, Ecuador, Peru, Venezuela.
Aims: To speed the process of economic integration of the members.

Asociación Latino Americano de Libre Comercio (ALALC) (or Latin American Free Trade Association – LAFTA) constituted Treaty of Montevideo, February 18, 1960.
Member States: Argentina, Bolivia, Brazil, Chile, Colombia, Ecuador, Mexico, Paraguay, Peru, Uruguay, Venezuela.
Aims: To create a common market among the members through the abolition of customs and tariffs.

Alliance for Progress constituted Charter of Punta del Este, 1961.
Member States: Argentina, Barbados,

Bolivia, Brazil, Chile, Costa Rica, Dominican Republic, El Salvador, Guatemala, Haiti, Honduras, Jamaica, Mexico, Nicaragua, Panama, Paraguay, Peru, Trinidad and Tobago, Uruguay, USA, Venezuela. Cuba was excluded in 1962.
Aims: To coordinate the cooperation and economic-social development of the members.

Benelux constituted Treaty of London, September 5, 1944. Treaty of The Hague, February 3, 1958.
Member States: Belgium, Luxembourg, Netherlands.
Aims: To form a customs and economic union.

Central American Common Market (CACM) constituted 1961.
Member States: Costa Rica, El Salvador, Guatemala, Honduras, Nicaragua.
Aims: To ensure freedom of movement for goods, persons and capital among the members, in progressive association with the ALALC.

Council for Mutual Economic Aid (COMECON) constituted Treaty of Moscow, January 15, 1949.

Member States: Bulgaria, Czechoslovakia, Cuba (since 1962), German Democratic Republic, Hungary, Poland, Rumania, USSR. Albania left in 1961 and Yugoslavia is now an associate.
Aims: To promote the planned development and economic progress of the members. At the session at Sofia, June 1974, the members stated their aim was also to develop cooperation with all countries regardless of their political and social regime and, in particular, with the EEC.

European Economic Community (EEC)
Origins: The beginning dates from 1950 when the French Foreign Minister, Robert Schumann, proposed that France and Germany should pool their coal and steel industries. Eventually the European Coal and Steel Community (ECSC) came into force on August 25, 1952, and included also Belgium, Italy, Luxembourg, and the Netherlands. After the Treaty of Rome in 1957 the European Economic Community (EEC), generally known as the Common Market, came into being together with the European Atomic Energy Community (EURATOM or EAEC). Both organizations were among the same six members. The task of the latter was to create conditions necessary to utilize nuclear discoveries and produce nuclear energy.
Member States: The six original members are: Belgium, France, Federal Republic of Germany, Italy, Luxembourg, and the Netherlands. On January 1, 1973, another three states – Denmark,

Ireland, and the UK – entered as part of the EEC. Norway applied for membership but the people voted against joining the EEC. The EEC also has agreements with many countries, some of which are purely trade agreements, others provide for trade and cooperation and are an association agreement. It has trade agreements with countries of EFTA; agreement with two state trading countries – China and Rumania; association agreements with Cyprus, Greece, Malta, and Turkey as well as trade agreements with Portugal, Spain, and Yugoslavia. There are agreements with Mediterranean countries of Africa and Asia; trade agreements with Asian countries – Bangladesh, India, Pakistan, Sri Lanka, and 10 other countries; agreements with 14 Latin American countries; agreements with Canada and the USA. The Lomé Convention covers the relation of the EEC with 53 countries in Africa, the Caribbean, and Pacific (ACP countries).
Aims: As well as the creation of a common market for coal and steel and nuclear structures the Community aims at putting into practice forms of cooperation in all sectors in order to attain customs, economic, and monetary unity by 1980.
Principal Organs: The organs, which were separate for each of the three communities, have now been unified and refer to all three, the EEC, ECSC, and EURATOM. The main ones are:
1. *European Parliament* is composed of 198 representatives elected by the Parliaments of the nine member states, in numbers proportional to the population: 36 each from France, Federal Republic of Germany, Italy, and the UK, 14 each from Belgium and the Netherlands, 10 each from Denmark and Ireland, and eight from Luxembourg. It controls the activities of the other organs of the Common Market and approves their balance sheets. Its headquarters are at Strasbourg.
2. *The Council of Ministers* consists of ministers from each member state, with the presidency held in rotation for a six-month period. It coordinates the economic policy of the Common Market, bringing it into line with that of the member states. It is the main decision-making body.
3. *The European Court of Justice* safeguards the law in the interpretation of treaties in legal terms. There are nine judges appointed by member governments, partially replaced every three years. A judge can be reappointed. Its headquarters are in Luxembourg.
4. *The Commission* is the executive body with headquarters in Brussel (Brussels).
Conference of Heads of State of Equatorial Africa constituted June 1959.
Member States: Chad, Congo, Gabon,

Central African Empire. Cameroun is an associate member.
Aims: To establish a customs union between members and cooperation in the political field.

Council of the Entente constituted May 1959.
Member States: Benin, Ivory Coast, Niger, Togo, Upper Volta.
Aims: A political and economic alliance that has led to a customs union between the members and a program of collaboration of institutions and administration.

Council of Europe constituted London, May 5, 1949.
Member States: Original members were Belgium, Denmark, France, Ireland, Italy, Luxembourg, Norway, Netherlands, Sweden, and the UK. Later Austria, Cyprus, Federal Republic of Germany, Iceland, Malta, Switzerland, Greece, and Turkey joined.
Aims: To promote greater unity between the members, to safeguard common principles and facilitate economic and social development.

Principal Organs: A Parliamentary Assembly, composed of 147 members elected by the national Parliaments in proportion to relative strength of the political parties; a Committee of Ministers composed of the Foreign Ministers of the member countries, which meets once a month; and a Joint Committee of Ministers and Representatives of the Consultative Assembly. The European Commission and European Court of Human Rights were established in 1950 and are two of the major achievements of the Council of Europe. The Council administers cultural and educational programs as well as a legal one.

Nordic Council constituted Copenhagen (København), March 16, 1952.
Member States: Denmark, Finland, Iceland, Norway, Sweden.
Aims: It functions as a consultative body to promote social and economic cooperation between the Parliaments of the member states.

East African Community (EAC) constituted 1967.
Member States: Kenya, Tanzania, Uganda.
Aims: To strengthen economic relations with a view to integration.

Economic Community of West African States (ECOWAS) constituted Treaty of Lagos, May 28, 1975.
Member States: Angola, Benin, Gambia, Ghana, Guinea, Guinea-Bissau, Ivory Coast, Liberia, Mali, Mauritania, Nigeria, Senegal, Sierra Leone, Togo, Upper Volta.
Aims: The initiative for the formation of ECOWAS came from Nigeria and its main object is to overcome the barriers between English-speaking and French-

speaking countries, rather than the development of economic cooperation.

European Free Trade Association (EFTA) constituted Convention of Stockholm, November 20, 1959.
Member States: Austria, Iceland, Norway, Portugal, Sweden, and Switzerland. Finland is an associate. Denmark and the UK withdrew in 1972 when they joined the EEC.
Aims: To work out a common trade policy and progressively abolish customs duties.

Arab League constituted Cairo, March 22, 1945.
Member States: Algeria, Bahrain, Democratic Republic of Yemen, Egypt, Iraq, Jordan, Kuwait, Lebanon, Libya, Morocco, Oman, Qatar, Saudi Arabia, Syria, United Arab Emirates, Yemen.
Aims: To promote cooperation among the members in the fields of common defense, economic policy, social security, culture, communications, and for the affirmation of Arab aspirations. An Arab common market has been in force since 1965 between Egypt, Iraq, Jordan, Kuwait, and Syria.
Principal Organs: A General Council, which meets twice a year; a Political Committee, made up of the Foreign Ministers of the member states; Economic Council; Defense Council; Scientific Council; and General Secretariat.

Organization Commune Africain et Malgache (OCAM) constituted Charter of Tananarive, June 25, 1966.
Member States: Benin, Central African Empire, Gabon, Mauritius, Niger, Rwanda, Senegal, Togo, Upper Volta. Cameroun, Chad, Congo, Madagascar, and Zaire have withdrawn.
Aims: To develop economic cooperation between the members.

Organization for Economic Cooperation and Development (OECD) constituted Convention of Paris, December 14, 1960.
Member States: Australia, Austria, Belgium, Canada, Denmark, Federal Republic of Germany, France, Greece, Iceland, Ireland, Italy, Luxembourg, Netherlands, Norway, Portugal, Spain, Sweden, Switzerland, Turkey, UK, and the USA. Finland, Japan, and Yugoslavia are associates.
Aims: To promote the development of world economy and maintain financial stability in the member countries.

Organization for African Unity (OAU) constituted in Addis Ababa, May 25, 1963.
Member States: All independent African countries except Rhodesia and the Republic of South Africa.
Aims: The political and economic integration of the African states.
Principal Organs: Assembly of heads of state, which meets once a year to decide the general policy of the organization; the Council of Ministers; and General Secretariat.

Colombo Plan constituted in Colombo, May 1950.
Member States: Afghanistan, Burma, Cambodia, India, Indonesia, Iran, Laos, Malaysia, Maldive Islands, Nepal, Pakistan, Philippines, Singapore, South Korea, Sri Lanka, Thailand, Western Samoa, in association with Australia, Canada, Japan, New Zealand, UK, and USA.
Aims: To promote the economic development of Southeast Asia by giving technical and financial aid from the Industrial countries.

South Pacific Commission (SPC) constituted Treaty of Canberra, February 6, 1947.
Member States: Australia, France, New Zealand, UK, USA, and Western Samoa and in addition Nauru joined in 1969 and Fiji and Tonga in 1970.
Aims: To promote the economic and social development of the Pacific Islands.

POLITICO-MILITARY ORGANIZATIONS

The phase of the "cold war" between the Western Powers and the Communist bloc, a little after the end of World War II, led to the formation of two opposing systems of military alliances. On the one hand were those linked with the USA: NATO in Europe, OAS in Latin America, CENTO in Central Asia, SEATO (dissolved in 1975) in Southeast Asia, and ANZUS in Australasia and Oceania. On the other hand were countries linked with the USSR by the Warsaw Pact. These alliances have remained though there have been steps toward international control of armaments, for example, the USA–USSR agreement for the nonproliferation of atomic experiments above ground. The equilibrium supporting peaceful coexistence between the superpowers is, nevertheless, an armed one.

Association of South East Asian Nations (ASEAN) constituted 1967.
Member States: Indonesia, Malaysia, Philippines, Singapore, Thailand.
Aims: To reinforce the military security and the economic stability of the member countries.

Australia, New Zealand, United States (ANZUS) constituted San Francisco, November 1, 1951.
Member States: Australia, New Zealand, USA.
Aims: A defensive military alliance.

Central Treaty Organization (CENTO) constituted in the Pact of Baghdad, February 24, 1955.
Member States: Iran, Pakistan, Turkey, UK, USA. Iraq withdrew in 1969.

Aims: A defensive military alliance.
North Atlantic Treaty Organization (NATO) constituted in the Treaty of Washington, April 4, 1949.
Member States: Belgium, Canada, Denmark, Federal Republic of Germany, France, Iceland, Italy, Luxembourg, Netherlands, Norway, Portugal, Turkey, UK, USA. Greece withdrew in 1974.
Aims: A defensive alliance and a common military organization of the member countries based on the principle that the presence of American forces in Europe is essential both for Europe and the USA. According to the "declaration of principles" of June 1974, the European states will supply three-quarters of the conventional weapons and the USA, aided by France and the UK, will provide atomic protection.
Principal Organs: The Atlantic Council, a deliberative body composed of the ministerial or diplomatic representatives of the member countries; a Military Committee, which is formed from the Heads of State and functions as the supreme authority; and a Secretariat.

Organization of the American States (OAS) founded in 1948 and constituted in the Charter of Bogotá of December, 1951.
Member States: Argentina, Barbados, Bolivia, Brazil, Chile, Costa Rica, Dominican Republic, El Salvador, Guatemala, Haiti, Honduras, Jamaica, Mexico, Nicaragua, Panama, Paraguay, Peru, Trinidad and Tobago, Uruguay, USA, Venezuela. Cuba was excluded in 1962.
Aims: To guarantee the security of the Americas through the peaceful solution of controversies and economic-social cooperation between the members. (See Alliance for Progress).

Union Européenne Occidentale (UEO) constituted in Paris, October 23, 1954.
Member States: Belgium, Federal Republic of Germany, France, Italy, Luxembourg, Netherlands, UK.
Aims: To guarantee the security of the member states through progressive military integration. UEO works in close contact with NATO.

Warsaw Pact constituted May 14, 1955.
Member States: Bulgaria, Czechoslovakia, German Democratic Republic, Hungary, Rumania, USSR. Albania withdrew in 1968.
Aims: To ensure military defense by the integration of armed forces and the political collaboration of members.
Principal Organs: Consultative Political Committee, with a representative from each member, United Supreme Command, with its headquarters in Moscow.

Placename Index

Opposite: the earth, photographed by
the astronauts of *Apollo 11*.

303

Aalborg 58 G3
Aarhus 58 G3
Aba 176 D5
Ābādān 112 D4
Abakan 121 M4
Abaya L., *lake* 168 G5
Abbai, *river* 168 G4
Abd al Kuri 177 J4
Abéché 168 F4
Abeokuta 168 D5
Aberdare Mts., *mountains* 168 G6
Aberdeen, *U.S.A., North Dakota* 208 H2
Aberdeen, *Scotland* 58 E3
Aberdeen, *U.S.A., Washington* 208 C2
Aberdeen L., *lake* 216 H2
Abidjan 168 C5
Abilene, *U.S.A., Kansas* 208 H4
Abilene, *U.S.A., Texas* 208 H5
Abitibi, *river* 216 J3
Abitibi, L., *lake* 200 F3
Abo, *region* 176 E3
Abomey 168 D5
Abrolhos, Arquipélago dos, *island group* 257 F4
Absaroka Ra., *mountains* 200 E3
Abū Dhabi 112 D4
Abū Kamāl 81 H3
Abut Hd., *cape* 277 D6
Aby, Lagune, *lake* 176 C5
Abyssinian Highlands 112 C5
Acámbaro 232 C2
Acapulco de Juárez 201 F5
Acapulco Trench, *sea feature* 201 E5
Acari, Serra, *mountains* 256 D2
Accra 168 C5
Achimota 168 C5
Acklins I., *island* 201 G4
Aconcagua, Co., *mt.* 201 B6
Aconquija, Nev. de, *mts.* 264 B1
Adafer, *region* 168 C4
Adama 177 G5
Adamoua, Massif de l', *mountains* 168 E5
Adam, Mt., *mountain* 264 C4
Adams, Mt., *U.S.A., mt.* 208 C2
Adams, Mt., New Zealand, *mountain* 276 F5
Adams Peak, *mountain* 136 F5
Adana 49 L5
Adapazari 81 F3
Adare, Cape, *cape* 292 L2
Ad Dahnā, *region* 112 D4
Ad Dammām 136 C3
Addis Ababa 168 G5
Adelaide 280 D5
Adelaide I., *island* 292 R2
Adelaide Pena., *peninsula* 216 H2
Adel-Esa, *region* 177 H4
Aden 112 D5
Aden, Gulf of, *gulf* 112 D4
Adigrat 177 G4
Adirondack Mountains, *mountains* 209 M3
Adi Ugri 177 G4
Admer, Erg d', *sand dunes* 168 D3
Admiralty G., *gulf* 272 E2
Admiralty Inlet, *Canada, inlet* 216 J1
Admiralty I., *island* 200 D3
Admiralty Is., *island group* 113 J6
Admiralty Mts., *mts.* 292 L2
Adoni 136 E4
Adoua, *river* 168 D4
Adrar 168 C3
Adrar des Iforas, *mts.* 168 D3
Adrar Edekel, *mountain* 176 D3
Adrar Sotuf, *region* 176 B3
Adriatic Sea 48 H4
Aduwa 177 G4
Aegean Sea 48 K5
Afghanistan 112 E4
Afikpo 176 D5
Aflāj, Al, *region* 136 B3
Afognak Is., *island* 200 C3
Afyon 81 F3
Agadès 168 D4
Agadir 168 C2
Agalega Is., *island group* 112 D6
Agassiz, C., *cape* 292 R2
Agaumdir, *region* 177 G4
Agboville 176 C5
Agen 80 C2
Agra 112 E4
Agrakhanskiy Poluostrov, *peninsula* 81 H2
Aguadas 233 F4
Aguadilla 233 G3
Agua Prieta 232 C1
Aguarague, Cord. de, *mountains* 256 C5
Aguascalientes 232 C2
Aguja, C. de la, *mts.* 233 F3
Aguja, Pta., *cape* 248 A3
Agulhas Bank, *sea bank* 169 E9
Agulhas Basin, *sea basin* 32 F5
Agulhas, C., *cape* 169 F9
Agulhas Negras, *mt.* 248 E5
Ahaggar, *mountains* 168 D3
Ahimanawa Ra., *mts.* 276 G4
Ahmadnagar 136 E4
Ahmar, Erg el, *sand dunes* 176 C3
Ahmar Mts., *mountains* 176 H5
Ahmedabad 112 E4
Ahuachapán 232 E3
Ahvāz 112 D4
Ahvenanmaa, *island group* 48 J2
Ain Salah 168 D3
Ain Sefra 168 C2
Aïn-Sefra, *region* 168 C3
Aïr ou Azbine, *mts.* 168 D4
Aitken, Mt., *mountain* 277 B8
Aix-en-Provence 80 C2
Aiyina C5
Ajaccio 48 H5
Ajedabya 177 F2
Ajjer, *mountains* 168 D3
Ajmer 112 E4
Ajo 208 E5
Akaroa 277 E6
Akaroa Harb., *harbour* 277 E6
Akchar, Dunes de l', *sand dunes* 176 B3
Akesu 112 F3
Aketi 168 F5
Akhdar, J. al, *Libya, mountains* 176 F2
Akhdar, J. al., *Muscat & Oman, mountains* 112 D4
Akhtyrka 59 K3
Akimiski I., *island* 200 F3
Akita 121 R6
Akkyr, G., *mountains* 49 N5
Aklavik 200 D2
Akola 136 E3
Akpatok I., *island* 217 L2
Akron 200 F3
Akseki 81 F3
Aksha 121 O4
Aksum 177 G4
Aktyubinsk 59 N3
Akureyri 58 C2
Alabama, *river* 200 F4
Alabama, *state* 209 K5
Al Aḥmadī 136 B3
Alajuela 233 E4
Al Amārah 136 B2
Alapayevsk 59 N3
Al Aqabah 81 G4
Al 'Arīsh 81 G4
Alaska, *state* 200 C2
Alaska, Gulf of, *gulf* 200 C3
Alaska Highway 216 C2
Alaska Pena., *peninsula* 200 C3
Alaska Ra., *mountains* 32 B2
Alatyr 59 L3
Alayskiy Khr., *mts.* 112 E4
Albacete 80 B3
Al Balyanā 177 G3
Albania 48 J5
Albany, *Australia* 280 B5
Albany, *U.S.A., Georgia* 209 L5
Albany, *U.S.A., New York* 209 N3
Albany, *river* 200 F3
Albatross B., *bay* 280 E3
Albatross Plateau, *sea feature* 283 E2
Albatross Pt., *cape* 276 F4
Albemarle Sd., *sound* 209 M4
Alberga, *river* 280 D4
Albert, *river* 273 G3
Alberta, *province* 216 F3
Albert, Lake, *see L. Mobutu Sese Seko* 177 G5
Albert Lea 209 J3
Albert Nile, *river* 177 G5
Albi 80 C2
Albina, Pta., *cape* 169 E7
Alborz, Reshteh-ye, *mts.* 112 D4
Albuquerque 208 F4
Albury 273 J7
Alcazarquivir 80 B3
Alcira 80 B3
Alcoa 209 L4
Alcoy 80 B3
Aldabra Is., *island group* 169 H6
Aldabra Ridge, *sea feature* 145 B3
Aldan 121 P4
Aldan, *river* 113 H2
Aldanskoye Nagor'ye, *highlands* 113 H3
Aleksandrovsk-Sakhalinskiy 121 R4
Alès 80 C2
Alessandria 80 D2
Ålesund 58 F2
Aleutian Basin, *sea feature* 283 B1
Aleutian Islands, *island group* 283 B1
Aleutian Trench, *sea feature* 283 B1
Alevina, M., *cape* 113 J3
Alexander Archo., *island group* 200 D3
Alexander Bay 169 E8
Alexander I., *island* 292 R2
Alexandra 277 C7
Alexandria, *Egypt* 168 F2
Alexandria, *U.S.A., Louisiana* 209 J5
Alexandria, *U.S.A., Virginia* 209 M4
Alexandrina, L., *lake* 273 G7
Aleysk 120 L4
Al Fayyūm 168 G3
Alfonse I., *island* 185 G3
Alfred & Marie Ra., *mountains* 272 E4
Algeria 168 C3
Al Ghurdaqah 177 G3
Algiers, *see El Djezair* 176 D2
Algoa B., *bay* 169 F9
Al Hasakah 81 H3
Al Hillah 136 B2
Al Hudaydah 112 D5
Al Hufūf 136 B3
Alicante 80 B3
Alice Springs 280 D4
Aligarh 136 E3
Al Ismā'īlīya 177 G2
Aliwal North 169 F9
Al Jawf, *Saudi Arabia* 136 A3
Al Jīzah, *see El Giza* 168 G2
Al Khārijah 168 G3
Alkmaar 58 F3
Al Kūt 136 B2
Al Lādhiqīyah 112 C4
Allahabad 112 F4
Allakh-Yun' 121 Q3
Allegheny, *river* 209 M3
Allegheny Mts., *mts.* 200 F4
Allentown 209 M3
Allepey 137 E5
Alliance 208 G3
Allier, *river* 48 G4
Al Līth 136 B3
Alma-Ata 112 E3
Al Madinah 112 C4
AlMafraq 81 G4
Al Mahallah al'Kubrā 168 G2
Al Manāmah 112 D4
Al Manṣūrāh 177 G2
Al Marj 177 F2
Almeria 80 B3
Al Minyā 168 G3
Al Mukhā 136 B4
Al Mūṣil 112 D4
Alor, *island* 113 H6
Aloysius, Mt., *mountain* 272 E5
Alpercatas, S. das, *mts.* 257 E3
Alpine 208 G5
Alpine-Himalayan System 24 F2
Alps, *mountains* 48 H4
Al Quṣayr 177 G3
Al Ramādī 168 H2
Alta 58 H1
Altamaha, *river* 209 L5
Altay, *mountains* 112 F3
Altiplano, *plateau* 248 C4
Altoona 209 M3
Altyn Tagh, *mountains* 112 F4
Al 'Uqalah 80 E4
Al Uqsur 81 G5
Alva 208 H4
Alvdal 58 G2
Al Wajh 112 C4
Al Zaqāzīq 177 G2
Amadeus, L., *lake* 280 D4
Amadjuak 217 K2
Amadjuak L., *lake* 200 G2
Amagasaki 113 H4
Amarillo 208 G4
Amazonas, *river* 248 D3
Amazon Basin, *region* 248 C3
Amazon, Mouths of the, *river mouths* 248 E3
Ambarchik 121 T3
Ambato 256 B3
Ambato, Sa., *mountains* 264 B1
Ambatolampy 169 H7
Ambatatondrazaka 169 H7
Ambergris Cay, *reef* 233 E3
Ambodifototra 169 H7
Ambositra 185 F5
Ambovombe 169 H8
Ambre, C. d', *cape* 169 H7
Amderma 59 N1
Ameca 232 C2
Amery Ice Shelf 292 F2
Amiens 58 F4
Amirante Is., *islands group* 145 B3
Amman 49 L6
Amravati 136 E3
Amritsar 112 E4
Amsterdam 48 G3
Amsterdam, I., *island* 145 C4
Amsterdam St. Paul Plateau, *sea feature* 145 D4
Am Timan 168 F4
Amu-Dar'ya, *river* 112 E4
Amundsen Gulf, *gulf* 200 D2
Amundsen Scott, *scientific base* 292 L1
Amundsen Sea 32 C5
Amur, *river* 113 H3
Anaconda 208 E2
Anadyr' 113 K2
Anadyr', *river* 113 K2
Anadyrskiy Zaliv, *bay* 113 L2
Anadyrskoye Ploskogor'ye, *tableland* 121 U3
Anaheim 208 D5
Anak, Krakatau, *island* 113 G6
Analalava 169 H7
Anambas, Kep., *island group* 137 H5
Anamur Br., *cape* 81 G3
Añatuya 264 B1
Anchorage 200 C2
Ancohuma, Nev. de., *mountain* 248 C4
Ancona 80 D2
Ancua, *mountain* 177 G4
Ancud, *island* 264 A3
Ancud, G. de, *gulf* 249 B7
Andaman Basin, *sea feature* 112 F5
Andaman Is., *island group* 112 F5
Andaman-Nicobar Ridge, *sea feature* 145 D2
Andaman Sea 112 F5
Andean Systems, *mts.* 24 D4
Anderson, *river* 216 E2
Andes 233 F4
Andes, *mountains* 248 B3
Andizhan 112 E3
Andorra 80 C2
Andorra, *state* 48 G4
Andrew Seamount, *sea feature* 145 B2
Andros, I., *Bahama Islands, island* 201 G4
Anegada Pass., *strait* 201 G5
Aného 176 D5
Aneto, P. de, *mountain* 48 G4
Angamos, Pta., *cape* 248 B5
Angara, *river* 112 F3
Angara Basin, *sea feature* 289 L1
Angara Shield, *plateau* 25 H2
Angarsk 121 N4
Angel de la Guarda, *island* 201 E4
Angers 58 E4
Anglem, Mt., *mountain* 277 B8
Anglesey, I. of, *island* 58 E3
Angmagssalik 217 O2
Angoche 169 G7
Angola 169 E7
Angoulême 80 C2
Anguilla, *island* 201 G5
An-hsi 112 F3
Anie, Pic d', *mountain* 80 B2
Anisiy, M., *cape* 121 Q2
Aniya, M., *cape* 121 R5
Anjouan, *island* 185 F4
Anjŭ 121 P6
An-k'ang 113 G4
Ankara 49 L5
Ankazoabo 169 H8
Ankober 177 G5
Ann, C., *cape* 217 K4
Annaba 168 D2
An'Nabk 81 G4
An Nafūd, *region* 112 D4
An Najaf 136 B2
Annapolis, *Canada* 217 L4
Annapolis, *U.S.A.* 209 M 4
Ann Arbor 209 L3
Anniston 209 K5
An-shan 113 H3
Antakya 81 G3
Antalaha 169 J7
Antalya 81 F3
Antalya Körfezi, *bay* 49 K5
Antananarivo 169 H7
Antarctica 33 G5
Antarctic Ice Cap 24 G5
Antarctic Pena., *peninsula* 292 R2
Antares Bank, *sea feature* 145 B5
Anti-Atlas, *mountains* 168 C2
Anticosti I., *island* 200 G3
Antigua 232 D3
Antigua, *island* 201 G5
Antipodes, Is., *islands* 33 K5
Antofagasta 248 B5
Antongil, B. d', *bay* 169 H7
Antrim Mts., *mountains* 58 E3
Antsirabe 185 F4
An-tung 113 H3
Antwerpen 48 G3
Anvers I., *island* 292 R2
Anyama 176 C5
An-yang 121 O6
Anzhero-Sudzhensk 121 L4
Aomori 113 J3
Aorangi Mts., *mountains* 276 F5
Aotea Harb., *harbour* 276 F3
Aouk, B., *river* 177 F5
Aouker, *region* 168 C4
Apalachee Bay, *bay* 209 L5
Apalachicola 209 K6
Aparri 137 K4
Apodi, Chapado do, *region* 257 F3
Appalachian Mountains, *mountains* 200 F4
Appennini, *mountains* 48 H4
Appleton 209 K3
Apucarana, Sa. da, *mts.* 257 D5
Apure, *river* 248 B2
Apuseni, Muntii, *mts.* 48 J4
Aqaba, G. of, *gulf* 49 L6
Aquidauana 256 D5
Arabian Basin, *sea feature* 145 C2
Arabian Peninsula, *region* 33 F3
Arabian Sea 145 C2
Arabian Shield, *sea feature* 25 F3
Aracaju 248 F4
Aracati 257 F3
Arad 81 E2
Arafura Sea 280 D2
Aragats, *mountain* 283 H3
Araguaia, *river* 256 D4
Araguari, *river* 257 D2
Arak 120 G6
Arakan Yoma, *mts.* 112 F4
Araks, *river* 49 M5
Aral'sk 112 E3
Aral'skoye More, *sea* 112 E3
Araras, Sa. das, *mts.* 257 D4
Ararat 273 H7
Ararat, Mt., *see Büyük Ağri Daği* 49 M5
Araripe, Sa. do, *mts.* 248 E3
Aras, *river* 49 M5
Arauca 256 C2
Arauca, *river* 233 F4
Aravalli Ra., *mountains* 136 E3
Araxá 257 E4
Arbay Hēre 121 N5
Archer, *river* 280 E3
Archer Bay 273 H2
Artic Bay, *trading post* 216 J1
Arctic Ocean 32 B1
Arḍ aş Şawwān, *region* 81 G4
Ardennes, *mountains* 58 F4
Arena, Pt., *cape* 208 C4
Arendal 58 G2
Arequipa 248 B4
Arezzo 80 D2
Argentina 249 C6
Argentino, L., *lake* 249 B7
Argentine Basin, *sea feature* 100 C7
Argun, *river* 113 G3
Arica 248 B4
Arid, C., *cape* 272 D6
Arima 233 G3
Aripuanā, *river* 256 C3
Arivonimamo 185 F4
Arizona, *state* 208 E5
Arkagala 121 R3
Arkansas, *river* 200 E40
Arkansas, *state* 209 J40
Arkansas City 208 H4
Arkhangel'sk 49 M2
Arles 80 C2
Armagnac, *region* 48 F4
Armavir 81 H2
Armenia 256 B2
Armidale 273 K6
Armstrong 216 F3
Arnhem 58 F3
Arnhem, C., *cape* 280 D3
Arnhem Land, *region* 280 D3
Aroánia Óri, *mountain* 81 E3
Arowhana, *mountain* 276 G4
Ar Rachidiya 168 C2
Arras 58 F3
Arrecife, Pto., *cape* 49 B3
Ar Rihāb, *region* 49 M6
Ar Rimāl, *region* 99 H3
Arrowsmith, Mt., *mt.* 277 D6
Arrowtown 277 C7
Artemovskiy 59 N3
Artesia 208 G5
Arthur's Pass, *mt. pass* 277 D6
Arti 59 N3
Aru, Kep., *island group* 113 H6
Arua 177 G5
Aruba, *island* 201 G5
Arunta, *see Simpson Desert* 280 D4
Arusha 185 E3
Arvida 217 K4
Arys' 120 J5
Asahigawa 113 J3
Asansol 137 F3
Asbest 59 N3
Ascension I., *island* 100 E5
Asedjrad, *mountains* 80 C5
Asekrem, *mountain* 176 D3
Ashburton, *New Zealand* 277 D6
Ashburton, *river* 280 B4
Ashburton Ra., *mts.* 280 D3
Asheville 209 L4
Ashkhabad 112 D4
Ashmore Reef, *reef* 272 D2
Ashuanipi L., *lake* 217 L3
'Āṣī, *river* 81 G3
Asinara 80 D3
Asino 121 L4
Asir 112 D5
Asmara 168 G4
Asosa 171 G4
Asoteriba, J., *mountain* 177 G3
Aspiring, Mt., *mountain* 277 C7
Assab 112 D5
Assiniboine, *river* 216 H4
Assiniboine, Mt., *mt.* 200 E3
Assumption, *island* 185 F3
As Suways 169 G3
Astoria 208 C2
Astove I., *island* 185 F4
Astrakhan' 49 M4
Asuncion 248 D5
Aswān 168 G3
Aswan Dam, *dam* 177 G3
Asyūt 168 G3
Atacama, Desierto de, *desert* 248 C5
Atacama, Puna de, *mts.* 248 C5
Atakora, Chaine de l', *mountains* 176 D4
Atakpamé 176 D5
Atar 168 B3
Atbara 168 G4
Atbara, *river* 177 G4
Atbasar 120 J4
Athabasca, *river* 216 F3
Athabasca, L., *lake* 200 E3
Atherton 273 J3
Atherton Plateau, *plateau* 280 E3
Athinai 48 J5
Athos, *mountain* 48 K5
Ati, J., *mountains* 176 E3
Atikonak L., *lake* 217 L3
Atka 121 S3
Atkarsk 59 L3
Atlanta 200 F4
Atlantic-Antarctic or Atlantic-Indian Ridge, *sea feature* 100 E7
Atlantic City 209 N4
Atlantic-Indian Antarctic Basin, *sea feature* 292 B2
Atlantic Ocean 289 O3
Atlas Saharien, *mts.* 168 C2
Atlixco 232 D3
At Tā'if 136 B3
Attawapiskat, *river* 216 J3
At Tih, *region* 81 G4
Attu, *island* 113 K3
Auckland 281 H3
Auckland Is., *islands* 33 K5
Augsburg 58 G4
Augusta, *Australia* 272 C6
Augusta, *U.S.A., Georgia* 209 L5
Augusta, *U.S.A., Maine* 209 O3
Augustus, Mt., *mt.* 280 B4
Aurès, *mountains* 48 G5
Ausangate, N., *mt.* 248 B4
Austin, *U.S.A., Texas* 201 F4
Austin, L., *lake* 272 C5
Austr. Alps, *mountains* 280 E5
Australian Antarctic Territory 292 J2
Australian Basin, *sea feature* 280 E4
Austr. Capital Territory 273 J7
Australian Shield, *plateau* 25 H4
Austral Ridge, *sea feature* 283 C3
Austria 48 H4
Autland de Navarro 232 C3
Avalon Pena., *peninsula* 216 M4
Aves, *island* 233 G3
Aves, Islas de, *island group* 233 G3
Aves Rise, *sea feature* 100 B4
Avignon 80 C2
Avon, *Australia, river* 272 C6
Awash, *river* 168 H5
Awatere, *river* 276 E5
Axel Heiberg Glacier 292 N1
Axel Heiberg I., *island* 289 Q2
Ayachi, Dj., *mountain* 176 C2
Ayacucho, *Peru* 256 B4
Ayaguz 120 L5
Ayak Küm Köl, *lake* 120 L6
Ayaviri 256 B4
Aydin 81 F3
Aygyn' 121 P4

Ayon, O., *island* 121 T2
Ayr, *Australia* 273 J3
Ayr, Scotland 58 E3
Ayutthaya 137 H4
Azao, Mt., *mountain* 168 D3
Azaouak, *river* 176 D4
Azefal, Dunes de l', *sand dunes* 176 B3
Azerbaydzhanskaya S.S.R., *republic* 120 G5
Azores, *islands* 100 D3
Azores-Cape St. Vincent Ridge, *sea feature* 100 D3
Azuero, Pena. de, *peninsula* 248 A2
Azul 264 C2
Azul, *river* 232 E3
Az Zallaf 80 D5
Az Zaqāziq 81 F4

Baba, *mountains* 81 E3
Bāb al Māndab, *strait* 168 H4
Bābol 120 H6
Back, *river* 216 H2
Backbone Ras., *mountains* 216 E2
Backstairs Pass., *strait* 273 G7
Bac Lieu 137 H5
Bacolod 137 K4
Badajoz 80 B3
Badiet ash Shām, *region* 112 C4
Badlands, *region* 200 E3
Bafatá 176 B4
Baffin Basin, *sea feature* 289 P2
Baffin Bay, *bay* 289 P2
Baffin-Greenland Rise, *sea feature* 289 P2
Baffin Island 200 G2
Bafia 176 E5
Bāfq 136 C2
Bagamoyo 185 E3
Bagé 264 C2
Baghdād 112 D4
Baghrash Kol, *lake* 121 L5
Bagoé, *river* 176 C4
Baguezane, Mts., *mts.* 176 D4
Bahama Islands, *island group* 201 G4
Baharīya Oasis 177 F3
Bahawalpur 136 E3
Bahia Blanca 249 C6
Bahia, Islas de la, *island group* 233 E3
Bahias C. dos, *cape* 264 B3
Bahraich 136 F3
Bahrain, *island* 112 D4
Bahr el Abyadh, *river* 177 G4
Bahr el Azraq, *river* 177 G4
Bahr el Ghazal, *region* 176 E4
Bahr el Ghazal, *river* 168 F5
Bahr el Jebel, *river* 168 G5
Baibokoum 176 E5
Bailey Deep, *sea feature* 24 J3
Bailundo 169 E7
Baiyuda Desert, *desert* 177 G4
Baja California, *peninsula* 201 E4
Bakal 59 N3
Baker, *U.S.A., Oregon* 208 D3
Baker Foreland, *cape* 216 H2
Baker Lake, *lake* 216 H2
Baker, Mt., *mountain* 200 D3
Bakersfield 208 D4
Bakhmach 59 K3
Baku 49 N5
Bala, Cerros de, *mts.* 256 C4
Balabac I., *island* 137 J5
Balakovo 59 L3
Balashov 59 L3
Balboa 233 F4
Balclutha 277 C8
Bald Head, *cape* 273 C7
Baldy Mt., *mountain* 208 G1
Baldy Peak, *mountain* 208 F5
Baleares, Islas, *island group* 48 G5
Baleia, Pta. da, *cape* 248 F4
Baley 121 O4
Bali 176 E5
Bali, *island* 113 G6
Balikesir 81 F3
Balikpapan 113 G6
Bali Trough, *sea feature* 145 E3
Balkhash 120 K5
Balkhash, Oz., *lake* 112 E3
Ballarat 280 E5
Ballard, L., *lake* 272 D5
Balleny Basin, *sea feature* 292 L2
Balleny Islands, *island group* 292 L2
Bally 136 F3
Balta 81 F2
Baltic Sea 48 J2
Baltic Shield, *plateau* 25 F2
Baltimore 200 G4
Baluchistan, *region* 112 E4
Bam 136 C3
Bamako 168 C4
Bambari 168 F5
Bañados de Atuel, *swamp* 264 B2
Bañados del Izozog, *swamp* 256 C4
Banalia 177 F5
Bananal, Ilha do, *region* 257 D4
Banās, Rās, *cape* 177 G3
Banda Aceh 112 F5
Banda, Laut, *sea* 113 H6
Bandama, *river* 176 C5
Bandar, *see Machilipatnam* 136 F4
Bandar 'Abbās 112 D4
Bandar-e Lengeh 136 C3
Bandar-e-Pahlavī 120 G6
Bandar Seri Begawan 113 G5
Bandundu 168 E6
Bandung 113 G6
Banff, *Canada* 216 F3
Bangalore 112 E5
Bangassou 168 F5
Bangka, *island* 113 G6
Bangka, Selat, *strait* 137 H6
Bangkok, *see Krung Thep* 137 H4
Bangladesh 112 F4
Bangor, *U.S.A.* 209 O3
Bangui, *Central African Empire* 168 E5
Bangweulu, L., *lake* 169 F7
Banhā 177 G2
Bani 233 F3
Bani, *river* 176 C4
Bani, Djebel, *mountains* 176 C3
Bani Mazār 177 G3
Bani Suwayf 168 G3
Banja Luka 80 E2
Banjarmasin 113 G6
Banjul 168 B4
Banjuwangi 137 J6
Banks I., *Australia, island* 280 E3
Banks I., *Canada, island* 200 D2
Banks Str., *strait* 273 J8
Ban Me Thuot 137 H4
B. Pakse 113 G5
Bantadji, Mt., *mountain* 184 C2
Bantaeng 113 G6
Banzare Coast, *region* 292 J2
Banzare Seamount, *sea feature* 292 F2
Barabinskaya Step', *region* 120 K4
Bărăganul, *region* 81 F2
Barahona 233 F3
Baranoa 233 F3
Baranof I., *island* 200 D3
Barbados, *island* 201 H5
Barbuda, *island* 201 G5
Barcaldine 273 J4
Barcelona, *Spain* 48 G5
Barcelona, *Venezuela* 248 C1
Barcelos, *Brazil* 256 C3
Barcoo, *river* 280 E4
Bardera 177 H5
Bareilly 112 E4
Bar el Ghazal, *river* 184 D2
Barentsovo, More, *sea* 289 K2
Bari 48 J5
Bariñas 233 F4
Barisal 112 F4
Barito, *river* 137 J6
Barkly Highway 272 G3
Barkly Tableland, *plateau* 280 D3
Barlee, L., *lake* 280 B4
Barlee Ra., *mountains* 280 B4
Barnaul 49 R3
Barnes Icecap 217 K1
Barquisimeto 248 C1
Barranquilla 248 B1
Barren, Îles, *island group* 185 F4
Barrington, Mt., *mt.* 280 F5
Barrow I., *island* 280 B4
Barrow, Pt., *Alaska, cape* 200 C2
Barrow Str., *strait* 200 F2
Barth Bank, *sea feature* 292 S3
Bartholomew Deep, *sea feature* 248 B5
Bartin 81 G3
Bartle Frere, Mt., *mt.* 273 J3
Barwon, *river* 280 E4
Basankusu 184 C2
Basilan I., *island* 137 K5
Baskatong, *lake* 209 M2
Baskerville, C., *cape* 272 D3
Basel 80 C2
Basoko 168 F5
Basra 112 D4
Bassas da India, *island* 185 E5
Bassein 112 F5
Basseterre, *island* 233 G3
Basso, Plat. de, *plateau* 177 F4
Bass Strait, *strait* 280 E5
Bastia 80 D2
Bata 168 D5
Batabano, G. de, *gulf* 233 E2
Batagay 121 Q3
Batan Is., *island group* 113 H4
Batha, *river* 177 E4
Bathurst, *Australia* 273 J6
Bathurst, C., *cape* 200 D2
Bathurst Inlet 216 G2
Bathurst Inlet, *inlet* 216 G2
Bathurst I., *Australia* 280 D3
Bathurst I., *Canada* island 200 E2
Batista, Chapada da, *region* 257 E3
Batna 168 D2
Baton Rouge 200 F4
Batouri 184 C2
Battambang 113 G5
Battle Harbour 217 M3
Batu, *mountain* 168 G5
Batumi 49 M5
Baubau 113 H6
Bauchi 184 B1
Baudo, Serrania, *mts.* 233 F4
Bauer Deep, *sea feature* 283 E3
Bauld, C., *cape* 200 H3
Bauru 264 D1
Bayamo 233 F2
Bayan Kara Shan, *mts.* 137 G2
Bay City, *U.S.A. Michigan* 209 L3
Bay City, *U.S.A., Texas* 209 H6
Baydag Bogdo, *mountain* 137 G1
Baydaratskaya Guba, *gulf* 120 J3
Baykal, Oz., *lake* 112 G3
Baytown 209 J6
Bazaruto, I. do., *island* 169 G8
Beagle Bay, *bay* 280 D3
Beal Ra., *mountains* 280 E4
Bear I., *Antarctica, island* 292 P2
Bear L., *lake* 208 E3
Beardmore Glacier 292 L1
Beata, C., *cape* 201 G5
Beatton River 216 E3
Beaufort Basin, *sea feature* 289 S2
Beaufort Sea 289 S2
Beaufort West 184 D6
Beaumont, *U.S.A.* 209 J5
Beaverhead Ra., *mts.* 208 E2
Beaverlodge 216 F3
Béchar 168 C2
Beddouza, Ras, *cape* 168 C2
Beechey Point 216 C1
Begicheva, O., *island* 112 G2
Beira 169 G7
Beirūt 49 L6
Bejaïa 176 D2
Belaya Tserkov' 81 F2
Belcher Is., *island group* 200 G3
Belém 248 E3
Belfast 48 F3
Belgaum 136 E4
Belgium 48 G3
Belgorod 59 K3
Belgorod-Dnestrovskiy 81 F2
Belitung 113 G6
Belize 201 F5
Belize, *state* 201 F3
Bellary 136 E4
Bella Vista, *Argentina* 264 B1
Belle Île, *island* 48 F4
Belle I., *island* 217 M3
Belle Isle, Str. of, *strait* 217 M3
Bellin 217 K2
Bellingshausen Sea 292 Q2
Bello 233 F4
Bellona Plateau, *sea feature* 283 B3
Belmopan 201 F5
Belogorsk 121 P4
Belo Horizonte 248 E4
Belomorsk 59 K2
Belomorsko-Baltiyskiy K., *canal* 59 K2
Beloretsk 59 N3
Belorusskaya S.S.R., *republic* 120 E4
Belo-sur-Tsiribihina 185 F4
Belovo 121 L4
Beloye More, *sea* 48 L2
Belozersk 59 K2
Bel'tsy 81 F2
Belukha, G., *mountain* 121 L5
Belyando, *river* 280 E4
Bemarah, Plat du., *plateau* 169 H7
Bemidji 209 J2
Benadir, *region* 185 F2
Benalla 273 J7
Bend 208 C3
Bendigo 273 H7
Bengal, Bay of, *sea* 145 D2
Bengal Plateau, *sea feature* 145 D2
Benghazi 168 E2
Ben Ghnema, Jebel, *mountains* 176 E3
Bengo, B. do, *bay* 184 C3
Benguela 169 E7
Beni, *river* 248 C4
Beni-Abbès 176 C2
Benin 168 D4
Benin, Bight of, *gulf* 168 D5
Benin City 168 D5
Ben Nevis, *New Zealand, mountain* 277 C7
Ben Ohau Ra., *mts.* 277 D7
Bentinck I., *Australia, island* 273 G3
Benue, *river* 168 D5
Beograd 48 J4
Berber 177 G4
Berbera 168 H4
Berberati 184 C2
Berdichev 81 F2
Berdyansk 81 G2
Berezniki 59 N2
Berezovo 120 J3
Bergamo 80 D2
Bergen, *Norway* 48 G2
Berhampur, *India, Orissa* 136 F4
Beringa, O., *island* 121 T4
Beringovskiy 121 U3
Bering Sea 283 B1
Bering Strait, *strait* 283 C1
Berkeley, *U.S.A.* 208 C4
Berkner I., *island* 292 S2
Berkshire Hills, *hills* 209 N3
Berlin 48 H3
Berlin, Mt., *mountain* 292 O2
Bermejo, *river* 248 D5
Bermuda, *island* 100 B3
Bern 48 G4
Bernier B., *bay* 216 J1
Bernier I., *island* 272 B4
Berri 273 H6
Berry Is., *island group* 209 M6
Berti Hills, *mountains* 177 F4
Besançon 80 C2
Beskidy Zachodnie, *mountains* 48 J4
Bessemer 209 K5
Bétaré-Oya 176 E5
Bethlehem, *Rep of South Africa* 184 D5
Betioky 169 H8
Betpak Dala, *steppe* 112 E3
Betroka 169 H8
Betsiboka, *river* 185 F4
Bettles 216 B2
Beverley, *Australia* 272 C6
Bey D., *mountain* 49 K5
Beyla 176 C5
Beypazari 81 F3
Beyşehir G., *lake* 48 K5
Bezhetsk 59 K3
Bezhitsa 59 K3
Béziers 80 C2
Bhagalpur 137 F3
Bhamo 112 F4
Bhavnagar 136 E3
Bhopal 112 E4
Bhuj 136 D3
Bhutan 112 F4
Bia, P., *mountain* 137 H4
Biak, *island* 280 D2
Bialystok 58 H3
Biarritz 80 B2
Bickerton I., *island* 272 G2
Bida 168 D5
Bi Doup, *mountain* 137 H4
Bielefeld 58 G3
Bienville, Lac, *lake* 217 K3
Big Belt Mts., *mts.* 208 E2
Biggar, *Canada* 216 G3
Bighorn, *river* 208 F2
Bighorn Mts., *mts.* 200 E3
Big I., *island* 217 K2
Big Smoky Valley, *region* 208 D4
Big Spring 208 G5
Big Trout L., *lake* 217 J3
Bijagós, Arqo. dos, *island group* 168 B4
Bikaner 136 E3
Bikin 121 Q5
Bilaspur 136 F3
Bilauktaung Ra., *mts.* 137 G4
Bilbao 48 F4
Biloela 273 K4
Bimberi, Mt., *mountain* 280 E5
Binga, Mte., *mountain* 185 E4
Bingerville 168 C5
Bintulu 137 J5
Birch Mts., *mountains* 200 E3
Birdsville 273 G5
Birhan, *mountain* 168 G4
Bīrjand 112 D4
Birkenhead, *New Zealand* 276 F3
Birksgate Ra., *mts.* 272 F5
Birmingham, *England* 48 F5
Birmingham, *U.S.A.* 200 F4
Birnin Kebbi 168 D4
Birni n'Konni 176 D4
Birobidzhan 121 Q5
Birsk 59 M3
Biscay, Bay of, *bay* 48 F4
Biscoe Bay, *bay* 292 N2
Biscoe Is., *island group* 292 R2
Biskra 168 D2
Bismarck 208 G2
Bismarck Archipelago, *island group* 113 J6
Bismarck, C., *cape* 200 K2
Bismarck Ra., *mts.* 280 E2
Bismarck Sea 280 E2
Bissau 168 B4
Bitola 81 E3
Bitterroot Range, *mts.* 200 E3
Biu 176 E4
Biwa Ko, *lake* 121 Q6
Biysk 121 L4
Bizerte 168 D2
Bjørnøya, *island* 289 L2
Blackall 273 J4
Black Belt, *region* 209 K5
Blackburn, Mr., *mt.* 216 C2
Black Diamond 216 F3
Black Hills, *mountains* 200 E3
Black Mesa, *tableland* 208 E4
Black Mts., *U.S.A., mts.* 208 E4
Black Ra., *mountains* 200 E4
Black Rock Desert, *desert* 208 D3
Black Sea 49 L4
Black Sugarloaf, *mt.* 273 K6
Black Volta, *river* 176 C5
Blagoveshchensk 121 P4
Blanc, Mt., *mountain* 48 G4
Blanca, Bahía, *bay* 249 C6
Blanche, L., *South Australia, lake* 273 G5
Blanco, C., *Argentina, cape* 249 C7
Blanco, C., *Costa Ruca, cape* 233 E4
Blanco, C., *U.S.A., cape* 200 D3
Blantyre 169 G7
Blenheim 276 E5
Bleue 137 G5
Blida 168 D2
Bloemfontein 169 F8
Bloomington, *U.S.A. Illinois* 209 K3
Bluefield 209 L4
Bluefields 233 E3
Blue Mts., *Australia mts.* 280 F5
Blue Mts., *New Zealand, mountains* 277 C7
Blue Mts., *U.S.A., Oregon, mountains* 200 E3
Blue Nile, *see Bahr el Azraq* 168 G4
Blue Ridge, *mountains* 200 F4
Bluff 277 C8
Bluff Pt., *cape* 272 B5
Blumenau 264 D1
Blytheville 209 K4
Bo 168 B5
Boa Vista 256 C2
Bobo Dioulasso 168 C4
Bobruysk 59 J3
Boby, Pic, *mountain* 169 H8
Bocas del Toro 233 E4
Bonifacio, Bocche di, *strait* 48 H5
Bochum 58 F3
Bodele, *region* 168 E4
Boden 58 H2
Bodensee, *lake* 58 G4
Bodø 58 G1
Bodoquena, Sa. da, *mts.* 264 C1
Boende 168 F6
Bogalusa 209 K5
Bogdanovich 59 N3
Bogdo Uula, *mountains* 112 F3
Bogong, Mt., *mountains* 273 J7
Bogor 137 H6
Bogotá 248 B2
Böhmerwald, *mountains* 48 H4
Bohol, *island* 137 K5
Bohol Sea 137 K5
Boise 208 D3
Bojador, Cabo, *cape* 168 B3
Bojnūrd 120 H6
Boké 176 B4
Boknfjord, *fjord* 58 F2
Bolama 176 B4
Bolivar 264 B2
Bolivia 248 C4
Bolobo 168 E6
Bologna 48 H4
Bologoye 59 K2
Bol'sheretsk 121 S4
Bol'shevik, O., *island* 121 N2
Bol'shezemel'skaya Tundra, *region* 120 H3
Bol. Balkhan, Khr., *mt.* 49 N5
Bol'shoy Kavkaz, *mts.* 49 M4
Bol. Shantar, O., *island* 113 H3
Bolsón de Mapimi, *region* 201 E4
Boma 169 E6
Bombay 112 E5
Bomi Hills, *mountains* 168 B5
Bomu, *river* 168 F5
Bon, C., *cape* 168 E2
Bonaire, *island* 201 G5
Bonaire Trench, *sea feature* 201 G5
Bonaparte Archipelago, *island group* 280 C3
Bonavista Bay, *bay* 217 M4
Bondo 184 D2
Bône, *see Annaba* 168 D2
Bone, Teluk, *bay* 113 H6
Bongor 176 E4
Bonn 48 G3
Bonny 176 D5
Bonthe 168 B5
Boothia, Gulf of, *gulf* 200 F2
Boothia Pena., *peninsula* 200 F2
Borama 177 H5
Borźs 58 G3
Borborema, Planalto da, *region* 248 F3
Bordeaux 48 F4
Borden I., *island* 200 E2
Borden Pena., *peninsula* 216 J1
Borisoglebsk 59 L3
Borku, *region* 168 E4
Borlange 58 G2
Borneo, *island* 113 G6
Bornholm, *island* 48 H3
Borō Horō-Ūla, *mts.* 120 L5
Borovsk 59 N2
Borshchovochnyy Khr., *mountains* 112 G3
Borūjerd 136 B2
Bory Tucholskie, *region* 58 H3
Borzya 121 O4
Bosporus, *see Karadeniz Boğazi* 81 F3
Boston, *U.S.A.* 200 G3
Boston Mts., *mountains* 200 F4
Botany Bay, *bay* 273 K6
Botev, *mountain* 81 F2
Bothnia, Gulf of, *gulf* 48 J2
Botoşani 81 F2
Botswana 169 F8
Botwood 217 M4
Bouaflé 168 C5
Bouaké 168 C5
Bouar 184 C2
Bou Arfa 176 C2
Boubandjida, *region* 176 E5
Bougainville, C., *cape* 272 E2
Bougainville, I., *island* 281 F2
Bougainville Reef, *reef* 273 J3
Bougainville Str., *strait* 281 F2
Bougie, *see Bejaïa* 80 C3
Boulder, *Australia* 272 D6
Boulder, *U.S.A.* 208 F3
Bounty Is., *island group* 19 K5
Bourarhet, Erg, *see Erg Bourarhet* 176 D3
Bourges 80 C2
Bourke 273 J6
Bou-Saâda 80 C3
Bouvetøya, *island* 292 C3
Bow, *river* 216 F3
Bowen 273 J3
Bowling Green 209 K4
Bowling Green, C., *cape* 273 J3
Bowman Bay, *bay* 217 K2
Boz D., *mountains* 81 G3
Bozeman 208 E2
Bozoum 168 E5
Brabant I., *island* 292 R2
Brač, *island* 48 J4
Bradford 48 F3
Brady 208 H5
Brahmaputra 112 F4
Brăila 81 F2
Branco, *river* 248 C2
Brandenburg 58 G3
Brandon, *Canada* 208 H2
Brandon Hd., *cape* 289 D3
Bransfield Str., *strait* 292 R2
Brasília 248 E4
Brassey Ra., *Australia, mountains* 272 D5
Brasstown Bald, *mt.* 209 L5
Bratislava 48 J4
Bratsk 112 G3
Braunschweig 58 G3
Brava 185 F2
Brazil 248 D3
Brazilian Basin, *sea feature* 100 D6
Brazilian Highlands, *mts.* 248 E5
Brazilian Shield, *plateau* 24 D4
Brazos, *river* 208 H5
Brazzaville 168 E6
Brdy, *mountains* 289 G4
Breaden, L., *lake* 272 E5
Breaksea Sound, *inlet,* 277 B7
Bream Bay, *bay* 276 F2
Breidhafjördhur, *bay* 48 D2
Bremen 48 H3
Bremerhaven 58 G3
Brenner, P., *pass* 80 D2
Brescia 80 D2
Brest, *France* 80 B2
Brest, *U.S.S.R.* 58 H3

Breton Sd., *inlet* 209 K6
Brett, C., *cape* 276 F2
Bria 168 F5
Bridgetown, *Australia* 272 C6
Bridgetown, *Barbados* 233 H3
Brie, *region* 80 C2
Brigham City 208 E3
Brighton 58 E3
Brindisi 58 E3
Brisbane 281 F4
Bristol, *England* 58 E3
Bristol Bay, *bay* 200 C3
Bristol Channel, *channel* 58 E3
Bristol I., *island* 292 A3
British Antarctic Territory 292 B2
British Columbia, *province* 216 E3
British Isles 32 E2
British Mts., *mountains* 200 D2
Brits 184 D5
Brno 48 J4
Broad Sd., *inlet* 273 J4
Brochet 216 G3
Brodeur Pena., *peninsula* 200 F2
Brody 81 F1
Broken Hill, *Australia* 280 E5
Bromley Plateau, *sea feature* 100 D6
Brooke Deep, *sea feature* 25 K3
Brooks Range, *mts.* 200 C2
Broome 280 C3
Broome, Mt., *mountain* 272 E3
Brothers, The, *island group* 177 J4
Browns Bay 276 F3
Brownsville 200 F4
Browse I., *island* 272 D2
Bruce Hwy. 273 J4
Bruce, Mt., *mountain* 280 B4
Brunei, *state* 113 G5
Brunner 277 D6
Brunner, L., *lake* 277 D6
Brunswick B., *bay* 272 D3
Brunswick, Pena de, *peninsula* 264 A4
Bruny I., *island* 273 J8
Brussel 48 G3
Bryan 209 H5
Bryansk 48 L3
Bü A Ağri Daği, *mountain* 81 H3
Bucaramanga 248 B2
Buccaneer Archo., *island group* 280 C3
Buchanan 168 B5
Buchanan Deep, *sea feature* 25 E4
Buchan Ness, *cape* 58 E3
Buckland Tableland, *plateau* 280 E4
Bucureşti 48 K4
Budapest 48 J4
Budd Coast, *region* 292 H2
Buenaventura 248 B2
Buenos Aires 249 D6
Buenos Aires, L., *lake* 249 B7
Buffalo 200 G3
Buffalo Head Hills, *mts.* 200 E3
Bug, *river* 48 J3
Buga 256 B2
Bagul'ma 59 M3
Buguruslan 59 M3
Bujumbura 168 F6
Bukama 169 F6
Bukantau, Gy., *mountain* 49 O4
Bukavu 168 F6
Bukittinggi 137 H6
Bukoba 185 E3
Būl, Kūh-e, *mountain* 49 N6
Bulagan 121 N5
Bulawayo 169 F8
Bulgaria 48 K4
Buller, *river* 276 E5
Buller, Mt., *mountain* 280 E5
Bullfinch 272 C6
Bulloo, *river* 280 E4
Bulls 276 F5
Bull Shoals Res., *reservoir* 209 J4
Bu Menderes, *river* 48 K5
Bunbury 280 B5
Bundaberg 273 K4
Bunia 177 G5
Burao 177 H5
Buraydah 177 H3
Burdekin, *river* 280 E4
Burdur 81 F3
Burdwan 112 F4
Burdwood Bank, *sea feature* 100 B7
Bureinskiy, Khr., *mts.* 113 H3
Burgas 81 F2
Burgeo 217 M4
Burgersdorp 284 D6
Burgos 80 B2
Burica, Pta., *cape* 233 E4
Burin Pena., *peninsula* 216 M4
Burke, *river* 273 H4
Burketown 273 G3
Burkhala 121 R3
Burlington, *U.S.A., Iowa* 209 J3
Burma 112 F4
Burnett, *river* 281 F4
Burnie 273 J8
Burra 273 G6
Burro, Serrianías del, *mountains* 232 C2
Bursa 49 K5
Būr Sa'id 177 G2
Burt Plain, *region* 272 F4
Buru, *island* 113 H6
Burundi 168 F6
Būshehr 136 C3
Busira, *river* 184 C3
Busselton 272 C6
Bustard Hd., *cape* 273 K4
Buta 168 F5
Butare 184 D3
Butte 208 E2
Butung, *island* 113 H6
Buy 59 L2
Buyr Nūr, *lake* 121 O5
Büyük Ağri Daği, *mt.* 49 M5
Buzachi, P-ov., *peninsula* 120 H5
Buzuluk 59 M3
Byam Martin, C., *cape* 217 K1
Byam Martin I., *island* 216 G1
Bydgoszcz 48 J3
Bylot I., *island* 200 G2
Byrd, *scientific base* 292 O2
Byrd Land 292 P1
Byron, C., *cape* 281 F4
Byro Plains, *region* 272 C5
Byrranga Gory, *mts.* 112 F2

Caala 169 E7
Caatinga, *region* 248 D3
Cabimas 256 B1
Cabinda 169 E6
Cabinda, *state* 169 E6
Cabinet Mts., *mountains* 208 D2
Cabonga, Rés., *reservoir* 217 K4
Caboolture 273 K5
Cabot Str., *strait* 200 G3
Cabrera, *island* 80 C3
Cacao, Canal de, *strait* 264 A3
Cachi, Nos. de, *mountain* 264 B1
Cachimbo, Sa. do, *mts.* 248 D3
Cachoeira do Sul 264 C2
Cádiz, *Spain* 48 F5
Caen 58 E4
Cagayan 113 H5
Cagliari 48 H5
Caguas 233 G3
Caiapó, Sa. do, *mts.* 257 D4
Caicos Is., *island group* 233 F2
Caicos Passage, *strait* 209 N7
Caird Coast, *region* 292 A2
Cairns 280 E3
Cairo, *Egypt* 168 G2
Cairo, *U.S.A.* 209 K4
Cajamarca 256 B3
Calabar 184 B2
Calabozo 233 G4
Calais 48 G3
Calalaste, Cord. de, *mountains* 264 B1
Calamar 233 F3
Calamian Group, *island group* 137 J4
Calapan 137 K4
Calcutta 112 F4
Caldwell 208 D3
Calğal Dağ, *mountain* 81 G3
Calgary 200 E3
Cali 248 B2
California, *state* 208 C4
California, Golfo de, *gulf* 201 E4
Callabonna, L., *lake* 273 H5
Callao 248 B4
Caltagirone 80 D3
Calvinia 169 E9
Camacupa 169 E7
Camagüey 201 G4
Camagüey, Archo. de, *island group* 233 F2
Ca Mau, Pte. de, *cape* 113 G5
Cambay, G. of, *gulf* 112 E4
Cambodia 113 G5
Cambrai 58 F3
Cambrian Mts., *mts.* 58 E3
Cambridge, *New Zealand* 276 F3
Cambridge Bay 216 G2
Camden 209 M4
Cameron Mts., *mts.* 277 B8
Cameroons Mt., *mt.* 168 D5
Cameroun 168 E5
Camiri 256 C5
Camooweal 273 G3
Campagna, *region* 80 D2
Campanquix, Cerros, *mountains* 256 B3
Campbell, C., *cape* 276 F5
Campbell I., *New Zealand, island* 292 L3
Campbell, Mt., *mountain* 216 D2
Campbellton 217 L4
Campeche 232 D3
Campeche, Bahía de, *bay* 201 F5
Campeche Bank, *sea feature* 201 F4
Cam-pha 113 G4
Campina Grande 257 F3
Campinas 249 E5
Campoalegre 233 F4
Campo Grande 256 D5
Campos 248 E5
Campos, *E. Brazil, reg.* 248 E4
Campos, *S. Brazil, reg.* 248 D5
Camrose 216 F3
Canada 200 D3
Canadian, *river* 200 E4
Canadian Shield, *plateau* 24 C2
Çanakkale Boğazi, *strait* 48 K5
Canal Beagle, *strait* 264 B4
Canal Casiquiare, *river* 256 C2
Cananea 208 E5
Canarias, Islas, *island grp* 100 E3
Canastra, Sa. da, *mts.* 248 E4
Canaveral, Cape, *cape* 201 F4
Canberra 280 E5
Candlemas I., *island* 292 A3
Canigou, Mt., *mountain* 80 C2
Çankiri 81 G3
Cannes 80 C2
Canning Basin, *region* 272 D3
Canouan 256 C1
Canso, C., *cape* 200 G3
Cantabrica, Cordillera, *mountains* 48 F4
Canterbury, *county* 277 D6
Canterbury Bight, *gulf* 277 E7
Canterbury Plains, *reg.* 277 D7
Can Tho 113 G5
Canton, *U.S.A.* 209 L3
Cape Barren I., *island* 272 J8
Cape Breton I., *island* 200 G3
Cape Coast 176 C5
Cape Dorset, *trading post* 217 K2
Cape Girardeau 209 K4
Cape Hope's Advance, *trading post* 217 L2
C. Johnson Depth, *sea feature* 283 A2
Cape Rise, *sea feature* 169 G9
Cape Town 168 E9
Cape Verde Basin, *sea feature* 100 D3
Cape Verde Is., *island group* 100 D4
Cape Verde Plateau, *sea feature* 100 D4
Cape York Peninsula, *peninsula* 280 E3
Cap-Haïtien 201 G5
Capoompeta, *mountain* 273 K5
Capri, *island* 80 D3
Capricorn Chan., *channel* 281 F4
Capricorn Group, *reefs* 273 K4
Caprivi Strip, *region* 169 F7
Capulin Mt., *mountain* 208 G4
Caquetá, *river* 256 B3
Carabaya, Cord. de, *mountains* 256 B4
Caracas 248 C1
Carajás, Sa. dos, *mts.* 257 D3
Caratasca, Laguna, *lake* 233 E3
Caravelas 248 F4
Carcar, Monti, *mountain* 177 H5
Carcassonne 80 C2
Carcross 216 D2
Cárdenas 232 D2
Cardiff 48 F3
Carey, L., *lake* 280 C4
Cariaco Trench, *sea feature* 233 G3
Caribbean Sea 201 F5
Cariboo Mts., *mountains* 200 D3
Caribou 216 H3
Carinhanha 248 E4
Caripito 256 C1
Carlisle 58 E3
Carlsbad 208 G5
Carlsberg Ridge, *sea feature* 145 B2
Carmen, *Colombia* 233 F4
Carmen, *Mexico* 232 D3
Carmen, *island* 208 E6
Carnarvon Ra., *W. Australia, mountains* 272 D5
Carnegie, L., *lake* 280 C4
Carnegie Ridge, *sea feature* 100 A5
Carolina 257 E3
Caroline Islands, *island group* 283 A2
Caroline-Solomon Ridge *sea feature* 283 B2
Caroni, *river* 233 G4
Carpathians, *mountains* 48 J4
Carpatii Meridionali, *Mti., mountains* 48 J4
Carpentaria, Gulf of, *gulf* 280 D3
Carpenter Ridge, *sea feature* 145 D2
Carranza, C., *cape* 249 B6
Carriacou, *island* 256 C1
Carson City 208 D4
Carson Sink, *region* 208 D4
Cartagena, *Colombia* 248 B1
Cartagena, *Spain* 80 B3
Cartago 233 F4
Carterton 276 F5
Cartier I., *island* 272 D2
Cartwright 217 M3
Caruarú 257 F3
Carúpano 256 C1
Caryapundy Swamp, *swamp* 273 H5
Casablanca, *see El-Dar-el-Beida* 176 C2
Cascade Range, *mts.* 200 D3
Caserta 80 D3
Casino 273 K5
Casper 208 F3
Caspian Sea 49 N4
Cassai, *river* 184 D4
Cassiar Mts., *mountains* 216 D2
Castellón de la Plana 80 C3
Castillo, Pampa del, *pampas* 264 B3
Castlecliff 276 F4
Castlemaine 273 H7
Castle Rock, *mountain* 277 C7
Castres 80 C2
Castries 233 G3
Catamarca 264 B1
Catanduva 257 E5
Catania 48 H5
Catastrophe, C., *cape* 280 D5
Cat I., *island* 201 G4
Catoche C., *cape* 201 F4
Catskill Mts., *mountains* 200 G3
Cauca, *river* 248 B2
Caucasus Mts., *see Bol'shoy Kavkaz* 49 M4
Cauquenes 264 A2
Caura, *river* 233 G4
Caviana, I., *island* 257 D2
Caxias 257 E3
Caxias do Sul 264 C1
Cayenne 248 D2
Cayman Is., *island group* 201 F5
Cayman Trench, *sea feature* 100 A4
Cay Sal Bank, *sea feature* 233 E2
Cebollera, Sa., *mountains* 80 B2
Cebu 113 H5
Cebu, *island* 113 H5
Cedar City 208 E4
Cedar Falls 209 J3
Cedar L., *lake* 216 G3
Cedar Rapids 209 J3
Cedros, *island* 201 E4
Ceduna 272 F6
Celaya 232 C2
Celebes, *see Sulawesi* 137 J6
Celebes Sea 113 H5
Celtic Sea 48 F4
Central African Empire 168 E5
Central Asian System 24 G2
Central Basin 25 J4
Central, Cord., *Bolivia, mountains* 256 C4
Central, Cordillera, *Colombia, mountains* 248 B2
Central, Cord., *Dominican Rep., mts.* 233 F3
Central, Cord., *Peru, mountains* 248 B3
Central Hwy. 273 J5
Centralia 209 K4
Central, Massif, *mts.* 48 G4
Central Ra., *mountains* 280 E2
Cerro de Pasco 248 B4
České Budějovice 80 D2
Cess, *river* 176 C5
Cessnock 273 K6
Cevennes, *mountains* 48 G4
Ceyhan, *river* 81 G3
Ceylon, *see Sri Lanka* 33 H3
Ceylon Rise, *sea feature* 145 D2
Chacabuco 248 B2
Chaco Austral, *region* 249 C5
Chaco Boreal, *region* 248 D5
Chaco Central, *region* 256 D5
Chad 168 E4
Chad Basin, *region* 25 F3
Chad, Lake, *lake* 168 E4
Chagai Hills, *mountains* 112 E4
Chagos Archipelago, *island group* 112 E6
Chala Shan, *mountains* 137 G2
Chaleurs, B. des, *bay* 217 L4
Chalky Inlet, *inlet* 277 B8
Challenger Deep, *sea feature* 25 J3
Challenger Depth, *sea feature* 283 B2
Chambal, *river* 137 E3
Chambéry 80 C2
Chamdo 112 F4
Chamo, L., *lake* 168 G5
Champlain, L., *lake* 200 G3
Chan-chiang 113 G4
Chandigarh 136 E2
Chandrapur 112 E4
Ch'ang Ch., *river* 113 G4
Ch'ang-ch'un 113 H3
Chang-p'ai Shan, *mts.* 112 H4
Ch'ang-sha 113 G4
Chang Tang, *plateau* 112 F4
Ch'ang-te 137 J3
Chang-yeh 121 M6
Channel Islands, *island group* 48 F4
Chanthaburi 137 H4
Chapada dos Parecis, *mountains* 248 C4
Chapala, L., de, *lake* 232 C2
Chaparral 233 F4
Chapayevsk 59 M3
Chaplina, M., *cape* 113 L2
Chapra 136 F3
Chaqui 256 C4
Charcot I., *island* 292 R2
Chardzhou 112 E4
Chari, *river* 168 E4
Charles, C., *cape* 200 G4
Charles I., *island* 217 K2
Charles Pk., *mountain* 272 D6
Charleston, *U.S.A., S. Carolina* 200 G4
Charleston, *U.S.A., West Virginia* 209 L4
Charleville, *Australia* 273 J5
Charlotte 209 L4
Charlottetown 200 G3
Charters Towers 273 J4
Chatham, *Canada, New Brunswick* 217 L4
Chatham Is., *island group* 281 J6
Chatham Rise, *sea feature* 283 B4
Chatham Str., *strait* 216 D3
Chattahoochee, *river* 209 K5
Chattanooga, *river* 209 K4
Chaunskaya Guba, *bay* 121 T3
Chayatyn, Khr., *mts.* 121 Q4
Cheboksary 49 M3
Chech, Erg, *sand dunes* 168 C3
Cheju Do, *island* 121 P6
Chela, Sa. da, *mountains* 184 C4
Cheliff, *river* 48 G5
Chelkar 120 H5
Chelyabinsk 49 O3
Chelyuskin 121 N2
Chelyuskin, Mys, *cape* 112 G2
Chen-chiang 137 J2
Ch'eng-chiang 137 H3
Cheng-hsien 113 G4
Chengshan Tow, *cape* 137 K2
Ch'eng-tu 112 G4
Chen-hsi 121 M5
Ch'en-hsien 112 G4
Cherangani Hills, *mts.* 177 G5
Cherbourg 58 E4
Cherchel 176 D2
Chercher, *region* 177 H5
Cherdyn 59 N2
Cheremkhovo 112 G3
Cherepovets 59 K2
Cherkassy 81 F2
Chernigov 59 J3
Chernikovsk 59 N3
Chernovtsy 81 F2
Chernysheva, Kryazh, *mountains* 49 O1
Cherokee 209 H3
Cherokees, L. O'The, *lake* 209 H4
Cherskogo, Khrebet, *mountains* 113 H2
Chesapeake B., *bay* 200 G4
Cheshskaya Guba, *bay* 59 L1
Chesterfield, Îles, *reefs* 281 F3
Chesterfield Inlet 216 H2
Chetumal 233 E3
Cheviot Hills, *mountains* 58 E3
Cheyenne 208 G3
Cheyenne, *river* 208 G3
Chia-mu-ssu 121 Q5
Chiang Mai 112 F5
Chiang-tu 137 J2
Chiba 113 J4
Chicago 200 F3
Chichagof I., *island* 200 D3
Ch'i-ch'i-ha-erh 113 H3
Chiclayo 256 B3
Chico, *Argentina, river* 249 C7
Chico, S. *Argentina, river* 264 B3
Chicoutimi 217 K4
Chidley, C., *cape* 200 G2
Chien-ou 137 J3
Chierh Shan 121 L5
Ch'ih-feng 121 O5
Chihuahua 200 C2
Chilcott I., *island* 273 K3
Childers 273 K5
Chile 249 B6
Chi-lin 113 H3
Chilka Lake, *lake* 112 F5
Chillan 249 B6
Chiloé, I. de, *island* 249 B7
Chilpancingo de los Bravos 232 D3
Chilterns, *hills* 58 E3
Chi-lung 137 K3
Chilwa, L., *lake* 169 G7
Chimbay 120 H5
Chimborazo, *mountains* 248 B3
Chimkent 112 E3
China 112 F4
Chi-nan 113 G4
Chinandega 233 E3
Chin-chiang 113 G4
Chinchilla 273 K5
Chin-chou 113 H3
Chinde 169 G7
Chindwin, *river* 137 G3
Ch'ing Hai, *lake* 112 G4
Ching-ku 137 H3
Chingola 184 D4
Ch'ing-tao 113 H4
Chin-hua 137 J3
Ch'in-huang-tao 121 O5
Chink Kaplankyr, *mts.* 49 O5
Chin-ling Shan, *mountains* 112 G4
Chipata 169 G7
Chiriquí, Golfo de, *gulf* 233 E4
Chirripó, *mountain* 201 F5
Chisimaio 168 H6
Chita 113 G3
Ch'i-t'ai 121 L5
Chitral 120 K6
Chittagong 112 F4
Chiu-chang 137 J3
Chiu-ch'uan 112 F4
Ch'iung-chou Hai-hsia, *strait* 137 H3
Chiung-hsia Shan, *mts.* 112 G4
Ch'iung-shan 137 J3
Chivilcoy 264 B2
Ch'i-yao Shan, *mountains* 137 H3
Cho-chou 137 J3
Choiseul I., *island* 280 F2
Choke Mts., *mountains* 168 G4
Chongjin 121 Q5
Chŏngju 121 P6
Chonos, Archipiélago de los, *island group* 249 B7
Chott Djerid, *seasonal lake* 168 D2
Chott ech Chergui, *seasonal lake* 176 D2
Ch. el Hodna, *seasonal lake* 80 C3
Chott Melrhir, *seasonal lake* 168 D2
Chou-ts'un 121 O6
Choybalsan 121 O5
Christchurch, *New Zealand* 281 H6
Christiana 169 F8
Christian, C., *cape* 217 L1
Christianshaab 217 M2
Christmas I., *island* 33 H4
Christmas Rise, *sea feature* 145 E3
Chu 136 E1
Chu, *river* 136 E1
Chubut, *river* 249 C7
Ch'u-ching 113 G4
Ch'ü-ching 137 H3
Chudskoye Oz., *lake* 48 K2
Chugach Mts., *mountains* 200 C2
Chü-hsien 137 J2
Ch'u-hsiung 137 H3
Chukchi Sea 289 B2
Chukotskiy Khr., *mts.* 113 K2
Chukotskiy P-ov., *peninsula* 113 L2
Chulym 120 L4
Chumpon 137 G4
Chun Deep, *sea feature* 24 E3
Ch'ung-ch'ing 113 G4
Chung-hsien 137 H2
Chuquicamata 256 B5
Churchill 200 F3
Churchill, *river* 216 G3
Churchill, C., *cape* 200 F3
Churchill L., *lake* 216 G3
Churchill Pk., *mountain* 200 D3
Churuguara 233 G3
Chusovoy 59 N2
Chyulu Ra., *mountains* 177 G6
Ciénaga 256 B1
Cienfuegos 233 E2
Cilacap 137 H6
Cilo Daği, *mountain* 49 M5
Cimarron, *river* 208 H4
Činčer, *mountain* 80 E2
Cincinnati 200 F4
Cinto, Mte., *mountain* 80 D2
Cirebon 137 H6
Cisco 208 H5
Cisneros 233 F4

Citlaltepec, Vol., *mt.* 232 D3
Ciudad Acuña 232 C2
Ciudad Bolívar 248 C2
Ciudad Camargo 232 C2
Ciudad Guzmán 232 C3
Ciudad Ixtepec 232 D3
Ciudad Juárez 200 E4
Ciudad Lerdo 232 C2
Ciudad Madero 232 D2
Ciudad Mante 232 D2
Ciudad Obregón 208 F6
Ciudad Victoria 232 D2
Clarence, *estuary* 277 E6
Clarence R., *river* 273 K5
Clarence Str., *Australia, strait* 272 F2
Clarence Str., *U.S.A., strait* 216 D3
Clarión, *island* 233 B3
Clarion Fracture Zone, *sea feature* 283 D2
Clarke Ra., *mountains* 280 E4
Clark Hill Res., *reservoir* 209 L5
Clarksburg 209 L4
Clarence I., *island* 289 S2
Clear, C., *cape* 48 E3
Clear Hills, *mountains* 200 D3
Clearwater L., *lake* 217 K3
Clearwater Mountains, *mountains* 208 D2
Clerke Reef, *reef* 272 C3
Clermont, *Australia* 273 J4
Cleveland, *U.S.A., Ohio* 200 F3
Cleveland, *U.S.A., Texas* 209 H5
Clinch Mts., *mountains* 209 L4
Clinton, *U.S.A., Oklahoma* 208 H4
Clipperton Fracture Zone, *sea feature* 283 D2
Clipperton I., *island* 283 D2
Cloates, Pt., *cape* 272 B4
Cloncurry 273 H4
Cloncurry, *river* 273 H3
Cloud Pk., *mountain* 200 E3
Cloudy Bay, *bay* 276 F5
Clovis 208 G5
Cluj 81 E2
Clutha, *river* 277 C7
Clyde, *river* 58 E3
Coari, Lago, *lake* 256 C3
Coastal Plain Basin, *reg.* 280 B5
Coast Mountains, *mts.* 200 D3
Coast Ra., *Australia, mountains* 273 K5
Coast Range, *U.S.A., mountains* 200 D3
Coatapec 232 D3
Coats I., *island* 200 F2
Coats Land, *region* 292 A2
Coatzacoalcos 232 D3
Cobalt 217 K4
Cobar 273 J6
Cobequid Mts., *mts.* 209 P2
Cobourg Pena., *peninsula* 272 F2
Cochabamba 248 C4
Cochilha Grande, *mts.* 249 D5
Cochin 136 E4
Cochrane 217 J4
Coco, *river* 233 E3
Coco, I. del., *island* 201 F5
Cocos Is., *islands* 145 D3
Cocos Ridge, *sea feature* 283 E2
Cod, Cape, *cape* 217 K4
Codfish I., *island* 277 B8
Coeur d'Alene 208 D2
Coff's Harbour 273 K6
Coiba I., *island* 201 F5
Coimbatore 112 E5
Coimbra 80 A3
Colac 273 H7
Col des Valles 232 D2
Coles, Pta. de, *cape* 256 B4
Colima 232 C3
College 216 C2
Collie 272 C6
Collier B., *bay* 272 D3
Collier Ras., *mountains* 272 C4
Collines de Normandie, *hills* 80 B2
Collinson Pena., *peninsula* 216 G1
Collinsville 273 J4
Colombia 248 B2
Colombian Basin, *sea feature* 201 G5
Colombo 112 E5
Colón, *Panama* 233 F4
Colorado, *Argentina, river* 249 C6
Colorado, *U.S.A., Arizona, river* 200 E4
Colorado, *U.S.A., Texas, river* 201 F4
Colorado, *state* 208 F4
Colorado Desert 208 D5
Colorado Plateau, *plateau* 200 E4
Colorado Springs 208 G4
Columbia, *U.S.A., Tennessee* 209 L5
Columbia, *river* 200 E3
Columbia Basin, *region* 216 F4
Columbia, Mt., *mountain* 200 E3
Columbus, *U.S.A., Georgia* 209 K5
Columbus, *U.S.A., Mississippi* 209 L5
Columbus, *U.S.A., Ohio* 200 F4
Columna, P. la, *mt.* 233 F4
Colville, *river* 216 B2
Colville, C., *cape* 276 F3
Colville Channel, *channel* 276 F3
Colville Ridge, *sea feature* 281 H5
Comalapa, *river* 232 D3
Coman, Mt., *mountain* 232 R2
Comitán de Domínguez 232 D3
Committee Bay, *bay* 216 J2
Commonwealth Territory 273 K7
Como, L. di, *lake* 80 D2
Comodoro Rivadavia 249 C7
Comoé, *river* 176 C5
Comore, Îles de, *island group* 169 H7
Comorin, C., *cape* 112 E5
Comoro Ridge, *sea feature* 169 H7
Conakry 168 B5
Concepción, *Argentina* 264 B1
Concepción, *Chile* 249 B6
Concepción, *Paraquay* 248 D5
Concepción del Uruguay 264 C2
Conception, Pt., *cape* 200 D4
Conchos, *river* 201 E4
Concord 209 N3
Concordia 249 D6
Condamine, *river* 280 F4
Congo *(Brazzaville)* 168 E6
Congo, *river* 184 C3
Congo Basin, *region* 25 F3
Conselheiro Lafaiete 257 E5
Constanta 48 K4
Constantine 168 D2
Constitución 264 A2
Contamana 256 B3
Contratación 233 F4
Conway Reef, *reef* 281 H4
Contwoyto Lake, *lake* 216 F2
Coober Pedy 272 F5
Cook Inlet, *inlet* 200 C2
Cook Is., *island* 293 A3
Cook Islands, *island group* 283 C3
Cooke, Mt., *mountain* 281 H6
Cooke, Mt., *mountain* 272 C6
Cook's Pass., *channel* 280 E3
Cook Str., *strait* 281 H6
Cooktown 280 F3
Coolgardie 280 C5
Cooper Ck., *see Barcoo* 273 G5
Coorong, The, *lagoon* 273 G7
Cooroy 273 K5
Coosa, *river* 209 K5
Coos Bay 209 C3
Cootamundra 273 J6
Copiapó 249 B5
Copper, *river* 216 C2
Copper Belt, *region* 169 F7
Coppermine 216 F2
Coquimbo 249 B5
Coral Harbour, *trading station* 217 J2
Coral Sea 280 F3
Coral Sea Basin, *sea feature* 281 F3
Coral Sea Plateau, *sea feature* 113 J6
Corantijn, *river* 256 D2
Cordilheiras, Sa. das, *mountains* 257 E3
Córdoba, *Argentina* 249 C6
Córdoba, *Spain* 80 B3
Córdoba, *Mexico* 232 D3
Córdoba, Sierra de, *mountains* 249 C6
Cordova 216 C2
Coringa Is., *island group* 273 J3
Cork 48 E3
Corner Brook 217 M4
Cornwallis I., *island* 216 H1
Coro 256 C1
Corocoro, Isla, *island* 256 C2
Coromandel Coast, *reg.* 136 F4
Coromandel Pena., *peninsula* 276 F3
Coromandel Ra., *mts.* 276 F3
Coronation Gulf, *gulf* 216 F2
Coronation I., *island* 292 S2
Coronel Pringles 264 B2
Coronel Suárez 264 B2
Corpus Christi 209 H6
Corrientes 249 D5
Corrientes, C., *Argentina cape* 249 D6
Corrientes, C., *Colombia, cape* 248 B2
Corrientes, C., *Cuba, cape* 233 E2
Corrientes, C., *Mexico, cape* 201 E4
Corrigin 272 C6
Corse, *island* 48 H4
Corse, C., *cape* 80 D2
Cortez Mts., *mountains* 208 D3
Çoruh, *river* 81 H3
Çorum 81 G3
Corumbá 248 D4
Corumbá, *river* 257 D4
Cosmoledo Is., *island group* 185 F3
Costa de Mosquitos, *reg.* 233 E3
Costa Rica 201 F5
Côte d'Azur, *region* 48 G4
Coteau, The, *region* 208 F1
Cotonou 176 D5
Cotopaxi, Vol., *mountain* 248 B3
Cottbus 58 G3
Council Bluffs 209 H3
Courtenay 208 B2
Coventry 48 F3
Cowan, L., *lake* 280 C5
Cowra 272 J6
Cox's Bazar 137 G3
Cozumel, I. de, *island* 233 E2
Craigs Ra., *mountains* 280 F4
Craiova 81 E2
Cranbrook, *Canada* 216 F4
Crary Mts., *mountains* 292 P2
Crateús 257 E3
Crato, *Brazil* 257 F3
Crazy Mts., *mountains* 200 E3
Cree L., *lake* 216 G3
Cres, *island* 80 D2
Crestone Pk., *mountain* 208 F4
Crete, Sea of 48 K5
Creus, C., *cape* 80 C2
Cristóbal Colón, Pico, *mountain* 248 B1
Crockett 209 H5
Croker I., *island* 272 F2
Cromwell 277 C7
Crooked I., *island* 209 N7
Crooked I. Pass., *strait* 209 N7
Cross, C., *cape* 184 C5
Cross L., *lake* 216 H3
Crossley, M., *mountain* 277 E6
Cross Sd., *inlet* 216 D3
Crowley's Ridge, *hills* 209 J4
Crowsnest Pass, *pass* 208 E2
Croydon, *England* 48 F3
Crozet, Îs., *island group* 145 B5
Crozier C., *cape* 292 L2
Cruz, C., *cape* 233 F3
Cruziero do Sul 256 B3
Cuando, *river* 184 D4
Cuango, *river* 184 C3
Cuba, *island* 201 F4
Cubango, *river* 169 E7
Cuchilla Grande, *mts.* 264 C2
Cúcuta 233 F4
Cuenca, *Ecuador* 248 B3
Cuenca, Serranía de, 4 *mountains* 48 F5
Cuernavaca 201 F5
Cuiabá 248 D4
Cuiabá, *river* 248 D4
Cuito, *river* 169 E7
Culebra Pk., *mountain* 208 F4
Culgoa, *river* 280 E4
Culiacán 208 F7
Culver Pt., *cape* 272 D6
Cuma 169 E7
Cumaná 256 C1
Cumberland, *river* 209 K4
Cumberland House 216 G3
Cumberland Is., *island group* 273 J4
Cumberland, L., *lake* 209 K4
Cumberland Pena., *peninsula* 200 G2
Cumberland Plateau, *plateau* 200 F4
Cumberland Sd., *inlet* 200 G2
Cuene, *river* 169 E7
Cunnamulla 273 J5
Curaçao, *island* 201 G5
Curacautin 264 A2
Curicó 264 A2
Curitiba 248 E5
Curtis Chan., *channel* 273 K4
Curtis I., *island* 273 K4
Curupira, Sa., *mountains* 256 C2
Curuzú Cuatiá 264 C1
Cuttack 112 F4
Cutts Mts., *mountains* 273 H4
Cuvier Basin, *sea feature* 145 E4
Cuvier I., *island* 276 F3
Cuzco 248 B4
Cyprus, *island* 49 L5
Cypress Hills, *mountains* 200 E3
Cyrenaica, *region* 185 F3
Czechoslovakia 48 H4
Czestochowa 58 H3

Daam Top, *mountain* 280 D2
Dabola 176 B4
Dacca 112 F4
Daet 113 H5
Dahlac Archo., *island group* 168 H4
Dahra, *region* 48 G5
Daito Is., *island group* 113 H4
Dakar 168 B4
Dakhla 168 B3
Dakhla Oasis 168 F3
Dal, *river* 48 J2
Dalaba 176 B4
Dalai Lama Ra., *mts.* 137 G2
Dalat 137 H4
Dalby, *Australia* 273 K5
Dalhart 208 G4
Dalhousie, C., *cape* 216 E1
Dallas 201 F4
Dallol Bosso, *river* 176 D4
Dalmatia, *region* 48 H4
Dalnerechensk 121 Q5
Daloa 176 C5
Dalrymple, Mt., *mt.* 273 J4
Daly, *river* 280 D3
Daly Waters 272 F3
Damanhûr 81 F4
Daman 112 E4
Damas 49 L6
Dāmāvānd, *mountain* 49 N5
Dampier Archo., *island group* 280 B4
Dampier Land, *region* 280 C3
Dampier, Sel., *strait* 280 D2
Dampier Str., *strait* 280 E2
Da Nang 113 G5
Danau Toba, *lake* 137 G5
Dannevirke 276 G5
Dante 168 J4
Danube, *see Donau, Duna, Dunărea and Dunay* 48 K4
Danville, *U.S.A., Illinois* 209 K3
Danville, *U.S.A., Virginia* 209 M4
Daoud 80 C3
Darbhanga 137 F3
Dar el Homr., *region* 168 F4
Dar es Salaam 169 G6
Dargaville 276 E2
Darién, G. del, *gulf* 201 G5
Darjeeling 112 F4
Darling, *river* 280 E5
Darling Downs, *region* 280 E4
Darling Ra., *mountains* 280 B5
Darnah 168 F2
Darnley Bay, *bay* 216 E2
Dar Nuba, *region* 168 F4
Darran Mts., *mountains* 277 C7
Dar Rounga, *mountains* 168 F5
Dart, C., *cape* 292 O2
Dartmoor, *moor* 58 E3
Dartmouth, *Canada* 217 L4
Daru 113 J6
Darwin 280 D3
Darwin, Cord., *mts.* 264 A3
Darwin, Mt., *Chile, mt.* 264 B4
Daryācheh-ye Namak, *see Namak* 49 N5
Daryācheh-ye Rezā'īyeh, *see Rezā'īyeh* 49 M5
Daryācheh-ye Sīstān, *see Sīstān* 136 D2
Dasht-e-Kavir, *desert* 112 D4
Dasht-e-Lūt, *desert* 112 D4
Dasht-e-Margo, *desert* 136 D2
Datu, Tg., *cape* 113 G5
Daugavpils 59 J3
Daulat Yar 136 D2
Dauphin 216 G3
Dauphin L., *lake* 217 H3
Davao 113 H5
Davao Gulf, *gulf* 137 K5
Davenport 209 J3
David 233 E4
David Seaknoll, *sea feature* 185 G2
Davis, *scientific base* 292 F2
Davis Inlet 217 L3
Davis Mts., *mountains* 208 G5
Davis Strait, *strait* 200 H2
Davlekanovo 59 M3
Dawes Ra., *mountains* 273 K4
Dawson 200 D2
Dawson, *river* 280 E4
Dawson Creek 216 E3
Dayr az Zawr 168 H2
Dayrūt 177 G3
Dayton 200 F4
Daytona Beach 209 L6
De Aar 169 F9
Dead Sea, *inland sea* 48 L6
Dean Funes 264 B2
Dearborn 209 L3
Dease Str., *strait* 216 G2
Death Valley, *valley* 200 E4
Débo, L., *lake* 176 C4
Deborah, Mt., *mountain* 216 C2
Debra Mark'os 177 G4
Debra Tabor 177 G4
Debrecen 81 E2
Decatur, *U.S.A., Alabama* 209 K5
Decatur, *U.S.A., Illinois* 209 K4
Deccan, plateau 112 E5
Deccan traps, *lava beds* 25 G3
Deception I., *island* 292 R2
Deering, Mt., *mountain* 272 E5
Deer Lake 217 M4
Deffa, ed., *region* 81 E4
De Grey, *river* 280 B4
Dehra Dun 136 E2
Deingueri, Mt., *mountain* 177 F5
Delano 208 D4
Delaware, *state* 209 M4
Delaware B., *bay* 209 M4
Delgado, C., *cape* 185 F4
Delhi 112 E4
Delicias 208 F6
Dellys 176 O2
De-Longa, O-va., *island group* 113 I2
Del Rio 208 G6
Dembidolo 177 G5
Deming 208 F5
Demirkazik, *mountains* 49 L5
Denezhkin Kamen', G., *mountain* 49 O2
Deniliquin 273 H7
Denison 209 H5
Denmark 272 C6
Denmark, *state* 48 H3
Denmark Strait, *strait* 289 N2
Denton 208 H5
D'Entrecasteaux Is., *island group* 280 F2
D'Entrecasteaux, Pt., *cape* 272 C6
Denver 200 E4
Dera Ismail Khan 136 E2
Derbent 81 J2
Derby, *Australia* 280 C3
Derwent, *Tasmania, river* 273 J8
Desau 58 G3
Deschutes, *river* 208 C3
Deseado 264 B3
Deseado, *river* 249 C7
Deserta Grande, *island* 176 B2
Desert Basin, *region* 280 C4
Des Moines 209 J3
Des Moines, *river* 209 J3
Desna, *river* 49 L3
Desolación, I., *islands* 249 B8
Desordem, Sa. da, *mts.* 256 E3
Desventurados, Islas de los, *island group* 32 C4
Detroit 200 F3
D.D.R. 48 H3
Devil River Pk., *mt.* 276 E5
Devil's Hole, *sea feature* 48 G3
Devils Lake 208 H2
Devon I., *island* 200 F2
Devonport, *Australia* 273 J8
Devonport, *New Zealand* 276 F3
Dey-Dey, L., *lake* 272 F5
Dezfūl 120 G6
Dhahran 177 J3
Dhaulagiri, *mountain* 112 F4
Dhulia 136 E3
Diamantina 248 E4
Diamantina, *river* 280 E4
Diamantina, Chapada, *region* 248 E4
Diane Bank, *island* 273 J3
Dibrugarh 112 F4
Dickinson 216 G4
Dickson 120 L2
Dicle, *river* 168 H2
Didinga Hills, *mountains* 168 G5
Diego Suarez 169 H7
Dieppe 58 F4
Digul, *river* 280 D2
Dijon 59 F4
Dika, M., *cape* 112 G2
Dikwa 168 E4
Dili 112 H6
Dillia, *river* 176 E4
Dimashq, *see Damas* 49 L6
Dimitrovgrad 59 M3
Dinār, Kūh-e *mountain* 177 J2
Dinara Planina, *mts.* 48 J4
Dindigul 136 E4
Diomede Is., *island grp.* 113 L2
Diomida, O-va., *island group* 113 L2
Diourbel 176 B4
Dipolog 133 H5
Direction, C., *cape* 273 H2
Diredâwa 168 H5
Dirk Hartogs I., *island* 280 B4
Disappointment, C., *Antarctica, cape* 292 R2
Disappointment, C., *S. Georgia, cape* 292 A3
Disappointment, C., *U.S.A., cape* 208 C2
Disappointment, L., *lake* 280 C4
Disaster Bay, *bay* 273 J7
Discovery B., *bay* 273 H7
Discovery Tablemount, *sea feature* 100 F7
Dishna 177 G3
Disko, *island* 200 H2
Disko Bugt., *bay* 217 M2
Dismal Swamp, *marsh* 209 M4
Diu 136 E3
Divisor, Serra de, *mts.* 256 B3
Diyarbakir 81 H3
Dixon Entrance, *channel* 200 D3
Dja, *river* 168 E5
Djerba, I. de, *island group* 176 E2
Djibouti 168 H4
Djibouti, *state* 168 H4
Djouf, El, *region* 176 C3
Djougou 176 D5
Djourab, *region* 177 E4
Djurdjura, *mountains* 48 G5
Dmitriya Lapteva, Proliv, *strait* 113 J2
Dnepr, *river* 48 K3
Dneprodzerzhinsk 81 G2
Dnepropetrovsk 49 L4
Dnestr, *river* 48 K4
Doce, *river* 248 E4
Dodge City 208 G4
Dodoma 169 G6
Dogger Bank, *sea feature* 48 G3
Doha 49 N7
Dois Irmãos, Sa. do, *mountains* 257 E3
Dolomitiche, A., *mts.* 48 H4
Dolphin & Union Str., *strait* 216 F2
Dombas 58 G2
Domel I., *island* 137 G4
Domeyko, Cord., *mts.* 256 C5
Dominica, *island* 201 G5
Dominica Pass., *channel* 233 G3
Dominican Rep. 107 C5
201 C5
Domuyo, *mountain* 264 A2
Don, *U.S.S.R., river* 49 L3
Donau, *river* 48 H4
Donbas, *region* 59 K4
Dondra Hd., *cape* 112 F5
Donegal Bay, *bay* 58 D3
Donets 49 L4
Donetskiy Kryazh, *mts.* 49 L4
Donggala 139 J6
Dong Hoi 137 H4
Dongola 168 G4
Donnybrook 272 C6
Dorchester, C., *cape* 217 K2
Dorre I., *island* 272 B5
Dortmund 48 G3
Douala 168 D5
Doubtful Sound, *inlet* 277 B7
Doubtless B., *bay* 276 E2
Dougherty Plain, *region* 209 L5
Douglas, *Rep. of South Africa* 169 F8
Douglas, *U.S.A., Alaska* 216 D3
Douglas, *U.S.A., Arizona* 208 F5
Douglas Ra., *mountains* 292 R2
Doukkala, *region* 48 E6
Dourada, Czchoeira, *fall* 257 E4
Dourados, Sa. dos, *mts.* 257 D5
Douro, *river* 80 B3
Dover, *England* 48 G3
Dover, *U.S.A.* 209 M4
Dover, Str. of, *strait* 58 F3
Dovrefj., *mountains* 58 G2
Dow, L., *lake* 169 F8
Dra, *river* 48 F6
Dragon's Mouth, *strait* 233 G3
Drakensberg, *mountains* 168 F9
Drake Passage, *sea* 292 R3
Drammen 58 G2
Drava, *river* 48 J4
Dre Chu, *river* 112 F4
Dresden 48 H3
Drina, *river* 48 J4
Drogobyč 81 E2
Dronning Maud Land, *territory* 292 B2
Drumheller 208 E1
Druskininkay 58 H3
Druzhina 121 R3
Drūz, Jabal ad, *mountain* 49 L6
Dryden 216 H4
Drysdale, *river* 280 C3
Drysdale I., *island* 272 G2
Dschang 176 E5
Dubawnt L., *lake* 200 E2
Dubayy 136 C3
Dubbo 273 J6
Dublin, *Rep. of Ireland* 48 F3
Dubrovnik 80 E2
Dubuque 209 J3
Duck Mt., *mountain* 208 G1
Dudinka 112 F2
Duero, *river* 48 F5
Duida, Co., *mountain* 233 G4
Duisburg 48 G3

Khmel'nitskiy 81 F2
Khomasplato, *plateau* 184 C5
Khopër, *river* 49 M3
Khorramshahr 136 B2
Khotin 59 J4
Khovy 81 H3
Khuff, Al, *mountains* 177 H3
Khulna 112 F4
Khyber Pass, *pass* 136 E2
Kibombo 168 F6
Kicking Horse Pass, *pass* 216 F3
Kidnappers, C., *cape* 276 G4
Kiel 48 H3
Kiel Canal, *canal* 48 H3
Kielce 58 H3
Kien Ko 137 H2
Kigali 168 G6
Kigoma 168 F6
Kikhchik 121 S4
Kikládhes, *island group* 48 K5
Kikwit 169 E6
Kilchu 121 P5
Kilcoy 273 K5
Kilimanjaro, Mt., *mt.* 168 G6
Killinek I., *island* 217 L2
Kilosa 169 G6
Kilwa Kivinje 169 G6
Kimberley, *Canada* 216 F4
Kimberley, *Rep. of S. Africa* 169 F8
Kimberley Plateau, *plateau* 280 C3
Kimberley Ra., *mts.* 272 C5
Kindersley 216 G3
Kindia 176 B4
Kindu 168 F6
Kineshma 59 L3
Kingaroy 273 K5
King Edward VIII Gulf, *gulf* 292 E2
King Edward VII Land, *region* 292 N2
King George I., *island* 292 S2
King George Sound, *inlet* 280 B5
King I., *Australia* 280 E5
King I., *Burma* 137 G4
Kg. Leopold & Qn. Astrid Coast, *region* 292 G2
King Leopold Ras., *mts.* 280 C3
King Sd., *inlet* 272 D3
Kings Peaks, *mountain* 208 E3
Kingston, *Canada* 209 M3
Kingston, *Jamaica* 201 G5
Kingston-upon-Hull 48 F3
Kingstown, *U.S.A.* 233 G3
Kingsville 208 H6
King William I., *island* 216 H2
King William's Town 169 F9
Kinkazan, *cape* 113 J4
Kinsha Kiang 137 G2
Kinshasa 168 E6
Kinyeti, *mountain* 168 G5
Kirensk 121 N4
Kirgizskaya S.S.R., *republic* 120 K5
Kirgizskiy Khr., *mts.* 112 E3
Kirikkale 81 G3
Kiriwina Is., *see Trobriand Is.* 280 F2
Kirkland Lake 217 J4
Kirkliston Ra., *mountains* 277 D7
Kirkwall 58 E2
Kirov, *Belorusskaya, S.S.R.* 59 K3
Kirov, *R.S.F.S.R.* 49 N2
Kirovabad 81 H3
Kirovograd 81 G2
Kirovsk 59 K1
Kirovskiy 121 S4
Kirs 59 M2
Kirşehir 81 G3
Kirthar Ra., *mountains* 112 E4
Kiruna 58 H1
Kisangani 168 F5
Kiselevsk 121 L4
Kishinev 48 K4
Kisir D., *mountain* 81 H3
Kislovodsk 81 H2
Kisumu 168 G6
Kitakyūshū 113 H4
Kitale 177 G5
Kitchener, *Canada* 217 J4
Kitega 184 D3
Kíthira, *island* 81 E3
Kitimat 216 E3
Kitwe 169 F7
Kivu, L., *lake* 168 F6
Kiyev 48 K3
Kizel 59 N2
Kizil Irmak, *river* 49 L5
Kizlyar 81 H2
Kizyl-Arvat 120 H6
Klagenfurt 80 D2
Klaipeda 58 H3
Klamath, *river* 208 C3
Klamath Falls 216 E4
Klamath Mts., *mountains* 200 D3
Klappan Ra., *mountains* 216 D3
Klar, *river* 48 H2
Klintsy 59 K3
Klyuchevskaya Sopka, *mountain* 113 K3
Klyuchi 121 T4
Knox, C., *cape* 216 D3
Knox Coast, *region* 292 H2
Knoxville, *U.S.A., Iowa* 209 J3
Knoxville, *U.S.A., Tennessee* 209 L4
Knysna 184 D6
Kōbe 113 H4
København 48 H3
Koblenz 58 F3
Kōchi 121 Q6
Ko-chiu 137 H3
Kodiak I., *island* 200 C3
Koforidua 168 C5
Kohat 136 E2
Koh-i-naba, *mountains* 120 J6
Kojonup 272 C6
Kokand 120 K5
Kokchetav 112 E3
Kokkola 58 H2
Koksoak, *river* 217 K3
Kokstad 169 F9
Kola 136 E4
Kolding 54 G3
Kolepom, *island* 113 H6
Kolguyev, O., *island* 289 J2
Kolhapur 136 E4
Köln 48 G3
Kolomna 59 K3
Kolomyya 58 J4
Kolpakovskiy 121 S4
Kolpashevo 120 L4
Kol'skiy P-ov., *peninsula* 289 K2
Kolwezi 169 F7
Kolyma, *river* 113 J2
Kolymskaya Nizmennost, *plain* 113 J2
Kolymskiy Khrebet, *mts.* 113 J2
Komadugu Gana, *river* 177 E4
Komandorskiye O-va., *island group* 113 K3
Kommunizma, Pik, *mountain* 112 E4
Kompong Cham 137 H4
Komsomolets, Zaliv, *bay* 120 H5
Komsomolets, O., *island* 121 M1
Komsomol'sk 113 H3
Kong Christian den IX's Land, *region* 200 J2
K. Frederik den VI's Kyst, *region* 200 H2
Kong Frederik den VIII's Land, *region* 200 J2
Konginskiye Gory, *mts.* 121 S3
Kongolo 168 F6
Konosha 59 L2
Konotop 59 K3
Konya 81 G3
Konya Ovasi, *plateau* 49 L5
Konzhakovskiy Kamen', G., *mountain* 49 O2
Kootenai, *region* 208 D2
Kopaonik, *mountains* 48 J4
Kopet Dag, Khr., *mts.* 49 O5
Kopeysk 59 N3
Korçë 81 E3
Korea B., *bay* 113 H4
Korea Str., *strait* 137 K2
Korf 121 T3
Korinthiakós Kólpos, *bay* 81 E3
Kórinthos 81 E3
Korkino 59 N3
Korosten 59 J3
Korsakov 121 R5
Koruteva, Sa., *mountains* 184 C4
Koryakskiy Khr., *mts.* 113 K2
Kosciusko, Mt., *mountain* 280 E5
Košice 58 H4
Kosti 177 G4
Kostroma 59 L3
Kostrzyn 58 G3
Kota Bharu 112 G5
Kota Kinabalu 169 H5
Kota Kota 169 G7
Kotel'nich 59 M2
Kotel'nyy, O., *island* 121 Q2
Kotka 58 J2
Kotlas 59 L2
Kotto, *river* 184 D2
Kotuy, *river* 121 N3
Koudougou 176 C4
Kouroussa 176 C4
Kovel' 58 J3
Kovroy 59 L3
Kowloon 137 J3
Koyp, G., *mountain* 49 O2
Koyukuk, *river* 200 C2
Kozhikode 112 E4
Kozhva 59 N2
Kra, Isthmus of, *isthmus* 137 G5
Kragujevac 81 E2
Krakatoa, *see Anak Krakatau* 137 H6
Kraków 48 J3
Kramatorsk 81 G2
Krasnoarmeyskoye 121 U3
Krasnodar 49 L4
Krasnokamsk 59 M2
Krasnotur'insk 59 N2
Krasnoufimsk 59 N3
Krasnovishersk 59 N2
Krasnovodsk 112 D3
Krasnoyarsk 112 F3
Kratie 113 G5
Kremenchug 81 G2
Krestovyy Pereval, *pass* 81 H2
Krishna, *river* 112 E5
Kristiansand 58 F2
Kristinehamn 58 G2
Kríti, *island* 48 K5
Krivoy Rog 49 L4
Kronotskiy P-ov., *peninsula* 121 T4
Kronprinsesse Märtha Kyst, *region* 292 B2
Kronprins Olav Kyst, *region* 292 E2
Kronshtadt 59 J2
Kroonstad 169 F8
Kropotkin 81 H2
Krugersdorp 169 F8
Krummel Deep, *sea feature* 248 B4
Krung Thep 112 G5
Kryazh Chernysheva, *mountains* 59 N1
Kryazh Polousnyy, *mts.* 113 H2
Krym, *peninsula* 49 L4
Krymskiye Gory, *mts.* 48 L4
Ksar el Boukhari 80 C3
Ksour Essaf 176 E2
Ksour, Mts. des, *mts.* 176 D2
Ksours, Mts. des, *mts.* 48 G6
Kuala Lumpur 112 G5
Kuang-chou 113 G4
Kuang-nan 137 H3
Kuan-hsien 137 H2
Kuantan 113 G5
Kuban', *river* 49 L4
K'u-ch'e 112 F3
Kuching 113 G5
Kudat 137 J5
Kudus 137 J6
Kuei-lin 137 J3
Kuei-p'ing 137 H3
Kuei-yang 113 G4
Kufra Oasis, *region* 168 F3
Kuhhā-ye Zagros, *mts.* 112 D4
Kuito 169 E7
Kukālār, Kūh-e, *mountain* 49 N6
Kulal, Mt., *mountain* 177 G5
Kulgera 272 F5
Kul'sary 59 M4
Kulundinskaya Step', *steppe* 112 E3
Kuma, *river* 81 H2
Kumamoto 113 H4
Kumara 277 D6
Kumasi 168 C5
Kumba 176 D5
Kumon Ra., *mountains* 137 G3
Kunashir, *island* 121 R5
Kundelungu Mts., *mts.* 184 D3
Kungur 59 N3
Kun-lun Shan, *mountains* 112 F4
K'un-ming 112 G4
Kuntsevo 59 K3
Kuopio 58 J2
Kupang 113 H6
Kura, *river* 49 N5
Kure 121 Q6
Kureyka, *river* 121 L3
Kurgan 112 E3
Kuria Muria Is., *island group* 112 D5
Kuril Ridge, *sea features* 283 B1
Kuril'sk 121 R5
Kuril'skiye O-va., *island group* 113 J3
Kuril Trench, *sea feature* 283 B1
Kurnool 136 E4
Kursk 49 L3
Kurskiy Zaliv, *bay* 58 H3
Kuruk Tagh, *mountains* 112 F3
Kuruman 169 F8
Kushiro 113 J3
Kuskokwim, *river* 200 C2
Kuskokwim Mts., *mts.* 200 C2
Kustanay 59 N3
Kutai, *river* 137 J6
Kutaisi 81 H2
Kutch, Great Rann of, *see Great Rann of Kutch* 112 E4
Kutch, G. of, *gulf* 112 E4
Kuwait 49 N6
Kuwait, *state* 49 M6
Kuybyshev, *Central R.S.F.S.R.* 120 K4
Kuybyshev, *West, R.S.F.S.R.* 120 H4
Kuybyshevskoye Vdkhr., *reservoir* 112 D3
Kuytun, G., *mountain* 112 F3
Kuzey Anadolu Dağlari, *mountains* 49 L5
Kuznetsk 59 L3
Kuznetskiy Alatau, *mts.* 49 S3
Kwa, *river* 169 E6
Kwangju 113 H4
Kwango, *river* 169 E6
Kwanza, *river* 169 E6
Kwilu, *river* 168 E6
Kyakhta 121 N4
Kyaukpyu 137 G4
Kyoga, L., *lake* 168 G5
Kyōto 113 H4
Kyrenia 81 G3
Kyūshū, *island* 113 H4
Kyūshū-Palau Rrdge, *sea feature* 283 A2
Kyzyl 121 M4
Kyzyl-Kum, Peski, *desert* 120 J5
Kzyl-Orda 120 J5

La Banda 264 B1
La Barca 232 C2
Labé 176 B4
Labe, *river* 58 G3
La Blanquilla, Isla, *island* 256 C1
Labrador, *region* 217 L3
Labuan, *island* 137 J5
Laccadive Trough, *sea feature* 145 C2
La Ceiba 233 E3
Lachlan, *river* 280 E5
La Columna, P., *mt.* 256 B2
la Coruña 80 A2
La Crosse 209 J3
Ladakh Ra., *mountain* 136 E2
Ladozhskoye Ozero, *lake* 48 K2
Lady Elliot I., *island* 275 K4
Ladysmith 169 F8
Lafayette, *U.S.A., Indiana* 209 K3
Lafayette, *U.S.A., Louisiana* 209 J5
Lafia 184 B2
Lågen, *river* 48 H2
Laghouat 176 D2
Lagos, *Nigeria* 164 D5
Lagos de Moreno 232 C2
La Grande 208 D2
La Guaira 248 C1
Laguna 264 D1
Laguna, I. da, *island* 257 D3
Lagune Aby, *lake* 184 A2
Lahad Datu 137 J5
Lahore 112 E4
Lahti 58 J2
La Junta 208 G4
Lake Charles 209 J5
Lake Eyre Basin, *region* 280 D4
Lake Harbour, *trading post* 217 L2
Lake River 217 J3
Lakselv 58 J1
Laksdahweep Islands *island group* 112 E5
La Laguna 176 B3
La Loche 216 G3
Lamar 208 G4
La Martre, Lac, *lake* 216 F2
Lambaréné 168 E6
Lambert Glacier 292 F2
Lambton, C., *cape* 216 E1
Lamé 176 E5
Lamesa 208 G5
Lamitan 137 K5
Lampi, *island* 137 G4
Lamu 168 H6
Lancaster Sd., *inlet* 200 F2
Lan-chou 112 G4
Lander, *river* 272 F4
Landes, *region* 48 F4
Landsborough 277 C6
Lands End, *Canada, cape* 200 D2
Land's End, *England, cape* 48 F3
Langres, Plateau de, *plateau* 80 C2
Lanín, Vol., *mountain* 78 A2
Lansing 209 L3
Lansdowne House 217 J3
L'Anse au Loup 217 M3
Lanzarote, *island* 176 B3
Laoag 113 H5
Lao-kay 112 G4
La Orchila, I., *island* 233 G3
La Oroya 256 B4
Laos 113 G5
La Paz, *Bolivia* 248 C4
La Paz, *Mexico* 232 B2
La Palma, *island* 168 B3
La Perouse Str., *strait* 113 J3
La Piedad 232 C2
La Plata 249 D6
Lappland, *region* 48 J1
Laptevykh, More, *sea* 289 E2
L'Aquila 80 D2
Lār 136 C3
Laramie 208 F3
Laramie Ra., *mountains* 200 E3
Laredo, *U.S.A.* 208 H6
La Rioja 264 B1
Lárisa 81 E3
Larnaca 81 G3
La Rochelle 58 E4
La Romana 233 G3
La Ronge 216 G3
La Ronge, Lac, *lake* 216 G3
Larrey Pt., *cape* 272 C3
Lars Christensen Coast, *region* 292 F2
Larsen Ice Shelf 292 R2
Larvik 58 G2
Las Cruces 208 F5
La Serena 264 A1
Las Flores 264 C2
Lashio 137 G3
La Sila, *mountain* 48 J5
Las Marismas 80 C3
Las Palmas, *Canary Is.* 168 B3
La Spezia 80 D2
Lassen Pk., *mountain* 208 C3
Last Mt., *mountain* 208 G1
Las Tres Marias, *island group* 201 E4
Las Vegas, *U.S.A., Nevada* 208 D4
Las Vegas, *U.S.A., New Mexico* 208 F4
Latacunga 256 B3
Latady I., *island* 292 R2
La Tortuga, Isla, *island* 233 G3
Latviyskaya S.S.R., *rep.* 58 H3
Launceston, *Australia* 280 E6
Laurentian Basin, *sea feature* 289 S1
Laurentian Mts. 200 G3
Laurentian Shield 200 E2
Lausanne 80 C2
Laut, *island* 113 G6
Lautaro 264 A2
Lava Beds, *region* 208 F5
Laval 80 B2
Lavapié, Pta., *cape* 249 B6
Laverton 280 C4
La Victoria 283 G3
Lawrence, *New Zealand* 277 C7
Lawton 208 H5
Leaf, *river* 200 G3
Leatherman Pk., *mt.* 208 E3
Lebanon, *state* 49 L6
Lebombo Mts., *mountains* 169 G8
Ledo, C., *cape* 184 C3
Leduc 216 F3
Leeds 48 F3
Leeuwin, C. 280 B5
Leeuwin, C., *cape* 280 B5
Leeuwin Sill, *sea feature* 280 B5
Leeward Islands, *island group* 201 G5
Lefroy, L., *lake* 272 D6
Legges Tor, *mountain* 275 J8
Leh 112 E4
Le Havre 48 G4
Leicester 48 F3
Leichhardt, *river* 280 D3
Leichhardt Ra., *mts.* 280 E4
Lei-chou pan-tao, *peninsula* 113 G4
Leigh Creek 273 G6
Leipzig 48 H3
Leisler, Mt., *mountain* 272 E4
Léman, L., *lake* 48 G4
Le Mans 80 C2
Lena, *river* 112 H2
Lengua de Vaca, Pta., *cape* 249 B6
Leninabad 120 J5
Leninakan 81 H3
Lenina, Pik, *mountain* 120 K6
Leningrad 48 K2
Leninogorsk, *R.S.F.S.R.* 120 L4
Leninski-Kuznetskiy 121 L4
Lenkoran 120 G6
León, *Mexico* 201 E4
León, *Nicaragua* 201 F5
León, *Spain* 80 B2
Leopold II, Lake, *See Mai-Ndombe* 177 E6
Lérida 80 C3
Lerwick 58 E2
Les Cayes 233 F3
Lesotho 169 F8
Lesozavodsk 121 Q5
Lesser Antilles, *island group* 201 G5
Lesser Slave L., *lake* 216 F3
Lesser Sunda Is., *island group* 113 H6
Lésvos, *island* 48 K5
Lethbridge 216 F4
Leticia 248 C3
Leti, Kep., *island group* 280 C2
Levelland 208 G5
Lévêque, C., *cape* 280 C3
Levier, B. du, *bay* 168 B3
Levin 276 F5
Lewis Range, *mountains* 216 F4
Lewiston, *U.S.A., Idaho* 208 D2
Lewiston, *U.S.A., Maine* 209 N3
Lexington, *U.S.A., Kentucky* 209 L4
Leyte, *island* 137 K4
Lhasa 112 F4
Liao-yang 121 P5
Liard, *river* 216 E2
Libenge 108 E5
Liberal 208 G4
Liberia 168 B5
Libnan, Jebel, *mountains* 81 G4
Libreville 168 D5
Libya 168 E3
Libyan Desert, *desert* 168 F3
Libyan Plateau, *plateau* 168 F2
Li-chiang 137 H3
Lichinga 169 G7
Lichtenburg 169 F8
Lidköping 58 G2
Liebig Ra., *mountains* 277 D6
Liechtenstein 48 H4
Lien-yun-kang 137 J2
Liepāja 58 H3
Lifi Mahuida, *mountain* 264 B3
Ligonha, *river* 185 E4
Ligurian Sea 48 H4
Lihou Reef and Cays, *reefs* 281 F3
Likasi 169 F7
Lille 58 F3
Lillehammer 58 G2
Lilongwe 169 G7
Lima, *Peru* 248 B4
Limassol 81 G3
Limay, *river* 264 B2
Limbe 185 E4
Limfjorden, *channel* 48 H3
Limmen, Bight, *gulf* 280 D3
Límnos, *island* 48 K5
Limoges 80 C2
Limón 233 E3
Limpopo, *river* 169 F8
Linares, *Chile* 264 A2
Linares, *Mexico* 232 D2
Linares, *Spain* 80 B3
Lin-ch'uan 137 J3
Lincoln, *U.S.A., Nebraska* 208 H3
Lincoln Sea 289 P1
Lindesay, Mt., *mountain* 209 E4
Lindesnes, *cape* 48 G3
Lindi 169 G6
Line Islands, *island group* 283 C2
Lin-fen 137 J2
Lingga, Kep., *island group* 137 H5
Ling-ling 137 J3
Lin-hsi 121 O5
Linköping 58 G2
Lin-tao 137 H2
Linz 58 G4
Lion, Golfe du, *gulf* 48 G4
Lipari, Isole, *island group* 48 H5
Lipetsk 49 L3
Lipez, Cord. de., *mts.* 256 C5
Lisala 168 F5
Lisboa 48 E5
Lisburne, C., *cape* 200 B2
Liski 59 K3
Lismore, *Australia* 273 K5
Lithgow 273 K6
Litovskaya S.S.R., *rep.* 58 H3
Little America V., *scientific base* 292 M2
Little Bahama Bank, *sea feature* 209 M6
Little Barrier I., *island* 276 F3
Little Belt Mts., *mts.* 216 F4
Little Colorado, *river* 208 E4
Little Karroo, *region* 184 D6
Little Missouri, *river* 208 G2
Little Rock 209 J5
Liu-chou 113 G4
Liulaka, *river* 177 F6
Liverpool, *Australia* 273 K6
Liverpool, *England* 48 F3
Liverpool Bay, *bay* 216 E1
Liverpool Plains, *region* 280 F5
Liverpool Ra., *mountains* 280 F5
Livingston 208 E2
Livingstone I., *island* 292 R2
Livingstone Mts., *mts.* 185 E3
Livramento 264 C2
Lizard Pt., *cape* 58 E4
Ljubljana 80 D2
Llano de los Caballos Mesteños, *region* 232 C2
Llano Estacado, *region* 200 E4
Llanos, *region* 248 C2
Llanos de Mojos, *region* 248 C4
Lloydminster 216 F3
Llullaillaco, Vol., *mt.* 248 C5
Lobatse 169 F8
Lobito 169 E7
Lobstick L., *lake* 217 L3
Lodeynoye Pole 59 K2
Lodi, *U.S.A.* 208 C4
Lódz 48 J3
Lofoten, *island group* 48 H1
Lofty Ra., *mountains* 272 C4

Logan 208 E3
Logan, Mt., *Canada, mt.* 200 C2
Logan Mts., *mountains* 216 E2
Logone, *river* 168 E4
Logroño 80 B2
Loire, *river* 48 G4
Loja, *Ecuador* 256 B3
Loko 176 E5
Loks Land, *island* 217 L2
Lomami, *river* 168 F6
Lomas Coloradas, *mts.* 248 B3
Lomas de Zamora 264 C2
Lombard, Serra, *mts.* 257 D2
Lombok, *island* 113 G6
Lomé 168 D5
Lomela, *river* 184 D3
Lomonosov (Harris) Ridge, *sea feature* 289 O1
London, *Canada* 217 J4
London, *England* 48 F3
Londonderry 58 E3
Londonderry, C., *cape* 280 C3
Longa, Proliv, *strait* 113 K2
Long Bay, *bay* 209 M5
Long Beach 200 E4
Longfellow, Mt., *mt.* 277 E6
Long Forties, *sea feature* 48 F3
Long I., *Bahama Is., island* 201 G4
Long I., *New Zealand, island* 277 B8
Long I., *U.S.A.* 200 G3
Longmont 208 F3
Long Pt., *New Zealand, cape* 277 C8
Long Ra. Mts., *mountains* 200 H3
Longreach 273 H4
Longs Pk., *mountain* 200 E3
Longview 208 C2
Lookout, C., *cape* 200 G4
Lookout Pt., *cape* 277 C8
Lookout Ridge, *mts.* 216 B2
Lopatka, Mys., *cape* 113 J3
Lopez, C., *cape* 168 D6
Lop Nor, *seasonal lake* 112 F3
Lorain 209 L3
Loralai 136 D2
Lorca 80 B3
Lord Howe I., *island* 281 F5
Lord Howe Rise, *sea feature* 283 B3
Lorengau 280 E2
Lorian Swamp, *swamp* 177 G5
L'Orne Bank, *sea feature* 283 C3
Los Andes 264 A2
Los Alamos 208 F4
Los Angeles, *Chile* 264 A2
Los Angeles, *U.S.A.* 200 E4
Los Iles de, *island group* 176 B5
Los Mochis 232 C2
Los Roques, Islas, *island group* 256 C1
Los Roques Trench, *sea feature* 233 G3
Los Teques 256 C1
Lota 264 A2
Lotagipi Swamp, *swamp* 177 G5
Lo-ting 137 J3
Louisburg 217 L4
Louisiade Archo., *island group* 281 F3
Louisiade Ridge, *sea feature* 281 F3
Louisiana, *state* 209 J5
Louis Trichardt 169 F8
Louisville 200 F4
Lourenço Marques, *see Maputo* 185 E5
Lousy Bank, *sea feature* 48 E2
Lovat', *river* 59 J3
Lower Hutt 276 F5
Lo-yang 113 G4
Loyauté, Is., *island group* 281 G4
Lualaba, *river* 169 F7
Luanda 169 E6
Luanda, I. de, *island* 184 C3
Luang Prabang 112 G5
Luangwa, *river* 169 G7
Luan Ho, *river* 121 O5
Luapula, *river* 184 D3
Lubang Is., *island group* 137 K4
Lubango 169 E7
Lubbock 208 G5
Lubilash, *river* 184 D3
Lublin 48 J3
Lubny 59 K3
Lubudi 184 D3
Lubumbashi 169 F7
Lu-chou 113 G4
Lucknow 112 F4
Lüderitz 169 E8
Ludhiana 112 E4
Ludogorie, *mountains* 81 F2
Ludvika 58 G2
Luebo 169 F6
Lufira, *river* 184 D3
Luga 59 J2
Lugenda, *river* 185 E4
Lugh Ferrandi 168 H5
Lukuga, *river* 184 D3
Luleå 58 H2
Lüneburger Heide, *heath* 58 G3
Lung-ch'i 137 J3
Lung-ling 137 G3
Lu-pin 121 O5
Lúrio, *river* 169 G7
Lusaka 168 F7
Lusambo 169 F6
Lü-ta 113 H4
Lutsk 81 F1
Lützow-Holmbukta, *bay* 292 D2
Luvua, *river* 184 D3
Luxembourg 48 G4
Luxembourg, *state* 48 G4
Luzon, *island* 113 H5
Luzon Str., *strait* 113 H4
L'vov 112 C3
Lyakhovskoye Ostrova 121 R2
Lydenburg 169 G8
Lyell, Mt., *mountain* 208 D4
Lyell Ra., *mountains* 276 E5
Lynchburg 209 M4
Lynn Lake 216 G3
Lyons, *Australia* 280 B4
Lys'va 120 H4
Lyttleton 277 E6
Ma'ān 81 G4
Maastricht 58 F3
Maaza Plat., *plateau* 177 G3
Macadam Plains, *region* 272 C5
Macapá 248 D2
Macarena, Cord., *mts.* 256 B2
Macau 113 G4
Macdonald, L., *seasonal lake* 272 E4
Macdonnell Ranges, *mountains* 280 D4
Macedon, *mountain* 273 H7
Maceió 248 F3
Macfarlane, L., *seasonal lake* 272 G6
Machala 256 B3
Machattie, L., *seasonal lake* 273 G4
Machilipatnam 112 F5
Ma Chu, *river* 137 G2
Macias Nguéma Biyoga, *island* 168 D5
Mackay 273 J4
Mackay, L., *seasonal lake* 280 C4
Mackenzie, *region* 216 E2
Mackenzie, *Canada, river* 200 D2
Mackenzie Bay, *bay* 200 D2
Mackenzie Mts., *mts.* 200 D2
Mackenzie Plains, *region* 277 D7
Macleod 216 F4
Macon, *U.S.A.* 209 L5
Macquarie, *river* 273 J6
Macquarie-Balleny Ridge, *sea feature* 292 L2
Macquarie I., *island* 292 K3
Macquarie Rise, *sea feature* 292 K3
Mac-Robertson Land, *region* 292 F2
Madagascar, *island* 33 G4
Madagascar, Republic of 169 H7
Madang 280 E2
Madeira, *island* 168 B2
Madeira, *river* 248 C3
Madeleine, Iles de la, *island group* 217 L4
Madinat al Shaab 112 D5
Madison 209 K3
Madiun 137 J6
Madrakah, Ra's al, *cape* 136 C4
Madras 112 F5
Madre de Dios, *river* 248 C4
Madre del Sur., Sa., *mountains* 201 F5
Madre, Laguna, *U.S.A.* 208 H6
Madre Occidental, Sierra, *mountains* 201 E4
Madre Oriental, Sierra, *mountains* 201 E4
Madre, Sa., *Mexico, mts.* 201 F5
Madre, Sa., *Philippines, mountains* 113 H5
Madrid, *Spain* 48 F5
Madura, *island* 113 G6
Madurai 112 E5
Mae Khong, *river* 112 G5
Maestra, Sa., *mountains* 200 G4
Maevatanana 169 H7
M. Yom, *river* 137 G4
Mafeking 169 F8
Mafeteng 184 D6
Mafia I., *island* 112 D6
Magadan 113 J3
Magallanes, Est. de, *strait* 249 C8
Magangué 256 B2
Magdagachi 113 H3
Magdalena, *river* 248 B2
Magdalena, Bahia, *bay* 232 B2
Magdalena, I., *island* 232 B2
Magdeburg 48 H3
Magellan Seamounts *sea features* 283 B2
Maggiore, L., *lake* 80 D2
Maglič I., *mountain* 48 J4
Magnetic I., *island* 275 J3
Magnitogorsk 49 O3
Magrath 216 F4
Magwe 137 G3
Mahābād 120 G6
Mahanadi, *river* 136 F3
Mahia Pena., *peininsula* 276 G4
Mahón 80 C3
Maiduguri 168 E4
Main, *Fed. Rep. of Germany, river* 80 D1
Main Barrier Ra., *mts.* 280 E5
Mai-Ndombe, *lake* 168 E6
Maine, *U.S.A., state* 209 N2
Maintirano 169 H7
Maiquetia 256 C1
Maire, Est. de le, *strait* 249 C8
Mainsi, C., *cape* 233 F2
Mait I., *island* 185 F1
Maitland 273 K6
Maiz, Is. del, *island group* 233 E3
Majene 137 J6
Maji 185 E2
Majunga 169 H7
Makarikari, *swamp* 169 F8
Makarov 121 R5
Makasar, Sel., *strait* 113 G6
Makeyevka 49 L4
Makhachkala 81 H2
Makinsk 120 K4
Makkah 112 C4
Makorako, *mountain* 276 G4
Makran, *region* 112 E4
Makteir, *region* 176 B3
Makurdi 176 D5
Malacca 112 G5
Malacca, Str. of, *strait* 112 F5
Málaga, *Colombia* 233 F4
Malaga, *Spain* 48 F5
Malaita I., *island* 281 G2
Malang 113 G6
Malanje 169 E6
Mala, Pta., *cape* 248 B2
Malaren, *lake* 48 J2
Malatya 81 G3
Malawi 169 G7
Malawi, Lake, *lake* 169 G7
Malay Pena., *peninsula* 112 G5
Malaysia 112 G5
Malazgirt 81 H3
Maldive Islands, *island group* 145 C2
Maldive Ridge, *sea feature* 145 C2
Maldonado 264 C2
Maldonado, Pta., *cape* 232 D3
Male 112 E5
Maléa, Akr., *cape* 81 E3
Malegaon 136 E3
Malekula, *island* 281 G3
Malí, *state* 168 C4
Malindi 168 H6
Malin Hd., *cape* 48 F3
Mallorca, *island* 48 G5
Malmesbury 169 E9
Malmö 48 H3
Malozoemel'skaya Tundra, *region* 49 N1
Malpelo 283 E2
Malta, *island* 48 H5
Malta Chan., *channel* 48 H5
Maluku, *island group* 113 H6
Maluku, Laut, *sea* 113 H6
Malyy Kavkaz, *mts.* 81 H3
Malyy Yenisey, *river* 121 M4
Mamoré, *river* 248 C4
Mamou 176 B4
Man 176 C5
Manacor 80 C3
Manado 113 H5
Managua 201 F5
Managua, L. de, *lake* 233 E3
Manakara 169 H8
Mānasarowar L., *lake* 136 F2
Manaus 248 C3
Manawatu, *river* 276 F5
Manawatu Gorge, *gorge* 276 F5
Mancha, La, *region* 80 B3
Manchester, *England* 48 F3
Manchester, *U.S.A.* 209 N3
Manchouli, *see Lu-pin* 121 O5
Manchuria, *region* 113 H3
Mandal 58 F2
Mandalay 112 F4
Mandan 216 G4
Mandara Mts., *mts.* 168 E4
Manding, *region* 168 C4
Manga, *region* 168 E4
Mangabeiras, Sa. das, *mountains* 257 E4
Mangakino 276 F4
Mangalore 112 E5
Mangaweka, *mountain* 276 G4
Mangoky, *river* 185 F5
Mangueni, Hamada, *plateau* 176 E3
Mangyshiak, P-ov, *peninsula* 49 N4
Manika, Plat. de la, *plateau* 184 D4
Manila 113 H5
Manisa 81 F3
Man, I. of, *island* 48 F3
Manitoba, *province* 216 H3
Manitoba, L., *lake* 200 F3
Manitoulin I., *island* 217 J4
Manizales 256 B2
Manjimup 272 C6
Mannar, G. of, *gulf* 112 E5
Mannheim 48 H4
Manokwari 113 H6
Manono 169 F6
Manresa 80 C3
Mansel I., *island* 200 F2
Mansfield, *U.S.A.* 209 L3
Manso, *river* 257 D4
Manta 256 A3
Mantiqueira, Sa. da, *mountains* 248 E5
Manukau Harb., *harbour* 276 F3
Manych-Gudilo, Ozero, *lake* 81 H2
Manychskaya Vpadina, *region* 81 H2
Manzanillo, *Cuba* 233 F2
Manzanillo, *Mexico* 232 C3
Manzano Mts., *mountains* 208 F5
Manzini 184 E5
Maouin Pena., *peninsula* 48 H5
Maple Creek 216 G4
Mapuera, *river* 256 D3
Maputo 169 G8
Mar del Plata 249 D6
Mar, Sa. do, *mountains* 248 E5
Maracá, I. de, *island* 248 D2
Maracaibo 248 B1
Maracaibo, L. de, *lake* 248 B2
Maracajú, Sa. de, *mts.* 256 D5
Maracay 248 C1
Maradi 168 D4
Marañuaca, Co., *mt.* 233 G4
Marajó, I. de, *island* 248 E3
Maramba 169 F7
Marañón, *river* 248 B3
Maraş 81 G3
Marau Pt., *cape* 276 H4
Marble Bar 272 C4
Marca, Pta. d, *cape* 184 C4
Mar Chiquita, *cape* 249 C6
Marcus I., *island* 113 J4
Marcus-Necker Rise, *sea feature* 283 B2
Mardan 136 E2
Mardin 81 H3
Mareeba 273 J3
Margaret, *river* 272 E3
Margarita, I. de, *island* 233 G3
Marguerite Bay, *bay* 292 R2
Margungu, *mountain* 184 D3
Maria Augustina Bank, *sea feature* 145 E3
Maria Elena 256 C5
Maria I., *island* 272 G2
Marianao 233 E2
Marianas, *island group* 283 B2
Marianas Ridge, *sea feature* 283 B2
Marianas Tr., *sea feature* 283 B2
Maria van Diemen, C., *cape* 281 H5
Marie Galante, *island* 233 G3
Mariental 169 E8
Mariinsk 121 L4
Marilia 257 D5
Marimas, Las, *region* 80 B3
Marion, *U.S.A., Illinois* 209 K4
Marion I., *island* 292 D3
Marion, L., *lake* 209 L5
Marion Reef, *reef* 281 F3
Maritsa, *river* 48 K4
Marittime, Alpi, *mts.* 48 G4
Marlborough, *county* 276 E5
Marlin 209 H5
Marmara, Sea of 48 K5
Maroantsetra 185 F4
Maroua 176 E4
Marquesas, *island group* 283 D3
Marquette 209 K2
Marra, Jebel, *mountains* 168 F4
Marrakech 168 C2
Marree 273 G5
Marsala 80 D3
Marseille 48 G4
Marshall Islands, *island group* 283 B2
Martaban, G. of, *gulf* 112 F5
Martha's Vineyard, *island* 200 G3
Martinborough 276 F5
Martinique, *island* 201 G5
Martinique Pass, *strait* 233 G3
Martin Vaz, *island* 100 D5
Marton 276 F5
Maryborough, *Australia Queensland* 273 K5
Maryborough, *Australia, Victoria* 273 H7
Maryland, *state* 209 M4
Masai Steppe, *steppe* 168 G6
Masaka 185 E3
Masan 121 P6
Masaya 233 E3
Masbate 113 H5
Mascara 80 C3
Mascarene Basin, *sea feature* 145 B3
Mascarene Ridge, *sea feature* 145 B3
Maseru 169 F8
Mashābih, J., *island* 177 G3
Mashhad 112 D4
Mashonaland, *region* 184 E4
Masindi 177 G5
Masoala, C., *cape* 169 J7
Masirah, J., *island* 112 D4
Massawa 168 G4
Massif Central, *mts.* 80 C2
Massif de L'Ouarsenis, *mountains* 80 C3
Massif du Tsaratanana, *mountains* 169 H7
Masterton 276 F5
Mata, Sa. de, *mountains* 256 C2
Matabeleland, *region* 184 D4
Matabele Plain, *region* 184 D4
Matadi 169 E6
Matagalpa 233 E3
Matagorda I., *island* 209 H6
Mataimoana, *mountain* 276 F4
Matakana I., *island* 276 G3
Matamata 276 F3
Matamoros, *Central Mexico* 232 C2
Matamoros, *East Mexico* 232 D2
Matanzas 200 F4
Mataram 137 J6
Mataura 277 C8
Matehuala 232 C2
Mathura 136 E3
Matochkin Shar, Proliv, *strait* 112 D2
Mato Grosso, Planalto do, *plateau* 248 D4
Matopo Hills, *mountains* 184 D5
Matrūh 177 F2
Matsue 121 Q6
Matsuyama 113 H4
Matterhorn, *Switzerland mountain* 48 G4
Matterhorn, *U.S.A., mountain* 208 D3
Matthew, *island* 281 H4
Maturin 256 C2
Maudheim, *scientific base* 292 B2
Maud Seamount, *sea feature* 292 C2
Maumere 137 K6
Maungahaumi, *mountain* 276 G4
Maungamangero, *mt.* 276 F4
Maungataniwha, *mt.* 276 G4
Mau Ra., *mountains* 168 G6
Maurice, L., *seasonal lake* 272 F5
Mauritania 168 B4
Mauritius, *island* 145 B4
Mauritius Basin, *sea feature* 145 B4
Mawson, *scientific base* 292 F2
Mawson Coast, *region* 292 F2
Mayadin 81 H3
Mayaguana, *island* 201 G4
Mayaguana Passage, *strait* 233 F2
Mayagüez 233 G3
Maya Mts., *mountains* 201 F5
Maykop 81 G2
Mayo Landing 216 D2
Mayor I., *New Zealand, island* 276 G3
Mayotte, *island* 169 H7
Mayoumba 168 E6
May Pen 233 F3
May Pt., C., *cape* 209 N4
Mazagan, *see El-Jadida* 176 C2
Mazandaran, *region* 49 N5
Mazar-i-Sharif 136 D2
Mazatenango 232 D3
Mazatlán 232 C2
Mazury, *region* 48 J3
Mbabane 169 G8
M'Baïki 176 E5
Mbale 177 G5
Mbandaka 168 E5
Mbarara 177 G6
Mbeya 169 G6
M'Bour 176 B4
Mbuji-Mayi 169 F6
McArthur, *river* 272 G3
McClintock Chan., *chan.* 200 E2
McClure Strait, *strait* 216 E1
McConnell Ra., *mts.* 216 E2
McCook 208 G3
McDouall Ra., *mountains* 272 F3
McIlwraith Ra., *mts.* 273 H2
McKinley, Mt., *mountain* 200 C2
McLennan 216 F3
McMurdo, *scientific base* 292 L2
McMurdo Sound, *inlet* 292 L2
McMurray 216 F3
Mdennah 176 C3
Mead, L., *lake* 208 E4
Meadow Lake 216 G3
Mealy Mts., *mountains* 200 H3
Mecca, *see Makkah* 136 A3
Medan 112 F5
Medellín 248 B2
Médenine 80 D4
Medford 208 C3
Medicine Bow Mts., *mountains* 208 F3
Medicine Hat 216 F3
Medina, *see Al Madinah* 136 A3
Mediterranean Sea 48 G5
Medjerda, Mts. de la, *mountains* 176 D2
Mednogorsk 59 N3
Medvezhiy, O-va, *island* 121 T2
Medvezh'yegorsk 59 K2
Meekatharra 272 C5
Meerut 136 E3
Meidob Hills, *mountains* 177 F4
Meknès 168 C2
Mekong, *river* 113 C4
Mekong, Mouths of the, *river mouths* 113 G5
Melanesia, *island groups* 283 A2
Melanesian Border Plateau, *sea feature* 283 B3
Melau 177 G4
Melbourne 280 E5
Melfort 216 G3
Melilla 168 C2
Melina, Mt., *mountain* 277 C7
Melitopol' 81 G2
Mellish Bank, *sea feature* 283 B2
Mellish Reef, *sea feature* 273 K3
Mellish Rise, *sea feature* 281 F3
Melville 208 G1
Melville C., *cape* 280 E3
Melville Hills, *mountains* 200 D2
Melville I., *Australia, island* 280 D3
Melville, I., *Canada, island* 200 E2
Melville Pena., *peninsula* 200 F2
Melville Sd., *inlet* 216 G2
Memphis, *U.S.A.* 200 F4
Mendocino, C., *cape* 200 D3
Mendocino Fracture Zone, *sea feature* 24 B3
Mendocino Seascarp, *sea feature* 283 C1
Mendoza 249 C6
Meng-tzu 112 G4
Menindee 273 H6
Menindee, L., *lake* 273 H6
Menorca, *island* 48 G5
Mentawai Kep., *island group* 137 G6
Mentawai Ridge., *sea feature* 145 D2
Mentawai Trench, *sea feature* 145 D2
Menzelinsk 59 M3
Menzies, Mt., *mountain* 292 F2
Meratus, Peg., *mountains* 137 J6
Merca 177 H5
Mercedario, C., *mt.* 264 A2
Mercedes, *Central Argentina* 264 C2
Mercedes, *East Argentina* 264 C2
Mercury Is., *island group* 276 F3
Mercy, C., *cape* 200 G2
Mergui 112 F5
Mergui Archo., *island group* 112 F5
Mérida, *Mexico* 200 F4
Mérida, *Venezuela* 256 B2
Mérida, Cord. de, *mts.* 264 B2
Meridian 209 K5
Mermaid Reef, *reef* 272 C3
Mernoo Bank, *sea feature* 277 F6
Meroë, *region* 177 G4
Merowe 108 G4
Merowe, *region* 108 F4
Merredin 272 C6
Mersin 81 G3
Meru, *mountain* 168 G6
Merzifon 81 G3
Mesa 208 E5
Mesabi Ra., *mountains* 209 J2
Meseta, *region* 168 C2
Meseta de Montemayor, *region* 264 B3
Meshchorskaya Nizina, *region* 59 L3
Messak Mellet, *mountain* 176 E3
Messak Set'tafet, *mts.* 176 E3
Messina, *Italy* 48 H5

Phoenix 200 E4
Phoenix Is., *island group* 283 C3
Phuket 137 G5
Phuket, *island* 137 G5
Phu Quoc, I. du, *island* 137 H4
Piacenza 80 D2
Piaui, Sa. dó, *mountains* 248 E3
Pickle Bank, *sea feature* 233 E2
Picton, *Canada* 276 E2
Picton, *New Zealand* 216 F5
Piedecuesta 233 F4
Piedras Negras 232 C2
Pielinen, *lake* 48 K2
Pierre 208 G3
Pietarsaari 58 H2
Pietermaritzburg 169 G8
Pietersburg 169 F8
Pietrosul, *mountain* 81 F2
Pilcomayo, *river* 248 C5
Pinar del Rio 233 E2
Pindhos, *mountains* 48 J5
Pine Bluff 209 J5
Pinega 59 L2
Pinega, *river* 49 M2
Pine I. Bay, *bay* 292 P2
Pine Islands, *Cuba, island group* 201 F4
Pingelly 272 C6
P'ing-lo, *China, Kwangsi* 137 J3
P'ing-lo, *China, Ningsia Hui Aut-Reg.* 137 H2
P'ing-ting 121 O6
Pinrang 137 J6
Pinto Butte, *mountain* 208 F2
Pioneer Mts., *mountains* 208 E2
Piotrków Trybunalski 58 H3
Pipípí, *mountain* 276 F4
Piracicaba 257 E5
Piraiévs 81 E3
Pirapora 257 E4
Pirongia, *mountain* 276 F3
Pisa 80 D2
Pissís Co., *mountain* 249 C5
Pita 176 B4
Pitcairn I., *island* 283 D3
Piteà 58 H2
Pittsburg, *U.S.A., Missouri* 209 J4
Pittsburgh, *U.S.A., Pennsylvania* 200 G3
Pittsfield 209 N3
Placentia Bay, *bay* 217 M4
Planalto do Mato Grosso, *see Mato Grosso* 248 D4
Planet Deep, *sea feature* 281 F2
Plasencia 80 B3
Plato Ustyurt, *region* 49 N4
Platte, *river* 200 F3
Plenty, Bay of, *bay* 281 H5
Ploesti 81 F2
Plovdiv 48 K4
Plymouth 58 E3
Plymouth, *island* 233 G3
Plzeň 58 G4
Po, *river* 48 H4
Pobedy, Pik, *mountain* 112 F3
Pocatello 208 E3
Pocos de Caldas 257 E5
Podkamennaya Tunguska, *river* 121 M3
Podol'sk 59 K3
Podporozh'ye 59 K2
Po Hai, *gulf* 113 H4
Pohokura, *mountain* 276 G4
Pointe-à-Pitre 233 G3
Pointe-Noire 168 E6
Poitiers 80 C2
Po-k'u-t'u 121 P5
Poland 48 J3
Polatli 81 G3
Poles'ye, *region* 48 K3
Pollock Reef, *reef* 272 D6
Polotsk 59 J3
Poltava 49 L4
Polyarnyy Ural, *mts.* 49 P1
Polynesia, *island groups* 283 C3
Ponce 201 G5
Pond Inlet 217 K1
Ponoy, *river* 48 L1
Ponta Grossa 264 C1
Ponta Porã 256 D5
Pontchartrain, L., *lake* 209 J5
Ponte Nova 257 E5
Pontianak 113 G6
Pool Malebo, *lake* 184 C3
Poopó, L. de, *lake* 248 C4
Poor Knights Is., *island group* 276 F2
Popacatepetl, *mountain* 201 F5
Popayán 256 B2
Poplar Bluff 217 J4
Porbandar 48 D3
Porcupine, *river* 200 C2
Porcupine Bank, *sea feature* 48 E3
Porcupine Mts., *Canada, mountains* 208 G1
Pori 58 H2
Porlamar 256 C1
Poronaysk 121 R5
Porpoise Bay, *bay* 292 J2
Portachuelo 256 C4
Portage la Prairie 216 H4
Port Alberni 208 B2
Portales 232 C1
Port Angeles 208 C2
Port Arthur, *U.S.A.* 209 J6
Port Augusta 273 G6
Port-au-Prince 201 G5
Port Blair 137 G4
Port-de-Paix 233 F3
Port Elizabeth 169 F9
Port-Gentil 168 D6
Port Harcourt 168 D5
Port Harrison, *see Inoucdjouac* 217 K3
Port Hedland 272 C4
Port Hope Simpson 217 M3
Port Huron 209 L3
Port Kelang 137 H5
Port Kembla 273 K6
Portland, *Australia, Victoria* 273 H7
Portland, *U.S.A., Maine* 200 G3
Portland, *U.S.A., Oregon* 200 D3
Portland, C., *cape* 273 J8
Portland I., *island* 276 G4
Portland Promontory, *cape* 217 K3
Portland Pt., *cape* 233 F3
Port Lincoln 280 D5
Port Lockroy 292 R2
Port Louis 185 G5
Port Menier 217 L4
Port Moresby 280 E2
Port Nelson 216 H3
Port Nicholson, *harbour* 276 F5
Port Nolloth 169 E8
Port-Nouveau-Quebec 217 L3
Porto 48 E5
Pôrto Alegre 249 D6
Porto Alexandre 169 E7
Porto Amboim 184 C4
Port of Spain 248 C1
Porto Novo 168 D5
Porto Santo 176 B2
Pôrto Velho 248 C3
Port Pegasus, *inlet* 277 B8
Port Pirie 280 D5
Port Radium 216 F2
Port Said, *see Būr Sa'īd* 177 G2
Port Shepstone 169 G9
Portsmouth, *England* 58 E3
Portsmouth, *U.S.A., Virginia* 209 M4
Port Sudan 168 G4
Portugal 48 E5
Posadas, *Argentina* 264 C1
Poso 113 H6
Poste-de-la-Baleina 217 K3
Poteriteri, L., *lake* 277 B8
Potgietersrus 169 F8
Poti 81 H2
Potiskum 168 E4
Potomac 209 M4
Potosi 248 C4
Poughkeepsie 209 N3
Poverty Bay, *bay* 276 G4
Powder, *river* 208 F2
P'o-yang Hu, *lake* 113 G4
Poza Rica 232 D2
Poznań 48 J3
Prachuap Khiri Khan 112 F5
Praha 48 H3
Pratt 208 H4
Precordillera, *mts.* 264 B1
Premier Downs, *hills* 272 E6
Prescott, *U.S.A.* 208 E5
Preservation Inlet, *inlet* 277 B8
Presidente Prudente 264 C1
Presque Isle 209 O2
Pretoria 169 F8
Prévaza 81 E3
Pribilof Is., *island group* 113 L3
Price 208 E4
Prichernomorskaya Nizmennost', *plain* 81 G2
Pridneprovskaya Nizmennost, *plain* 48 K3
Prieska 169 F8
Prikaspiyskaya Nizmennost', *plain* 49 N4
Prikubanskaya Nizmennost', *plain* 49 L4
Priluki 59 K3
Prince Albert, *Canada* 216 G3
Prince Albert Pena., *peninsula* 216 F1
Prince Albert Sd., *inlet* 216 F1
Pr. Alfred C., *cape* 200 D2
Pr. Charles I., *island* 200 G2
Prince Edward-Crozet Ridge, *sea feature* 145 A5
Prince Edward I., *island* 200 G3
Prince Edward Is., *island group* 145 A5
Prince George 216 E3
Pr. of Wales, C., *cape* 200 B2
Prince of Wales I., *Canada, island* 200 E2
Prince of Wales I., *U.S.A., island* 200 D3
Prince of Wales Str., *strait* 216 F1
Pr. Patrick I., *island* 200 D2
Prince Regent Inlet, *inlet* 216 H1
Prince Rupert 200 D3
Princes Highway 273 J7
Princess Charlotte Bay, *bay* 273 H2
Princess Elizabeth Land, *region* 292 G2
Principe, *island* 168 D5
Prinsesse Astrid Kyst, *region* 292 C2
Prinsesse Ragnhild Kyst, *region* 292 D2
Prins Harald Kyst, *region* 292 D2
Priozersk 59 J2
Pripolyarnyy Ural, *mts.* 49 O2
Pripyat', *river* 48 K3
Privolzhskaya Vozvysh., *plateau* 49 M3
Progreso 232 E2
Prokop'yevsk 112 F3
Prome 112 F5
Proserpine 273 J4
Providence 209 N3
Providence, C., *cape* 281 G6
Providence Is., *island group* 169 J6
Providencia, I. de, *island* 233 E3
Provo 208 E3
Prut, *river* 48 K4
Prydz Bay, *bay* 292 F2
Przemyśl 81 E2
Przheval'sk 120 K5
Pskov 59 J3
Pucallpa 256 B3
Pudozh 59 K2
Puebla 201 F5
Pueblo, *U.S.A.* 208 G4
Puerto Armuelles 233 E4
Puerto Ayacucho 257 C2
Pto. Aysén 264 A3
Pto. Barrios 233 E3
Puerto Berrío 233 F4
Pto. Cabello 233 G3
Puerto Carreño 256 C2
Pto. Cortés 233 E3
Pto. La Cruz 233 G3
Puerto Montt 249 B7
Puerto Natales 264 A4
Puerto Plata 201 G5
Puerto Rico 201 G5
Puerto Rico Trench, *sea feature* 201 G5
Puerto Santa Cruz 249 C8
Puget Sd., *inlet* 208 C2
Pukekohe 276 F3
Puketeraki Ra., *mts.* 276 E6
Puketoi Ra., *mountains* 276 F5
Pullman 208 D2
Puna de Atacama, *region* 248 C5
Puna 112 E5
Puná, I., *island* 248 A3
Punakha 112 F4
Punjab, *region* 112 E4
Puno 256 B4
Punta Arenas 249 B8
Punta, C. de, *mountain* 233 G3
Puntarenas 233 E3
Puntas Negras, Co., *mountain* 264 B1
Purcell Mts., *mountains* 200 E3
Puri 137 F4
Pursat 137 H4
Purus, *river* 248 C3
Pusan 113 H4
Pushkin 59 J2
Putaruru 276 F4
Putjak Djaja, *mountain* 280 D2
Putorana, Gory, *mts.* 112 F2
Putumayo, *river* 248 B3
Pyasina, *river* 121 L2
Pyatigorsk 81 H2
Pyong Yāng 112 H4
Pyramid Lake, *lake* 208 D3
Pyrenees, *mountains* 48 F4

Qa'āmīyāt, Al., *region* 136 B4
Qabr al Hindī, Ra's, *cape* 136 C3
Qasā, J. al, *mountains* 177 J4
Qaşbah, Ra's, *cape* 81 G4
Qatar 112 D4
Qattara Depression, *region* 168 F3
Qazvīn 120 G6
Qena 168 G3
Qeshm 136 C3
Qizān 136 B4
Qom 112 D4
Quairading 272 C6
Qu'Appelle, *river* 208 G1
Queanbeyan 273 J7
Quebec 200 G3
Quebec, *province* 217 K3
Queen Alexandra Range, *mountains* 292 L1
Queen Bess, Mt., *mt.* 216 E3
Queen Charlotte Is., *island group* 200 D3
Queen Charlotte Sound, *Canada, inlet* 216 E3
Queen Charlotte Sd., *New Zealand, inlet* 276 F5
Queen Charlotte Str., *strait* 208 B1
Queen Elizabeth Islands, *island group* 200 E2
Queen Mary Land, *region* 292 G2
Queen Maud Gulf, *gulf* 216 G2
Queensland, *state* 280 E4
Queenstown, *Australia* 273 J8
Queenstown, *New Zealand* 277 C7
Queenstown, *Rep. of South Africa* 169 F9
Quelimane 169 G7
Que Que 169 F7
Querétaro 232 C2
Quetta 112 E4
Quezaltenango 232 D3
Quezon City 13 D4
Quibdó 233 F4
Quilán, C., *cape* 264 A3
Quillacollo 256 C4
Quill Lakes, *lakes* 216 G3
Quilmes 264 C2
Quillota 264 A2
Quilon 137 E5
Quilpie 273 H5
Quincy 209 J4
Qui Nhon 113 G5
Quirimba, Ilhas, *island group* 185 F4
Quita Sueño Bank, *sea feature* 233 E3
Quito 248 B3
Qulansīyah, Ra's, *cape* 177 J4
Quorn 273 G6
Qus 177 G3

Raahe 58 J2
Raba 113 G6
Rabat 168 C2
Rabaul 281 F2
Race, C., *cape* 200 H3
Racine 209 K3
Radom 58 H3
Rae 216 F2
Rae Isthmus, *isthmus* 216 J2
Raeside, L., *lake* 280 C4
Raetea, *mountain* 276 E2
Raetihi 276 F4
Rafsanjān 136 C2
Raglan 276 F3
Raglan Harb., *harbour* 276 F3
Raglan Ra., *mountains* 276 E5
Ragusa 80 D3
Raijua, *island* 272 D2
Raine Entrance, *channel* 273 H2
Raine I., *island* 273 H2
Rainier, Mt., *mountain* 200 D3
Rainy L., *lake* 216 H4
Raipur 136 F3
Rajahmundry 136 F4
Rajang 137 J5
Rajkot 136 E3
Rakaia, *river* 277 E6
Raleigh 209 M4
Rall Amane, *region* 176 B3
Ramapo Deep, *sea feature* 283 B2
Rāmhormoz 48 B2
Rampur 136 E3
Ramree I., *island* 137 G4
Rancagua 264 A2
Randers 58 G3
Ranfurly 277 D7
Rangiora 277 E6
Rangitaiki, *river* 276 G4
Rangitata, *river* 277 D6
Rangitikei, *river* 276 F4
Rangitoto Ra., *mts.* 276 F4
Rangoon 112 F5
Rantekombola, Bk., *mt.* 280 B2
Raoui, Erg er, *sand dunes* 176 C3
Rapid City 208 G3
Raqqah 81 G3
Rasa, Pta., *cape* 249 C7
Rashid 177 G2
Rasht 112 D4
Raskoh, *mountains* 48 D3
Raso, C., *Brazil, cape* 248 E2
Rason, L., *lake* 272 D5
Rasskazovo 59 E3
Rat Is., *island group* 113 K3
Ratlam 136 E3
Raukumara, *mountain* 276 H3
Raukumara Ra., *mts.* 276 G4
Raumati 276 F5
Rawalpindi 112 E4
Rawāndiz 81 H3
Rawlins 208 F3
Rawson 249 C7
Ray, C., *cape* 217 M4
Ray Mts., *mountains* 216 B2
Raychikhinsk 121 P5
Raymondville 208 H6
Raz, Pte. du, *cape* 48 F4
Ré, Î. de, *island* 80 B2
Reading, *U.S.A.* 209 M3
Real, Cord., *mountains* 256 C4
Reaside, L., *seasonal lake* 272 D5
Rebiana Sand Sea, *sand dunes* 168 E3
Recherche, Archo. of the, *island group* 280 C5
Recife 248 F3
Reconquista 264 C1
Recovery Glacier 292 A2
Red, *U.S.A., Louisiana, river* 200 F4
Red, *U.S.A., N. Dakota, river* 200 F3
Red Basin, *region* 112 G4
Red Deer 216 F3
Reddickton 217 M3
Redding 208 C3
Red Hill, *mountain* 276 E5
Red Hills, *U.S.A., mts.* 209 K5
Redondo, Pico, *mountain* 233 G4
Red Sea 168 G3
Red Sea Rift, *sea feature* 25 G3
Redwater 216 F3
Reefton 277 D6
Regensburg 80 D2
Reggio di Calabria 80 D3
Regina 208 G1
Registan, *region* 136 D2
Rehoboth 169 E8
Reims 58 F4
Reindeer L., *lake* 200 E3
Reinosa, *Mexico* 232 D2
Rembang 137 J6
Renmark 273 H6
Rennell Ridge, *sea feature* 281 F3
Rennes 58 E4
Rennick Bay, *bay* 292 L2
Reno 208 D4
Republican, *river* 208 H3
Rep. of Ireland 48 F3
Republic of South Africa 169 F8
Repulse Bay, *trading post* 217 J2
Resistencia 264 C1
Resolute 216 H1
Resolution I., *Canada, island* 200 G2
Resolution I., *New Zealand, island* 277 B7
Resolution L., *lake* 217 L3
Réunion, *island* 145 B4
Revda 59 N3
Revelstoke 216 F3
Revilla Gigedo, Is., *island group* 283 D2
Reykanes Ridge, *sea feature* 100 D2
Reykjavik 48 D2
Rey Malabo 168 D5
Rezā'īyeh 120 G6
Rezā'īyeh, Daryācheh-ye, *lake* 49 M5
Rezekne 59 J3
Rharsa, Chott el, *seasonal lake* 176 D2
Rhein, *river* 48 G4
Rhin, *river* 80 C2
Rhodesia, *see Zimbabwe* 169 F8
Rhône, *river* 48 G4
Riau, Kep., *island group* 137 H5
Ribeira, *river* 264 D1
Ribeirão Prêto 248 E5
Riberalta 248 C4
Richards Deep, *sea feature* 248 B5
Richardson Mts., *Canada, mountains* 216 D2
Richardson Mts., *New Zealand, mountains* 277 C7
Richelieu, *river* 209 N2
Richland 208 D2
Richmond, *New Zealand* 276 E5
Richmond, *U.S.A., Indiana* 209 L4
Richmond, *U.S.A., Virginia* 209 M4
Richmond Ra., *mountains* 276 E5
Riding Mountain, *mts.* 208 G1
Rif, El, *region* 168 C2
Riga 48 K3
Rijeka 80 D2
Rihn, *river* 58 F3
Rimini 80 D2
Rimouski 217 L4
Riobamba 256 B3
Rio Branco 256 C3
Rio Bravo del Norte, *river* 232 C1
Rio Caribe 233 G3
Rio Claro, Sa. do, *mts.* 257 D4
Rio Cuarto 264 B2
Rio de Janeiro 248 E5
Río de las Balsas, *river* 201 F5
Río de la Plata, *estuary* 249 D6
Río de Oro, B. de, *bay* 176 B3
Río Gallegos 264 B4
Rio Grande 249 D6
Rio Grande, *Panama, river* 233 E3
Rio Grande, *U.S.A., river* 201 E4
Rio Grande de Santiago, *river* 256 C2
Río Grande do Sul 264 C2
Riohacha 233 F3
Rio Negro, Embalse del, *lake* 264 C2
Rio Piedras 233 G3
Ríosucio 233 F4
Rivera 264 C2
Riverina, *region* 280 E5
Riversdale 184 D6
Riverton 277 C8
Riviera, *region* 80 C2
Riyadh 112 D4
Rizhskiy Zaliv, *bay* 48 J3
Rkiz, L., *lake* 176 B4
Road Town 233 G3
Roan Mt., *mountain* 209 L4
Roanne 80 C2
Roanoke 209 M4
Roanoke, *river* 209 M4
Roberts, Mt., *mountain* 273 K5
Robinson Ras., *mts.* 280 B4
Robson, Mt., *mountain* 200 E3
Roca Partida, *island* 233 B3
Rocas, *island* 248 F3
Rocas Alijos, *island group* 232 B2
Rocha 264 C2
Rochefort 80 B2
Rochester, *U.S.A., Minnesota* 209 J3
Rochester, *U.S.A., New York* 209 M3
Rockall Deep, *sea feature* 48 E3
Rockall Oceanic Bank, *sea feature* 48 E3
Rock & Pillar Ra., *mts.* 277 C7
Rockford 209 K3
Rockhampton 280 F4
Rock Pt., *cape* 276 E5
Rock Springs 208 F3
Rocky Mountains, *mts.* 200 D3
Rocky Mountain System, *mountains* 24 B2
Ródhos 81 F3
Ródhos, *island* 48 K5
Rodopi Planina, *mts.* 48 J5
Rodriguez I., *island* 145 C3
Roebourne 272 C4
Roes Welcome Sd., *inlet* 216 J2
Rogagua, Lago, *lake* 256 C4
Rogoaguado, Lago, *lake* 256 C4
Rojo, C., *Mexico, cape* 232 D2
Rojo, C., *Puerto Rico, cape* 233 G3
Røldal 58 F2
Roma, *Australia* 273 J5
Roma, *Italy* 48 H5
Roma, *island* 280 C2
Romanche Gap, *sea feature* 100 E4
Romanzof, C., *cape* 200 B2
Roncador Cay, *reef* 233 E3
Roncador, Sa. do, *mts.* 248 D4
Ronda, Sa. de, *mountains* 80 B3
Rønne 58 G3
Ronne Entrance, *channel* 292 R2
Roosevelt I., *island* 292 M2
Roper, *river* 280 D3
Roraima, Mt., *mountain* 248 C2
Rosalind Bank, *sea feature* 233 E3
Rosa, Monte, *mountain* 48 H4
Rosario 249 C6
Roseau 233 G3
Roseburg 208 C3
Rosemary Bank, *sea feature* 48 E2
Rosenberg 209 H6
Roskilde 58 G3
Roslavl' 59 K3
Ross, *New Zealand* 277 D6
Ross Dependency, *territory* 292 M2
Rossel I., *island* 273 K2
Ross Ice Shelf 292 M1
Ross I., *Ross Dependency, island* 292 L2
Ross River 216 D2
Ross Sea 292 M2
Rostock 58 G3

Shendi 177 G4
Shenton, Mt., *mountain* 272 D5
Shen-yang 113 H3
Shepparton 273 J7
Sherbro I., *island* 176 B5
Sherbrooke 217 K4
Sheridan 216 G4
Shetland Islands, *island group* 48 F2
Shibām 136 B4
Shibīn al Kawm 177 G2
Shickshock Mts., *mountains* 217 L4
Shifā, Jabal ash, *mts.* 49 L6
Shigatse 137 F3
Shigh-men 113 G4
Shikarpur 136 D3
Shikoku, *island* 113 H4
Shilka, *river* 133 G3
Shillong 137 G3
Shimanovsk 121 P4
Shimonoseki 113 H4
Shindand 136 D2
Shingle Pk., *mountain* 276 E5
Shinyanga 185 E3
Shiono-misaki, *cape* 121 Q6
Shīrāz 112 D4
Shire, *river* 169 G7
Shiriya-saki, *cape* 121 R5
Shizuoka 113 H4
Shkhara, *mountain* 81 H2
Shkoder 81 E2
Shoalwater B., *bay* 273 K4
Sholapur 112 E5
Shoshone Mts., *mts.* 208 D4
Shostka 59 K3
Shreveport 209 J5
Shumagin Is., *island grp.* 200 C3
Shumikha 59 N3
Shuya 59 L3
Shyok, *river* 136 E2
Siahan Ra., *mountains* 136 D3
Sialkot 136 E2
Siam, Gulf of, *gulf* 112 G5
Šiauliai 58 H3
Šibenik 80 D2
Siberian Plain, *plain* 25 G2
Siberut, *island* 137 G6
Sibir'skiye Uvaly, *marsh* 112 E2
Sibiu 81 F2
Sibolga 112 F5
Sibu 137 J5
Sibuyan Sea 113 H5
Sicilia, *island* 48 H5
Sicilian Chan., *channel* 48 H5
Sidi Barrāni 177 F2
Sidi-bel-Abbès 168 C2
Sidi Ifni 168 B3
Siem Reap 137 H4
Siena 80 D2
Sierra Leone 168 B5
Sierra Leone Basin, *sea feature* 100 E4
Sierra Leone, C., *cape* 176 B5
Sierra Nevada, *Spain, see Nevada, Sierra* 48 F5
Sierra Nevada, *U.S.A., see Nevada, Sierra* 200 D4
Siglufjördhur 58 C1
Signal Pk., *mountain* 208 E5
Siguiri 176 C4
Sikasso 168 C4
Sikhote Alin, *mountains* 113 H3
Silao 232 C2
Silifke 81 G3
Siljan, *lake* 58 G2
Silkeborg 58 G3
Silver Bank, *sea feature* 233 F2
Silver Bank Pass., *channel* 233 F2
Silver City 208 F5
Sim 59 N3
Simcoe, L., *lake* 217 K4
Simeuluë, *island* 112 F5
Simferopol' 49 L4
Simla 136 E2
Simplon P., *pass* 80 D2
Simpson Desert, *desert* 280 D4
Simpson Pena., *peninsula* 216 J2
Sinai, *peninsula* 168 G3
Sincé 233 F4
Sind, *desert* 176 D3
Sinfra 176 C5
Singapore 113 G5
Singaraja 137 J6
Sinkiang, *region* 112 F3
Sinop 81 G3
Sinop Burun, *cape* 49 L4
Sioux City 208 H3
Sioux Falls 200 F3
Sioux Lookout 216 H3
Siple, Mt., *mountain* 292 O2
Sira Dağlari, *mountains* 48 K5
Sir Edward Pellew Group, *island group* 280 D3
Sirik, Tg., *cape* 137 J5
Sirjān, *region* 136 C3
Sir Sanford, Mt., *mt.* 216 F3
Sirte Desert, *desert* 168 E2
Sirte, Gulf of, *gulf* 168 E2
Siskiyou Mts., *mountains* 208 C3
Sistān, D.-ye, *lake* 136 D2
Sitka 216 D3
Sitwe 112 F4
Sivas 81 G3
Siwa 177 F3
Siwa Oasis 168 F3
Sjaelland, *island* 48 H3
Skagerrak, *channel* 48 H2
Skagway 216 D3
Skeena, *river* 200 D3
Skellefteå 58 H2
Skelton Glacier 292 L2
Skikda 168 D2
Skíros, *island* 81 F3
Skopje 48 J4
Skovorodino 121 P4
Skye, *island* 48 F3
Slamet, G., *mountain* 137 H6
Slave, *river* 216 F3
Slavyansk 81 G2
Sliven 81 F2
Slobodskoy 59 M2
Slot, The, *channel* 281 F2
Slutsk 59 J3
Slyudyanka 121 N4
Smela 81 F2
Smith, C., *cape* 217 K2
Smoky Hill, *river* 208 G4
Smoky Hills, *mountains* 200 E4
Smokensk 48 K3
Smolikas, Óros, *mt.* 48 J5
Snake, *river* 200 E3
Snake Ra., *mountains* 208 E4
Snake River Canyon, *gorge* 208 D2
Snake R. Plain, *plain* 200 E3
Snares, The, *island group* 292 L3
Sneeuw Gebergte, *mts.* 113 H6
Snowdon, *mountain* 58 E3
Snowy Mts., *mountains* 273 J7
Snyder 208 G5
Soaker, Mt., *mountain* 277 B7
Soavinandriana 185 F4
Sobar, *river* 168 G5
Sobral 257 E3
So-ch'e 112 E4
Sochi 81 G2
Society Islands, *island group* 283 C3
Sockling, C., *cape* 216 C2
Socorro, *island* 257 B3
Socotra, *island* 177 J4
Söderhamn 58 H2
Södertälje 58 H2
Sodo 185 E2
Sofiya 48 J4
Sogamosto 233 F4
Sognefj., *fjord* 48 G2
Sogo Hills, *mountains* 185 E2
Sokodé 168 D5
Sokota 177 G4
Sokoto 168 D4
Solander I., *island* 277 B8
Solikamsk 59 N2
Solimões, *river* 248 C3
Solomon Islands, *island group* 281 F2
Solomons Basin, *sea feature* 281 F2
Solomon Sea 281 F2
Solov'yevsk 121 P4
Solund 58 F2
Sol'vychegodsk 59 L2
Somalia 168 H5
Somali Basin, *sea feature* 145 B3
Somerset 273 H2
Somerset I., *island* 200 F2
Somuncurá, Mesa Volcanica de, *tableland* 264 B3
Son, *river* 136 F3
Sondre Stromfjord 289 O2
Song Bo, *river* 137 H3
Songkhla 112 G5
Song Nhi Ha, *river* 137 H3
Sonoita 208 E5
Sonson 233 F4
Sonsonate 232 E3
Soo Canals, *canals* 209 L2
Sopron 80 E2
Sorell, C., *cape* 273 J8
Sorocaba 257 E5
Soroki 81 F2
Soroti 168 G5
Sørøya, *island* 58 H1
Sosnogorsk 59 M2
Sosnowiec 58 H3
Sos'va 59 N2
Souk-Ahras 176 D2
Sources, Mt. aux, *mt.* 169 F8
Souris 216 G4
Souris, *river* 208 G2
Sous, *river* 48 E6
Sousse 168 E2
Southampton 48 F3
Southampton, C., *cape* 200 F2
Southampton I., *island* 200 F2
S. Andaman, *island* 137 G4
South Atlantic Ocean 100 D5
South Australia, *state* 280 D4
South Australian Basin, *sea feature* 283 A3
South Bend 209 K3
Southbridge 277 E6
South Cape, *New Zealand, cape* 277 B8
South Carolina, *state* 209 L5
South China Sea 113 G5
South Dakota, *state* 208 G3
S. E. Cape, *Australia, Tasmania cape* 280 E6
South-Eastern Atlantic Basin, *sea feature* 100 E6
South-Eastern Indian Ridge, *sea feature* 145 D4
South-Eastern Pacific Basin, *sea feature* 283 E3
South-Eastern Pacific Plateau, *sea feature* 283 D3
South-East Indian Basin, *sea feature* 145 E4
Southern Alps, *mts.* 281 H6
Southern Indian Lake, *lake* 216 H3
Southern Ocean 292 O2
Southern Pine Hills, *hills* 209 K5
South Esk Tableland, *tableland* 272 E3
South Fiji Basin, *sea feature* 283 B3
S. Fiji Ridge, *sea feature* 283 B3
South Georgia, *island* 100 D7
South Henik Lake, *lake* 216 H2
South Honshu Ridge, *sea feature* 283 A2
South Island, *island* 281 G6
South Korea 113 H4
South Madagascar Ridge, *sea feature* 145 B4
South Nahanni, *river* 216 E2
South Negril Pt., *cape* 233 F3
South Orkney Islands, *island group* 292 S2
South Pacific Ocean 292 O3
South Platte, *river* 208 G3
South Polar Plateau, *plateau* 292 A1
Southport, *Australia* 273 K5
South Sandwich Islands, *island group* 292 R2
South Sandwich Trench, *sea feature* 292 A3
S. Saskatchewan, *river* 200 E3
South Shetland Islands, *island group* 292 R2
South Taranaki Bight, *bay* 276 F4
South Tasmania Ridge, *sea feature* 292 K3
South Tent, *mountain* 208 E4
South Wellesley Is., *island group* 273 G3
South West Africa, *see Namibia* 184 C5
S. West C., *Australia, cape* 273 J8
Southwest Cape, *New Zealand, cape* 277 B8
South-Western Pacific Basin, *sea feature* 283 C3
South-West Indian Ridge, *sea feature* 145 B4
S. West I., *island* 273 J3
Sovetsk 58 H3
Sovetskaya Gavan' 121 R5
Sozimskiy 59 M2
Spain 48 F5
Spanish Town 233 F3
Spartanburg 209 L5
Spassk Dal'niy 121 Q5
Spence Bay 216 H2
Spencer Gulf, *gulf* 280 D5
Spenser Mts., *mountains* 277 E6
Split 80 E2
Spokane 216 F4
Sporádhes, *island group* 48 K5
Spornoye 121 S3
Springbok 169 E8
Springfield, *U.S.A. Illinois* 209 K4
Springfield, *U.S.A., Mass.* 209 N3
Springfield, *U.S.A., Missouri* 209 J4
Springfield, *U.S.A., Ohio* 209 L4
Springfontein 184 D6
Spring Mts., *mountains* 208 D4
Springs 169 F8
Springsure 273 J4
Spruce Knob, *mountain* 209 M4
Spurn Head, *cape* 58 F3
Sredinnyy Khr., *mts.* 113 J3
Sredne-Kolymsk 121 S3
Sredne-Russkaya Vozvyshennost, *hills* 49 L3
Sredne Sibir'skoye Ploskogor'ye, *plateau* 112 F2
Sredniy Ural, *mountains* 49 O3
Sri Lanka 112 F5
Srinagar 112 E4
Ssu-mao 137 H3
Ssu-p'ing 121 P5
Stanley 249 D8
Stanovoy Khr., *mountain* 113 H3
Stanovoye Nagor'ye, *plateau* 112 G3
Stanthorpe 273 K5
Stara Planina, *mountains* 48 K4
Staraya Russa 59 J3
Stara Zagora 81 F2
Star Pk., *mountain* 208 D3
Stavanger 58 F2
Stavropol', *U.S.S.R., Stavropol'* 81 H2
Stavropol'skaya Vozvyshennost', *hills* 81 H2
Stawell 273 H7
Steens Mt., *mountain* 208 D3
Stefanie, L., *lake* 185 E2
Stefansson I., *island* 216 G1
Stepanakert 120 G6
Stephens, C., *cape* 276 E5
Stephenson I., *island* 276 E2
Stepnyak 120 K4
Sterling 208 G3
Sterlitamak 120 H4
Stewart I., *island* 281 G6
Stikine, *river* 200 D3
Stikine Mts., *mountains* 200 D3
Stillwater 208 H4
Stirling Ra., *mountains* 280 B5
Stockholm 48 J2
Stoke-on-Trent 48 F3
Stokes Ra., *mountains* 272 F3
Stonington I., *island* 292 R2
Storavan, *lake* 48 J2
Storsjön, *Sweden, C. Jamtland, lake* 58 G2
Strand 184 C6
Strasbourg 48 G4
Stratford, *New Zealand* 276 F4
Streaky B., *bay* 280 D5
Stromboli, *island* 48 H5
Stryy 81 F2
Stuart Bluff Ra., *mts.* 272 F4
Stuart Highway 272 F3
Stuart Ra., *Australia, mountains* 280 D4
Stuart Mts., *New Zealand, mountains* 277 B7
Sturt Creek, *river* 280 C3
Sturt Desert, *desert* 280 E4
Sturt, Mt., *mountain* 273 H5
Sturt Plain, *plain* 280 D3
Stuttgart 48 H4
Suakin 168 G4
Sucre 248 C4
Sudan 168 F4
Sudbury, *Canada* 217 J4
Sudd, *region* 168 G5
Sudety, *mountains* 48 H3
Sue, *river* 184 D2
Suez, *see As Suways* 177 G3
Suez Canal, *canal* 168 G2
Suez, G. of, *gulf* 168 G3
Su-fu 112 E4
Sukarnapura, *see Jayapura* 113 J6
Sukhe Bator 121 N4
Sukhona, *river* 49 M2
Sukhumi 81 H2
Sukkur 112 E4
Sula, Kep., *island group* 113 H6
Sulaiman Ra., *mountains* 112 E4
Sulawesi, *island* 113 G6
Sulina 81 F2
Sulitjelma, *mountain* 48 J1
Sulphur Springs 209 H5
Sulu Archo, *island group* 113 H5
Sulu Sea 113 G5
Sulzberger B., *bay* 292 N2
Sumatra, *island* 112 F5
Sumatra Trough, *sea feature* 145 D2
Sumba, *island* 113 G6
Sumbawa, *island* 113 G6
Sumen 81 F2
Sumy 59 K3
Sundarbans, *swamp forest* 136 F3
Sunda, Selat., *strait* 113 G6
Sunda Shelf, *sea feature* 25 H3
Sundsvall 58 H2
Sung-hua Ch., *river* 113 H3
Sunnmør, *region* 58 F2
Superior 209 J2
Superior, L., *lake* 200 F3
Sūr, *Oman* 112 D4
Sura, *river* 59 L3
Surabaya 113 G6
Surakarta 113 G6
Surat, *India* 112 E4
Surat Thani 112 F5
Surigao 113 H5
Surimo 169 F6
Surinam 248 D2
Suriname, *river* 256 D2
Surt 176 E2
Sušak 80 D2
Susanville 208 C3
Susquehanna, *river* 209 M3
Susuman 121 R3
Sutlej, *river* 112 E4
Suva 281 H3
Suzu-misaki, *cape* 121 Q6
Svalbard, *island group* 289 L2
Sverdlovsk 49 O3
Sverdrup Is., *island grp.* 200 E2
Svetogorsk 59 J2
Svir', *river* 59 K2
Svyatoy Nos, M., *cape* 121 R2
Swain Reefs, *reefs* 281 F4
Swakopmund 169 E8
Swan, *river* 280 B5
Swan Hill 273 H7
Swan Is., *island group* 233 E3
Swan River 216 G3
Swansea 58 E3
Swartberge, *mountains* 169 F9
Swaziland 169 G8
Sweden 48 H2
Swellendam 184 D6
Swift Current 216 G3
Swire Deep, *sea feature* 25 J3
Switzerland 48 G4
Sydney, *Australia* 280 F5
Sydney, *Canada* 217 L4
Syktyvkar 59 M2
Sylt, *island* 58 G3
Syracuse, *U.S.A.* 209 M3
Syr-Dar'ya, *river* 112 E3
Syria 112 C4
Syzran' 59 M3
Szczecin 48 H3
Sze-fang Shan, *mountains* 137 H3
Szeged 81 E2
Szombathely 80 E2

Tabas 136 C2
Table Cape, *cape* 276 H4
Table Hill, *mountain* 277 B8
Table Mt., *mountain* 169 E9
Tabora 168 G6
Tabriz 49 M5
Tabūk 81 G4
Ta-ch'ing Shan, *mountain* 113 G3
Tacloban 137 K4
Tacna 256 B4
Tacoma 200 D3
Tacuarembó 264 C2
Tademait, Pleateau du, *plateau* 48 G6
Tadmur 81 G3
Tadzhikskaya S.S.R., *republic* 120 J6
Taegu 113 H4
Taejon 113 H4
Taganrog 49 L4
Taganrogskiy Zaliv, *bay* 81 G2
Tagula I., *island* 273 K2
Tahan, G., *mountain* 137 H5
Tahat, *mountain* 168 D3
Tahiti, *island* 283 C3
Tahoe Lake, *Canada, lake* 216 G1
Tahoe, Lake, *U.S.A., lake* 208 C4
Tahoua 176 D4
Ta-hsing-an-ling Shan-mo, *mountains* 113 G3
T'ai-chung 113 H4
Taieri, *river* 277 D7
T'ai-hang Shan, *mountains* 112 E4
Taihape 276 F4
T'ai-hsien 137 J2
Tainan 113 H4
Taínaron, Akr., *cape* 48 J5
T'ai-pei 112 H4
Taitao, Pena. de, *peninsula* 249 B7
Taiwan, *island* 113 H4
T'ai-wan Hai-hsia, *strait* 113 G4
Ta'izz 112 D5
Tajo, *river* 48 F5
Tajumulco Vol. de, *mt.* 201 F5
Tak 137 G4
Takahe, Mt., *mountain* 292 P2
Takapuna 276 F3
Takilgan 137 G2
Takitimu Mts., *mountains* 277 B7
Takla Makan, *desert* 112 F4
Takoradi 168 C5
Talak, *region* 168 D4
Talara 248 A3
Talar-i-Band 136 D3
Talaud, Kep., *island group* 113 H5
Talca 249 B6
Talcahuano 249 B6
Taldom 59 K3
Taldy-Kurgan 120 K5
Ta-li, *China, Shensi* 137 H2
Ta-li, *China, Yunnan* 112 G4
Taliang Shan, *mountains* 137 H3
Ta-lien 121 P6
Talkalakh 181 G3
Tallahassee 209 L5
Tallinn 48 K2
Talou Shan, *mountains* 113 G4
Taltal 264 A1
Tamale 168 C5
Tamanrasset 168 D3
Tamatave 169 H7
Tambov 112 D3
Tamgak, Monts., *mts.* 176 D4
Tamiahua, Laguna de, *lake* 232 D2
Tampa 201 F4
Tampa Bay, *bay* 209 L6
Támpere 58 H2
Tampico 232 D2
Tamworth, *Australia* 273 K6
Tana 58 J1
Tana, *Kenya, river* 168 G6
Tana, Lake, *lake* 168 G4
Tanana 216 B2
Tanana, *river* 200 C2
Tandil 264 C2
Tandou L., *lake* 273 H6
Tanezrouft, *region* 168 C3
Tanezrouft n-Ahenet, *region* 168 D3
Tanga 169 G6
Tanganyika, Lake, *lake* 169 F6
Tanger 188 C2
T'ang-ku 137 J2
Tanglha Range, *mountains* 112 F4
Tangra Tso, *lake* 137 F2
T'ang-shan 113 G4
Tang-t'u 137 J2
Tanimbar, Kep., *island group* 113 H6
Tanjungkarang 137 H6
Tannu Ola, Khr., *mts.* 112 F3
Ţanţā 168 G2
Tanzania 169 G6
T'ao-an 121 P5
T'ao-nan 121 P5
Tapachula 232 D3
Tapajós, *river* 248 D3
Tapanui 277 C7
Ta-pa Shan, *mountains* 113 G4
Tapieh Shan, *mountains* 137 J2
Tapirapecó, Sa., *mts.* 233 G4
Tapti 136 E3
Tarabulus 168 E2
Taradale 276 G4
Tarakan 113 G5
Taranaki, *county* 276 F4
Taranţo 80 E3
Taranto, Golfo di, *gulf* 48 J5
Tararua Ra., *mountains* 276 F5
Tarawa 281 H1
Tarawera, L., *lake* 276 G4
Tarawera, Mt., *mountain* 276 G4
Tarbagatay, Khr., *mts.* 121 L5
Tarbes 80 C2
Taree 273 K6
Tarfaia 176 B3
Tårgu Mureş 81 F2
Tarim Darya, *river* 120 L5
Tarkhantut, M., *cape* 81 F2
Tarkwa 176 C5
Tarnów 58 H3
Taroom 273 J5
Tarouadji, Mts., *mts.* 176 D4
Taroudant 176 C2
Tarran Hills, *mountains* 273 J6
Tarso Taho, *mountain* 177 E3
Tarso Tiéroko, *mountain* 176 E3
Tarso Tourari, *mountain* 176 E3
Tartu 58 J2
Tarţus 81 G3
Tasedjibest, *mountain* 176 D3
Tashauz 120 H5
Tashkent 122 E3
Tasman B., *bay* 281 H6
Tasmania, *island and state* 280 E6
Tasman, Mt., *mountain* 277 D6
Tasman Mts., *mountains* 276 E5
Tasman Pena., *peninsula* 273 J8
Tasman Sea 281 F5
Tassili n'Ajjer, *plateau* 168 D3
Tassili Oua-n-Ahaggar, *plateau* 176 D4
Tassili Tin Eggolé, *plateau* 176 D3
Tasueh Shan, *mountains* 137 H2
Tatarskiy Proliv, *strait* 113 J3
Tatnam, C., *cape* 200 F3
Tatry, *mountains* 81 E2
Ta-t'ung, *China, Anhwei* 137 J2
Ta-t'ung, *China, Shansi* 121 O5
Taubaté 257 E5
Taumarunui 276 F4
Taupo 276 G4
Taupo, L., *lake* 281 H5
Taurakawa, *mountain* 276 F4
Tauranga 276 G3
Tauranga Harb., *harbour* 276 F3
Tauroa Pt., *cape* 276 E2
Tauyskaya Guba, *gulf* 121 R4

Vidin 81 E2
Viedma 264 B3
Viedma, L., *lake* 249 B7
Vientiane 113 G5
Vietnam 113 G5
Vigan 137 K4
Vignemale, P. de, *mt.* 80 B2
Vigo 80 A2
Vijawada 136 F4
Vik 58 C2
Viking Bank, *sea feature* 58 F2
Vila 281 G3
Vila Luso 169 E7
Vil'kitskogo, Proliv, *strait* 112 G2
Villa Ängela 264 B1
Villa Dolores 264 B2
Villaggio Duca degli Abruzzi 168 H5
Villahermosa, *Mexico* 232 D3
Villa María 264 B2
Villa Mercedes 264 B2
Villa Montes 256 C5
Villarrica, *Paraguay* 264 C1
Villavicencio 233 F4
Vil'nyus 48 K3
Vilyuy, *river* 121 P3
Vilyuysk 121 P3
Viña del Mar 264 A2
Vincennes 209 K4
Vindhya Range, *mts.* 112 E4
Vinh 113 G5
Vinnitsa 48 K4
Vinson Massif, *mts.* 292 Q2
Virgenes, Cabo, *cape* 249 C8
Virginia, *U.S.A.* 209 J2
Virginia, *state* 209 M4
Virgin Is., *island group* 201 G5
Visayan Sea 137 K4
Visby 58 H3
Viscount Melville Sound, *channel* 200 E2
Vishakhapatnam 136 F4
Visokoi I., *island* 292 A3
Vitebsk 48 K3
Viti Levu, *island* 281 H3
Vitim, *river* 113 H3
Vitimskoye Ploskogor'ye *tableland* 121 O4
Vitória, *Brazil* 248 E5
Vitória da Conquista 257 E4
Vityaz' Deep, *sea feature* 113 J3
Vladimir 49 M3
Vladivostok 113 H3
Vogelkop, *peninsula* 113 H6
Voi 168 G6
Volga, *river* 49 M4
Volgo-Donskoy K., *canas* 49 M4
Volgograd 49 M4
Volkhov 59 K2
Vologda 59 K2
Vólos 81 E3
Volta, *river* 168 D5
Volta L., *reservoir* 168 C5
Volta Noire, *river* 168 C4
Volta Rouge, *river* 176 C4
Vol'sk 59 L3
Voríai Sporádhes, *island group* 81 E3
Vorkuta 59 O1
Voronezh 49 L3
Voroshilovgrad 49 L4
Vosges, *mountains* 48 G4
Vost. Chink Ustyurta, *mountains* 49 O4
Vostochnyy Sayan, *mts.* 112 F3
Vostok 292 G2
Votkinsk 59 M3
Vrangelya, O., *island* 289 B2
Vryburg 184 D5
Vryheid 169 G8
Vyatka, *river* 59 M3
Vyaz'ma 59 K3
Vyborg 59 J2
Vychegda, *river* 49 N2
Vyshniy-Volochek 59 K3
Vytegra 59 K2

Wabash, *river* 209 K4
Wabowden 216 H3
Waccasassa B., *bay* 248 D4
Waco 208 H5
Waddenzee, *channel* 58 F3
Waddington, Mt., *mt.* 200 D3
Wādī 'Arabah, *valley* 81 G4
Wadi Halfa 112 C4
Wadi Sirhān, *region* 112 C4
Wādīyan, Al, *region* 49 M6
Wad Medani 168 G4
Wager Bay 216 H2
Wager Bay, *bay* 216 J2
Wagga Wagga 280 E5
Wagin 272 C6
Wāhāt al Khārijah, Al, *oasis* 177 G3
Waiau 277 E6
Waiau, *New Zealand, Nelson, river* 277 E6
Waiau, *New Zealand, Otago, river* 277 B7
Waigeo, *island* 113 H6
Waiheke I., *island* 276 F3
Waihi 276 F3
Waihou, *river* 276 F3
Waikare L., *lake* 276 F3
Waikare Moana, *lake* 276 G4
Waikato, *river* 276 F4
Waikouaiti 277 D7
Waikouaiti Downs, *hills* 277 D7
Waimate 277 D7
Waimea Plain, *plain* 277 C7
Waingapu 137 K6
Wainwright, *Canada* 216 F3
Wainwright, *U.S.A.* 216 B1
Waipa, *river* 276 F4
Waipawa 276 G4
Waipukurau 276 G4
Wairarapa, L., *lake* 276 F5
Wairau, *river* 276 E5
Wairoa 276 G4
Wairoa, *New Zealand, Auckland, river* 276 E3
Wairoa, *New Zealand, Hawkes Bay, river* 276 G4
Wairua, *river* 276 F2
Waitaki, *river* 277 D7
Waitaki Plains, *plain* 277 C7
Waitara 276 F4
Waitoa 276 F3
Waiuku 276 F3
Wakatipu, L., *lake* 277 C7
Wakayama 121 O6
Wake I., *island* 283 B2
Wakkanai 121 R5
Waldburg Ra., *mountains* 272 C4
Wales I., *island* 216 J2
Walgreen Coast, *region* 292 P2
Wallabi Group, *island group* 272 B5
Wallaby I., *Australia, Wellesley Is., island* 273 G3
Wallaroo 273 G6
Walla Walla 208 D2
Wallel, T., *mountain* 177 G5
Wallowa Mts., *mountains* 208 D2
Walpole, *island* 281 G4
Walvis Bay 169 E8
Walvis or Cape Basin, *sea feature* 100 F6
Walvis Ridge, *sea feature* 100 E6
Wanaka, Lake, *lake* 277 C7
Wandels Sea 289 N1
Wanganui 281 H6
Wanganui, *river* 276 F4
Wangaratta 273 J7
Wan-ch'üan 113 G3
Wang-yeh-miao 121 P5
Wankie 169 F7
Warangal 136 E4
Warburton, *river* 280 D4
Warburton Ra., *mts.* 272 E5
Warner Ra., *mountains* 208 C3
Waroona 272 C6
Warrego, *river* 280 E4
Warrego Ra., *mountains* 273 J5
Warrenton 184 D5
Warri 176 D5
Warrnambool 273 H7
Warszawa 48 J3
Warta, *river* 48 J3
Warwick, *Australia* 273 K5
Wasatch Range, *mts.* 208 E4
Wash, The, *gulf* 58 F3
Washington, *U.S.A., D.C.* 200 G4
Washington, *state* 208 C2
Waterbury 209 N3
Waterford 58 E3
Watertown, *U.S.A., New York* 209 M3
Watertown, *U.S.A., S. Dakota* 208 H3
Watkins, Mt., *mountain* 48 C1
Watling I., *see San Salvador* 233 F2
Watsa 184 D2
Watson Lake 216 E2
Wausau 209 K3
Waxahachie 209 H5
Weald, The, *region* 58 F3
Webi Shebeli, *river* 177 H5
Weddell Sea 292 S2
Wedgeport 217 L4
Weggs, C., *cape* 217 K2
Wei-chang 121 O5
Wei Ho, *river* 137 H2
Wei-hsien 137 J2
Wei-shan Hu, *lake* 137 J2
Welcome Kop, *mountain* 169 E9
Weld Ra., *mountains* 272 C5
Welkom 169 F8
Welland C., *canal* 217 K4
Wellesley Is., *island grp.* 280 D3
Wellington, *Australia* 273 J6
Wellington, *N. Zealand* 281 H6
Wellington, *Rep. of South Africa* 169 E9
Wellington, *county* 276 F4
Wellington Chan., *chan.* 216 H1
Wellington, I., *island* 249 B7
Wells, L., *lake* 272 D5
Wells, Mt., *mountain* 280 C3
Wenatchee 208 C2
Wen-chou 113 C4
Wentworth 273 H6
Weser, *river* 58 G3
Wessel, C., *cape* 280 D3
Wessel Is., *island group* 280 D3
West African Shield, *plateau* 24 E3
West Australian Basin, *sea feature* 145 D3
W. Australian Ridge, *sea feature* 145 E4
West Berlin 48 H3
West Butte, *mountain* 208 F2
West Caroline Basin, *sea feature* 113 H5
Western Australia, *state* 280 C4
Western Ghats, *mts.* 112 E5
Western Hwy. 273 H7
Western Port, *bay* 273 J7
West Falkland, *island* 249 C8
West Ice Shelf 292 G2
West Indies, *island grps.* 201 G4
Westland, *county* 277 C6
West Palm Beach 209 L6
Westport, *New Zealand* 276 D5
West Virginia, *state* 209 L4
Wetar, *island* 113 H6
Wetaskiwin 216 F3
Wexford 48 F3
Weyburn 216 G4
Whakapunaki, *mountain* 276 G4
Whakatane 276 G3
Whale, *river* 217 L3
Whales, Bay of, *bay* 292 M2
Whangerei 276 F2
Whangarei Harbour, *harbour* 276 F2
Wharton Deep, *sea feature* 145 D3
Wheeler Pk., *mountain* 208 E4
Wheeling 209 L3
Whichaway Nunataks, *mountains* 292 A1
Whidbey Is., *island grp.* 272 G6
Whidbey Pt., *cape* 272 G6
White, *Canada, river* 216 C2
White, *U.S.A., Arkansas, river* 209 J4
White, *U.S.A., S. Dakota, river* 208 G3
White B., *bay* 217 M4
Whitehorse 216 D2
White I., *island* 276 G3
White L., *lake* 272 E4
White Mts., *U.S.A., California, mountains* 200 E4
White Mts., *U.S.A., New Hampshire, mountains* 200 G3
White Nile, *see Bahr el Abyadh* 177 G4
White Nile, *see Bahr el Jebel* 168 G5
White Volta, *river* 168 C5
Whitmore Mts., *mts.* 292 P1
Whitney, Mt., *mountain* 200 E4
Whitsunday I., *island* 280 E4
Whyalla 280 D5
Wichita 200 F4
Wichita Falls 208 H5
Wichita Mts., *mountains* 208 H5
Wick 58 E2
Wicklow Mts., *mountains* 58 E3
Wien 48 H4
Wr. Neustadt 80 E2
Wiesbaden 80 D1
Wight, I. of, *island* 58 E3
Wilhelm II Land, *region* 292 G2
Wilkes, *scientific base* 292 H2
Wilkes Barre 209 M3
Wilkes Coast, *region* 292 J2
Wilkes Land, *district* 292 J2
Wilkie 216 G3
Wilkins Str., *strait* 292 R2
Willamette, *river* 208 C3
Willemstad 201 G5
William, Mt., *mountain* 273 H7
Williamsburg 209 M4
Williamsport 209 M3
Willis Group, *island group* 273 K3
Williston, *U.S.A.* 208 G2
Willmar 209 H2
Wilmington, *U.S.A., Delaware* 209 M4
Wilmington, *U.S.A., N. Carolina* 200 G4
Wilson, C., *cape* 217 J2
Wilson, Mt., *mountain* 208 F4
Wilson's Promontory, *cape* 280 E5
Windhoek 169 E8
Windom Pk., *mountain* 208 F4
Wind R. Ra., *mountains* 200 E3
Windsor, *Canada, Newfoundland* 217 M4
Windsor, *Canada, Ontario* 217 J4
Windward Islands, *island groups* 201 G5
Windward Pass., *chan.* 201 G5
Winisk 217 J3
Winneba 176 C5
Winnipeg 200 F3
Winnipeg, L., *lake* 200 F3
Winnipegosis 216 G3
Winnipegosis, L., *lake* 200 F3
Winslow 208 E4
Winston-Salem 209 L4
Winter Harbour, *bay* 216 F1
Winton, *Australia* 273 H4
Winton, *New Zealand* 277 C8
Wisconsin, *river* 209 J3
Wisconsin, *state* 209 J2
Wisla, *river* 48 J3
Wloclawek 58 H3
Wollaston, C., *cape* 216 F1
Wollaston L., *lake* 200 E3
Wollaston Pena., *peninsula* 216 F2
Wollongong 280 F5
Wolstenholm 217 K2
Wolverhampton 48 F3
Wŏnsan 121 P6
Wonthaggi 273 J7
Woodlark I., *island* 280 F2
Wood Mt., *mountain* 208 F2
Woodroffe, Mt., *mt.* 280 D4
Woods, Lake of the, *lake* 200 F3
Woodward 208 H4
Woody Hd., *cape* 276 F3
Wooramel, *river* 272 C5
Worcester, *Rep. of South Africa* 169 E9
Worcester, *U.S.A.* 209 N3
Worthington 209 H3
Wrangell 216 D3
Wrangell Mts., *mts.* 200 C2
Wrath, C., *cape* 48 F2
Wrigley 216 E2
Wrigley Gulf, *gulf* 292 O2
Wroclaw 48 J3
Wu-Chiang, *river* 137 H3
Wu-chou 113 G4
Wu-ch'uan 121 O5
Wu-chung P'u 121 N6
Wu-han 113 G4
Wu-hsi 113 H4
Wu-hsien 113 H4
Wu-hu 137 J2
Wukari 176 D5
Wu Liang Shan, *mts.* 137 H3
Wuppertal 80 C1
Wurno 176 D4
Würzburg 80 D2
Wu-t'ung ch'iao 137 H3
Wu-wei 137 H2
Wuyi Shan, *mountain* 113 G4
Wyndham, *Australia* 280 C3
Wyndham, *New Zealand* 277 C8
Wynniatt B., *bay* 216 F1
Wynyard 216 G3
Wyoming, *state* 208 F3
Wyoming Ra., *mountains* 208 E3
Wyville-Thomson Ridge, *sea feature* 289 M2

Xai-Xai 169 G8
Xieng Khouang 131 H4
Xingu, *river* 248 D3

Ya-an 112 G4
Yablonovyy Khrebet, *mountains* 112 G3
Yagodnoye 121 R3
Yakima 208 C2
Yakutat 216 D3
Yakutat Bay, *bay* 216 D3
Yakutsk 113 H2
Yallourn 273 J7
Yalta 81 G2
Ya-lu 121 P5
Yalu, *river* 121 P5
Yalutorovsk 59 O3
Yamagata 121 R6
Yamal, P-ov, *peninsula* 112 E2
Yambi, Mesa de, *tableland* 256 B2
Yamma Yamma, L., *seasonal lake* 273 H5
Yamuna, *river* 112 E4
Yanbu'al Baḩr 112 C4
Yang-ch'u 113 G4
Yankton 208 H3
Yano-Indigirskaya Nizmennost', *plain* 113 H2
Yanskiy 121 Q3
Yanskiy Zaliv, *bay* 121 Q2
Yaoundé 168 E5
Yap, *island* 113 H5
Yap Ridge, *sea feature* 113 H5
Yap Trench, *sea feature* 113 H5
Yaqui, *river* 208 F6
Yarega 59 M2
Yarí, *river* 233 F4
Yaritagua 233 G3
Yarkand, *see So-ch'e* 121 K6
Yaroslavl' 112 D3
Yarumal 233 F4
Yasanyama 168 F5
Yass 273 J6
Yatta Plat., *plateau* 185 E3
Yavarí, *river* 256 B3
Yavi, Co., *mountain* 256 C2
Yazd 112 D4
Yazoo, *river* 209 J5
Yazun Burnu, *cape* 81 G3
Ydzhid Parma, *mountain* 49 O2
Yebala, *region* 48 F5
Yegor'yevsk 59 K3
Yeh-ma Shan, *mountains* 120 B4
Yelets 59 K3
Yelgava 58 H3
Yelizavety, M., *cape* 113 J3
Yellowhead Pass, *pass* 216 F3
Yellowknife 216 F2
Yellow Sea 113 H4
Yellowstone, *river* 200 E3
Yemen Arab Republic 112 D5
Yemen, Republic of 112 D5
Yenakiyevo 59 K4
Yen-ch'ang 137 H2
Yen-ch'eng 121 P6
Yen-ch'i 121 L5
Yenisey, *river* 112 F2
Yeniseysk 121 M4
Yeniseyskiy Zaliv, *bay* 121 L2
Yen-t'ai 137 K2
Yeo L., *lake* 272 D5
Yeppoon 273 K4
Yerevan 49 M5
Yergeni, *mountain* 59 L4
Yerofey-Pavlovich 121 P4
Yerupaja, *mountain* 248 B4
Yesil, *river* 49 L5
Yevpatoriya 81 G2
Yeysk 59 K4
Yin-ch'uan 137 H2
Yin-hsien 113 H4
Yirga-Alam 177 G5
Yogyakarta 113 G6
Yokohama 113 H4
Yokosuka 121 Q6
Yola 168 E5
York, *Australia* 272 C6
York, C., *cape* 280 E3
York Factory 216 H3
York, K., *cape* 200 G2
Yorkton 216 G3
Yoshkar Ola 59 L3
Young 273 J6
Younghusband Pena., *peninsula* 273 G7
Young Ra., *mountains* 277 C7
Youngstown 209 L3
Yozgat 81 G3
Yüan-ling 137 J3
Yucatan, *peninsula* 201 F5
Yucatan Basin, *sea feature* 201 F5
Yucatan Channel, *chan.* 201 F4
Yudomo Mayskoye Nagor'ye, *mountains* 121 Q4
Yugorskiy P-ov., *peninsula* 49 O1
Yugorskiy Shar, *bay* 59 N1
Yugoslavia 48 J4
Yukagirskoye Ploskogor'ye, *tableland* 113 J2
Yukon, *province* 216 D2
Yukon, *river* 200 C2
Yü-lin, *China, Hai-nan* 113 G5
Yü-lin, *China, Shensi* 121 N6
Yuma 208 E5
Yü-men 121 M5
Yumenshih 121 M6
Yungas, *region* 248 C4
Yün-hsien 137 J2
Yun-ling Shan, *mountains* 112 F4
Yurimaguas 256 B3
Yuryuzan' 59 N3
Yuzhno-Sakhalinsk 113 J3
Yuzh. Anysyskiy Khr., *mountain* 121 T3
Yuzhnyy Bug, *river* 48 K4
Yuzhnyy, M., *cape* 121 S4
Yuzh. Ural, *mountains* 49 O3

Zàbaykal'sk 121 O5
Zacatecas 232 C2
Zacatecoluca 233 E3
Zadar 80 D2
Zagorsk 59 K3
Zagreb 48 H4
Zāhedān 136 D3
Zaire, *river* 168 F5
Zaire, *state* 168 E6
Zākhō 81 H3
Zambeze, *river* 169 G7
Zambezi, *river* 169 F7
Zambia 169 F7
Zamboanga 113 H5
Zamora, *Mexico* 232 C3
Zanesville 209 L4
Zanzibar 169 G6
Zanzibar I., *island* 169 G6
Zap. Dvina, *river* 48 K3
Zapadno-Sibir'skaya Nizmennost', *plain* 112 E2
Zapadnyy Chink Ustyurta, *escarpment* 49 N4
Zapadnyy Sayan, *mts.* 112 F3
Zaporozh'ye 49 L4
Zaragoza, *Spain* 48 F5
Zaraza 233 G4
Zaria 176 D4
Zarzis 176 E2
Zaskar Mts., *mountains* 136 E2
Zaysan, Oz., *lake* 112 F3
Zemio 177 F5
Zemlya Frantsa Iosifa, *island group* 112 D2
Zeya 121 P4
Zeya, *river* 121 P4
Zhdanov 49 L4
Zhelaniya, Mys, *cape* 112 E2
Zhigansk 121 P3
Zhiguli, *mountains* 49 N3
Zhitomir 59 J3
Zhmerinka 81 F2
Ziel, Mt., *mountain* 280 D4
Ziguinchor 176 B4
Zile 81 G3
Zilling Tso, *lake* 137 F2
Zimbabwe-Rhodesia 184 D5
Zinder 168 D4
Zitácuaro 232 C3
Zlatoust 59 N3
Zomba 169 G7
Zonguldak 81 F3
Zuénoula 176 C5
Zürich 48 H4
Zwai, L., *lake* 177 G5
Zwickau 58 G3
Zyryanka 121 S3
Zyryanovsk 120 L5

Index

Opposite: a Toda tribal village in the
Nilgiri Hills in southern India.

Page references in *italics* refer to illustrations and captions.

A

Picture Credits

134	Foto Pontis
135(L)	Photo Felix Greene © Aldus Books
135(R)	Photo J. Allan Cash
136-7	© Geographical Projects Limited
138-9(T)	Japan National Tourist Organization
138(B)	Popperfoto
139(B)	© Associated Press
140	Picturepoint, London
141(T)	Jane Burton/Bruce Coleman Ltd.
141(B)	Dubontin/Explorer
142	Courtesy Malayan Rubber Fund Board
143	© Geographical Projects Limited
144	British Crown Copyright reserved
145(T)	Photo J. Allan Cash
145(BL)	Photo Ceylon Tea Centre, London
145(BR)	FAO photo
146	Camera Press, London
147(T)	Ishitawajima-Harima, Heavy Industries Co., Ltd.
147(CL)	Emil Schulthess
147(B)	C.S. Services Limited
148-9	Marcus Brooke/Colorific!
150	Guglielmo Mairani
151(T)	Picturepoint, London
151(B)	*Daily Telegraph* Colour Library
153	Photo courtesy Ford Foundation
154	Ginette Laborde
155	Photo J. Allan Cash
158	Three Lions, Inc.
160	Victor Englebert/Susan Griggs Agency
162	Desmond Harney
163	© Geographical Projects Limited
164,	Giorgia Gualco/Bruce Coleman Inc.
165(TL)	Giorgia Gualco/Bruce Coleman Inc.
165(TR)	Robert Yarnall Richie
165(B)	Dr. Edward S. Ross
166	© Geographical Projects Limited
167	Popperfoto
168-9	© Geographical Projects Limited
170	Naud/AAA Photo
171(T)	Photo Mirella Ricciardi from *Vanishing Africa*, Collins Publishers, London
171(B)	Leonard Lee Rue/Bruce Coleman Ltd.
172(B)	The Magadi Soda Co. Ltd.
173	Syndication International Ltd., London
174(T)	Alan Hutchison
175(L)	British Museum/Photo Michael Holford © Aldus Books
175(R)	C. Blanc-Pattin/Explorer
176-7	© Geographical Projects Limited
178-9(T)	United Nations
178(B)	Camera Press, London
179(B)	Dipl. Inc. Richard Gerlach, Berlin
180(T)	Ethiopian Tourist Organization (Bernheim)
180(B)	Unesco/Studio Raccah
181(T)	Colorific!
181(B)	By courtesy of De Beers Consolidated Mines Ltd.
184-5	© Geographical Projects Limited
187	Paul Henry Mellinghaus, Müchen
188	Victor Englebert/Susan Griggs Agency
189(T)	E. Haeberlin
190	Picturepoint, London
191	Popperfoto
192	Picturepoint, London
193	Malawi Department of Information
194(T)	Courtesy Alice Mertens
194(B)	Supplied by Dr. H.J. Heinz, University of Witwatersrand, Johannesburg
196	Photo J. Allan Cash
197	Wide World Photos, Inc.
198	Lee E. Battaglia/Colorific!
200-1	© Geographical Projects Limited
202	Syndication International Ltd., London
203(T)	Robert Estall
203(B)	Photo Ray Dean © Aldus Books, by courtesy of The British Trawlers' Federation Ltd.
204-5	Howard Sochurek
206(L)	Saskatchewan Government photo
206(R)	Sonia Halliday
207	Picturepoint, London
208-9	© Geographical Projects Limited
210	Lowell J. Georgia/Photo Researchers Inc.
211,	Josef Muench, F.P.S.A.
212(T)	Josef Muench, F.P.S.A.
212(B)	Courtesy Museum of Fine Arts, Boston. M. and M. Karolik Collection
213	© Geographical Projects Limited
214(T)	B.L. Sage/Ardea, London
214(B)	Brian Hawkes/Natural History Photographic Agency
215	Robert Estall
216-7	© Geographical Projects Limited
218	United States Information Service, London
219(T)	C. Reubmeester, *Life* © Time Inc.
219(B)	Monsanto Company, St. Louis, Mo.
220(L)	Courtesy of Kaiser Aluminum and Chemical Corporation
220(R)	United States Information Service, London
221	International Nickel Company of Canada Limited
222(L)	William W. Bacon/Rapho-Guillumette
222(R)	Picturepoint, London
223	Van Bucher/Photo Researchers Inc.
224	Mary Fisher/Colorific!
225	Photo J. Allan Cash
226	Barnaby's Picture Library
228	Alan Hutchison © Moser
230	L.L.T. Rhodes/*Daily Telegraph* Colour Library
231	Picturepoint, London
232-3	© Geographical Projects Limited
234	Popperfoto
235(L)	Tate & Lyle Refineries Limited
235(R)	Photo Anne Bolt
236	H. Grathwohl/Zefa
237(T)	The Venezuelan Embassy, London
237(B)	R. Pierer/Zefa
238(L)	The John Judkyn Memorial, Freshford Manor, Bath/Photo Mike Busselle © Aldus Books
238(R)	Leonard McCombe © Time Inc.
239(T)	Keystone
239(B)	Picturepoint, London